*Cities of Canada*

# CITIES
# OF CANADA

VOLUME ONE:

*Theoretical, Historical and Planning Perspectives*

*George A. Nader*

TRENT UNIVERSITY

*Macmillan of Canada*

Library of Congress Catalogue Card No. 74-10295


ISBN 0-7705-1029-9

*Printed in Canada for*
The Macmillan Company of Canada

# Contents

FOR CATHY

# *Preface*

The organization of the book into three parts reflects its three principal goals: to provide a description of the major forces which operate on the contemporary urban system in terms of both inter-urban relationships and the internal structure of cities; to describe the historical evolution of the Canadian urban system; and to examine solutions to the present and future problems which face Canada's cities. In *CITIES OF CANADA, Volume II, Profiles of Fifteen Metropolitan Centres*, these foci are drawn together in the examination of selected metropolitan centres.

Part I presents a theoretical framework within which many aspects of the contemporary Canadian city can be understood. Chapter I is concerned with inter-city relationships and examines the major forces which shape the external urban system at both national and regional levels. Chapter 2 is concerned with theories that explain the internal structure of urban areas, while Chapter 3 examines the same problems but with a greater empirical emphasis. The particular importance of the city centre warrants special consideration and Chapter 4 is entirely devoted to this area.

Part II recognizes the importance of viewing the contemporary Canadian urban system from an evolutionary standpoint and accordingly spans the period from the forts, fishing bases, trading posts and missions of the earliest era to the megalopolitan agglomerations of the present day. The history of Canadian cities may be divided into several clearly differentiated eras, each of which has left its unique imprint on the urban scene and it is only in this way that some of the apparently unrelated attributes of the present-day urban system can be understood. Chapter 5 is concerned not explicitly with the urban system but rather with the major formative forces which influenced the early fortunes of Canadian cities, both as a group and individually. Chapter 6 describes the development of Canadian cities until 1867 while Chapter 7 focuses primarily on the development of the national urban system after confederation.

Part III concentrates on urban problems; Chapter 8 examines Canada's institutional-governmental system and the possibilities which it affords for the solution of urban problems, while Chapter 9 analyzes the nature of these problems and the policies which have been utilized in dealing with them.

A book of this kind must inevitably draw on the work of others but I have thought it best to avoid an elaborate footnote system; instead, a number of selected references are included for each chapter in order to provide the student with material for further reading.

It is impossible to thank all those who have in some way contributed to the book but I would particularly like to acknowledge the many people in organizations across Canada who generously provided answers to numerous requests for information, both in person and by letter. I am especially grateful to: Mr. N. Dant, Provincial Planning Director, Alberta; Mrs. P. J. Drake, Planning Information Officer, City of Calgary; Mr. B. Elwood, Director of Research, Metropolitan Toronto Planning Board; Mr. C. A. Louis, Plans Administration Branch, Ministry of Housing, Ontario; Mr. J. G. Masterton, Planning Department, City of Edmonton; Mr. A. Melamed, Housing and City Planning Department, City of Montreal; Mr. L. H. Morasch, Transportation Department, City of Calgary; and Mrs. G. Stoner, Office Leasing Department, A. E. LePage Limited. I would also like to acknowledge the help of Professors Elwood Jones and Douglas McCalla of the History Department, Trent University, for commenting on chapters five, six and seven. I am much indebted to my own students who have used various chapters in their courses and whose comments and reactions have been both illuminating and helpful; special thanks are due to Messrs. Mark Betteridge, Paul Henry and Ronald Watkins (now with the Ministry of State for Urban Affairs). I should like to thank Mrs. Kerry Taylor for her particularly helpful comments on various aspects of the book. Responsibility for errors is, of course, mine alone.

I am most grateful to Mrs. I. Smith and Mrs. J. Takacs of Oxford University for their cartographic expertise in drawing the maps, and to Mrs. C. Brunger for the competent and expeditious typing of the original manuscript.

Finally, I owe a considerable debt to my wife; she has helped not only by reading the first draft of the book but by her constant encouragement despite the numerous disruptions and inconveniences which inevitably resulted from its preparation. This book is appropriately dedicated to her.

George A. Nader

Peterborough
January, 1975

# PART ONE
## *Modern Urban Structure*

# 1.
# The External Urban System: National and Regional

Urbanization is a socio-economic process in which the territorial units of human organization become more specialized and therefore more interdependent, and in which the social system becomes more complex. An urban system can therefore be defined as a *complex system of interdependent, specialized parts.* The urbanization process is the result of economic or technological factors, but the development of an urban society is inevitably accompanied by simultaneous changes in social organization. In all societies and periods of history the city has been recognized as the most efficient vehicle for the development and assimilation of technological advances, which have in turn produced changes in the prevailing social structure; the history of cities is almost synonymous with the history of man's economic, cultural and social development.

Cities are the essential focal points of economic development; an economically advanced country is invariably urbanized, and it is the city that coordinates and controls the economy. The coincidence of the major production inputs (labour, capital, technology) within a city creates an ideal economic climate; the proximity of specialist functions encourages a high level of interaction because of the low costs of exchange, and this in turn enhances productivity, innovation and other facets of economic progress. Although cities may be the principal production centres and channels for distributing goods, their most essential function is to control the various aspects of a society—economic, political, cultural, military and religious. The importance of these control functions is evidenced in societies at every level of urbanization and at every period in history by the concentration of services (tertiary industries) in cities.

Regardless of the particular forces at work in a society, the urbanization process is spatially manifested in an urban system which, at every phase of its evolution, is a reflection of the current levels of social and economic development. At each stage in its development from hamlet to metropolis, an urban settlement forms an integral part of a larger socio-economic system, within which it functions and on which it depends for its survival. It is a truism that urban areas are not self-supporting, and must therefore depend on the export of a proportion of their production in order to pay for the import of those goods which they cannot provide for themselves. A city's *basic* activities are those which produce goods for export, while activities which produce goods that are consumed within the city are termed *nonbasic* or *service*. Although in practice such a division is technically difficult to determine, the basic-nonbasic differentiation exemplifies the interdependency which exists between urban and rural areas on the one hand, and within the urban system on the other. Although in some way every urban centre in a country is dependent on every other centre, it is convenient for analytical purposes to divide these external relations into two components: national and regional. Since each city functions at both levels, its economic structure will depend on its competitive position in the national urban system and also on its role within its region.

## The National Urban System

Since national economic development depends upon the functional specialization of a country's territorial units, the national space economy may be disaggregated into its principal elements and viewed as a system of regions. Each region performs specialized functions within the national economy, and it therefore follows that all regions depend on interregional exchanges of goods and services. Indeed, specialization in production is inevitably accompanied by dependence on others for some products, and consequently the more specialized are a region's productive functions the greater is its need for exchange. These exchanges are mostly channelled through a relatively small number of large cities or metropolitan centres, which accordingly function as the brokers or exchange points between their regions and the larger economic system and are therefore the chief organizing forces acting on the space economy of their dependent regions. This inter-metropolitan system forms the super-structure of a modern country's urban system and may be termed the national urban system.

In industrial countries a consistent relationship has been demonstrated between dimensions of the urban system and economic development, and the spatial structure of the urban system at any period may be viewed as a function of the technology for moving people, goods and information. Employing a simple three-stage model of economic development (early industrial, industrial and post-industrial) it is possible to distinguish corresponding changes in the structure of the urban system.

In the early stages of a country's economic development it is generally true that only a few areas are industrialized. The main reason for this selective development is the presence of interregional differences in the economic returns from industrial investment. In the typical underdeveloped country, where capital is scarce, transportation costs are high, natural resource endowments vary from one part of the country to another, and where profit is the principal objective, industrial investment is initially restricted to the best-endowed areas. The early industrial stage is therefore characterized by a dual economy: urban-industrial development in a few rich regions and traditional economies in the rest of the country. At this stage, a primate urban system usually exists. An exceptionally high proportion of the urban population is found in one or two large cities, with only a few medium-sized cities, and often a large number of small cities scattered throughout the country. There are, however, many exceptions, which are generally related to the diversity of factors capable of affecting the structure of the urban system; these include non-economic forces, the size of the country and its history of urbanization.

As national development proceeds the less-developed areas of the country receive increased capital investment for several reasons. Improvements in transportation enhance the returns on investment; new resource exploitations become possible with technological advance; the greater capital accumulation in the country permits investments in less accessible areas for long-term rather than short-term profitability; and, finally, diseconomies associated with congestion or the full development of their most profitable resources encourage a transfer of capital from more highly developed areas. The transfer of capital and other factors of production does not necessarily lead to an equalization of economic activities among all regions; indeed, empirical evidence indicates that a heartland-periphery relationship frequently exists. The "heartland," usually the first area to be industrialized, exercises an economic sovereignty over the less-developed "periphery" regions, and encourages their development in a manner which furthers its own interests. For example, the discovery of petroleum and gas resources in Alberta did not lead to an influx of secondary manufacturing into the province but rather to the export of energy to the eastern industrial region. The northeastern United States provides an excellent example of the strength and persistence of a heartland economy; in Canada, the Quebec-Windsor axis (which accounts for almost 80 per cent of Canada's manufacturing production) performs a similar role. The growth of medium-sized cities in the periphery results in a more balanced distribution of cities in terms of population. This pattern frequently conforms to the rank-size rule according to which a city's population can be expressed as a function of its rank in the national urban hierarchy; for example, the second-largest city may be one-half the size of the largest, the third-largest city one-third the size of the largest, and so on.

In a post-industrial economy all regions are fully integrated, with regional functional specializations and a considerable degree of interdependence prevailing. Extensive interregional exchanges are facilitated by other structural alterations within the urban system. The spatial organization of the economy becomes increasingly metropolitan-dominated as these exchanges are channelled through the inter-metropolitan communications network. Increasingly, the metropolitan rather than the regional economy becomes the meaningful subsystem of the national economy. The metropolitanization of post-industrial society is accompanied by a simplification of the hierarchical structure of the national urban system; in effect the movement of goods and information from one part of the country to another now requires fewer intermediary centres. This is due to the increased concentration of activities in metropolitan areas, and also to the extension of their territorial influences.

METROPOLITANISM

Although large urban centres became common in the nineteenth century, metropolitanism is essentially a twentieth-century phenomenon. Traced back to its Greek origin the word "metropolis" means "mother city." Its most distinctive characteristic is the ability to dominate other cities and thus to extend its social, cultural and economic orbit over a wide geographical area. It functions as a nerve centre for its region through the control of communications and the centralization of executive operations in commerce, finance and government.

According to the definition used by Statistics Canada a census metropolitan area is "the main labour market area of a continuous built-up area having 100,000 or more population. . . . The main labour market area corresponds to a commuting field or a zone where a significant number of people are able to travel on a daily basis to workplaces in the main built-up area." In reality a metropolitan economic system extends beyond the census metropolitan area or "commuter shed" to include outlying settlements (within a radius of about one hundred miles) whose economies are closely tied to the metropolitan centre. Within this metropolitan region there are fewer and less frequent interconnections between outer and inner zones than exist within the metropolitan area.

Metropolitan status is not just a matter of size. For example, in terms of both functional structure and geographical sphere of influence the Kitchener metropolitan area (pop. 227,000 in 1971) and the city of Peterborough (pop. 58,000) are basically similar, while Sudbury (pop. 155,000), which had 24 per cent of its labour force engaged in mining in 1971, is unique among Canadian metropolitan areas. Obviously there is no single criterion which adequately defines the socio-economic concept of metropolitanism; population size, economic structure and geographical sphere of influence are three of the most important indices of this special status, but there is little agreement among social scientists on how best to apply them to the definition of a metropolitan area.

There are five main stages through which an urban centre usually passes before achieving metropolitan status. In the first stage most towns are unifunctional and a single activity provides the economic *raison d'être*. In the second stage, that of a service centre, the urban economy is diversified by the addition of a number of regional service functions such as distributing, wholesaling and marketing; the town is merely an outpost of a distant metropolis, but is able to act as an agent for the local population because of its centrality to the latter and/or its strategic location on a major long-distance transportation route. In the third stage the town becomes a primary manufacturing centre, by intercepting products originating within its region and processing them (e.g., flour-milling or meat-packing) before they are despatched to their ultimate markets. The fourth stage, graduation to a secondary manufacturing centre, is achieved by the expansion of its industrial base to include the manufacture of goods previously imported into its region; this import-substitution phase is critically dependent on the size and wealth of its hinterland population. The acquisition of control functions for the regional economy marks the fifth stage, as the urban centre becomes a regional metropolis; it functions as the region's economic decision-maker through its financial and governmental institutions and as the clearing house for ideas through its newspapers, radio and television stations and other communications media. A final stage, the achievement of national metropolitan status, is reserved for only a few cities and is characterized by the appropriation of control over one or more vital sectors of the national economy, normally through the localization of financial and corporate head offices.

COMMUNICATIONS AND METROPOLITANISM

Much of the metropolitanization which has taken place in post-industrial societies has been the direct result of advances in communications. Widespread social and economic changes in industrial location, business organization, life styles and occupations may be traced to communications technology; it is mainly these changes that have promoted the vitality of metropolitan centres.

Two complementary forces in particular have stimulated the reorganization of regional economies around metropolitan centres: the development of rapid, long-distance communications has encouraged the concentration of growth in a few large cities, while improvements in medium-distance communications have extended the area that can be integrated into a single metropolitan complex. At every point in time the most modern communications facilities are largely confined to metropolitan centres: at present these include international airports, integrated road and rail terminals (including facilities for handling piggyback operations), and access to computer terminals. Nationally, the increasing demand for speed in both passenger and freight transportation, and the economies associated with the geographical concentration of transportation terminals, have combined to encourage the metropolitanization of a wide variety of economic functions. Regionally, improvements in transportation have prompted an increasing proportion of activities to concentrate within the metropolitan centre, where advantage may be taken of the inter-metropolitan communications system, while at the same time close contact can be maintained with the outlying settlements.

The metropolitan region is largely the result of outward expansion from an urban core, which is produced by two forces: a short-distance decentralization of activities and residences within the metropolitan area, and the extension of a centralized economic influence. over outlying and formerly independent towns and villages, transforming or modifying their functions and integrating them into the larger economic system. The extension of a metropolitan centre's influence generally encourages the increased specialization of those settlements which are brought within its economic sphere. Thus, a rural service centre may become a dormitory suburb or an industrial town, depending on the needs of the metropolis and its own location and resources.

The rapid transfer of information is, perhaps, the most important of the factors which enable extensive metropolitan regions to function as integrated economic systems. For the sake of increased efficiency a manufacturing firm may centralize its office functions and locate its plant in the metropolitan periphery; close coordination between the two is maintained by a variety of communications devices such as the telephone, teleprinters and facsimile transmitters. Less evident are other centre-periphery relationships; because of its unrivalled communicational advantages, the metropolitan core acts as the control centre for widely separated, peripheral settlements with varying degrees of self-sufficiency. Characteristically, the peripheral settlements in a metropolitan region interact relatively little, but share a common, centripetal orientation to the metropolitan core. This is not, however, to deny the continued, though reduced, importance of local travel for shopping, entertainment and similar purposes. For the peripheral localities, the most vital commodities which the metropolitan core has to offer are intelligence and expertise; it is the principal source of the specialized financial, legal, administrative and other services which they periodically require.

Although its boundaries are generally tenuous, the metropolitan region represents the spatial expression of a fundamental reorganization of the social and economic systems of developed countries. Its extent and shape are functions of communications technology, and cannot therefore be adequately defined in physical terms. The structural relationships within the region are too diverse to allow the drawing of definitive boundaries. In some cases, particularly between centre and periphery, there is no apparent physical interaction but nevertheless invisible ties link the centre to branch plants, local banks and other facilities in the periphery. The commuting area of the metropolis is useful as a definition of its day-to-day sphere of influence, but there is also a "week-end" metropolitan region, within which cottages, ski resorts and other recreational facilities used by metropolitan residents are located; centripetal commuting and centrifugal cottaging both identify aspects of the territorial extent of the modern metropolis. Its economic influence is also felt in the surrounding rural areas where agricultural production is integrated into the metropolitan economic system. For example, agricultural land use is most intensive near metropolitan centres, and dairying and market gardening are especially important.

MODERN INDUSTRIAL LOCATION

Location analysis attempts to explain the spatial distribution of economic activity. Classical location theory deals with the location of the individual firm, and is primarily concerned with the minimization of transportation costs. If these costs are at a minimum, it is assumed that profits will be maximized *when all other factors are held constant*. In fact, geographical variations in factors such as price and processing costs, combined with the lack of perfect knowledge among entrepreneurs, imperfections in the operation of the free market and the pursuit of non-economic goals, largely negate the ability of classical location theory to explain the modern space economy.

The modern emergence of a large number of "footloose" industries has had an important bearing on present locational patterns. A footloose industry is essentially one which is not forced by transportation costs to locate near sources of raw materials or markets; in other words, transportation costs are of secondary importance and a firm is therefore relatively free to locate anywhere within a wide geographical area. This type of industry owes its existence mainly to advances in transportation technology (trucking, for example) which have reduced the relative contribution of transfer costs to the final product price. A number of other factors have also played a part: the declining importance of raw material inputs in many manufacturing processes; the decreasing reliance on any particular raw material; the increasing importance of light industries; the growth of precision-goods industries; and the universal use of electricity as a source of power. In general, the commercial value of manufactured products has risen faster than the costs of raw materials and transportation, and the latter now play relatively minor roles in the locational decision. The importance of savings in production systems now generally outweighs that of savings in transportation, the traditional concern of location analysis.

In practice very few industries are free to locate anywhere they wish; the freedom of footloose industries has simply permitted firms to select locations on the basis of criteria other than transportation costs. The rate at which these industries have located in metropolitan areas has exceeded the prediction of conventional location analysis, and is better understood in terms of the importance of *agglomeration economies*, that is, the savings that accrue to firms locating in areas of concentrated economic activity. In modern economies, agglomeration factors often constitute the single most important influence on the location of industry. There are three types of agglomeration economies: internal economies of scale, localization economies and urbanization economies.

*Internal economies of scale* refer to reductions in the average cost of the finished product resulting from an increased rate of production. Higher rates of production and concomitant cost savings may be achieved through the use of more expensive equipment, or through the use of a larger work force which permits operators to perform their most specialized functions on a full-time basis. In some industries, the economies that can be achieved by large-scale production are so great that there is a tendency for plants to be located in areas where such operations are possible, generally the major population centres. In economic terms, savings through concentrated large-scale production are greater than the transportation savings that can be achieved through the geographical dispersal of a number of small plants. Transportation costs are not, however, unimportant, and the optimal location of a large plant is frequently close to the largest market for its product. In Canada this often means southern Ontario, the country's largest consumer-industrial market. Since the optimum size for each of a firm's major functions may vary, it is often the case that a firm achieves maximum economies of scale by the physical separation of its establishments. Thus, a brewery firm may achieve significant scale economies in finance, marketing and management by becoming a national distributor, and these office functions are likely to be located in one centre. At the same time, its production plants may be optimally dispersed (because of transportation costs) in accordance with the regional distribution of population.

*Localization economies* are savings which result when firms engaged in the manufacture of similar products locate in the same area. In this case the economies of scale are external to any one firm but internal to the localized industry as a whole. The reduction in the cost of the final product stems from a number of factors. These include the establishment of specialized component or intermediate-product firms, which are each able to achieve a scale of production (and therefore economies) greater than that of any one final-product firm (for example, manufacturers of carburettors or spark plugs for Detroit's automobile industry); the development of waste-product firms, such as chemical plants that use the by-products of petroleum refining; the development of a large labour force skilled in the particular industry; the support of research and development facilities that may be too expensive for a single firm; and the lower costs of raw materials because of cooperative purchases or common transportation terminals where specialized facilities are needed. For instance, localization economies are important in most branches of the clothing industry where firms are typically small because the variability of demand makes long production runs uneconomical.

*Urbanization economies* are savings made in a variety of industries by firms which locate in urban rather than rural areas, and in larger rather than smaller communities. For a given rate of production the average costs incurred by such firms will be lower. Transfer economies represent one type of savings; whether engaged in similar or dissimilar activities, firms which locate in the largest urban centres share a pool of transportation facilities which are generally superior to those available in the smaller centres. On a local scale this is exemplified by the industrial park, where diverse manufacturing plants achieve savings by sharing transportation facilities which they would be unable to finance individually; on a national scale large airports, integrated freight terminals and other transportation facilities set metropolitan areas apart from smaller communities. A second group of savings are commonly a function of the size of a community. These may include a large and diversified labour market; lower average costs for many of the public services that are particularly important to industry, such as water, sewage disposal and electricity; and access to a variety of professional, banking, financial and other commercial services. Especially important to smaller firms are the external economies afforded by urban locations—such things as renting rather than buying equipment, sub-contracting part of the production process, reducing inventory levels because of the proximity of wholesalers, and employing the services of accountants, lawyers and other professionals on a part-time or contractual basis. Finally, as technological inputs become increasingly important and as product specialization increases, there is a marked orientation to market centres, in particular the largest urban centres.

Agglomeration economies are not the only economic reasons for the drawing power of the larger urban centres. Inevitably imperfect knowledge of present conditions and uncertainty about the future encourage some firms to select locations on the basis of maximum sales rather than greatest profit. When this is the case, some loss of profit is regarded as the price paid for a reduced risk of business failure and the long-term possibility of scale economies supported by an increased output. Particularly for firms producing "unstandardized" products, proximity to a large consumer market is often an essential prerequisite. Rapidly changing styles in women's fashions, for example, require clothing manufacturers to locate close to their most important purchasers in order to match production schedules and designs to the changing demand.

A number of economic factors combine to maintain the importance of the large established industrial areas, including locational inertia and inter-industry linkages. Locational inertia refers to the disinclination of established firms to seek more profitable locations, the principal disincentive being that relocation costs must be recovered from the additional profits of the alternative site. In most cases such costs can be recovered only over a long period of time and the more uncertain the future, the greater is the perceived risk, and the less likely the plant is to relocate. In instances where a few firms dominate a particular industry, as is the case with steel production, it is often possible for firms to pass on to the customer the additional cost of a sub-optimal location. The interest-rate structure also favours the maintenance of the prevailing spatial pattern, since an established firm generally finds it cheaper to borrow money in its local area. Finally, since location decisions are generally made in isolation, without knowledge of the future locational decisions of competitive or complementary firms, there is a tendency to conform to the existing pattern. This is reinforced by the considerable degree of locational interdependence among modern firms. The increasing complexity of the manufacturing process has fostered the development of so many intermediate-product manufacturers that, within some industries, they may account for the majority of employment.

Since in most cases the future is unpredictable, few firms actually go to extreme lengths in order to find the site of maximum profitability. In the absence of certain knowledge of the optimum location, firms may be satisfied with the modest objective of simply being profitable; this is generally termed "satisficing" behaviour as opposed to the "optimizing" behaviour of profit maximization. In such circumstances a firm generally prefers a market location and other locations must be shown to have clear cost advantages in order to warrant consideration. If a firm is satisfied with simply being profitable, it is likely that greater importance will be attached to non-economic factors; since an optimum location is not being sought, such things as managerial preferences for metropolitan living may be decisive factors. Also as the location decision becomes increasingly complex, firms may be unable to make optimal decisions, and the criteria examined may not be the appropriate economic ones. For example, access to market or technical information may be given priority over production costs in the evaluation of alternative locations.

In summary, it appears that at present more factors favour centralization than decentralization, and on the basis of past trends it seems likely that the future industrial pattern will be a reinforcement of the existing structure. In practice the locational decision is influenced by a complex of social, economic and technological factors, which may be highly interrelated but not always in a quantifiable manner. The difficulty of choosing an optimum location is confounded by the uncertainty of future changes in the critical factors. The basic paradox in the location of industry is that although these decisions are long-term or future-oriented, they are in practice strongly influenced by existing conditions and short-term considerations. Historical advantage is therefore one of the most important factors controlling the spatial distribution of industry. The size of an urban area is itself an attraction for industry; although there are exceptions, it is probably appropriate to describe the locational process as one of "success breeding success."

MODERN BUSINESS ORGANIZATION

Modern locational patterns are closely related to certain changes in the organizational structure of business enterprises. The size of the firm, the types of goods marketed, the production methods, and many other aspects of the way in which modern businesses are organized directly influence the spatial distribution of economic activity. Increasingly, firms are producing goods which are very susceptible to changes in consumer tastes, and so an important part of their operation is to maintain contacts and exchanges of information with a growing number of experts who trade specialized intelligence. On the other hand, many of a firm's activities, such as production, require few contacts with individuals outside the firm.

By the 1890s the typical Canadian manufacturing firm was still family-owned, the factory system had only just begun to develop, and most firms were one-product, one-plant operations. In contrast, many of today's largest firms are multi-product, multi-plant enterprises, frequently organized so that some of their four major functions of production, financing, management and marketing, are physically separate. Scale economies and optimum locations vary for each of the four functions, and the modern firm can, therefore, maximize its profits as much by a "mix of locations" as by a "mix of products." Also, because of differences in scale economies for its different functions, it is common for a large firm to sell a variety of products. Thus, if spare capacity (i.e., because the market may be saturated for its main product) should exist in a firm's marketing division, it might profitably expand its line to include other products. It is not uncommon, therefore, for a petroleum company to finance a new town or for a liquor company to market drugs.

Although office functions (management, marketing and financing) have always been essential to large-scale factory production, the physical separation of office and plant is of more recent origin, and has come about largely as the result of improvements in instantaneous communications systems such as the telephone. Consequently the factory, formerly the symbol of the metropolis, has in the last few decades been replaced by the office tower. Although industrialization was initially responsible for much metropolitan development, the most valuable asset of a modern metropolis is its potential for communication, and its most specialized role is as a transactions centre. The production facilities of large firms may be located in the periphery of the metropolitan region, or thousands of miles away, but the executive and decision-making personnel gravitate towards the metropolitan core, the centre of the communications system.

The metropolitanization of office functions has stemmed from the modern firm's urgent need for rapid access to current information. There are increasingly fewer standardized products. A new product (or production technique) might in the past have assured a firm a head start of many years over its competitors; today, however, as a result of modern advertising, marketing and production techniques, it might be only a matter of months before the market is saturated with similar products manufactured by its competitors. If its product is demonstrably better, a single firm can quickly capture a major share of the market, and no competitive enterprise can therefore afford to be without facilities for duplicating as well as pioneering products.

The principal purpose of the head office is to coordinate and control the increasingly complex affairs of a modern firm. A drop in the banking interest rate, a revaluation of currencies, revisions of the corporation tax structure and the like will all have immediate repercussions on the operations of a variety of Canadian firms, and in this situation the speed of reaction may well be decisive. Informed and specialized advice is frequently essential to the decision-making process of the modern firm, and since it is generally uneconomical for the necessary resource personnel to form part of the permanent staff, their advice must be solicited as and when the need arises. In this respect, the resources of the metropolis are without equal. Once decisions have been made, instructions can be relayed instantly to widely separated plants or offices, where they are executed by administrative staff.

A little understood consequence of the concentration of head offices in the national metropolitan centre is the effect on the distribution of other activities within the national space economy; Toronto and Montreal, for example, contain two-thirds of the head offices of the three hundred largest companies (by sales and assets) operating in Canada and 99 per cent of the assets of chartered banks. The economies of scale enjoyed by multi-plant firms are to a large extent the result of the centralization of the head office functions, including marketing, financing, management, research, and product innovation and design. Branch plant diseconomies of scale (because of their small size) can be largely offset by such economies, and so the existing geographical dispersion of production workers need not be altered and decentralization may actually be encouraged. However, the major growth in employment has recently occurred in central office functions. Moreover, the scope for innovation by branch plants is largely circumscribed by the nature of the responsibilities granted to them by their parent companies, and their roles therefore tend to remain fixed within the larger context of the parent company's profitability. Accordingly, major economic impulses almost always originate in the national metropolitan centres.

METROPOLITAN ECONOMIC STRUCTURE

Compared to other urban areas diversification is, perhaps, the most distinctive characteristic of metropolitan economies; it is a reflection both of their greater number of specialized functions and of their greater self-sufficiency. Export or basic industries typically form only a small proportion of the total spectrum of metropolitan functions, and most employment tends to be in activities which are primarily oriented to the local market. The predominance of these service or nonbasic activities is the principal reason for similarities in functional structure among metropolitan areas. In general, the nonbasic proportion increases with city size, so that as metropolitan areas get larger, they tend to increase in functional similarity; Toronto and Montreal, for example, are more similar to each other in functional structure than they are to any other metropolitan area.

There are several reasons for the relative importance of nonbasic functions in large cities. First, increases in population make it possible for a growing number of locally-oriented activities to find an adequate market. For instance, a rise in population might increase the volume of building construction to the point where it becomes possible for a small factory to manufacture door knobs, which were previously imported. Second, consumption patterns may change as the expanded market enables a wider range of goods and services to be produced locally. In this case the emergence of live theatre might persuade some people to forego previously imported services (e.g., weekend holidays) for theatre performances. Third, as city size and therefore functional complexity increase, the need for supporting services also grows. In a small town there might be no need for public transportation facilities, but it is doubtful whether Toronto could function adequately without its public transit system. It is important to note that in metropolitan areas the higher cost of supporting services, such as transit systems, is normally compensated for by the increased productivity of export industries, which results from the high level of functional specialization.

Despite their general functional similarity, metropolitan areas, like all other cities, may be distinguished from each other by the nature of their basic industries. The classification of cities according to their functional structure has most frequently been based on employment or labour force data. Approximately a dozen industrial groupings have been used in the various classification studies, but the considerable diversity of metropolitan economies makes such a small number totally inadequate for the analysis of functional differentiations among metropolitan areas. Many of the most commonly observed functional differences are associated with the heartland-periphery relationships which characterize the space economy of most advanced countries. "Heartland" cities (for example, those lying between Quebec and Windsor in Canada) frequently specialize in manufacturing, while "periphery" cities (those in the rest of Canada) serve mainly as regional centres, and therefore tend to specialize in trade, transportation and community services. The heartland-periphery distinction emphasizes the persistence of a close economic relationship between city and region; despite their size and relative self-sufficiency, metropolitan areas, with very few exceptions, bear the imprints of their regional economies.

Compared to the national average, metropolitan areas are specialized in all but the primary industries (Table 1.1). Total employment in metropolitan areas is actually higher than might be expected on the basis of their share of national population. This is accounted for by higher participation rates (i.e., the labour force expressed as a percentage of the population aged 15 years and over) and by the higher proportion of their populations in the working age group because of selective in-migration (see, for example, Table 1.2), and both factors are related to the greater employment opportunities in metropolitan areas. In 1971, for example, the twenty-two census metropolitan areas accounted for 55 per cent of the national population but for 60 per cent of those between 20 and 44 years and for 59 per cent of the national labour force; the participation rate for the metropolitan areas was 61 per cent compared to the national average of 58 per cent.

Mainly as a result of national trends in production and consumption patterns, most metropolitan economies have recently experi-

TABLE 1.1 *Labour force by industry (percentage distribution), Census Metropolitan*

| Industry | St. John's | Halifax | Saint John | Chicoutimi-Jonquière | Quebec | Montreal | Ottawa-Hull | Toronto | Hamilton | St. Catharines-Niagara | Kitchener |
|---|---|---|---|---|---|---|---|---|---|---|---|
| Primary | 1.8 | 0.6 | 1.0 | 2.0 | 0.9 | 0.5 | 1.0 | 1.0 | 1.8 | 2.6 | 1.0 |
| Manufacturing | 7.0 | 8.3 | 16.3 | 24.4 | 12.3 | 25.6 | 7.9 | 25.3 | 34.5 | 33.0 | 39.0 |
| Construction | 7.1 | 5.1 | 6.6 | 4.8 | 5.9 | 4.7 | 5.8 | 6.2 | 6.3 | 5.6 | 6.1 |
| Transportation, communications & other utilities | 10.8 | 8.5 | 12.4 | 6.2 | 6.2 | 9.5 | 6.2 | 7.5 | 4.9 | 6.2 | 3.9 |
| Wholesale Trade | 6.9 | 4.5 | 5.4 | 2.2 | 3.3 | 4.7 | 2.6 | 5.5 | 4.0 | 2.4 | 3.6 |
| Retail Trade | 12.9 | 11.2 | 12.6 | 11.1 | 10.6 | 10.3 | 9.7 | 11.2 | 11.1 | 11.1 | 10.3 |
| Finance, insurance and real estate | 3.3 | 5.0 | 4.6 | 2.6 | 4.2 | 5.7 | 4.3 | 6.8 | 4.0 | 3.0 | 4.8 |
| Community, business & personal services | 30.0 | 27.6 | 26.2 | 26.4 | 29.1 | 24.5 | 24.9 | 24.1 | 23.3 | 24.9 | 21.8 |
| Public administration and defence | 11.0 | 22.6 | 7.3 | 8.3 | 17.3 | 5.2 | 30.2 | 5.4 | 3.7 | 4.2 | 3.5 |
| Unspecified | 9.2 | 6.6 | 7.6 | 12.0 | 10.2 | 9.3 | 7.4 | 7.0 | 6.4 | 7.0 | 6.0 |
| Total | 100.0 | 100.0 | 100.0 | 100.0 | 100.0 | 100.0 | 100.0 | 100.0 | 100.0 | 100.0 | 100.0 |

SOURCE: Census of Canada, 1971 and Statistics Canada.
Figures in italics indicate above average for all CMA's.

enced a shift of employment from goods-producing to service-producing industries. In 1946 39.8 per cent of the Canadian work force was engaged in service industries; by 1956 the proportion had risen to 48.5 per cent and between 1961 and 1971, the proportion increased from 55.5 per cent to 62.6 per cent. These industrial trends have been accompanied by corresponding changes in the occupational structure of the work force, the most important employment increases recently being in white-collar occupations including pro-

Areas (CMA's) and Canada, 1971

| London | Windsor | Sudbury | Thunder Bay | Winnipeg | Regina | Saskatoon | Calgary | Edmonton | Vancouver | Victoria | All CMA's | Canada | CMA's as % of Canada |
|---|---|---|---|---|---|---|---|---|---|---|---|---|---|
| 2.9 | 1.6 | 24.1 | 3.5 | 0.8 | 1.9 | 3.7 | 6.9 | 3.7 | 2.9 | 3.0 | 1.9 | 8.3 | 13.4 |
| 22.2 | 33.0 | 12.9 | 15.9 | 18.2 | 9.5 | 9.8 | 11.2 | 11.4 | 16.6 | 8.8 | 21.3 | 19.8 | 63.5 |
| 5.9 | 5.1 | 8.0 | 7.1 | 5.1 | 5.5 | 6.3 | 8.9 | 8.4 | 6.8 | 6.3 | 6.0 | 6.2 | 56.7 |
| 6.2 | 5.9 | 5.6 | 13.8 | 11.3 | 10.7 | 9.2 | 8.7 | 9.3 | 10.5 | 6.8 | 8.3 | 7.8 | 62.8 |
| 4.2 | 3.0 | 2.8 | 4.3 | 6.2 | 5.0 | 5.9 | 5.4 | 5.3 | 6.1 | 2.9 | 4.8 | 4.0 | 70.0 |
| 11.1 | 11.8 | 10.0 | 11.8 | 12.5 | 14.3 | 13.2 | 11.6 | 12.0 | 12.0 | 12.9 | 11.2 | 10.7 | 61.8 |
| 6.2 | 4.0 | 2.7 | 3.0 | 5.3 | 5.7 | 4.2 | 5.5 | 4.4 | 5.9 | 4.8 | 5.4 | 4.2 | 77.2 |
| 28.7 | 24.5 | 20.2 | 27.2 | 25.7 | 27.1 | 35.0 | 28.0 | 27.6 | 26.9 | 28.2 | 25.4 | 23.7 | 63.4 |
| 6.1 | 4.1 | 4.3 | 6.5 | 8.2 | 13.9 | 6.9 | 7.0 | 10.4 | 4.7 | 18.8 | 8.0 | 7.4 | 63.4 |
| 6.5 | 7.0 | 9.4 | 6.9 | 6.7 | 6.4 | 5.8 | 6.8 | 7.5 | 7.6 | 7.5 | 7.7 | 7.9 | 57.4 |
| 100.0 | 100.0 | 100.0 | 100.0 | 100.0 | 100.0 | 100.0 | 100.0 | 100.0 | 100.0 | 100.0 | 100.0 | 100.0 | 59.0 |

fessional, technical, clerical, service and recreational categories. Changes in occupational structure are to some extent the result of technological improvements in the industrial production process. Because of increasing automation the proportion of white-collar employment in the manufacturing industry has risen steadily in the last few decades, while the increasing complexity of business operations has promoted the growth of professional and commercial services. Changing consumption patterns have contributed to the

TABLE 1.2 *Estimated net migration (1966-1971) to Calgary by sex and five-year age group compared to the actual populations of Calgary and Canada in 1971 (percentage distribution)*

| Age | Net Migrants Male | Net Migrants Female | Calgary 1971 Male | Calgary 1971 Female | Canada 1971 Male | Canada 1971 Female |
|---|---|---|---|---|---|---|
| 0 - 4 | 4.8 | 5.8 | 9.5 | 9.1 | 8.6 | 8.2 |
| 5 - 9 | 6.7 | 8.4 | 10.8 | 10.5 | 10.7 | 10.2 |
| 10 - 14 | 5.5 | 4.8 | 10.8 | 10.3 | 11.0 | 10.5 |
| 15 - 19 | 15.5 | 25.3 | 9.2 | 9.2 | 10.0 | 9.6 |
| 20 - 24 | 29.9 | 28.8 | 9.7 | 10.2 | 8.7 | 8.8 |
| 25 - 29 | 14.5 | 7.3 | 8.4 | 8.3 | 7.4 | 7.3 |
| 30 - 34 | 7.0 | 4.6 | 6.8 | 6.7 | 6.1 | 6.0 |
| 35 - 39 | 4.1 | 2.3 | 6.9 | 6.3 | 6.0 | 5.7 |
| 40 - 44 | 2.7 | 2.2 | 6.5 | 6.1 | 5.9 | 5.8 |
| 45 - 49 | 1.9 | 1.9 | 5.4 | 5.5 | 5.7 | 5.8 |
| 50 - 54 | 0.8 | 1.2 | 4.3 | 4.4 | 4.8 | 4.9 |
| 55 - 59 | 1.7 | 1.5 | 3.4 | 3.6 | 4.4 | 4.5 |
| 60 - 64 | 2.1 | 2.0 | 2.6 | 2.9 | 3.5 | 3.7 |
| 65 - 69 | 1.7 | 1.9 | 2.0 | 2.2 | 2.7 | 3.1 |
| 70 + | 1.1 | 2.0 | 3.7 | 4.7 | 4.5 | 5.9 |
| Total | 100.0 | 100.0 | 100.0 | 100.0 | 100.0 | 100.0 |
| Sex split | 52.5 | 47.5 | 49.8 | 50.2 | 50.0 | 50.0 |

SOURCE: Census of Canada 1971 and City of Calgary

further growth of the service industry, since increases in personal income have in general meant that the proportion of consumer spending devoted to services has risen. Finally, because productivity has increased faster in the goods-producing industries than in service industries, there has been a net shift of employment to the latter. If past productivity trends were to continue, an equal increase in the future demand for both goods and services would result in a faster growth of employment in service industries; in fact, rising incomes make it probable that the future increase in demand for services will exceed that for goods.

The products of service industries are not as readily transported as those of the goods-producing sector, and are generally consumed locally. Marked differences in the service consumption potential of metropolitan and non-metropolitan areas are partly responsible for the uneven geographical distribution of service employment. A small town may receive televised plays and the services of a general medical practitioner, but only the metropolis can support a live theatre or a brain surgeon. The larger populations, higher incomes and more diversified economies of metropolitan areas are encouraging increasingly high concentrations of service employment; in the case of finance, insurance and real estate services, which include high-order functions, 77 per cent of national employment in 1971 was accounted for by the twenty-two metropolitan areas (Table 1.1) with Toronto and Montreal together accounting for 41 per cent.

METROPOLITAN GROWTH

Although metropolitan areas as a whole are growing faster than the rest of Canada, the pattern is uneven (Table 1.3). Two main factors may be isolated from the complex of forces which determine an individual city's growth rate—changes in the exploitation potential of its regional resources, and its industrial composition. The discovery of new resources (oil in Alberta), the decline in demand for a region's resources (wheat in Saskatchewan) or changes in accessibility to inputs and markets (southern Ontario's strategic location with respect to increasingly important American markets and capital) may significantly affect the growth rate of particular metropolitan areas. Another important determinant of growth rate is the "industry mix" of a metropolitan economy. Changes in demand and variations in the rate of productivity normally produce differential rates of growth among a country's industries; on this basis, they can be classified into slow-growth and fast-growth industries when compared to the national average. Whether the former or latter predominate in a particular city may be very relevant to its growth experience; for example, an above-average number of slow-growth industries will usually produce an overall economic growth rate below the national average. The industry mix of a particular metropolitan area may also be favourable simply because it is large and diversified. Toronto's exceptional magnetism for new firms is related not only to its particular industrial specifications but also to its large size and diversified economy.

The growth of metropolitan areas has so far been explained largely in terms of the advantages which they offer to producers of goods and services; in the traditional economic view of the spatial distribu-

TABLE 1.3 *Population of census metropolitan areas (1971 limits), 1951-1971*

| CMA | Population | | Percentage Rate of Increase | | | | |
|---|---|---|---|---|---|---|---|
| | 1951 | 1971 | 1951-56 | 1956-61 | 1961-66 | 1966-71 | 1951-71 |
| Calgary | 142,315 | 403,319 | 41.2 | 38.8 | 18.5 | 22.0 | 183.4 |
| Chicoutimi-Jonquière | 91,161 | 133,703 | 21.0 | 15.7 | 4.2 | 0.6 | 46.7 |
| Edmonton | 193,547 | 495,702 | 42.0 | 30.9 | 18.2 | 16.5 | 156.1 |
| Halifax | 138,427 | 222,637 | 23.2 | 13.4 | 8.6 | 6.1 | 60.8 |
| Hamilton | 281,901 | 498,523 | 21.1 | 17.4 | 14.0 | 9.0 | 76.8 |
| Kitchener | 107,474 | 226,846 | 19.8 | 20.3 | 24.2 | 18.0 | 111.1 |
| London | 167,724 | 286,011 | 17.1 | 15.4 | 11.9 | 12.7 | 70.5 |
| Montreal | 1,539,308 | 2,743,208 | 18.9 | 21.1 | 16.0 | 6.7 | 78.2 |
| Ottawa-Hull | 311,587 | 602,510 | 18.0 | 24.3 | 15.7 | 13.9 | 93.4 |
| Quebec | 289,294 | 480,502 | 13.5 | 15.4 | 15.3 | 10.0 | 66.1 |
| Regina | 72,731 | 140,734 | 25.4 | 24.7 | 16.4 | 6.3 | 93.5 |
| St. Catharines-Niagara | 189,046 | 303,429 | 23.3 | 10.6 | 10.7 | 6.3 | 60.5 |
| St. John's | 79,562 | 131,814 | 14.9 | 16.7 | 10.2 | 12.1 | 65.7 |
| Saint John | 80,689 | 106,744 | 9.5 | 11.0 | 6.2 | 2.4 | 32.3 |
| Saskatoon | 55,679 | 126,449 | 31.0 | 31.0 | 21.3 | 9.1 | 127.1 |
| Sudbury | 80,543 | 155,424 | 33.9 | 18.1 | 7.3 | 13.7 | 93.0 |
| Thunder Bay | 73,713 | 112,093 | 18.9 | 16.5 | 5.8 | 3.8 | 52.1 |
| Toronto | 1,261,861 | 2,628,043 | 24.6 | 22.1 | 19.3 | 14.8 | 108.3 |
| Vancouver | 587,635 | 1,082,352 | 18.4 | 19.0 | 12.7 | 16.0 | 84.2 |
| Victoria | 118,380 | 195,800 | 17.4 | 14.5 | 10.2 | 11.7 | 65.4 |
| Windsor | 182,619 | 258,643 | 14.1 | 4.2 | 9.7 | 8.5 | 41.6 |
| Winnipeg | 357,229 | 540,262 | 15.5 | 15.5 | 6.8 | 6.2 | 51.2 |
| Total | 6,402,425 | 11,874,748 | 21.0 | 19.9 | 14.9 | 11.1 | 85.5 |
| Rest of Canada | 7,607,004 | 9,693,567 | 9.5 | 7.3 | 4.2 | 3.9 | 27.4 |

SOURCE: Census Division of Statistics Canada

tion of activities, it is people who follow the jobs. It is important to note, however, that in modern societies a growing proportion of the population is free to choose both where and how it will live. Because of the growing importance of consumer goods and services, the production system is becoming increasingly market-oriented, and the evolving space economy may soon become as dependent on where people choose to live as on where producers prefer to locate.

Many migrants to metropolitan centres are attracted primarily by the consumption opportunities. These are typically young adults, who may be motivated by cultural, amenity or other non-economic factors, but who generally anticipate improved employment prospects. The desire for proximity to natural amenities is also becoming an increasingly important factor in the location decision of households. As the average amount of leisure time increases, many people are choosing to live in areas where the climate and natural environment provide maximum opportunity for outdoor recreation. In the United States the amenity factor has been one of the principal reasons for the net shift of population to states such as California, Florida and Arizona. In Canada, British Columbia has, since the Second World War, had a growth rate well above the national average; between 1966 and 1971 the province grew by 16.6 per cent compared to the national average of 7.8 per cent and 72 per cent of its growth was the result of the net in-migration of people. Throughout the postwar period the province has had an unemployment rate substantially above the national average and the principal reason (unlike that of the Atlantic provinces) has been the large number of young adults who do not have secure positions on moving to the region but who are attracted by a combination of attractive environment and optimism about future job expectations. Vancouver has shared proportionately in the province's growth, since it combines employment opportunities with an attractive natural setting.

In the Canadian prairies, the urban environment provides a particularly sharp contrast to the sometimes harsh natural surroundings, which may account for the fact that a substantial amount of the recent growth of cities such as Saskatoon can be directly attributed to the in-migration of "suitcase" farmers. With the introduction of highly mechanized methods, the amount of farm labour needed has been sharply reduced, and many farmers are free to spend most of the year in the city. In the spring and fall when the farm work is heaviest the farmer will commute on weekdays to his farm, which may be as much as one hundred miles away. The reasons for this practice are similar to those which apply to the general migrant population: the advantages of better shopping and entertainment facilities (especially during the winter), better educational opportunities for children, employment openings for wives, and the possibilities of part-time employment in winter.

## The Regional Urban System

At the national level inter-urban exchanges are channelled through a small number of specialized nodes (jet airports, railway divisional points and other transportation foci) which are normally found in metropolitan centres, but at the regional level movement is more frequent, more complex and more multi-directional. Within the region, movement tends to be on an individual rather than an aggregate basis; the types of goods and services demanded frequently require that the consumer travel to the centre where these are supplied. Unlike the interaction which takes place within the national urban system, the operation of the regional economy necessitates a considerable amount of "on the ground" travel by individuals. The "friction of distance" is therefore greater at the regional level and is the principal reason for the tendency of regional urban systems to develop a regular hierarchical-spatial pattern.

Central place theory attempts to explain the regularities which occur in the distribution of settlements within regional urban systems. It is not a general theory of urban location, and does not, therefore, attempt to explain all the factors which govern the size, number and distribution of towns. It is primarily intended to offer some explanation of how a system of urban centres evolves in response to regularities in spatial behaviour in the purchase of consumer goods and services. Although a substantial proportion of the range of urban functions is accounted for by this group of consumer goods and services, there are other specialized functions which do not involve direct contact between producer and consumer and which may be of considerable importance in particular cities—for example, many types of manufacturing. Although other theories have been developed to explain the locational characteristics of some of these activities (e.g., industrial location theory), central place theory is the only one which generates a geometrically regular spatial model. In order to explain the hierarchical-spatial structure of particular regional urban systems, it is useful to use the central place model as an idealized, initial framework upon which unique regional characteristics such as topography, population density, transportation routes, historical development and economic specializations may be superimposed.

## CENTRAL PLACE THEORY

Central place theory is based on the belief that there are certain principles which govern the spatial behaviour of people in response to their demands for a wide variety of goods and services. Because of the costs (money, time and the like) involved in travel it is assumed that people will react in such a way as to minimize the overall distance which they must travel in order to obtain all the goods which they require—in minimizing the aggregate distance travelled (i.e., travel costs), a consumer actually maximizes the number of goods and services which he is able to obtain with a fixed disposable income.

The central place model is a generalized statement about the spatial arrangement of service centres at the regional level and is logically derived from a few basic assumptions about consumer behaviour, the operation of individual firms and the nature of the spatial environment. The assumptions made about the spatial behaviour of consumers are of necessity generalizations based on individual behaviour patterns and are therefore subject to variation, but when viewed collectively consumer behaviour exhibits a number of regularities. Since goods must be supplied profitably by businesses, some assumptions about the operation of a firm must also be incorporated. Furthermore, since central places are located in space, assumptions must also be made about the natural as well as the cultural features of the environment.

Because it is a deductive theory the central place model must first be seen to be internally logical, that is, as the unique outcome of a few basic assumptions, although this does not mean that the assumed conditions will correspond exactly to real-world conditions. In the social sciences all assumptions or generalizations are necessarily abstractions from reality and are therefore less-than-exact representations of the real world. If the model is internally logical then the test of its relevance to the understanding of regional urban systems will be essentially whether or not the assumptions correspond closely to reality.

Central place theory has been developed from four basic assumptions: consumers are rational and will obtain a good (or service) at the nearest centre at which it is supplied; each good has a distinctive economic range, which is the maximum distance that a consumer will travel for the purchase of the good; population is distributed uniformly over an isotropic plain (i.e., there are no areal variations in physical or cultural features and transportation is therefore equally practicable in all directions); and the spatial arrangement of central places is such that each consumer is within the economic range of all goods that are supplied. It is implicitly assumed that the trade area of each good will contain a population large enough to support the profitable operation of a firm supplying that good; in other words, each firm must draw on a minimum or "threshold" population to ensure its profitability. A further important assumption of central place theory is that the number of centres of each rank will be the minimum required to ensure that all consumers are within the economic range of all the goods that are supplied. This final constraint is a prerequisite for both the emergence of a hierarchical arrangement of central places and a unique solution of the spatial pattern. In a situation where as many central places arise as can be supported (i.e., a number equal to the number of threshold populations for each good) there will be neither an hierarchical arrangement nor a unique or optimal spatial model. The assumption that the minimum number of central places will emerge appears to be closer to the real-world conditions than is the assumption that the maximum number of centres will develop. Because of agglomeration economies there is a tendency for central place establishments to cluster. For example, consumers achieve transportation savings by making multi-purpose trips to a single centre and therefore favour centres at which a variety of goods are available. It should be noted that the existence of an urban hierarchy implies that there is a stepped gradation of functions and therefore discrete levels or ranks of towns. Thus, all the functions performed by a hamlet (the lowest rank) are also performed by a village (the next higher rank) in addition to a number of village functions which are not provided by hamlets; towns (the next higher rank) perform all the functions provided by villages in addition to a number of town functions. . . .

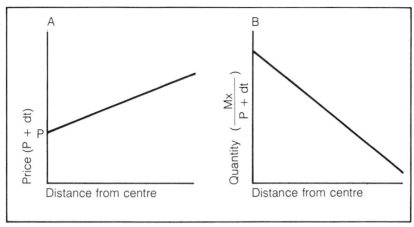

FIGURE 1.1   Price of goods and quantity purchased in relation to distance from a central place. A: The delivered price increases with distance. B: The quantity which can be purchased with a fixed income declines with distance.

THE CENTRAL PLACE MODEL

The ideal trade area of a good, and therefore of a central place, is circular. The price that a consumer pays for a good is

$$P + dt$$

where $P$ = price at the store, $d$ = distance in miles from the store, and $t$ = the travel cost per mile. Assuming that each consumer has a maximum ($Mx$) that he is willing to spend on each good, the quantity ($Q$) purchased will decline with distance (Figure 1.1), since the price of the good increases with distance; that is,

$$Q = \frac{Mx}{P + dt}$$

When $P + dt$ equals $Mx$ only one item is purchased and that distance marks the economic range of the particular good. Since travel is equally costly in all directions on the isotropic plain, the trade area of the central place supplying that good is circular. The range of a good is generally a function of the value of the article and the frequency of demand. Infrequently demanded and expensive items such as fur coats have an extensive range and are termed high-order goods, while frequently demanded and inexpensive items such as food have a smaller range and are classed as low-order goods.

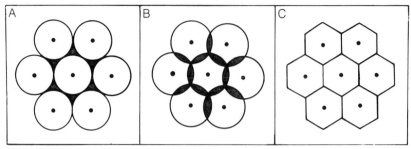

FIGURE 1.2   The optimal arrangement of central places and their market areas according to Christaller's marketing principle. A: The most economical arrangement of non-overlapping circular market areas. Unserved areas are shaded. B: The minimum overlapping of circles in order to eliminate unserved areas. Areas in which consumers are within the economic range of two centres are shaded. C: Hexagonal market areas result if each consumer is allocated to the nearest central place.

When the first-order central places (that is, those centres supplying the highest-order goods) and their circular market areas are arranged tangentially so as to pack as many as possible into a given area without overlapping, they form a triangular-hexagonal pattern. When these circles are allowed to overlap to the minimum extent necessary in order to eliminate unserved areas, the circular market areas become hexagonal while the central places remain distributed in a triangular-hexagonal pattern. Assuming that these smaller hexagonal market areas still contain the threshold population necessary for firms to supply this good profitably, the spatial arrangement of central places and of their market areas will then be optimal (Figure 1.2).

In central place theory it is postulated that first-order (A) centres supply all goods of all ranges, and that second-order (B) centres will arise in those areas which are beyond the range of certain lower-order goods supplied by the A centres. The optimal location of a B centre is at the mid-point of the equilateral triangle formed by three A centres, since it is here that the first unserved areas arise (Figure 1.3b). The lower-order good which gives rise to B centres may be termed the second-order hierarchical marginal good and B centres will have market areas equal to those of A centres for the second-order hierarchical marginal good (Figure 1.3c). The B centres will also provide all goods of a lower order than their hierarchical marginal good and further centres of successively lower rank are established by the application of the same rules as those governing the

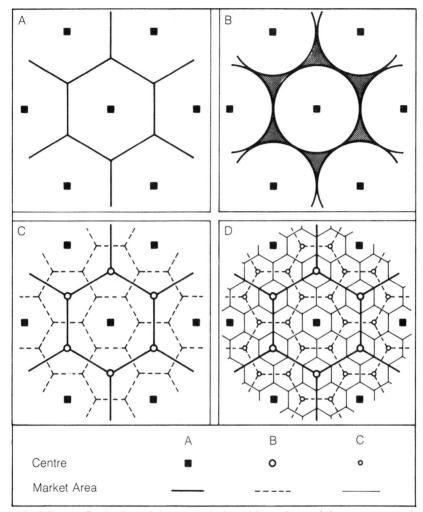

FIGURE 1.3   Derivation of the central place hierarchy and the arrangement of market areas according to Christaller's marketing principle. A: Hexagonal market areas of A centres. B: Unserved areas for lower-order goods emerge first at the mid-point of each group of three A centres. C: B centres are therefore optimally located at each of these mid-points. D: The location of A, B and C centres and their market areas.

existence of *B* centres. The method is repeated until the lowest-order centres, hamlets, have been located. Figure 1.3d shows the location and trade areas of *A*, *B* and *C* centres.

As a result of the geometrical arrangement of the central place system, at each successively lower rank there is an orderly increase in the number of centres and a constant rate of decrease in the spacing of centres. The number of *market areas* corresponding to each level of the hierarchy increases by a rule of threes: 1, 3, 9, 27, 81, 243, 729 for a 7-rank system. If the market areas of the hierarchical marginal goods alone are considered (that is, the lower-order market areas of higher-order centres are excluded) the progression is then equivalent to the number of *centres* at each rank: 1, 2, 6, 18, 54, 162, 486. The progression of centres by a rule of threes is known as the $k = 3$ network or the *marketing principle*, and the geometrical solution is such that the area is served by the minimum number of centres which will permit all consumers to be within economic range of all goods. The distances between centres increase by the $\sqrt{3}$ for each higher rank. For example, in the original formulation of the theory Christaller[1] hypothesized that the smallest central places would be 7 kilometres apart, the second-largest centres would be 12 kilometres ($7 \times \sqrt{3}$) apart, the third-largest 21 kilometres ($12 \times \sqrt{3}$) apart, and so on. The precise distances are not important, since in reality they are a function of population density, transportation technology and other variables, but they serve to illustrate the regular relationship between the spacing of centres and the level of the hierarchy.

Other central place systems have been postulated and include those which conform to the *transport principle* ($k = 4$ network) and the *administrative principle* ($k = 7$ network). Neither of these is of general or universal importance; in the first instance the isotropic plain is modified by transportation routes (and therefore as many places as possible lie along the routes connecting the higher-order centres), and in the second by political jurisdictions (where all lower-order centres must be dominated exclusively by one higher-order centre).

RELEVANCE OF THE MODEL

Central place theory, like any other theory, may be criticized not only on the soundness of the model's internal logic but also in terms of the degree to which its assumptions correspond to reality and whether it excludes other important factors.

1 W. Christaller (trans. C. W. Baskin), *Central Places in Southern Germany* (Englewood Cliffs, N.J.: Prentice-Hall, 1966).

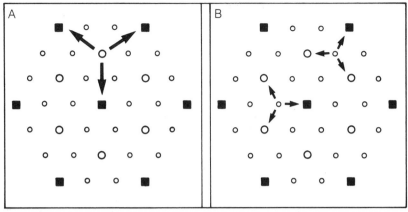

FIGURE 1.4   The sharing of lower-order central places according to Christaller's marketing principle. A: Each B centre is shared among three A centres. B: Each C centre is shared among two B centres and an A centre.

In its ideal form the central place model cannot be found in the real world, regardless of whether the theoretical assumptions obtain. *The theoretical progression of the various ranks of centres (and therefore their spacing) is possible only in an infinitely expanding set of central place systems.* The $k = 3$ network results from the fact that each high-order centre shares each of its six surrounding lower-order centres with two competing centres (Figure 1.4). The number of central places at each successively lower rank is therefore derived as follows:

$$\frac{1 \times 6}{3} = 2; \quad \frac{(1 + 2) \times 6}{3} = 6; \quad \frac{(1 + 2 + 6) \times 6}{3} = 18;$$

$$\frac{(1 + 2 + 6 + 18) \times 6}{3} = 54. \ldots$$

This obviously assumes a continuously expanding set of central place systems and the ideal arrangement therefore cannot be achieved, simply because the 1, 2, 6, 18 . . . progression would be unstable in a finite world.

It is doubtful whether the assumption of equal market area size in the case of each good is valid. For the highest-order good this assumption is valid since only one type of centre—the first-order central place—provides this good. For all lower-order goods, which by definition are provided by centres at two or more levels of the hierarchy, the assumption of equal market areas is invalid, since in reality high-order centres have larger market areas than low-order centres for the same goods. This comes about because consumers achieve transportation savings by purchasing low-order goods on trips made to high-order centres primarily in order to purchase high-order goods; typically, shopping trips are multi-purpose. *The minimization of travel costs, and therefore the maximization of benefits, will not be achieved by visiting the nearest centre where each good is available but rather by combining purchases on a fewer number of trips to high-order centres.* This problem was recognized in the original formulation of the theory but was ignored in the construction of the model, since different sizes of market areas for the same good would have resulted in geometrical irregularities in the spacing of central places. The error of assuming an equal size of market area for low-order goods is revealed by the frequent absence of the expected number of low-order centres within specified distances of large centres.

Central place theory is based on the assumption that a consumer's spatial behaviour is deterministic; specifically that a good will be purchased at the nearest centre at which it is provided. In addition to the evidence of multi-purpose trips to high-order centres described above, there is reason to question the assumption of deterministic behaviour, which implicitly assumes that individuals possess perfect knowledge of the availability of goods. (It is also possible to question other aspects of perfect competition, such as uniform price, standardized products, and uniform size of firm, but these will be ignored and the discussion restricted to spatial behaviour characteristics.) The deterministic character of spatial behaviour is more evident in some environments than in others. In areas of low population density where centres are widely spaced, it is likely that spatial behaviour will be more nearly deterministic, since distances to centres are relatively great. Errors are therefore costly, and the knowledge of the goods offered at the various centres is likely to be a significant element in the determination of consumer behaviour. In areas of high population density centres are more closely spaced and consumer movements become more probabilistic and less deterministic. Since the distances to a large number of competitive centres do not vary significantly, the savings that can be made by shopping consistently at the nearest centre for each good are relatively minor, and consumers are consequently motivated by factors other than distance minimization. Under these circumstances consumers do not attempt to maintain a clear register of where particular goods are available and therefore choose among competing centres on the basis of other variables. Accordingly, the more closely centres are spaced, the more closely consumer behaviour corresponds to the postulates of the gravity model than to the central place model. The gravity model assumes that the probability of a consumer from a particular area *(i)* travelling to a particular centre *(j)* is in direct proportion to the size of that centre ( $S_j$ ) and in inverse proportion to its distance ( $D_{ij}$ ). The attraction value of a particular centre is therefore $\dfrac{S_j}{D_{ij}}$ and

the total attraction of all competing centres is $\displaystyle\sum_{j=1}^{n} \dfrac{S_j}{D_{ij}}$ . When the attraction value of a particular centre is expressed as a fraction of the total attraction of all centres (including the centre itself), i.e.,

$$\frac{\dfrac{S_j}{D_{ij}}}{\displaystyle\sum_{j=1}^{n} \dfrac{S_j}{D_{ij}}}$$

it is equivalent to the probability of a trip $(T_{ij})$ being made to that centre. The gravity formula of consumer trip distribution is therefore

$$T_{ij} = \frac{\dfrac{S_j}{D_{ij}}}{\displaystyle\sum_{j=1}^{n} \dfrac{S_j}{D_{ij}}}$$

A further shortcoming of central place theory is the static nature of the model. Once established, a central place system does not remain unaltered if the conditions under which it evolved undergo change. The number, type and distribution of central places will theoretically be the optimal arrangement required to serve a region efficiently with a given array of goods at a particular point in time. If conditions change it is presumed that the central place system will adjust; in practice, such adjustments will result in the distortion of the spatial-hierarchical system postulated by the theory.

MODERN CHANGES IN CENTRAL PLACE SYSTEMS

The form of the central place system which develops in a region is essentially dependent on four conditions: the density of the rural population, the quality of goods demanded, the size of firms, and the mode of transportation. The effects of these on the system are such that fewer centres will be required if there is a decrease in rural population density, an increase in demand for high-order-goods, an increase in the size of firms, or an improvement in transportation.

When rural population density declines (a common occurrence in advanced economies) centres are forced to increase their market area in order to draw upon a constant trading population. In other words, the spacing of centres increases and therefore fewer centres are required in any area.

The quality of goods and services demanded by the rural population is directly related to the prevailing level of income. High-order goods consume a greater proportion of the expenditure of high-income households than of low-income households. High-order goods require high threshold populations and are therefore provided only by large centres. A rise in the average income of rural households would therefore increase the demand for higher-quality goods and would result in greater patronage of large centres than small centres. This would cause a decline in the number of centres at the lower levels of the hierarchy while the higher-order centres might either increase or remain stable in number. Changes in taste, when not caused by a rise in income, may account for the same transformations in the central place system; the adoption of an urban culture by rural households partly explains why small villages and towns are by-passed in favour of a trip to the city.

In general, there has recently been a steady increase in the size of most establishments which provide central goods and services. Increased size results in scale economies which in turn make it possible for larger establishments to sell goods at lower prices than smaller establishments. Large outlets are generally found in high-order centres, since it is only in such locations that the required threshold populations exist. The lower prices made possible by the establishment of large stores and the use of modern advertising methods help to expand the competitive range of large centres at the expense of small centres. In fact, the market areas of small centres may shrink to the point where some of their traditional functions are no longer supported by the required threshold population. In such cases there will be an upward hierarchical shift of functions; for example, some of the goods formerly provided by villages will no longer be offered by centres below the rank of towns.

The economic range of a good is determined in part by the time-cost distance, and therefore changes in transportation technology will require adjustments to the spatial-hierarchical arrangement of centres. It is evident that recent changes in transportation, including the increasing use of the automobile and more paved highways, have produced substantial reductions in the cost of local travel. The economic range of each good has therefore increased, and in practice this has resulted in the decline of small centres. As consumer sensitivity to distance decreases, the smaller centres lose one of their most important assets, their convenience, and they are accordingly unable to withstand the economic competition of larger centres. It is important to bear in mind that marked changes may be expected in those areas where the regional urban system evolved during a period when the horse and buggy was the fastest means of transportation. In a later automobile-oriented society, consumer mobility may increase to the point where for the same travelling time consumers may be within reach of up to twenty times as many centres as during the horse-and-buggy era. In this case it would be natural for the consumer to prefer the larger centre and for some of the smaller centres to be eliminated.

In most regions of advanced countries it is common for all four of the above factors to work towards a reduction in the number of central places, and in particular of low-order centres. A variety of other factors, mainly technological in nature, have also worked to reduce the number of central places. Because of technological advances in communications fewer trips are necessary in order to obtain the same array of goods and services; telephone calls, which are not as sensitive to distance, have replaced many trips, and the overall effect has been to reduce the number of short-distance trips and to extend the market area of large centres. Many low-order functions have been virtually rendered placeless or have been centralized in large centres. For example, telephone, electricity and other bills are commonly paid by mail thus eliminating what used to be a low-order trip, while television has displaced many place-oriented activities such as visits to theatres or community centres. The number of shopping trips made by an average household has

TABLE 1.4 *Changes in number, proportion and spacing of trade centres by functional class, Saskatchewan, 1941-1961*

| Type of centre | 1941 Number | % | 1961 Number | % | Characteristic spacing of trade centres (miles apart) of same class 1941 | 1961 |
|---|---|---|---|---|---|---|
| Primary wholesale and retail | 2 | 0.2 | 2 | 0.3 | 144.0 | 144.0 |
| Secondary wholesale and retail | 5 | 0.6 | 9 | 1.2 | 119.8 | 67.5 |
| Complete shopping | 26 | 2.9 | 29 | 3.7 | 40.4 | 39.5 |
| Partial shopping | 57 | 6.3 | 85 | 10.9 | 25.9 | 22.5 |
| Full convenience | 171 | 18.9 | 100 | 12.7 | 15.4 | 19.8 |
| Minimum convenience | 287 | 31.8 | 150 | 19.4 | 10.3 | 13.5 |
| Hamlet | 358 | 39.3 | 404 | 51.8 | 9.1 | 9.6 |
| Total | 906 | 100.0 | 779 | 100.0 | | |

SOURCE: Gerald Hodge, "The Prediction of Trade Center Viability in the Great Plains."

also been reduced because of the widespread availability of personal transportation (automobile), refrigerators, freezers, storable foods, credit facilities and other conveniences, as well as by the increasing proportion of households with working wives. Typically, fewer trips are made and a greater range of goods is obtained on each outing; both factors work in favour of the larger centre, since con-sumers achieve transportation savings by obtaining as many goods as possible on a single trip to a high-order centre.

One of the best-documented studies of changes in the spatial-hierarchical structure of regional urban systems has been made in Saskatchewan by Gerald Hodge.[2] (Later studies of eastern Ontario and Prince Edward Island by the same author supported the original conclusions.) Between 1941 and 1961 the number of centres in Saskatchewan declined by 14 per cent but the reduction had a differential impact on the several levels of the hierarchy and the result was a thinning out of the weaker, smaller centres. In the four highest-order ranks the number of centres increased from 90 to 125, or by 39 per cent, while the number in the three lowest-order ranks declined from 816 to 654 or by 20 per cent. Table 1.4 illustrates the

2 Gerald Hodge, "The Prediction of Trade Center Viability in the Great Plains," *Papers and Proceedings of the Regional Science Association*, vol. 15 (1965), 87-115.

TABLE 1.5 *Rate of decline\* among small trade centres in relation to distance from large centres† in Saskatchewan, 1941-1961*

| Distance from large centre (miles) | Hamlet | Minimum convenience | Full convenience | Partial shopping | All small centres |
|---|---|---|---|---|---|
| Within 10 | 55 | 81 | 43 | 100 | 61 |
| 10 - 15 | 51 | 65 | 50 | 29 | 55 |
| 15 - 20 | 36 | 38 | 24 | 29 | 38 |
| All locations (provincial average) | 46 | 58 | 34 | 23 | 51 |

SOURCE: Hodge, "The Prediction of Trade Center Viability in the Great Plains."
*in percentages
†complete shopping and other higher-ranking centres

specific changes which occurred at each level of the hierarchy, and demonstrates the greater stability of higher-order centres. Hodge found that the probability of decline among lower-order centres was directly related to their distance from higher-order centres; Table 1.5 illustrates the higher death rate of small centres within the nearer distance-zones from large centres (top three ranks).

The results of Hodge's study bear out the hypothesis that declining rural population density, increased household incomes, growth of large firms, and improved transportation (all of which had occurred in Saskatchewan between 1941 and 1961) will result in an upward hierarchical shift of functions and therefore in fewer centres, a decline in the number of low-order centres, and an increase in the number of high-order centres. The effect of these changes (as demonstrated in Saskatchewan) will be a marked alteration in the spatial-hierarchical structure. A closer spacing of high-order centres will result from an increase in their number while a wider spacing of lower-order centres will be produced by a reduction in their numbers (Table 1.4). The reduction in the average market area of high-order centres is actually accompanied by an increase in their average market area population, since the disappearance of low-order centres increases the proportion of the surrounding population which is drawn to the high-order centres.

There is clear evidence that the hierarchical-spatial structure of regional urban systems is altered as a result of changes in the variables which form the basic assumptions of central place theory, yet

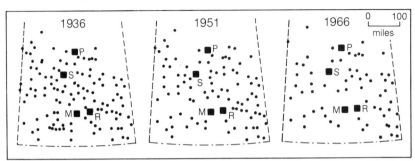

FIGURE 1.5   Changes in the distribution of trade centres in Saskatchewan, 1936 to 1966. These centres are classified as independent trade centres and are banking towns with locally published newspapers. Excluding the four cities of Regina (R), Saskatoon (S), Moose Jaw (M) and Prince Albert (P), the number of centres declined from 115 in 1936 to 89 by 1951 and to 62 by 1966.

*Source:* C. C. Zimmerman and G. W. Moneo, *The Prairie Community System* (Agricultural Economics Research Council of Canada, 1971).

the latter yields a static rather than a dynamic model of regional urban systems. There is no theoretical way of making the central place model dynamic, since centres once established tend to persist in their location in one form or another long after their original function has been altered. Thus, real-world regional urban systems which have undergone change can only be adequately understood in terms of their historical evolution.

Figure 1.6 illustrates a hypothetical example of how a central place system will adjust to the types of changes described above. It is assumed that at one time the central place system had achieved equilibrium and that the hierarchical-spatial arrangement of centres conformed to the theoretical model (Figure 1.6a). Assuming that the isotropic plain has been retained but that the range of each good has been increased because of such factors as rural depopulation, rising incomes, larger business establishments and improved transportation, the optimal arrangement for the same region will be as shown in Figure 1.6b; it should be noted that the central place system has been "stretched out," i.e., for the same area there are fewer, more widely-spaced centres. Only the metropolis is presumed to be constant in location, and there is a general lack of conformity between the hierarchical-spatial structures of the two systems. There is no theoretical solution to the problem, but Figure 1.6c illustrates one possible adjustment of the pre-existing system to the new optimal

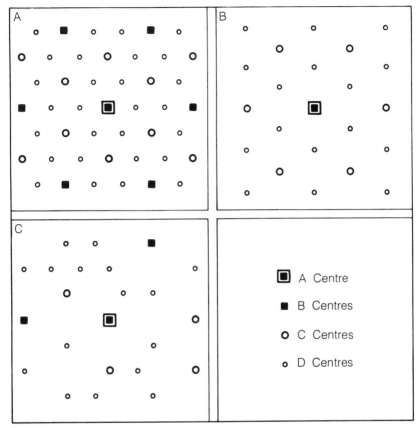

FIGURE 1.6   Adjustment of a hypothetical central place system to conditions which require fewer centres. A: Initial optimal arrangement. B: Future optimal arrangement. C: One possible outcome of the adjustment of the initial central place system to the future optimal arrangement.

arrangement, in which the existing centres have maintained or changed rank approximately in relation to their distance from the new optimal locations. It is important to note that the final solution is neither optimal according to central place theory nor predictable without historical explanation. It is therefore to be expected that in any region which has undergone changes in those conditions which form the fundamental elements of a central place system, the spatial-hierarchical arrangement of centres will not conform to the postulates of the theory, even though the theoretical principles remain valid.

# 2.
# *Internal City Structure*

The growth of cities in most societies can be generally attributed to the introduction of specialized functions, particularly those of an economic nature. Such divisions of labour or sectoral changes in the economy are manifested spatially by a clustering of specialized functions at points which enjoy production advantages; this in turn results in the development of urban settlements. As urban areas grow in size and functional complexity (from hamlet to metropolis), the efficient performance of their specialized functions is enhanced by internal areal specializations. The reasons for this internal differentiation into functional zones are generally similar to those which explain inter-city specializations and the spatial clustering of economic activities.

The forces which encourage the arrangement of urban activities into a mosaic of functional zones are mainly economic, but natural, social and cultural factors play important though variable roles in particular cities. Thus, differences in natural terrain, historical evolution and transportation systems, as well as variations in the impact of social, economic and cultural forces make each city's land use pattern unique. Although the complexity of land use arrangements within cities prohibits the development of a universal model of spatial structure, it is nevertheless clear that common land use processes can be identified within cities belonging to the same economic system. Thus, the internal structure of North American cities largely results from the operations of the "market"; the land use patterns which emerge are the outcome of competition between potential users, so that each site is generally occupied by the highest bidder.

40

Historically there have been two classical approaches to the theory of urban spatial structure: land use theory, which is based on economic principles, and descriptive land use models, which are derived largely from empirical observations. Urban land use theorists, who are usually economists, have been particularly concerned with the deductive development of highly abstract models based on severely limiting assumptions about the natural environment, land use forces and the competitive process. In contrast, descriptive land use models, used mainly by sociologists, geographers and land economists, have been largely derived inductively from observed patterns in cities, and are therefore capable of incorporating many non-economic factors.

## Land Use Theory

Classical land use models developed by location theorists are based on a number of central assumptions. It is postulated that the urban environment consists of a single-centred city on a featureless plain (often referred to as a transport surface or an isotropic plain) with equal transportation access in all directions. It is further assumed that location decisions are made by "economic man," a rational being who is interested in the maximization of some benefit such as profit, satisfaction or utility. Human geographers concerned with location analysis are increasingly resorting to the use of such economic landscapes in order to analyse the nature of man-man relationships in space.

Urban land use theory was developed as an extension of the agricultural location theory initially formulated by Von Thünen[1] in 1826. Although many of the principles of agricultural location theory are inapplicable in the urban context, strong parallels do exist between urban and agricultural land markets.

AGRICULTURAL LAND USE THEORY

Four major assumptions form the basis of agricultural location theory: there is one market centre where all agricultural products are sold; the price received for each product is determined at a level which equates supply with demand; uniform fertility prevails and as a result production costs and yield per acre are everywhere equal for the same product; transportation costs are directly related to distance

1 P. Hall, ed., *Von Thünen's Isolated State* (Oxford: Pergamon Press, 1966).

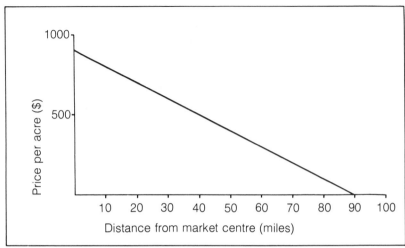

FIGURE 2.1   Profit curve for wheat farming.

and are equal in all directions. As a result of variations between products in yield per acre, price, and transportation costs, a pattern of land use zones emerges through a bidding process which ensures that each use comes to occupy that area for which it is able to pay a higher rent than competing uses. Simultaneously, the method produces a model of land use and land rent.

The development of the agricultural land use-land rent model can be explained in a very simplified form by first examining the locational competition among producers of the same commodity and, secondly, that among producers of different commodities. Assuming that each acre yield of wheat costs $100 to produce, $10 per mile to transport and has a selling price of $1,000, the farmer's profit at various distances from the market will be as shown in Figure 2.1. Assuming that the land is to be rented, competing farmers will bid up to but not more than the amount of the profits indicated for each location. If it is assumed that the production cost of $100 per acre includes a reasonable or "normal" profit, then the profits shown in Figure 2.1 are really "excess profits." In equilibrium, the bid or rent paid for land at each location will therefore be that indicated by the profit curve which thus becomes a bid-rent curve along which all profits are normal; a farmer will be indifferent as to his location along the bid-rent curve, since his profit remains the same whether he pays $800 per acre at 10 miles or $400 per acre at 50 miles. Bid-rent curves

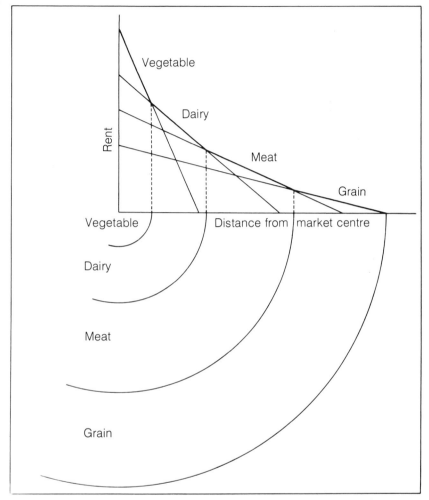

FIGURE 2.2 Bid-rent curves and land use arrangements for competing agricultural products (hypothetical).

may be similarly determined for other products as shown in Figure 2.2. The land rent at each location is equivalent to that of the highest bidder among the potential users, and the overall rent gradient is shown by the bold outer line. Land values are therefore determined by the land uses which result from competition among potential users. Since in the bid-rent formula (Bid-rent = market price -

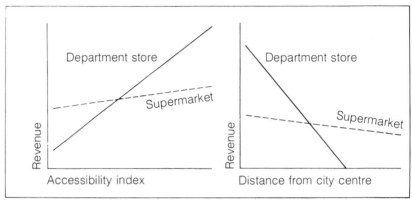

FIGURE 2.3    Revenue of a department store and a supermarket in relation to the degree of accessibility and to distance from the city centre. (Revenue is here expressed per unit of land occupied.)

production costs - transportation costs) only the costs of transportation are allowed to vary with distance from the market centre, a concentric arrangement of land values and land uses results when the bid-rent gradients are rotated around the market centre (Figure 2.2).

URBAN LAND USE THEORY

The agricultural model can be usefully extended to the urban environment, but with two important modifications. First, in the urban context it is the consumer who normally bears the cost of transportation, and so constant production levels (yields per acre in the case of agricultural production) cannot be assumed for all locations. In other words, urban goods and services are not transported from the place of production to a single market centre but rather the revenue or sales volume of a particular firm will vary according to its location with respect to consumers; the revenue of an urban firm is therefore a function of its accessibility to a potential market. (Accessibility may be defined as the number of people who can be assembled at a given point within a given period of time, and is therefore a function of both population density and the mode of transportation.) Although the revenue of all firms generally rises in accordance with increases in accessibility, some uses are able to take greater advantage of this than others. Figure 2.3 illustrates hypothetically the relationship between revenue and accessibility for two types of firm, a supermarket and a department store, respectively low-accessibility and high-accessibility uses. The operating profit of a firm is equal to its

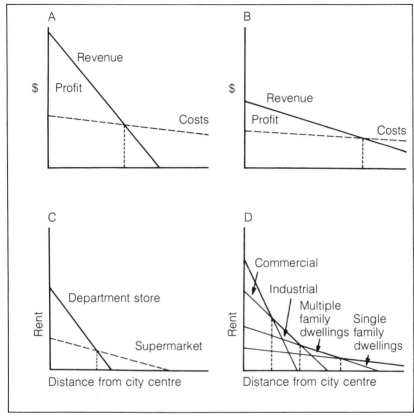

FIGURE 2.4   Derivation and structure of urban bid-rent curves in relation to distance from the city centre. A: Operating profit of a department store. B: Operating profit of a supermarket. C: Bid rents (equal to operating profits) of a department store and a supermarket. D: Generalized structure of urban bid-rent curves.

revenue less operating costs (the latter frequently varies as a function of the former) and at a particular location is equivalent to its maximum bid-rent for that site. Since accessibility generally declines with distance from the city centre (the point of maximum accessibility to consumers), decreasing profits would result if the same firm located at increasingly distant points from the centre. The bid-rent curve is accordingly steeper for high-accessibility uses than for low-accessibility uses, and the general structure of urban bid-rent curves is similar to that of agricultural land uses. (Figure 2.4).

The second and more important consideration is that the locational decision of some urban uses is not related to profit maximization. Residential locations are chosen to maximize satisfaction, which involves a combination of the amount of land and the commuting costs which a given income level can support. The form of the residential bid-rent curve does, however, bear a general similarity to other curves, since the maintenance of a similar level of satisfaction at more distant locations from the city centre usually requires that a greater amount of land be occupied (and therefore that lower prices or bid-rents be acceptable) to compensate for the increase in time and cost of commuting. Since the rich are better able to bear commuting costs, they are less location-bound than the poor, and a pattern of inner-city poor and outer-city rich therefore evolves; the poor live on expensive land but occupy small lots, while the rich consume large amounts of cheap land on the periphery. Public land uses are not generally located in order to maximize profit or to minimize cost but rather to maximize utility. Schools, hospitals, churches, parks, administrative offices and an array of public and semi-public uses cannot be included within the profit-maximization model of the real estate market. Although their locations are partly determined by the land values which result from competition among profit-oriented land users, they cannot be explained by urban land use theory. The value of a downtown park cannot, for example, be costed in dollars, since its benefits can only be measured in terms of such intangibles as mental health, happiness and general emotional well-being.

In summary, the arrangement of land uses in a city is seen as the outcome of competition for accessibility; because of the "friction of distance" (i.e., the time-cost distance between interacting agents), the ultimate distribution of land users is not random but rather the result of competition for proximity to the least-cost location, which is the point of highest accessibility for the dispersed population. Since each user will attempt to locate as close to the city centre as profitability, satisfaction or utility will permit and and since all users cannot occupy the same site, urban space becomes a scarce commodity and is therefore sold to the highest bidder in the real estate market. Firms accordingly bid on the basis of their ability to pay for accessibility, which is a function of both the economic range of the good or service they offer and the intensity with which the site is used. In practice all urban land users trade off space for accessibility; those that can operate with the smallest space requirements and which benefit from high accessibility (e.g., offices) offer the highest bid-rents and therefore locate close to the city centre, while those with the largest space requirements, almost regardless of their accessibility requirements (e.g., a golf course), bid the lowest rents and locate on the edge of the city.

Although urban land use theory provides illuminating insights into urban spatial structure, the resulting model has two serious drawbacks: the limited assumptions on which it is based, and its deterministic nature. In reality the land use process encompasses a complex array of social, economic and technological forces, in addition to the influence of the natural environment and random effects. There are, in fact, no simple causal ties between land use forces and land use patterns, and the spatial structure of every city is more complex than the zonal arrangement postulated by land use theory.

The highly idealized arrangement of the urban land use model (Figure 2.5a) can be made more realistic by simply relaxing three of the limiting assumptions concerning the urban landscape: uniform topography, equal transportation in every direction, and a single market centre. For example, the presence in every city of some topographical features such as rivers, lakes or mountains would inevitably distort the concentric land use pattern. Thus, the land use system of a port city would not be concentrically arranged around a single centre; as the city grew in size the centre of population would inevitably shift away from the original nucleus, which might remain the most accessible point only by virtue of the development of a system of fast-access radial routes, and the original transportation assumptions would, therefore, no longer apply. If the transportation network of a city consisted of major radial routes, the land use-land rent system would form a radial-concentric pattern because of the higher accessibility potentials along such routes (Figure 2.5b). Circumferential highways would further modify the accessibility surface, and necessitate the relaxation of a third assumption: the single market centre. The intersections of radial and circumferential highways would become secondary centres and the land use-land rent pattern would form a complex mosaic (Figure 2.5c).

Although the limiting assumptions related to the landscape detract from the practical contributions of the urban land use model, more fundamental shortcomings are associated with its assumptions concerning costs of operation, revenue and profit levels of urban firms. One feature which sets urban firms apart from agricultural activities

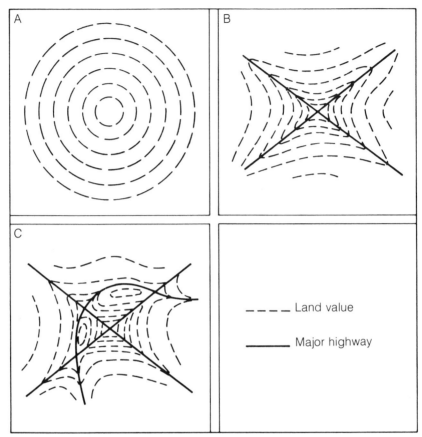

FIGURE 2.5   Hypothetical land value (and land use) patterns. A: An isotropic plain. B: A radial highway system. C: A radial-circumferential highway system.

is the importance assigned to externalities in making the locational decision. Externalities are the effects of one land use on neighbouring land uses; these effects may be either beneficial (positive externalities) or injurious (negative externalities) but by definition they cannot be "internalized" by the initiating use. Urban activities occupy such small areas and are so closely juxtaposed that they do not have the space to internalize these positive and negative effects, which inevitably spill over from each use to neighbouring uses. It is a truism that in cities everything is related to everything else. Externalities exist at various scales but are omnipresent within cities: the unpleasant aromas of a stockyard might be detectable within a radius of several miles, while the negative effects of a weed-ridden yard or unpainted house might only affect its immediate neighbours.

All urban activities are sensitive to external effects; each use is positively attracted to some and repelled by others. Competitive, complementary or like activities may, for example, cluster in order to achieve production economies or increases in revenue; such activities are subject to horizontal linkage. Thus reductions in transfer costs result where direct linkages exist between establishments, with the output of one forming the input of another. The revenue of one firm may also be indirectly dependent on proximity to quite different types of activity; restaurants and other service establishments, for example, may cater to the downtown office work force. Firms dealing in the same type of merchandise, such as shoe stores, generally increase their revenue (and their accessibility) when they locate close to each other, because of the advantages of comparison shopping to consumers. In a similar way households, which are obviously not profit-oriented (although maintenance of house value is a consideration), maximize their satisfaction by locating among compatible uses. Thus, high-income families can increase their satisfaction by locating in districts which contain only expensive housing; private golf courses may be permitted, but not a shopping centre. In short, there are two accessibility considerations for all urban users, the first to the wider population (the city), and the second to neighbouring uses; in modern cities either of these may be the more important for a particular use.

Besides the positive and negative effects generated by each activity there is another area in which externalities play an important role in the determination of land use patterns. Certain facilities necessary for the support of some activities may be too expensive for any one firm to provide or it may be impossible for a firm to internalize all the benefits; in any event, because of the existence of such externalities many location decisions are dependent on a pooling of private resources or, as is more often the case, some assistance from public authorities. These facilities are often referred to as infrastructure, and include roads, sewers and water mains, as well as more specialized assets such as airports. The decisions to build these facilities in particular places, whether made by private groups or by a

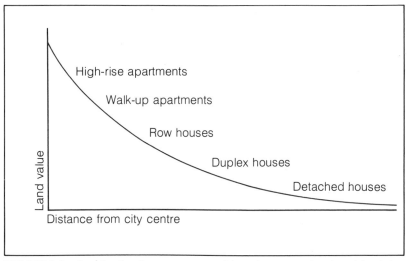

FIGURE 2.6   An idealized arrangement of housing types (and residential density) in relation to land value and distance from the city centre.

public authority, are primary decisions; these in turn instigate a chain of location decisions, and the final land use pattern can only be satisfactorily explained by reference to the whole sequence of events.

The relevance of land use theory is also limited by its assumption of constant production costs; in the classical model only revenue and rent are allowed to vary. Production costs may, however, vary according to the scale of operation, the capital outlay, the area of land occupied per unit of production, and the level of technology. For example, a retail firm may operate profitably at a location where the land value is higher than the theoretical bid-rent of the retail industry, if it reduces its production costs and/or increases its accessibility through economies of scale, advertising and the like. Firms are capable of maintaining or achieving profitability by substituting among a number of production inputs, one of which, but not necessarily the most important, is land rent. The substitution principle accounts for the existence of all uses (at a generalized level such as industrial or residential) at all distances from the city centre (Figure 2.6).

Deliberately excluded from urban land use theory are many factors, mainly non-economic, which have a largely predictable influence on location decisions; these include social and cultural values, technology, and legal and institutional structures. Also excluded are the economic factors which influence those urban firms whose products are marketed outside the local area; in such cases their locations may be only incidentally related to accessibility to the local market (they may, for example, be influenced by the land rent structure which is determined by competition among other land uses).

## Descriptive Land Use Models

There are three well-known models of urban structure (Figure 2.7): the concentric zone (Burgess). sector (Hoyt) and multiple nuclei (Harris and Ullman) models.[2] These models are generalizations of actual land use patterns observed in North American cities, and differ from those of urban location theory, which are deduced from a limited number of assumptions concerning the operation of the urban land market. This is reflected in the diversity of the variables which have been employed to explain the postulated land use patterns: economic, social, psychological, ethnic, historical, topographical and other factors.

### CONCENTRIC ZONE THEORY

Burgess generalized the land use structure of cities into five concentric zones: (1) the central business district, (2) the zone in transition, an area of mixed land uses which is being invaded by businesses and factories from the central zone, (3) the zone of workingmen's (low-income) housing, (4) the zone of better residences, and (5) the commuters' zone which extends beyond the built-up area and includes outlying settlements. He viewed the concentric arrangement of land uses as the net result of a dynamic process of physical urban growth. As urban expansion progresses there is a tendency for each zone to expand into the area of the next outer zone in a series of ecological stages, from invasion to succession. Although the zone in transition most typically evidences invasion characteristics, all zones are viewed as transitional in the long run.

Burgess himself recognized that certain factors could distort the simple concentric arrangement (such as the presence of rivers, can-

2 E. W. Burgess, "The Growth of the City," in R. E. Park and E. W. Burgess, eds., *The City*; H. Hoyt, *The Structure and Growth of Residential Neighborhoods in American Cities*; and C. D. Harris and E. L. Ullman, "The Nature of Cities."

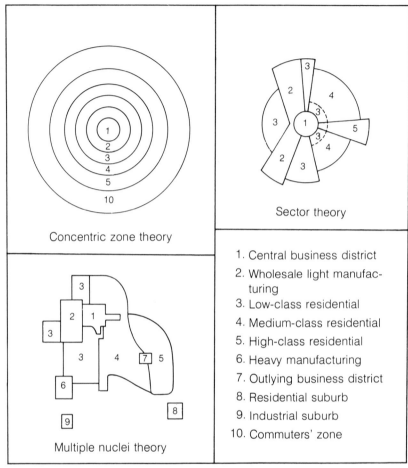

Concentric zone theory

Sector theory

Multiple nuclei theory

1. Central business district
2. Wholesale light manufacturing
3. Low-class residential
4. Medium-class residential
5. High-class residential
6. Heavy manufacturing
7. Outlying business district
8. Residential suburb
9. Industrial suburb
10. Commuters' zone

FIGURE 2.7   Descriptive models of urban land use.

*Source:* C.D. Harris and E.L. Ullman, "The Nature of Cities,"
*Annals of the American Academy of Political and Social Science,*
242 (1945).

als, railways and other natural and man-made barriers) but maintained that the underlying, organizing principles would remain important in all cities. In fact, his model best describes the pre-1920, pre-automobile North American industrial city where most activities were highly concentrated in the city centre, and is far less relevant to modern metropolitan areas. It should, however, be noted that the concentric zone model bears considerable similarity to the land use model of urban location theory, even though the two are respectively dynamic and static models.

## SECTOR THEORY

The sector theory was developed specifically in order to explain the residential pattern of the American city, particularly the location and movement of high-income housing, but Hoyt recognized that other types of land use also followed sectoral rather than concentric distribution patterns. Industrial land uses, for example, often develop linearly along railways, rivers, canals and ocean or lake shores. In his initial formulation of the theory, Hoyt advanced a number of reasons for what he termed "the sector theory of neighborhood change." Historically, high-income areas developed along the fastest transportation routes, such as streetcar and suburban railway lines. Once established, a high-income area tends to migrate outwards by accretions to its outer edge, thus following a definite sectoral path; to some extent this is the natural direction of expansion, since the land is normally vacant. The trend is often emphasized by the efforts of real estate developers and speculators who, in anticipation of sectoral expansion, place a high price on the land or restrict it to expensive housing and compatible uses. The sectoral pattern may also result from the tendency of high-income housing to spread towards high ground and along amenity areas such as water fronts (river, lake or ocean) where these have not already been appropriated by industry.

In formulating the sector theory of city structure, Hoyt emphasized that a particularly important characteristic of urban expansion is its tendency to develop along fast radial routes and around specialized transportation facilities, but he also recognized that concentric zonal patterns exist within each sector. Within residential sectors, this is due to variations in the age and modernity of buildings; old, obsolescent housing in the inner ring of high-income sectors will "filter down" to lower-income households which often consist of older, retired persons, young single adults, or childless couples. Thus, the distributional patterns of most housing groups (defined in terms of social, economic, cultural or ethnic characteristics) vary on a sectoral basis, with distinct concentric gradations moving out from the city centre.

MULTIPLE NUCLEI MODEL

The multiple nuclei model is based on the premise that urban land use patterns are in reality far more complex than the simple arrangements postulated by the concentric and sector theories. The complexity of these patterns is presumed to be a function of the grouping of activities around not one but several discrete centres or nuclei. These foci may result either from the coalescence of formerly separate communities into a single metropolitan area or from the establishment of a major facility, such as an iron and steel plant; in either case, the larger the city, the more numerous and specialized will be the nuclei. Harris and Ullman offered four explanations for the emergence of separate nuclei and their associated land use patterns: certain activities which require specialized facilities may have only a limited number of potential sites (for example, many manufacturing plants need flat land with access to water or rail transportation); complementary or like activities tend to cluster together; some activities are repelled by others; and certain activities, such as bulk storage, have low rent-paying ability and are unable to compete with other uses for the more desirable sites.

Perhaps the most important contribution of the multiple nuclei model is the emphasis which it places on factors unrelated to accessibility, such as site characteristics, historical development and the presence of externalities. The more realistic approach of this model, particularly its inclusion of the unique factors of site and history, has, however, a serious shortcoming: the physical arrangement of land uses is capable of almost infinite variation. This absence of a distinctive form makes it necessary to regard each city's land use system as unique, and the model fails, therefore, to provide an overview of urban spatial structure. The multiple nuclei theory may be more accurately described as a collection of general statements about land use relationships than as a model of urban form.

## Conclusion

Land use theory provides a useful model which highlights certain economic principles of urban spatial structure but which is not a complete theory of city structure. The basic economic assumption which the theory makes is that each site will be developed to the "highest and best use," that is, the one which can afford to pay the highest price among competing uses. Although the economic princi-

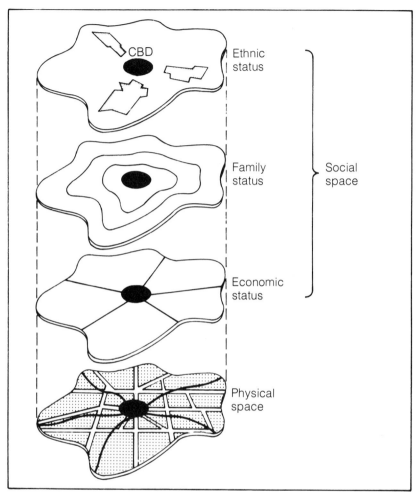

FIGURE 2.8   A spatial model of urban social structure.

*Source:* R.A. Murdie, *Factorial Ecology of Metropolitan Toronto, 1951-1961,*
          Research Paper 116, Department of Geography, University of
          Chicago (University of Chicago Press, 1969).

ples can be extended to more realistic environments which are less
constrained than the single-centre, featureless plain, the model soon
becomes distorted to the point where almost infinite variations are
possible. A further criticism is that other important factors, both of
an economic (externalities and input substitutions) and non-

economic (social, cultural and technological) nature are not considered. Although the effects of these factors are quite predictable they cannot be fully incorporated into a single theory of land use. In part this is due to the operational impossibility of reducing the complex interrelationships among urban land uses to a finite set of equations in the case of any large city. Since no use can be optimally located without the simultaneous location of other uses (because of the influence of externalities) a general theory of land use is impossible even for hypothetical, "instant" cities; the millions of potential sites (since urban activities occupy "points" compared to the "areas" of agricultural activities) would require nearly infinite sets of equations. Land use theory is ultimately capable only of providing insights into the nature of urban spatial structure, and in this respect the urban land use model described above has considerable value.

Although each of the three descriptive land use models isolates certain underlying land use principles, none of them adequately describes the reality of internal city structure; nor is it possible to sum the relevant elements of each into a general theory of urban land use. However, with specific reference to urban social structure it has been suggested that the three models complement one another, since each describes one of the three important dimensions of social differentiation within cities. Thus, social rank and economic status are sectorally arranged, demographic structure and family status vary concentrically, and particular ethnic characteristics exhibit segregated patterns (Figure 2.8). The super-imposition of these three surfaces therefore represents a partial model of urban social space. In the final analysis, all three models are partial theories of city structure, simplicity being at once their most important asset and their chief limitation.

# 3.

# Urban Land Use Structure

At first glance the land use distributions of urban areas seem rather haphazard, and this impression is strengthened by the marked variation in spatial structure from one city to another. In fact, urban land use patterns exhibit a considerable degree of regularity and owe their differences largely to variations in the characteristics of the natural environment, the historical timing of major growth periods, the size of cities and the types of functions performed by them.

The land use structure of a particular city may be quite adequately explained in terms both of the methods currently used for moving people, goods and information and also of the legacy of past technologies. The mosaic of functional zones which characterizes the urban spatial system is largely a function of the size of the city and the available means of transportation. As a city grows in size the horizontal linkages which exist among like or complementary uses (e.g., the output of one may form the input of another) generally encourage their segregation within a common "functional zone" in order to increase their productivity, satisfaction or utility. Because of the overall interdependency of urban activities areal specializations would require commensurate levels of efficiency in inter-zonal circulation; for example, the tendency of workplaces to amass within a specific area is limited by the degree to which workplace and home can be conveniently separated. It is, therefore, the facility with which movement occurs within the city that determines the practical extent of the spatial separation of various urban activities. Accordingly, the cheaper and more efficient the transportation, the greater will be the potential spatial differentiation of a city by function.

Although it is obviously difficult to establish simple cause-and-effect relationships, many of the modern changes in urban spatial structure are clearly rooted in technological advances in transportation, communication and production.

## Technology and Urban Structure

Until the middle of the nineteenth century cities were severely limited in terms of their physical dimensions and internal structure by transportation technology; journeys were on foot for the majority of residents, "on hoof" for the few wealthy people, and goods were generally moved by horse and cart. The foot-and-hoof city rarely exceeded a radius of about three miles, or an hour's walking distance. Even Imperial Rome, the largest of the ancient cities of Europe, covered only about eight square miles. Because of the inadequacy of intra-urban transportation different land uses such as factories, shops and homes were juxtaposed; in other words, the inter-zonal transfer costs resulting from functional segregation generally outweighed any possible intra-zonal savings. This pattern is well illustrated by the common coincidence of a medieval craftsman's activities in one building: workshop at the back, showroom at the front and residence on the upper floor. In addition the guild quarters, the guild church and other fraternity institutions were usually located in the neighbourhood where the majority of guild members lived and worked.

The major nuclei of the nineteenth-century city were the terminals of long-distance transportation routes; factories, warehouses and other goods-handling activities tended to circumvent the inadequacy of intra-urban transportation by locating at river, rail, canal or ocean transportation terminals. Houses and tenements were generally built within easy walking distance of factories and other workplaces, and increases in the urban population were more often accommodated in higher density development than in horizontal spread.

Until the 1860s, all the major transportation advances in Canada took place in the long-distance (inter-urban) systems. The dredging of river channels and the construction of canals and railways had greatly improved the efficiency of long-distance transportation, and the telegraph had been developed as an efficient means of sending information across thousands of miles. Internal transportation, however, was still largely medieval in character, and most exchanges depended on one of the three basic means—foot, horse and cart. In the late 1840s the first public transportation systems were inaugurated in Canada; in 1847 the eight-mile Montreal and Champlain Railroad between Montreal and Lachine provided a commuter service, and in 1849 a horse-drawn omnibus service was introduced between Yorkville (then a high-income suburb outside the city) and King Street in Toronto. In 1861 horse-drawn streetcars made their appearance for the first time in Toronto and Montreal, heralding an era of extensive and, on the whole, well-integrated public transit systems. Although they greatly increased the efficiency of intraurban movement the main effect of the horse-drawn streetcar was to support the growth of high-income suburbs. In 1884 North America's first electric streetcar was introduced during the ten-day Agricultural Fair in Toronto; the line ran between the Exhibition grounds and the terminus of the city's horse-drawn car service at Strachan Avenue. Two years later Canada's first commercial electric street railway, (1¹/₂ miles in length) was opened in Windsor and in the following year (1887) the first inter-city electric railway was opened along the seven-mile route (originally built in 1881 as a horse-car route) between Thorold and St. Catharines. During the 1890s the electric cars rapidly supplanted the horse-drawn cars in most cities and a number of inter-city railways were also built. After 1880 the expansion of the telephone network added to the growing intra-urban communications system.

The electric streetcar, the telephone and the increasingly widespread use of electricity were probably the most important technological developments in the three decades before the First World War. Together they made it possible for residential areas to spread outwards from the city centre much farther than ever before, while on the other hand, because of the inadequacy of goods transportation methods, factories remained concentrated at rail and water terminals. Particularly as a result of the rapid extension of streetcar service after 1890, homes and workplaces became increasingly separated in most Canadian cities. High- and low-income suburbs developed along streetcar lines, and gave rise to the characteristic radial or star-like urban patterns of this period. In larger cities such as Toronto intercity railways (appropriately called radials in Ontario), promoted the attenuation of urbanized areas along a few major axes, although their use was not as widespread in Canada as in the United

Courtesy Toronto Transit Commission

*A present-day Toronto street-car.*

States. Some service activities, notably retailing, also began to decentralize in response to the development of residential suburbs. At first, stores were mainly local in nature and were situated near streetcar stops for the convenience of people returning home from work; gradually they became more numerous and eventually merged to form continuous commercial ribbons. Strip retail developments on Main Street in Winnipeg, Queen Street in Toronto and Hastings Street in Vancouver, for example, were greatly expanded after the introduction of the first streetcars.

Although in use by the turn of the century, it was not until about 1920 that the internal combustion engine began to revolutionize the land use structure of cities. In terms of the land use system the most important characteristic of the car is its door-to-door convenience; since the entire trip may be made without resorting to any additional form of transportation, the location decision of an urban user may be made on a correspondingly flexible basis and will produce a more

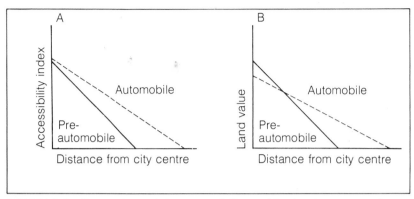

FIGURE 3.1 Comparison of the accessibility and land value curves of an automobile city and a pre-automobile city with similar populations.

concentric than radial pattern of development—a return to the concentric form of the medieval city (albeit on a much enlarged scale) which evolved in response to the flexibility of foot travel. Trucks also became increasingly common after 1920, and their use was a major factor in the decentralization of goods-handling activities. Although motor buses were widely introduced in the 1920s it was not until after the Second World War that they supplanted the fixed-route systems of the electric streetcar and trolley bus—so successfully that Toronto is now the only Canadian city where streetcars are still in use.

The automobile has significantly altered the traditional accessibility, density and land value surfaces in cities. In absolute terms the advent of the automobile increased accessibility levels throughout the city (i.e., during a given period of time a greater number of people could be assembled at each site in the city than at the same site in the pre-automobile era) but in relative terms accessibility increased more in the periphery than in the centre of the city (Figure 3.1a). As a result of the more uniform nature of the accessibility surface, land values in the post-automobile era should theoretically be reduced at the city centre and increased in the outer areas, assuming a constant population or demand for urban land (Figure 3.1b). In fact, land values have rarely been reduced at the city centre (even after discounting the effect of inflation) principally as a result of the increases in total population which have occurred in almost every city. If the level of transportation technology remains un-

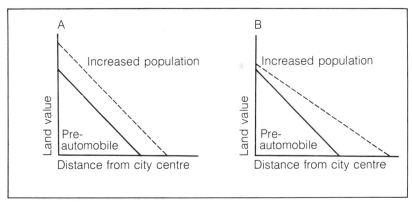

FIGURE 3.2   Impact of an increase in population on the land value curve of a pre-automobile city. A: Before the advent of the automobile.
B: Accompanied by the advent of the automobile.

changed any expansion of the population will commonly produce a fairly uniform increase in the price of land at all distances from the centre (Figure 3.2a). The combined effects of population growth and the advent of the automobile on the land value curve of most cities is illustrated in Figure 3.2b.

The availability of advanced communications systems has fostered a growing propensity for firms to substitute communications for transportation (for example, a telephone call instead of a personal visit). The substantial reduction in the costs of transporting goods, people and information has conferred a "footloose" status on most urban activities, which simply means that such activities are relatively free to choose locations on the basis of criteria other than transportation costs. In practice, greater locational freedom has led to a more even spread of activities but with a definite bias towards peripheral development.

The "spread city" has not produced a dilution of functional areal differentiation, but rather an increasing segregation of land uses. The modern tendency towards increased areal specialization is the indirect result of a general reduction in transportation costs; since the accessibility of each site to the wider population has been increased, this element of the location decision has declined in importance relative to that of proximity to related uses. In other words, as a result of transportation improvements, inter-zonal transfer costs have been more reduced than intra-zonal transfer costs, and many

TABLE 3.1 *Employment distribution by place of work, Metropolitan Toronto Planning Area, 1956-1964*

| Place of work | 1956 | | 1960 | | 1964 | |
|---|---|---|---|---|---|---|
| | No. | % | No. | % | No. | % |
| City of Toronto | 467,500 | 70.6 | 448,900 | 63.7 | 436,300 | 58.1 |
| (Central area) | (300,700) | (45.2) | (297,200) | (42.2) | (284,000) | (37.8) |
| York and East York (inner boroughs) | 63,500 | 9.6 | 58,400 | 8.3 | 56,700 | 7.5 |
| Etobicoke, North York and Scarborough (outer boroughs) | 99,000 | 15.0 | 167,400 | 23.7 | 218,700 | 29.2 |
| Rest of planning area | 32,000 | 4.8 | 30,400 | 4.3 | 39,200 | 5.2 |
| Total | 662,000 | 100.0 | 705,100 | 100.0 | 750,900 | 100.0 |

SOURCE: Metropolitan Toronto Planning Board

complementary or like activities are now able to achieve external or agglomerative economies by clustering. Since transportation costs will never fall to zero, it can be assumed that functionally interdependent firms will continue to exploit these economies by locating close to each other. This phenomenon is not, however, unique to business concerns but applies equally to residences. People with similar socio-economic characteristics cluster in order to increase their satisfaction with their living environment; in effect, they achieve external aesthetics or neighbourhood prestige by locating close to each other. As a result neighbourhoods become more internally homogeneous and differences between the neighbourhoods become more marked; the larger the urban area, the greater is the segregation of its inhabitants by income, occupation, ethnicity, religion and so on. Because they have been more recently developed, suburban neighbourhoods are also more homogeneous than inner residential districts.

Probably the most important characteristic of the modern metropolis is the trend towards decentralization, evidenced by a relative decline in the importance of the central area for most urban activities. Technological, economic and social forces have combined to promote reduced densities throughout the metropolitan area and, on balance, have encouraged a proportional shift of functions to the periphery, particularly since the outward movements of various activities, such as housing, retailing and manufacturing tend to reinforce each other. Historical data on place of employment for the documentation of changing intra-urban workplace patterns are not generally available in Canada. However, Table 3.1 indicates the changes that occurred in metropolitan Toronto between 1956 and 1964; these patterns are similar to those which have been observed for metropolitan areas in the United States.

The decentralization of activities as a result of technological advances in production is perhaps most evident in the manufacturing industry. New production methods and the increasing proportion of the market devoted to highly manufactured goods (such as electronic or precision equipment) have generally increased the price of finished products relative to the costs of transportation and greater emphasis has accordingly been placed on internal economies of scale, automation, horizontal assembly-line techniques and other facets of the production process, and less on the transportation of raw materials and finished goods. Technological innovations have also affected the mode of operation and therefore the locational pattern of many other urban activities including retail stores, wholesale establishments and offices.

Freedom to choose among many suitable locations is becoming an increasingly relevant factor in both business and household decision-making as a result of reduced accessibility differentials and the variety of production methods. By substituting among various inputs each user can operate profitably at a number of locations. For example, a particular manufacturer might choose between two equally profitable methods of operation: a large single-storey plant in the suburbs where he might employ a large amount of cheap land, low labour inputs, and large capital outlays; or a multi-storey or loft building in the city centre where he might employ high labour inputs, low capital investments and a small amount of land. In practice, technological advances have favoured the suburban alternative, but the substitution principle accounts in part for the observed existence of most types of land use at all distances from the city centre.

The most important factor favouring peripheral locations is probably not the push of the city centre (high land values, congestion) but the pull of the suburbs, where the most obvious attraction is the

Photo by Earl Kennedy, Specialized Photographic Services

*Winnipeg's Symington Yards—an integrated road and rail terminal.*

availability of large amounts of vacant land. Public restrictions (zoning, for example) tend to be less stringent, while the undeveloped state of the site allows the builder a considerable degree of latitude in the construction and design of his plant. Suburban sites for a single building (e.g., a shopping centre) or for a complex of buildings (e.g. an industrial park) are often close to fifty times the size of a typical city block—for example, the 108-acre Sherway Gardens Shopping Centre in Toronto and the 296-acre tract for the Canadian Mint in Winnipeg. Apart from the flexibility of vacant land, a number of other factors favour the suburbanization of activities: low land values, little congestion and proximity to modern transportation facilities including airports, expressways and integrated rail-and-road terminals.

## Manufacturing Land Use

Historically, manufacturing has evidenced a strong and consistent trend towards decentralization; almost without exception the central industrial zones of metropolitan areas have been declining both absolutely and relatively for more than fifty years. The modern suburbanization of manufacturing is related to the growth of trucking after 1920, but even by the turn of the century there was already some evidence of decentralization associated with the construction of suburban railway terminals and circumferential or belt lines. The availability of streetcar lines frequently encouraged this trend, which was most evident in the case of nuisance industries such as meatpacking, and space-consuming operations such as railway-car repair shops. Even in the new cities such as Calgary, Edmonton, Saskatoon and Winnipeg, the process of decentralization was clearly under way by the outbreak of the First World War.

As with other urban uses, the present distribution of manufacturing in any metropolitan area can only be explained in terms of the locational forces operating at each significant period of its history. In Canada, there have been three particularly important periods during which similar locational forces applied: the water transportation era up to the 1850s, the railway era up to the First World War, and the modern highway era. Prior to 1850, few Canadian cities had experienced any significant industrial development; although Montreal and Quebec had the most important and diversified industrial structure. In those cities with navigable water frontage, including Montreal, Toronto and Hamilton, the railway terminals of the subsequent era were located close to the harbour to facilitate the transfer of goods from one mode of transportation to the other.

*The Coca-Cola Ltd. plant in Winnipeg's Inkster Industrial Park.*

Towards the end of the nineteenth century the rapid growth of the Canadian manufacturing industry stimulated the development of an industrial concentration in the railway-harbour area of these cities — a pattern reinforced by the inadequacy of intra-urban goods transportation. In the prairies little industrial development had preceded the arrival of the railway, which in every instance determined the subsequent industrial pattern. After 1920 the increasing use of trucking freed many plants from their former locational ties with the long-distance transportation terminals, while later developments such as modern expressways and highway systems, containerization, piggy-back rail operations (the transportation of truck trailers on railway flat-cars) and air transportation, also encouraged the shift to the suburbs. In sum, the cost of intra-urban transportation is no longer an important factor in the location decision of most manufacturing concerns.

The internal shift of manufacturing employment is the net result of a complex process during which new firms are set up, firms move from one part of the city to another, firms cease to function or leave the metropolitan area, and differential rates of growth exist between those firms which are advantageously located and those which are poorly located. On the whole, the benefits of a suburban location for modern firms are much greater than those of a central site; because of the advantages of single-storey buildings for modern assembly-line methods, manufacturing plants have become extensive users of land and the availability of large tracts of cheap vacant land in the suburban fringe has become one of the strongest forces promoting decentralization. An additional attraction is the fact that property taxes are frequently lower in suburban municipalities. In addition, transportation costs are often lower for suburban plants; this is particularly true in the case of firms serving regional or national markets since suburban sites often enjoy easier access to the national or intermetropolitan transportation system, but it applies also to some locally oriented industries. Finally, it is in the suburbs that an increasing proportion of the manufacturing work force lives. It is also worth noting the growing importance of prestige factors in some suburban locations; national and international firms are particularly aware of their public image and, where possible, well-landscaped grounds and attractive buildings are used to advantage.

Despite widespread decentralization, the central industrial zone of metropolitan areas has remained an important though increasingly specialized employment district. In Metro Toronto (Municipality of Metropolitan Toronto), for example, about one-fifth of metropolitan industrial employment is in the old, pre-1920 manufacturing district which lies south of Queen Street, between the Don Valley in the east and Dufferin Street in the west. As a result of selective migration central manufacturing firms are typically small, except for a few large plants which remain tied to the area either because of their need for specialized transportation facilities or because of excessive relocation costs (an inertia factor).

For some manufacturing firms the central area may be an optimal location; when this is the case, it can usually be traced to their dependence on external economies. They may, for example, require access to the general services, specialized facilities and markets of the city centre. Many complementary or similar firms jointly share specialized facilities such as showrooms, while plants engaged in the manufacture of new or unstandardized products need to be in close contact with clients, buyers and suppliers who either operate in the city centre or are most easily assembled there. By taking advantage of external economies the production costs of a small firm in the city centre may be low enough to compete with those of larger suburban plants. This can be achieved in a number of ways: by renting rather than purchasing equipment and accommodation (the latter usually in low-rent loft buildings); by using the services of transportation companies rather than providing its own (particularly if the firm ships less-than-carload lots); by retaining the services of specialists such as lawyers and accountants on a part-time or contractual basis; by subcontracting work which might require expensive equipment; by reducing its stock of raw materials because of the proximity of wholesalers; by not providing many employee conveniences, such as snack bars and parking space, because these are readily available in the area.

In many respects the central city functions best as a "business nursery" or "incubator." The new firm is generally short of capital and tries to devote as much as possible of what is available to the actual production of goods. Accordingly, it is very dependent on external services which can be used quickly and inexpensively when the need arises. As the firm grows and production expands it is often more economical to internalize many of these services, and as a result the firm may then decide to move to the periphery; because of their larger size and distance from the city centre, suburban plants generally need to be less dependent on external services than their central area counterparts. Not all small central area firms are, however, newly established ventures which will later move to suburban locations. Many firms, particularly those in the communication-oriented industries, choose a permanent central location.

Communication-oriented firms are those which manufacture unstandardized products and which, therefore, need to have immediate access to buyers and suppliers; examples of such firms are found in the clothing and job-printing industries. Speed is essential if the firm is to survive; it may, for example, be only a matter of hours between the receipt and delivery of a job-printing order, while a women's clothing manufacturer may have to switch lines completely at very short notice. Another characteristic of these firms is the unpredictability or variability of the demand with which they must cope. The maintenance of sufficient stocks and equipment to meet such fluctuations would be beyond the financial ability of most firms, and they therefore rely heavily on wholesalers, rental equipment and subcontractors. The uncertainty of outlook makes long production runs uneconomical and frequently impossible, and as a result communication-oriented firms are usually small and dependent on external economies. In some cities the concentration of a large number of similar firms in the central area promotes complex interdependencies which benefit all firms and which make it difficult for any one firm to move away; in the clothing industry, for example, jobbers, designers, cutters, wholesalers, showrooms, equipment

TABLE 3.2 *Manufacturing employment, downtown and metropolitan Winnipeg,
1966*

| Industrial group | Downtown No. | % | Metropolitan No. | % | Downtown as % of metropolitan |
|---|---|---|---|---|---|
| Textile and clothing | 4,804 | 40.5 | 5,640 | 14.4 | 85.0 |
| Printing and publishing | 2,984 | 25.2 | 3,685 | 9.4 | 80.1 |
| Food and beverages | 1,448 | 12.2 | 8,954 | 22.8 | 16.3 |
| Other | 2,621 | 22.1 | 20,982 | 53.4 | 12.5 |
| Total | 11,857 | 100.0 | 39,261 | 100.0 | 30.2 |

SOURCE: Metropolitan Corporation of Greater Winnipeg

renters and the manufacturers themselves are highly interdependent. The newspaper industry is an example of a communication-oriented industry which despite large plant sizes is attracted to downtown locations because of its dependence on immediate personal contact with a large and often unpredictable number of news sources. Its goods-handling operations and deliveries are usually made at off-peak periods (at night or mid-afternoon) and thus avoid the drawbacks of traffic congestion in the central area. Table 3.2 illustrates the very specialized nature of manufacturing in downtown Winnipeg, where the textile-clothing and printing-publishing industries together accounted for 65.7 per cent of manufacturing employment in 1966; for both industries more than 80 per cent of metropolitan employment was located downtown.

Because of the importance of goods-handling operations, the distributional pattern of the wholesale industry is similar to that of manufacturing and has been decentralizing at a particularly rapid rate; the importance of truck transportation, congestion in the city centre and the suitability of one-storey buildings for wholesaling operations have been the most compelling factors. The outward shift of manufacturing has itself contributed to a similar movement among wholesalers specializing in producer goods. The central area has retained a certain amount of wholesaling activity, mainly of the type which involves direct selling to buyers as a primary function; in these cases clustering in the city centre facilitates the comparison shopping of both metropolitan and out-of-town buyers. In contrast, the warehouses of national distributors are almost always located on the periphery of metropolitan areas.

## Residential Land Use

The residential location decision results from the interaction of two generally opposing forces: minimization of the time-cost distance to work (centripetal force), and the maximization of living space (centrifugal force). Rising incomes, almost universal car ownership and the decentralization of employment, have greatly expanded the number of potential locations available to households by reducing the time-cost of commuting. This greater locational freedom has increased the consumption of cheap land on the periphery, and as a result suburbs are spreading outwards at progressively lower population densities. The basic pattern of residential land use has, however, remained unchanged.

One of the main reasons for the spread of households to low-density, peripheral locations is only indirectly related to lower transportation costs. The North American goals of privacy, child-oriented family life and home ownership have encouraged the development of house-centred activities and made the individual households more self-sufficient than ever before. Largely because of improvements in communications, an increasing number of leisure activities are now placeless, that is, they do not involve physical movement outside the home. These include the use of newspapers, books, television and radio as sources of entertainment and information; the use of the telephone to reduce the need for many social and other outings; and large back yards, perhaps with a swimming pool, which provide opportunities for play, entertainment and relaxation. In many instances, the journey to work has remained the only frequent outing (excluding the generally short shopping and school trips), thus increasing the level of commuting costs which some households are willing to tolerate. These trends are directly reflected in the increased importance of "house and lot" features in the location decision; consideration of the site, size, and design of the house, neighbourhood quality and other local elements have gained in significance at the expense of location with respect to the workplaces of household members.

APARTMENT DISTRIBUTION

One of the most conspicuous features of the contemporary metropolitan landscape is the high-rise apartment building. In the 1960s the construction of apartments rose steeply, in marked contrast to the dominance of single-family housing in the 1950s; in metropolitan

TABLE 3.3 *Apartment buildings by height (number of floors), Metro Toronto, 1959–1973*

| Number of Floors | Number of buildings | | | | | | | |
|---|---|---|---|---|---|---|---|---|
| | 1959 | 1961 | 1963 | 1965 | 1967 | 1969 | 1971 | 1973 |
| 2 - 5 | 2951 | 3103 | 3199 | 3215 | 3224 | 3226 | 3220 | 3213 |
| 6 - 9 | 161 | 283 | 419 | 468 | 497 | 521 | 537 | 552 |
| 10 - 14 | 48 | 57 | 87 | 142 | 194 | 241 | 303 | 346 |
| 15 - 19 | 4 | 7 | 8 | 34 | 76 | 121 | 175 | 220 |
| 20 - 24 | — | — | — | 5 | 23 | 43 | 70 | 93 |
| 25 - 29 | — | — | — | 3 | 7 | 14 | 21 | 38 |
| 30 + | — | — | — | — | 1 | 5 | 6 | 11 |
| Total | 3164 | 3450 | 3713 | 3867 | 4022 | 4171 | 4332 | 4473 |

SOURCE: Metropolitan Toronto Planning Board

areas the shift was even more significant. Although data are not available for most Canadian cities, it is clear that a substantial proportion of the recently built apartment units were located in high-rise structures—this was particularly the case for metropolitan Toronto (Table 3.3). Within a relatively short period, the apartment boom has had a considerable impact on the structure of the housing market, which in turn has affected the urban spatial pattern.

The principal reason for the recent increase in apartment construction is related to changes in the age structure and household composition of the population. Typically, about one-half of all home purchases are made by people in the 25-34 age bracket and the low birth rate of the 1930s and early 1940s therefore caused a decline in the home-buying market during the 1960s. Also at this time, the members of the postwar baby boom were in the below-25 age group, which characteristically exhibits a high demand for rental accommodation; by the early 1970s members of this group were in the home-buying age bracket. There is, therefore, some reason to expect that apartments will in future constitute a smaller proportion of the new housing stock; for example, between 1970 and 1973 single-detached houses increased from 37 per cent to 49 per cent of the total number of dwelling units constructed in Canada, while apartments declined from 48 per cent to 40 per cent during the same period.

Other reasons for the recent boom indicate that the demand for apartments will probably continue, although at a rate below that of the mid — 1960s peak. Since the Second World War there has been a consistent increase in the proportion of one- and two-person households, due both to the growing number of retired people in the population and to the trend towards household formation at an earlier average age; among these groups the demand for rental accommodation is generally high. In Canada the number of one-person households (excluding roomers or boarders in private homes, lodging houses or institutions) increased from 9.3 per cent of all households in 1961 to 11.4 per cent in 1966 and to 13.4 per cent in 1971; in metropolitan areas the incidence of one-person households is much above the national average because of selective in-migration. The high cost of serviced land and improvements in construction techniques for multi-storey structures have made it more economical for developers to meet these rental demands by building high-rise apartments rather than detached or other low-density housing. Partly as a result of this, the cost of rental accommodation has recently increased at a slower rate than that of home ownership; for example, between 1961 and 1973 the former increased by 26.4 per cent compared to 107.0 per cent for the latter and 50.4 per cent for the overall consumer price index.

The changing life styles of many small households, which are frequently childless, have also contributed to the demand for apartments. For these people apartment living is often more convenient, particularly since it does not involve the physical tasks of house maintenance, snow removal, lawn mowing and so on. The generally wider acceptance of apartment living is also evident from the recent evolution of a new type of housing in Canada, the condominium. A residential condominium is a building complex where an individual owns and is wholly responsible for the space contained within a dwelling unit (an apartment, a row house or even a detached house), while the balance of the structure—the exterior walls and the land — are owned jointly by all the homeowners. Normally the maintenance and upkeep of the jointly owned property (landscaping, lawn mowing, snow removal, roof repairs, exterior decorating, janitorial services and the like) are supervised by a group elected by the homeowners, with the costs apportioned to each dwelling unit on some pre-arranged basis (e.g., in proportion to the floorspace within

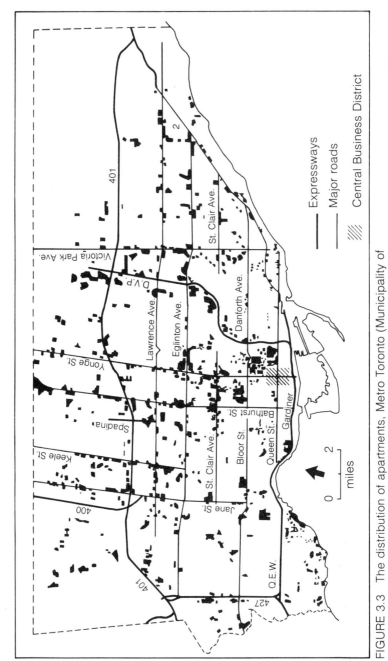

FIGURE 3.3  The distribution of apartments, Metro Toronto (Municipality of Metropolitan Toronto)

Source:  Metropolitan Toronto Planning Board.

each unit). Particularly in Toronto, the condominium concept, which is normally applied to row housing, has been extended in many instances to high-rise buildings.

The locational pattern of recent apartment construction has been quite different from the previously existing spatial structure. Traditionally, apartments have been located on the fringe of the central business district and along major arterial routes, in order to accommodate the former dependence of apartment dwellers on access to employment by public transit or on foot. Although these locations have remained important, the most striking feature of recent apartment construction is the large proportion built in the suburbs, often near highways and expressways (see Figure 3.3). The drawbacks associated with central apartment locations are partly economic and include such factors as the high price of land, high tax rates, demolition costs, and practical difficulties in assembling large parcels of land and in obtaining the rezoning approvals which are frequently required. Other deterrents are the generally unattractive environment, the lack of parks and other amenities, and traffic congestion. When the demand for apartments is considerable, as it was during the 1960s, the generally slow rate at which older, central areas can be redeveloped is itself a factor promoting suburban development. Suburban locations also have a number of economic advantages, such as low-priced land, large vacant areas, less stringent zoning controls, and lower tax rates. Also important are the particular demands of the new apartment population. For economic, demographic or personal reasons many households choose or are forced to rent apartments, but nevertheless maintain a desire for suburban living; this is illustrated by the well-known differences in age structure between central and suburban apartment populations (Table 3.4). The twenty-storey suburban apartment building is quite often simply a compromise between supply economics and consumer demand, and it is frequently the case that these high-rises have been built at fairly low densities per gross acre, which may even approximate the density in older single-family housing areas in the city centre. Other factors which have promoted the development of suburban high-rises are the premiums or higher rents that some people are willing to pay for apartments on upper floors (principally because of the view) and the greater range of facilities available in such buildings, which may include recreation rooms, health clubs and swimming pools.

TABLE 3.4 *Age structure of population in apartments built between 1960 and 1966, Metropolitan Winnipeg, 1966*

| | Age Group | | | | | |
| | 0 - 17 % | 18 - 20 % | 21 - 64 % | 65+ % | Total % | Total No. |
| --- | --- | --- | --- | --- | --- | --- |
| Central apartments | 4.0 | 3.9 | 75.5 | 16.6 | 100.0 | 3,791 |
| Suburban apartments | 17.0 | 4.4 | 69.7 | 8.9 | 100.0 | 10,024 |
| Census metropolitan area | 34.4 | 5.6 | 50.9 | 9.1 | 100.0 | 508,759 |

SOURCE: G.A. Nader, "Some Aspects of the Recent Growth and Distribution of Apartments in the Prairie Metropolitan Areas."

Contrasts between suburban and central apartment populations correspond to the general inner-outer differences: in the central area population densities are higher and there are proportionately more retired persons, young single adults, and married couples without children. Differences in population structure are also reflected in the types of accommodation available: apartment buildings in central areas generally have larger numbers of bachelor and one-bedroom units. Middle-income housing is contrary to the predictions of classical land use models such as the concentric zone theory and, to a lesser extent, of urban location theory. Both economic and social factors account for their success: the increasing number of one- and two-person households at both ends of the adult age scale (the groups that are traditionally located centrally), and the willingness of a growing number of people to exchange the private space of a single-family house for convenient access to work, shopping, entertainment and other specialized facilities of the city centre. The changing structure of downtown employment is also a relevant factor; the number of unskilled and semi-skilled jobs has declined while office and other white-collar jobs have increased. The large numbers of young, female workers employed in downtown offices and other service industries are reflected in the age-sex structure of modern, central-area apartment populations (see Table 4.1).

## Commercial Land Use

Commercial activities include retailing, business services, and a variety of office functions such as finance, insurance and real estate. Although wholesaling fits into the commercial category, its loca-

British Columbia Government Photograph

*Vancouver's West End.*

tional pattern resembles that of the manufacturing industry because of the extent of its goods-handling operations. Government functions, on the other hand, frequently share the same locational constraints as commercial activities because of their need to be accessible to the population at large. Although commercial uses are among the most conspicuous elements of the urban landscape, they occupy only a small proportion of developed land because of their very intensive nature; this proportion usually amounts to between 3 per cent and 5 per cent, although the percentage declines with distance from the city centre (for example, Table 4.5). Two of the major categories of commercial land use—retailing and offices—will be examined in the following sections.

RETAILING

The retail structure of North American cities includes both nucleated shopping areas (centres) and ribbon or string-street developments. Whether planned or unplanned, retail centres generally form a five-level hierarchy: the central business district, regional centres, community centres, neighbourhood centres and isolated stores. This hierarchical organization, which is particularly evident in the case of planned shopping centres, is not matched by marked regularities in spatial distribution. However, the intra-urban pattern of retail centres can usually be explained in terms of variations in population density, income and accessibility, as well as by the changing locational preferences of modern retailers.

Unlike retail centres, commercial ribbons are not generally characterized by hierarchical patterns. First of all, there are marked differences between long established and newly developed ribbons. Old ribbons have traditionally depended on their accessibility to pedestrians, and their origins can frequently be traced to stores which were built along streetcar (and later bus) routes, where they could intercept pedestrians between the transit stop and their homes. These ribbons have continued to perform local or neighbourhood functions and are characterized by the repetition of a few convenience stores (drug, hardware, grocery and similar stores) at regular intervals along the street. Modern commercial ribbons have developed in association with automobile traffic and are usually found along highways and major urban arterials. Highway ribbons cater mainly to the demands of passing traffic; typical commercial outlets include motels, service stations and restaurants. Some urban arterial functions also cater to the same transient demand, while others depend on attracting special-purpose shopping trips from within the urban area. Discount stores, furniture stores, automobile dealers and other extensive users of land locate on urban arterials because they require accessibility to the metropolitan market but cannot afford the high rents of the city centre. Urban arterials frequently take on a very specialized character when similar establishments locate in the same area; this is, for example, the case with medical districts, furniture districts and automobile rows. This specialization is generally the result of linkages between establishments; in the case of automobile rows (Danforth Avenue in Toronto, for instance) the concentration of dealerships is an attraction for consumers, who generally prefer to do some comparative shopping.

The changing retail pattern is characterized by two related elements: decentralization and a trend towards the establishment of planned shopping centres. The outward movement of population, accompanied by declining population densities, rising incomes and

TABLE 3.5 *Retail floor space by type, Metropolitan Toronto Planning Area,*
*1953-1971*

| Type | 1953 | | 1966 | | 1971 | |
|------|------|------|------|------|------|------|
| | sq.ft. | % | sq.ft. | % | sq.ft. | % |
| Strip retail | 19,840,000 | 97.7 | 21,253,000 | 63.4 | 22,049,000 | 56.5 |
| Shopping centres | 466,000 | 2.3 | 12,276,000 | 36.6 | 16,963,000 | 43.5 |
| Total | 20,306,000 | 100.0 | 33,529,000 | 100.0 | 39,012,000 | 100.0 |

SOURCE: Metropolitan Toronto Planning Board

high car-ownership rates, has naturally encouraged a similar shift of retailing outlets. The consumer preference for automobile-based shopping trips and the advantages of a single-storey structure for the handling of goods, have together produced one of the most distinctive features of modern North American cities — the planned shopping centre.

SHOPPING CENTRES

Probably the most important of the recent changes in urban retail structure is the growth of planned shopping centres, which in Canada date from the early 1950s (from the 1930s in the United States). In metropolitan Toronto, for example, the first five centres, which together covered a floor area of less than 200,000 square feet, were opened in 1952, and by 1971 this had increased to 313 centres with a total floor area of almost 17 million square feet; during the intervening period almost 90 per cent of the net increase in Toronto's retail space was located in shopping centres, which accordingly expanded their share of total retail floorspace in the metropolitan area from 2.3 to 43.5 per cent (Table 3.5). Similar trends are evident in all Canadian cities which have grown significantly since 1950.

Planned shopping centres come in a wide range of sizes (Table 3.6 and Figure 3.4), but they can generally be functionally classified into a three-level hierarchy: regional, community and neighbourhood. Regional centres typically contain more than 300,000 square feet, with at least one full-line or major department store, and serve a trade area population of at least 100,000; community centres have at least 100,000 square feet, with a variety store, a junior department

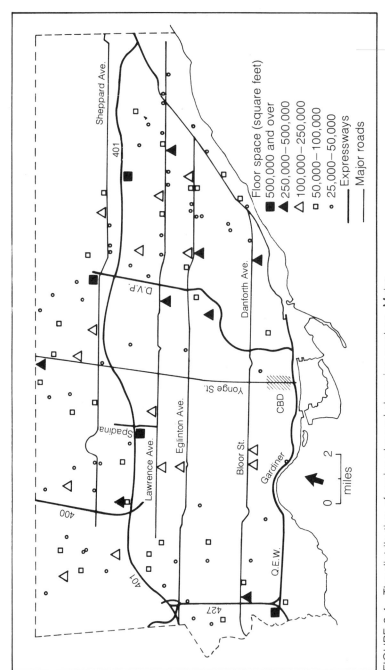

FIGURE 3.4 The distribution of major planned shopping centres, Metro Toronto (Muncipality of Metropolitan Toronto).

*Source:* Metropolitan Toronto Planning Board.

TABLE 3.6 *Shopping centres by date of construction and by size, Metropolitan Toronto Planning Area, 1971*

| Year | Growth of shopping centres, 1952-1971 | | Shopping centres by size, 1971 | |
| | Floorspace (sq.ft.) | No. of centres | Size (sq.ft.) | No. of centres |
|---|---|---|---|---|
| 1952 | 195,000 | 5 | under 12,000 | 74 |
| 1953 | 466,000 | 13 | 12-25,000 | 97 |
| 1956 | 2,297,000 | 34 | 25-50,000 | 75 |
| 1959 | 4,512,000 | 93 | 50-100,000 | 31 |
| 1961 | 7,002,000 | 123 | 100-250,000 | 23 |
| 1964 | 10,772,000 | 173 | 250-500,000 | 11 |
| 1966 | 12,601,000 | 227 | over 500,000 | 3 |
| 1969 | 14,360,000 | 278 | Total centres | 313 |
| 1971 | 16,963,000 | 313 | | |

SOURCE: Metroplitan Toronto Planning Board

store or a discount department store as the chief tenant, and serve a trade area population of between 25,000 and 150,000; in a neighbourhood centre the principal tenant is normally a supermarket or a drug store and the trade area population may be as low as 5,000. If it is large enough, a regional centre may also function as the equivalent of a central business district. For example Yorkdale (1.39 million square feet), functions as a first-order centre for many people outside Toronto. Table 3.7 illustrates the general characteristics of planned shopping centres in Calgary.

The planned centre with its acres of parking space has decided advantages over the traditional shopping street. The widespread ownership of refrigerators and freezers, the increasing availability of storable foods, and the growing number of working wives have reduced the frequency of shopping trips and increased the number of purchases made during a single outing. The weekly shopping trip is typically made for the purchase of high-volume, mass-merchandise items such as those sold in food, hardware and drug stores; for this type of shopping dispersed stores are obviously less convenient than the shopping centre's agglomeration of complementary stores. Rising incomes have increased consumer expenditure on high-quality goods, and this has favoured shopping centres in general and the

TABLE 3.7 *Shopping centres in Calgary: general characteristics and retail sales (percentage distribution) by type of store and type of ownership*

| | Regional centre | Community centre | Neighbourhood centre |
|---|---|---|---|
| | General Characteristics | | |
| Principal tenant: | Major department store(s) | Junior department store | Supermarket |
| Acreage: | Min.: 30 acres | Min.: 8 acres | Ave.: 2.5 acres |
| Gross leasable area | Min.: 300,000 sq. ft. | Min.: 90,000 sq. ft. | Ave.: 27,600 sq. ft. |
| | Retail Sales, 1966 | | |
| *Type of store* | | | |
| Food | 12.2 | 20.0 | 67.5 |
| General merchandise | 56.6 | 13.0 | — |
| Clothing | 6.9 | 6.0 | 2.9 |
| Drug | 0.7 | 1.3 | 7.0 |
| Other | 23.6 | 59.7 | 22.6 |
| Total | 100.0 | 100.0 | 100.0 |
| *Type of ownership* | | | |
| Independent* | 9.4 | 15.9 | 37.4 |
| Chain | 90.6 | 84.1 | 62.6 |
| Total | 100.0 | 100.0 | 100.0 |

SOURCE: City of Calgary
*In 1966 independently owned stores accounted for 45.7% of metropolitan retail sales.

larger centres in particular; the incidence of higher incomes among suburban as compared to central residents has itself encouraged retail decentralization. Changes in marketing methods (especially the growth of mass advertising) and in retail organization have contributed to a more rapid expansion of sales in chain stores than in independently owned stores; between 1966 and 1971, for example, chain stores increased their national sales by 56 per cent compared to only 23 per cent for independent stores. These trends generally favour shopping centres, where chain stores have an above-average representation (see Table 3.7). Supply factors have also encouraged the development of shopping centres; these include the easier handling of goods in single-storey buildings and the economies of scale associated with the development and management of a large unit.

*Sherway Gardens shopping centre at the intersection of Highway 427 and the Queen Elizabeth Way, Metropolitan Toronto.*

DOWNTOWN RETAILING

As retailing has become increasingly decentralized the city centre has diminished in relative importance for all retail functions, and has experienced an absolute decline in some categories such as food, for which distance and automobile access are important factors in determining where the consumer will shop. The decline of downtown retailing is also related to the changing functional structure of the city centre and to changes in the central resident population. A significant number of retail stores, which on the whole are extensive users of land, have been forced out by more intensive uses; for example, many furniture and discount stores and automobile dealerships have moved out of the central area and have reassembled along major urban arterials in suburban locations. As a result of selective migration both the number of people living in the central area and their average income have declined, and their importance to downtown retailing has consequently diminished.

The city centre now functions at three levels of retail specialization: as a convenience centre for the large, daytime work force; as a
mass-merchandise centre for the central area population; and as a
specialty centre for the metropolitan population. Several studies
have shown that about one-third of all shopping trips made in the
central business district originate from downtown workplaces. This
close relationship between downtown retailing and employment is
exemplified by the number of underground shopping plazas which
have been incorporated into recently built office towers in many
large Canadian cities, particularly Montreal, Toronto and Vancouver. The transient hotel population is also becoming increasingly
important to the survival of downtown retailing. In cities such as
Quebec and Victoria visitors account for a large proportion of downtown retail sales, but the impact of tourist expenditure is also apparent in a number of other centres. For example, the specialty shops on
Sparks Street in Ottawa, the department stores on St. Catherine
Street in Montreal, and the Queen-Yonge intersection in Toronto
rely heavily on visitor spending. The role of downtown as a specialty
centre for the metropolitan population has remained important,
however, particularly in the case of those goods which are normally
bought after some comparison shopping. The one-of-a-kind retail
outlet (for example, a store specializing in imported glassware or
furniture) can exist almost anywhere in the metropolitan area by
relying on advertising and its reputation; on the other hand, stores
selling shoes, ladies' clothing and other widely available items with a
rapid turnover usually find it more profitable to cluster together. For
these stores the downtown is the prime location because of its
superior accessibility to the metropolitan population.

OFFICES

Office functions, which include a wide variety of activities with
different locational preferences, are as a group among the most
centralized of major land uses. They include government administration offices, the headquarters and administrative offices of private
corporations, banking and other financial institutions, real estate
companies, insurance companies, a variety of business services, and
some community services such as medical offices. It is difficult to
discuss the locational pattern of offices in terms of a land use classification, and it is usually more meaningful to differentiate on the basis
of their activity patterns. In many cases, for example, decision-

making (head office) functions are centralized, while routine operations are decentralized.

Because of a lack of historical data it is difficult to trace the evolution of the intra-urban distribution of office employment. Although it is possible to analyse the locational pattern of pure office functions such as banking and insurance, little is known about the geographical distribution of offices attached to manufacturing and other firms. On the basis of the evidence available, it appears that offices were not an important element of the urban land use system before the First World War; after 1920 their numbers began to increase and have undergone a period of marked acceleration since the end of the Second World War. Modern office functions have evolved in response to the rising consumer demand for services, the growth of government administration and the proportional shift of employment in the goods-producing industries from technical production to supervisory, executive and other service functions. The spread of goods-handling operations to the suburbs after 1920 was a significant factor in the physical separation of plant and office, since the latter remained close to the financial community, which had itself developed around the early concentration of factories and wholesalers near the transportation terminals of the city centre.

The intra-urban locational patterns of the various office functions are most easily explained in terms of their need for accessibility to consumers, employees, associates and competitors. Activities which require access to the total metropolitan population and to out-of-town visitors generally prefer central sites; the offices of lawyers and architects, for example, are more centrally located than are real estate offices and branch banks. The larger the staff, the more likely it is that the office will be situated in the city centre; maximum accessibility to the metropolitan population is often essential for adequate staffing, particularly if large numbers of women (who are usually more dependent on public transportation) are employed. Those functions which periodically require immediate, personal contact with a wide number of specialized professional and business services generally locate in downtown areas where such services are most readily available. In contrast, relatively self-sufficient operations, routine administrative or processing functions, and locally oriented offices often choose suburban locations.

Within the metropolitan region the city centre is the preeminent office district. It accommodates the national and regional headquarters of major industrial, commercial and financial firms; especially conspicuous are the growing numbers of banks, trust companies, investment brokers and other financial institutions. Federal, provincial and municipal governments and their agencies occupy a major share of downtown office space, although their presence is most evident in a few cities such as Ottawa, Quebec and Victoria. Due to the increasing importance of decision-making and administration in both public and private spheres there has been the proliferation of professional services: lawyers, architects, engineers, systems analysts and others. These professionals draw their clientele from private companies, government agencies and the public, and therefore locate in the city centre in order to maximize accessibility to their market.

Excluding those organizations which choose central locations simply in order to maximize their accessibility to the metropolitan population, offices are generally located here for two related reasons—a need for frequent personal contact with individuals and organizations outside the firm, and the existence of functional linkages with a variety of other businesses. Typical of city centre offices are the corporate headquarters which depend on face-to-face communication in much of their daily business, and therefore tend to locate close together. Even the largest company cannot economically internalize all the specialist skills that it might require from time to time to deal with its problems, and it must therefore depend on having ready access to a wide range of professional consultants. A downtown location is also important in terms of its convenience for out-of-town businessmen, who may have neither the time nor the inclination to visit scattered suburban offices. Finally, in many communication-intensive activities, there is no adequate substitute for personal contact; difficult negotiations and the exchange of complex ideas are not easily handled by other forms of communication. In general, improvements in telecommunications (even the picture telephone and teleconferencing facilities) have not diminished the need for face-to-face contact; rather, they have increased the amount of information which can be exchanged in a given period of time so that firms can satisfy an increased proportion of their nearly infinite demand for information. The *proportion* of communication which takes place in the form of face-to-face contact may decline in the future but the absolute amount is likely to increase.

Recent advances in communications have encouraged many firms to decentralize their office functions either partially or totally, and to use their suburban offices for programmed decision-making functions, including routine administration or bookkeeping (e.g., the recording of stocks, purchases, sales and salary payments). These are largely internal operations and the external contacts which they require can be adequately made by telephone, teleprinter or letter. The very fact that such offices can substitute communication for transportation allows them to locate anywhere within the metropolitan area. In large companies it is often impractical to decentralize the entire office operation because of the need to maintain some personal contacts; in such cases routine or repetitive functions are generally transferred to the suburbs while the variable, non-programmed executive functions remain in the city centre. There are instances in which the entire office function of a large firm is decentralized; this is particularly likely in the case of bookkeeping firms such as insurance companies, which do not deal directly with the public but maintain extensive files on their customers. Moreover, non-programmed problems form a relatively minor proportion of the total office load of these firms and their executive and administrative functions are therefore almost inseparable.

Apart from the reduction in transfer costs brought about by improvements in communications technology, decentralization is related to advances in production methods, notably electronic data processing. The mechanization of many office operations has reduced the need for staff or conversely has increased the floorspace required per employee. The space required for the storage of files, machines and other equipment (ideally arranged horizontally on one floor) means that these functions are extensive users of land, and they have accordingly moved to lower-priced suburban land. The reduction in staff size is itself a factor contributing to the shift to the periphery where the majority of a firm's employees may reside, particularly since the remaining workers tend to be on average higher paid and male. In Toronto, the customers' accounts section of many major firms as well as some government departments, including the Ontario Health Insurance Plan, are located in suburban areas. The suburbanization of office functions has led to the evolution of office parks, which are patterned after industrial parks and which are potentially capable of rivalling downtown office clusters. Because of the agglomeration economies which it offers, an office park complex is capable of attracting many of the marginal downtown offices. One of the largest office parks in Canada is Toronto's Flemingdon Park.

Improvements in communications, transportation and methods of operation have contributed to the locational freedom of offices and have accordingly increased the importance of prestige factors in the locational decision. In practice, prestige factors may encourage either centralization or decentralization depending on the nature of the firm involved. The modern office skyscraper is generally a prestige location in the downtown area. Some of Canada's best-known and most attractive buildings are occupied by and named after the major banks; they include Toronto-Dominion Centre and Commerce Court in Toronto and the Royal Bank's cruciform tower in Montreal's Place Ville Marie. The larger cities may even have prestige office streets; University Avenue in Toronto and Dorchester Boulevard in Montreal are well-known examples. Among the most footloose are insurance companies, which are generally willing to locate their head offices in any large but inexpensive building which is named after the company; the preferred locations are therefore on major thoroughfares at the edge of the central business district (for example, University Avenue and Bloor Street in Toronto and Broadway in Winnipeg) or on landscaped grounds in the suburbs. In suburban locations many firms take advantage of the low land values to increase expenditure on the architectural design of their building and the landscaping of the site, particularly if it is visible from a nearby highway.

# 4.
# The City Centre

The city centre or central area is a unique functional zone within the urban area, often defined in superlative terms relative to the rest of the city: it is the most accessible point, the most intensively developed area, the largest employment district, the largest generator of traffic, and it has the highest land values. However, the feature which is most immediately evident to even the casual visitor is its functional diversity. It is the main financial, commercial, governmental, cultural and entertainment centre within the urban area, and its buildings constitute a unique record of the city's history. This is the district which is most familiar to visitors and residents alike, and which, to a considerable extent, is the image-maker for the whole city. The downtown area epitomizes inter-city differences and the distinctive character which is unique to each metropolis.

The city centre can be defined in a number of ways. "Central city" refers to the area enclosed by the political boundaries of the municipality which is the historic core of the metropolitan area (the City of Toronto, for example). Although much larger than and therefore not an adequate substitute for the city centre, it is frequently used when statistical data are not available for smaller areal units. The central business district (CBD), on the other hand, is generally the smallest geographically defined zone within the city centre. It is characteristically the area within which commercial uses are dominant and therefore excludes residential, industrial and institutional uses, even though some of these may deliberately seek a central location. In this chapter "city centre" defines an area whose boundaries lie somewhere between the CBD and the central city, more extensive than the

TABLE 4.1 *Age-sex population structure (percentage distribution) of a modern apartment district and a declining industrial district in central Winnipeg, 1971*

| | Apartment district* | | Industrial district† | | Metropolitan area | |
|---|---|---|---|---|---|---|
| Age | Male | Female | Male | Female | Male | Female |
| 0 - 4 | 1.0 | 0.9 | 3.8 | 3.5 | 4.0 | 3.9 |
| 5 - 9 | 0.4 | 0.5 | 3.5 | 3.1 | 4.7 | 4.5 |
| 10 - 14 | -0.5 | 0.5 | 2.8 | 3.5 | 4.7 | 4.6 |
| 15 - 19 | 3.0 | 4.3 | 3.5 | 3.5 | 4.6 | 4.8 |
| 20 - 24 | 8.1 | 11.6 | 3.9 | 3.5 | 4.8 | 5.0 |
| 25 - 34 | 8.9 | 6.6 | 5.9 | 5.0 | 6.7 | 6.6 |
| 35 - 44 | 3.9 | 4.1 | 6.3 | 3.7 | 5.6 | 5.7 |
| 45 - 54 | 4.3 | 6.5 | 7.3 | 4.0 | 5.4 | 5.9 |
| 55 - 64 | 4.6 | 8.3 | 9.7 | 4.2 | 4.2 | 4.8 |
| 65 + | 7.6 | 14.4 | 15.4 | 3.9 | 4.1 | 5.4 |
| Total (%) | 42.3 | 57.7 | 62.1 | 37.9 | 48.8 | 51.2 |
| Total (No.) | 1830 | 2495 | 3130 | 1910 | 263,750 | 276,510 |

SOURCE: Census of Canada, 1971
*South of the commercial core (Census Tract No. 14)
† North of the commercial core (Census Tracts Nos. 24 and 25)

former and more "centred" than the latter; it is often conterminous with the high-density historical core of the pre-automobile or pre-streetcar era.

## Population

The inner city population differs from the metropolitan average in three respects: age and family composition, income and ethnic character. Relative to the rest of the city the central population contains higher proportions of young adults, retired persons, non-family households, low-income earners and minority ethnic groups. It is, however, possible to recognize areal segregations within the central area, and in most cities there exist at least two distinct residential areas with very different socio-economic and demographic characteristics: a modern high-rise apartment district and a declining skid row district. Table 4.1 illustrates the age-sex structure of these two districts in the city of Winnipeg.

Every large Canadian city has its skid row, usually limited to a few blocks within a more extensive residential area. The latter can generally be recognized by the coincidence of a number of indices: low

*Apartment development along the valley bluff on the North Saskatchewan River, Edmonton.*

incomes, high unemployment rates, low educational levels, a disproportionately large number of adult males and welfare recipients, the presence of large numbers of minority ethnic groups, and high rates of juvenile delinquency, drug addiction and alcoholism. The district functions as a reception area for unskilled rural or foreign immigrants, a rental area for low-income households and, in some cities, as a winter residence for seasonally employed workers. The amenities of the district include cheap hotels, rooming houses and missions, as well as pawnshops, second-hand clothing shops, pool halls and beer parlours. The unattractive aspect of the area is compounded by its usual location close to the old commercial-industrial zone.

The other main residential area within the city centre is the more recently developed high-rise apartment district. This is usually located at the edge of the CDB in order to accommodate some of the residential needs of the growing number of white-collar workers in the downtown area. Apartments are not, however, located on all sides of the CBD; developers generally avoid old industrial-commercial areas and instead favour established high-income residential districts whose social prestige is a prime locational inducement. Apartment developments are often located near natural amenities such as rivers, beaches and parks where these adjoin the downtown area — for example, the valley bluffs of the North Saskatchewan River in Edmonton, the slopes of Mount Royal in Montreal, and the beaches and parks of Vancouver's West End.

Since most high-income housing was originally built in the more attractive areas of the city centre, these districts usually combine most of the social, economic and natural locational factors favoured by apartment developers.

## Functional Structure

Although still the paramount employment centre within the metropolitan region, the city centre is undergoing a process of selective growth and decline. Employment gains have been made in office and other service functions but its importance for manufacturing, wholesaling and other goods-handling activities has declined considerably. While it has remained the optimal location for first-order functions, the nature of these functions has changed. The functional structure of the city centre is becoming more specialized than at any time in the past; it is evolving as a transaction centre or business forum, at the expense of its role as a consumer market for shopping, entertainment and cultural pursuits. Retailing, for example, can no longer be considered a primary function of the city centre, and downtown retail shops increasingly cater to the downtown work force rather than to the metropolitan population. Far more people now enter the city centre for work or work-related business than for any other reason. Since the central area has retained its preeminent accessibility for people rather than for the distribution of goods, it has become the prime location for contact-dependent or "confrontation" industries.

Despite the growing number of office and other white-collar jobs, the city centre has not maintained its proportionate share of total metropolitan employment. As well as the decentralization of many goods-handling industries, a number of consumer services have followed the outward movement of population; as the suburban population has grown, an increasing number of former first-order functions have found it economically feasible to locate outside the city centre. This is well illustrated by the changing distributional pattern of the retail industry. Since 1961 nearly all new department stores in Canadian cities have been located in the suburbs, and for the nine largest metropolitan centres the CBD's share of total department store sales declined from 84.6 per cent in 1961 to 57.4 per cent by 1966 and to 39.0 per cent by 1971.[1] Although most specialty

1 By permission of the Hudson's Bay Company from unpublished data supplied by Statistics Canada.

TABLE 4.2 *Components of average daily transient room demand, Ottawa, 1968*

| Location | Purpose of visit | | | | | | | | | |
|---|---|---|---|---|---|---|---|---|---|---|
| | Conventions | | Federal-generated business | | General business | | Tourists | | Total | |
| | No. | % | No. | % | No. | % | No. | % | No. | % |
| Downtown | 206 | 80.2 | 353 | 90.1 | 353 | 49.2 | 304 | 35.8 | 1,216 | 54.9 |
| Suburban | 51 | 19.8 | 39 | 9.9 | 365 | 50.8 | 545 | 64.2 | 1,000 | 45.1 |
| Total | 257 | 100.0 | 392 | 100.0 | 718 | 100.0 | 849 | 100.0 | 2,216 | 100.0 |

SOURCE: Hammer, Green, Siller Associates, *Ottawa Central Area Study, 1969* (Ottawa: 1969)

stores still prefer central locations, the differences between down-town and suburban retailing have diminished; sales in Toronto's Yorkdale shopping centre, for example, exceed CBD sales in a number of census metropolitan areas.

As a result of the substantial increase in their numbers, hotels have recently emerged as a principal support of the downtown economy. After the Second World War new hotels and motels were built mainly along the major suburban highways for the convenience of motorists. Since the mid-1960s there has been a definite trend to-wards the construction of large downtown hotels in almost every major city in Canada. This is related to the general growth of tourism, and more specifically to the increasing numbers of business travellers and conventions. In 1972, for example, three hundred and fifty conventions and trade shows were held in metropolitan To-ronto, attracting a total of 245,000 out-of-town delegates. Conven-tions held in metropolitan areas generally prefer the city centre for several reasons: the large number of hotel rooms in the area; the variety of facilities available for meetings and display; access to a wide range of shopping, entertainment and tourist attractions; and the concentration of these features within a relatively small area—an advantage for the many convention delegates who travel by air and are therefore pedestrians during their visit. The importance of con-ventions and business visitors to downtown hotels is illustrated for Ottawa in Table 4.2. The expansion of downtown hotel space in major metropolitan centres was exemplified in Toronto by the re-cent completion (1972) of two hotels, with a combined total of 2,200 rooms, adjacent to the new City Hall; convention facilities were incorporated into both. Montreal's Place Bonaventure complex, which was opened in 1967, exemplifies the modern trend towards the development of a downtown convention centre; it was specifically designed to cater to conventions and trade shows and contains a wide assortment of meeting rooms, including a hall which seats more than 17,000 persons, as well as a 400-room hotel.

Although it is generally accepted that central area employment is declining, the situation within the CBD is not as readily apparent. Information on North American CBD employment is scanty at best, and most hypotheses are therefore based on fragmentary evidence. It is widely held that a redistribution of jobs in central areas has increased the level of employment in the CBD and contributed to a general decline in the rest of the area. This is supported by the city centre's gains in office and service functions and its losses in the manufacturing and wholesaling sectors; the office booms which have been experienced in most major metropolitan centres since the 1950s are cited as confirmatory evidence of the growth of CBD employment. The opposing view is that CBD employment has remained stable or declined slightly; this is generally supported by historical data on the number of persons entering the downtown area during the morning rush hours. The use of this index is based on the assumption that such trips will be predominantly journeys-to-work; in metropolitan Toronto, for example, it was found that 90 per cent of persons entering the central area between 7 a.m. and 9 a.m. were on their way to work. Between 1951 and 1971 the number of people entering Toronto's downtown (approximately the CBD) between 7 a.m. and 9 a.m. remained fairly constant (Figure 4.1); three-year running averages are used to compensate for random variations which are generally related to the day chosen for the annual count. For the same period the total number of people entering and leaving the downtown between 6:30 a.m. and 11:30 p.m. followed a generally similar pattern although an upward trend has been evident since 1965 (Figure 4.1). Similar data for cities in the United States would suggest that the hypothesis of a redistribution of central area employment in favour of the CBD is probably untenable.

Despite the evidence based on traffic patterns it is probably the case that most Canadian cities have experienced increased downtown or CBD employment. Although historical information is not available for most cities there is sufficient evidence to support the hypothesis that there is a redistribution of city centre employment in favour of the CBD. In Vancouver, for example, downtown employ-

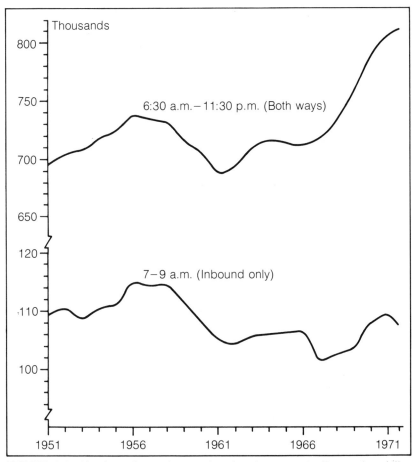

FIGURE 4.1   Number of people crossing the downtown traffic cordon daily, Toronto, 1951-1972 (three-year running averages).

*Source:* Toronto Transit Commission.

ment has grown steadily since the post-1950 boom in office development, and increased from 73,000 in 1955 to 88,000 in 1965 and to 91,000 in 1970. Toronto's CBD employment increased from 122,000 in 1956 to 134,000 in 1970. The apparent contradiction between the boom in office development and the stabilization or slow growth of CBD employment is primarily the result of two factors: the decline in employment experienced by almost every industrial category except for office and personal services; and the fact that office employment has not increased as fast as office floor-space because improved working environments and the greater use of machinery have combined to increase the average office space per worker.

In general office functions have emerged as the bastion of the CBD economy and the growth of office employment has in most cities offset the declines in other sectors. The changing functional structure is clearly reflected in available data on floorspace changes: office and personal service functions are expanding, retail functions have remained stable or declined slightly while manufacturing and wholesaling functions have generally declined (see, for example, Table 4.9).

GOVERNMENT FUNCTIONS

The most commonly used method of delimiting the CBD[2] classifies government functions as non-CBD uses; but in reality government services constitute one of the major sources of employment in the city centre (and often the CBD) of most metropolitan areas. The importance of a downtown location for government functions is the result of historical, economic and political factors. For historical reasons city halls and legislative buildings are mainly located in the core of metropolitan areas; Vancouver (city hall) and Regina (legislative building) are notable exceptions. Locational inertia and tradition have encouraged the continuation of these functions on their original sites, but some government activities prefer central locations for the same economic reasons that apply to private offices: maximum accessibility to residents and workers from the metropolitan region; the need for face-to-face contact with a variety of professional consultants and agencies; and, in many cases, the locational affinity which exists between legislative and executive-administrative functions. The concentration of government employment downtown cannot, however, be satisfactorily explained by historical or economic factors alone, since political considerations form an important element of the locational decision.

The downtown area is characteristically regarded by municipal politicians as a civic showcase, and considerable energy is devoted to

2 R. E. Murphy and J. E. Vance, Jr., "Delimiting the CBD."

Courtesy Toronto Fire Department

*City Hall, Toronto.*

the maintenance of a concomitant air of economic and cultural vitality. In the planning literature, for example, the downtown area is often referred to as the heart of the city, and by analogy the economic and cultural health of the urban area is assumed to be dependent on that of the city centre. All levels of government are very sensitive to the political implications of the locations chosen for important public buildings. Increasingly, government functions are being regarded as essential to the maintenance of an adequate level of downtown employment. As well as their direct contribution to the work force, they indirectly support many related and ancillary services (the "multiplier effect"). Even government functions of a purely bookkeeping nature are frequently not decentralized. Public buildings are also used to enhance the appearance of the downtown; Toronto's City Hall is an outstanding example, but several Canadian cities have carried the concept further by their use of civic centre plans. The greatest popularity of the civic centre concept was during

TABLE 4.3 *Core-frame structure in terms of floor space, Central Business District, Regina*

| Land Use | Internal distribution | | | Core-frame split | | | |
|---|---|---|---|---|---|---|---|
| | Core % | Frame % | Total CBD % | Core % | Frame % | Total CBD % | Total CBD '000 sq. ft. |
| Retail | 21.1 | 12.2 | 17.5 | 71.2 | 28.8 | 100.0 | 1,344.8 |
| Personal services | 10.4 | 18.0 | 13.5 | 45.1 | 54.9 | 100.0 | 1,041.9 |
| Hotels, entertainment | 16.9 | 5.4 | 12.2 | 81.7 | 18.3 | 100.0 | 935.5 |
| Public administration and utilities | 10.9 | 12.7 | 11.7 | 55.0 | 45.0 | 100.0 | 898.0 |
| Finance, insurance and real estate | 6.2 | 5.4 | 5.9 | 62.0 | 38.0 | 100.0 | 454.0 |
| Wholesale | 0.8 | 5.6 | 2.7 | 17.6 | 82.4 | 100.0 | 210.9 |
| Business services | 2.5 | 1.3 | 2.0 | 73.0 | 27.0 | 100.0 | 156.9 |
| Manufacturing | 0.6 | 3.8 | 1.9 | 18.2 | 81.8 | 100.0 | 150.0 |
| Residential | 5.8 | 15.4 | 9.7 | 34.6 | 65.4 | 100.0 | 750.2 |
| Other | 16.9 | 15.1 | 16.2 | 61.0 | 39.0 | 100.0 | 1,246.4 |
| Vacant | 7.9 | 5.1 | 6.7 | 68.9 | 31.1 | 100.0 | 517.6 |
| Total (%) | 100.0 | 100.0 | 100.0 | 58.7 | 41.3 | 100.0 | 7,706.2 |
| Total ('000 sq. ft.) | 4,520.3 | 3,185.9 | 7,706.2 | | | | |

SOURCE: City of Regina

the decade before the First World War but it experienced a minor revival after the Second World War. Among Canadian cities, Edmonton's is both the most ambitious and the most successful scheme.

The importance of government employment in any city centre is related to its political status, economic base and the size of the urban population. Ottawa provides an outstanding example of a government-dominated city centre; the federal government accounts for two-thirds of central area employment, and in terms of office employment alone the proportion rises to four-fifths. In Quebec City, Victoria and Halifax the proportions are also high because of their status as provincial capitals, their moderate size and their considerable dependence on government functions. However, even in Toronto, which has one of the most diversified urban economies in Canada, the various levels of government account for more than one-third of downtown office space; the provincial government is the principal employer, with approximately 10,000 downtown employees.

Finally, churches, theatres, museums, universities and other institutional and public buildings add significantly to downtown employment and activity in particular cities.

## Spatial Structure

The city centre can be divided into the CBD-core, the CBD-frame and the periphery. The core is primarily commercial in nature; characteristically its activities include offices, department stores, specialist retail stores, nightclubs and theatres. Land uses are typically intensive and high-rise office towers are common. In contrast, the frame covers a relatively extensive area characterized by low and medium-rise (walk-up) buildings, and by the more traditional functions of the city centre — manufacturing, wholesaling, high-density housing, and transportation terminals for both passengers and freight. This is approximately the area which Burgess [3] termed the "zone in transition" because he believed the core functions would in time spread outward into the frame; this has not proven to be the case and the two areas have developed quite separate functional roles (see Table 4.3). Although the two zones are quite different in both function and

3 E. W. Burgess, "The Growth of the City," in R. E. Park and E. W. Burgess, eds., *The City*.

physical structure, their areal extents are not easy to define. Beyond the CBD is the peripheral zone which is predominantly occupied by residential and other low-order uses (e.g., Table 4.9).

THE CENTRAL BUSINESS DISTRICT

In the case of its three major functions the CBD is unrivalled by any other part of the city: as an employment centre, a shopping centre and an entertainment-cultural centre. The reasons for its paramount importance in these areas are partly historical. For some time after their establishment most towns were small enough to be contained within the area of the modern CBD; it was therefore the location of many early functions which would later increase in importance, including commercial, industrial, governmental and institutional organizations. Locational inertia has encouraged many of these activities to remain downtown, but because of the area's centrality to the growing population it has continued to attract new first-order functions (those which depend on maximum accessibility to the metropolitan population). The localization of activities in the CBD was particularly prevalent during the pre-automobile era when many functions were tied to long-distance transportation terminals in the city centre. Until the widespread introduction of electric streetcars in the 1890s almost all employment, including retailing and other consumer services, was centrally located.

Accessibility is the most important and distinctive characteristic of the CBD; for the total metropolitan population it is the most easily reached area, particularly when some form of public transportation is used. As a result there are more competitors for its available space and its land values are accordingly higher than anywhere else in the city. As a consequence of this competition, change has always been a characteristic of the CBD, which throughout its history has experienced a continuous replacement of lower-intensity by higher-intensity uses. More recently, many CBD functions have moved out to peripheral locations, which the growth of the suburban population and preferences for automobile-based trips have made economically feasible.

Since accessibility and therefore land values fall off very quickly with distance from the peak intersection, the CBD generally covers only a small fraction of the total urbanized area (frequently less than half of one per cent). Although the extent of the CBD is related to the size of the urban population, the relationship is not always direct; for

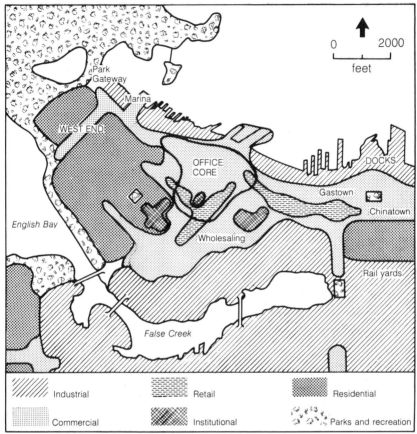

FIGURE 4.2 Functional areas within the downtown peninsula, Vancouver.

*Sources:* W. Smith and Associates, *Downtown Vancouver Transit Concepts* (1972), and City of Vancouver.

example, in Saskatoon (pop. 126,000) it covers about 170 acres, while in Montreal (pop. 2,743,000) it is about 550 acres. This less than proportionate increase is a result of the limitations imposed on the dimensions of the CBD by the pedestrian scale of distance, and its maximum extent is usually about one square mile. Such a large area seldom functions as a unit since the average walking distance for both shoppers and workers tends to be between 500 and 600 feet (one or two blocks), regardless of the size of the downtown area. Thus, as the CBD increases in size and functional complexity, specialized land-use zones emerge. The more extensive the area, the greater will be the internal differentiation.

Specialized functional areas are distinctive elements in every metropolitan CBD, although they are more evident in larger urban centres such as Montreal, Toronto and Vancouver than in small cities such as Saskatoon or St. John's. Clustering is an economic necessity in the CBD because many transfers of goods and information are made on foot and so distances of only a few blocks between interdependent establishments become quite significant. Inefficiency will obviously increase as a function of size if uses are distributed on a random basis, and in large cities office, retail, entertainment and other uses therefore form distinct functional zones within the CBD; this is illustrated for Vancouver in Figure 4.2.

The process by which the CBD becomes differentiated into functional zones can be explained in terms of two principal requirements of each activity: accessibility to the metropolitan population and locational affinity between uses. Some uses are more dependent on convenient access to the metropolitan population than others, and therefore seek out the most accessible sites. It is important to note that intra-CBD accessibility differences cannot be satisfactorily measured in terms of the physical capacity of transportation systems, in which there is frequently no significant variation from one area to another; in fact, the Bloor-Yonge intersection, which is at the extreme edge of Toronto's CBD, is far more accessible in time-cost terms to the metropolitan population than Queen-Yonge and Bay-King, the two most highly valued locations. The intra-CBD distribution of the "daytime" population (which is itself a function of the existing land use pattern) is a far more meaningful measure of accessibility; internal functional differentiation is in turn dependent on the accessibility potentials of the different sites.

The second factor, locational affinity, refers to the agglomeration or external economies which some uses achieve by clustering. (Some uses are repelled by others and locational antipathy is also a factor.) Thus, functional zonations are determined jointly by accessibility and locational affinity. Collectively, uses may be located at varying distances from the peak land value intersection (PLVI) according to their rent-paying ability, but they will not be concentrically arranged around it. For example, theatres in a given city may be able to compete successfully for land between 500 and 1,000 feet from the

PLVI but because of the importance of agglomeration economies (advertising, comparison shopping), a theatre district will ordinarily emerge in only one sector of this concentric zone. Although the actual land use pattern of a particular CBD is strongly influenced by historical factors (e.g., the original site of City Hall or the railway station), certain common patterns are evident. The PLVI, for example, is most frequently located within the retail core, which therefore acts as the pivotal point for the various functional districts.

Typically, the areal extent of the CBD has remained relatively stable in most large cities, where growth has tended to be vertical rather than horizontal. Although frequently regarded as a prestige location, the skyscraper is both an economical and a logical building choice within the CBD. Construction economics favour the use of high-rise buildings where land values and/or the costs of municipal services are high; both conditions frequently obtain when new structures are to be built downtown. For most office functions the greatest benefits of the skyscraper are its concentration of large numbers of people in a small area and associated agglomeration economies; for example, the Toronto-Dominion Centre and Place Ville Marie each contain more than 15,000 workers on an areal base which is only a fraction of a typical city block. The speed with which personal contact can be established between functionally interdependent firms is increased when they are distributed vertically, and the use of elevators and underground passages means that thousands of people in adjacent towers are only a few minutes away from each other. Other economies of scale benefit all firms, whether or not they are functionally related; these include the shared costs of security and maintenance as well as the availability of ancillary services such as restaurants and convenience shops. Provided that they do not generate inefficiencies elsewhere in the system (as when the carrying capacities of roads and public facilities are exceeded), high-density developments minimize the need for pedestrian movement and so enhance the CBD's accessibility, which is its most valuable asset.

Despite the stabilization of its areal extent and its emphasis on vertical growth, the CBD is constantly shifting its position in response to functional changes (e.g., the rise of offices and the decline of manufacturing) and the nature of the redevelopment process. These shifts may cover a distance of only a few blocks during a period of many years, but they are nevertheless very significant in an area of such intensive development, where buildings have a long structural life and where land values may fall by as much as a half within one block of the PLVI. The shifts are in part explained by the locational decisions of new and expanding CBD functions. New buildings are not normally located in the core of the CBD for several reasons: the sites may be already occupied by optimally located uses; no vacant lots may be available; lots that are available may not be large enough; assembling a large tract of land under multiple ownership may involve delays, frustrations, exorbitant expenses and possible failure; it is often more economical to rent old buildings for sub-optimal uses than to demolish and re-build for more modern functions (e.g., a department store building might be taken over by a discount furniture store); the core is usually congested; and finally, land is much cheaper on the edge of the CBD. The location of a new large building or complex on one side of the CBD (e.g., Place Ville Marie in Montreal) encourages other uses to locate near by, and the cumulative effect is to produce an area whose modern appearance contrasts sharply with the old buildings of the core.

In most cities it is relatively easy to identify the direction in which the CBD is advancing (zone of assimilation) and the district which it is abandoning (zone of discard). The two areas differ both in physical appearance and functional structure. There are really three zones: the advancing front, the abandoned area and the old, stable core. The old core retains the more traditional and stable CBD functions such as department stores, specialty shops and entertainment facilities. The advancing front is characterized by the newest CBD functions, especially offices, while the abandoned area is typically occupied by declining and marginal CBD functions, including manufacturing, warehousing, and wholesaling. Frequently, the old core retains the greatest functional diversity and attracts the largest number of pedestrians. This is the area which stays alive when the offices are closed; every city exhibits this contrast in night life between the multi-functional old core and the uni-functional new core.

The geographical shift of the CBD is generally towards high-income residential areas and away from the old industrial districts. The zone of discard may be characterized by "barriers" (rivers, railways, steep slopes) which prevent the expansion of the CBD in that direction; more frequently it is the land uses in the vicinity of these barriers which discourage new development, which may include wholesaling, warehousing, manufacturing and low-income housing.

Courtesy City of Montreal, Department of Public Relations

*Place Jacques Cartier in Montreal, with restored cobblestone paving.*

A number of factors favour the shift of CBD functions towards the more expensive residential areas—the prestige of such districts, their superior environmental amenities, the low coverage of buildings and the presence of large lots, which make it easier to assemble and clear land; and the economic advantages of convenient access for high-income households. The first visible sign of CBD encroachment is often widespread conversion; large single-family houses are refurbished, subdivided and occupied by a variety of professional and service offices including real estate agencies, medical centres, lawyers, engineers and other professionals. In later stages, redevelopment takes place and the new multi-storey buildings house headquarters offices, hotels and other increasingly important CBD activities. The zone of assimilation has a comparatively attractive appearance; rising land values and rising rents encourage the upkeep of buildings even when redevelopment is certain. In contrast, the zone of discard is characterized by commercial and residential blight;

at its worst, there are acres of surface car parks, numerous unoccupied buildings and skid row conditions. A few cities have had some success in rehabilitating such areas. In part this has stemmed from the discovery of their tourist potential. Boutiques, quaint restaurants, antique shops, and the restoration of historic buildings have revivified Vancouver's Gastown, Old Montreal and Old Quebec, and these areas have now been designated historic precincts to preserve their character and to prevent wholesale redevelopment.

## The CBD—Frame

In comparison with the core, the frame is characterized by less intensive development, lower land values, older buildings and blighted conditions. It shares in the high accessibility of the core but not to the same extent; it is usually not as well served by public transit systems but it may be more accessible for those who travel by automobile, particularly during peak travel hours. The functional and spatial structures of the frame can be best explained in terms of its historical relationship with the core of the CBD.

Three main types of activities are generally located in this area: former CBD functions, marginal CBD functions, and activities which are closely related to CBD functions. Manufacturing, wholesaling and warehousing are typical of those activities which were at one time tied to the city centre by their need for access to long-distance transportation terminals; these can be generally classified as former CBD functions. Some activities for which a central location is optimal may be unable to pay the high rents of the core and may therefore prefer to locate on its periphery; these marginal CBD functions include extensive users of land (furniture stores and automobile dealerships, for example) and those activities whose business is not increased appreciably by a more central location (for example, medical centres, which locate in areas that are central to the metropolitan population, but which derive little benefit from proximity to other CBD uses). Finally, many functions located in the frame complement or are related to CBD functions; included in this category are off-street parking facilities, wholesaling and transportation terminals.

To some extent the frame's blighted appearance is due to its location in the economic shadow of the core. This is analogous to the well-known phenomenon of an urban shadow, which is the effect that cities have on the land use system of surrounding rural areas. Because rural land produces higher returns when urbanized, much land is taken out of agriculture long before it is needed for urbanization. Land speculation of this type is usually rife in the vicinity of most large urban centres. As a result, these areas are frequently characterized by scattered urban development (including urban sprawl) and blighted conditions of an economic and/or physical nature. In the frame, similar effects are generated by the presence of the CBD; although it may be *certain* that only a small proportion of the land will be developed for CBD uses, there is often *uncertainty* about which specific areas will be chosen for such redevelopment. Under these conditions, land speculation is inevitable: land values remain high while the carrying charges (property taxes, interest charges and the like) are paid by renting buildings to sub-optimal users or by using the cleared land for parking lots. It should be added that the property tax system encourages such speculation, since taxes will generally be lower when a building is allowed to deteriorate structurally or when it is demolished (see page 339).

Although the frame may be divided into a number of functional zones, these are not as clearly differentiated as in the case of the CBD. This is due both to the lower land values, which obviate the need for high-density development, and also due to the nature of the area's functions. Many activities, particularly small manufacturing firms, are not functionally tied to any specific uses or location but depend instead on the general availability of downtown services. Because of their need for a considerable amount of space, tight clusters are impractical for some establishments. Other activities, although they benefit from clustering, depend on their customers travelling by car; as a result, continuity is not essential. Finally, the prevailing low-density development discourages internal trips on foot and functional zones are therefore not constrained by the pedestrian scale of distance.

Excluding residential areas, which have been described above, several functional zones can usually be distinguished within the frame: wholesale-warehousing, light manufacturing, specialized retailing, specialized services, and institutional uses. Two specialized retail districts frequently evolve as a result of consumer preferences for comparative shopping; automobile rows and furniture districts. One of the more recent but increasingly common functional zones is the medical service centre, which is located in the frame for several reasons: the need for convenient accessibility to the metropolitan population, reliance on the automobile as the principal means of transportation for both staff and patients, the economic advantages

TABLE 4.4 *Employment by place of work and by major land use, Metro Toronto, 1970*

| Land use | Downtown core | | Central area | | City of Toronto | | Metro Toronto | |
|---|---|---|---|---|---|---|---|---|
| | No. | % | No. | % | No. | % | No. | % |
| Offices | 78,890 | 58.9 | 135,550 | 42.5 | 170,550 | 36.4 | 214,858 | 23.3 |
| % of Metro | (36.7) | | (63.1) | | (79.4) | | (100.0) | |
| Retail and personal services | 39,982 | 29.9 | 74,375 | 23.3 | 113,354 | 24.2 | 227,655 | 24.7 |
| % of Metro | (17.6) | | (32.7) | | (49.8) | | (100.0) | |
| Industry, storage and warehousing | 5,924 | 4.4 | 69,817 | 21.9 | 121,158 | 25.7 | 362,182 | 39.3 |
| % of Metro | (1.6) | | (19.3) | | (33.5) | | (100.0) | |
| Institutional | 5,864 | 4.4 | 23,492 | 7.4 | 34,628 | 7.4 | 66,299 | 7.2 |
| % of Metro | (8.8) | | (35.4) | | (52.2) | | (100.0) | |
| Transportation, communication and utilities | 994 | 0.7 | 12,229 | 3.8 | 22,026 | 4.7 | 37,162 | 4.1 |
| % of Metro | (2.7) | | (32.9) | | (59.3) | | (100.0) | |
| Other | 2,284 | 1.7 | 3,508 | 1.1 | 7,469 | 1.6 | 12,460 | 1.4 |
| % of Metro | (18.3) | | (28.2) | | (59.9) | | (100.0) | |
| Total | 133,938 | 100.0 | 318,971 | 100.0 | 469,185 | 100.0 | 920,516 | 100.0 |
| % of Metro | (14.6) | | (34.6) | | (51.0) | | (100.0) | |

SOURCE: Metropolitan Toronto Planning Board

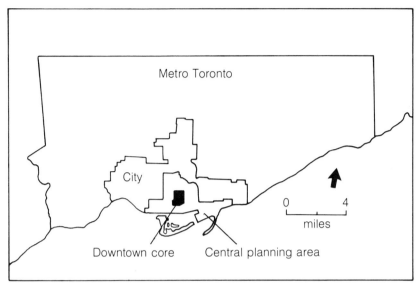

Reference map for Table 4.4

gained by clustering (for example, the sharing of laboratory facilities), and the relatively few functional linkages with other downtown uses. Within the manufacturing industry, clothing firms are the most likely to cluster together. Because of the low weight of the equipment used and of the finished product, their operations are particularly suited to the old loft buildings which are so common in the frame. Localization is further encouraged by the functional interdependencies that are characteristic of firms in the industry; in Toronto, for example, more than a hundred firms are located within one block of the Spadina-Adelaide intersection. The wholesaling-warehousing district frequently adjoins the inter-city transportation terminals; in many cases these districts developed in association with spur lines constructed by the major railways.

## Toronto: A Case Study

Descriptive data on the functional structure and historical evolution of Canadian city centres are generally lacking except in the case of Toronto, which has recently undergone considerable downtown redevelopment and concerning which a substantial body of information exists. From this it is possible to gain some insight into the three principal questions concerning the central area: what are its

TABLE 4.5 *Developed urban area by land use (percentage distribution), Metropolitan Toronto Planning Area, 1971*

| Land use | Downtown core | Central Planning Area | City of Toronto | Metro Toronto | Metropolitan Toronto Planning Area |
|---|---|---|---|---|---|
| Residential | 3.9 | 17.5 | 50.7 | 49.6 | 42.5 |
| Commercial | 63.0 | 13.5 | 9.0 | 4.9 | 3.9 |
| Industrial | 5.9 | 20.2 | 9.8 | 10.8 | 10.6 |
| Institutional | 24.1 | 13.1 | 7.9 | 6.7 | 5.5 |
| Transportation and utilities | 1.1 | 19.5 | 9.8 | 10.3 | 13.0 |
| Open space | 2.0 | 16.2 | 12.8 | 17.7 | 24.5 |
| Total (%) | 100.0 | 100.0 | 100.0 | 100.0 | 100.0 |
| Total (acres) | 445 | 6,710 | 23.212 | 125,103 | 196,945 |

SOURCE: Metropolitan Toronto Planning Board

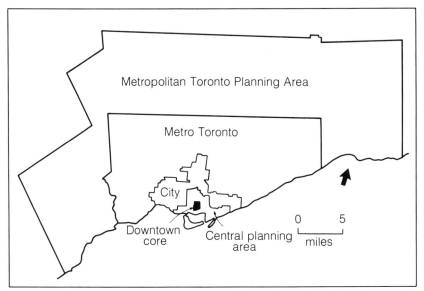

Reference map for Table 4.5

specialist functions? how are these spatially arranged? and what changes, both functional and spatial, are currently taking place?

Tables 4.4 and 4.5 illustrate for employment and land use respectively the types of functional specializations that occur within both the downtown core and the central area as a whole. Downtown is primarily important for office, retail and personal service employment; although the central area exhibits similar specializations it is of relatively greater importance for manufacturing, wholesaling, transportation and institutional activities. Commercial and institutional land uses predominate in the downtown core while in the rest of the central area industrial, transportation and residential uses are relatively more important. Table 4.6 indicates the types of functional change presently occurring within the downtown core, the central area and the City of Toronto. (Although employment data do exist for 1970 the sub-groups are not strictly comparable with previous data because of changes in the basis of classification, viz. by land use instead of by industry.) Alterations in the employment profile of all three central districts are representative of the major changes occurring in all city centres: declining employment in goods-handling activities (e.g., manufacturing, wholesaling and transpor-

TABLE 4.6 Employment by place of work and by industry, City of Toronto, 1960-1964*

| Industrial category | Downtown core | | | Central Area | | | City of Toronto | | |
|---|---|---|---|---|---|---|---|---|---|
| | 1960 | 1964 | % change | 1960 | 1964 | % change | 1960 | 1964 | % change |
| Manufacturing and construction | 15,208 | 13,396 | −11.9 | 73,846 | 67,262 | −8.9 | 137,228 | 128,282 | −6.5 |
| Transportation, storage and wholesale | 13,956 | 11,064 | −20.8 | 55,318 | 46,474 | −16.0 | 75,551 | 66,657 | −11.8 |
| Retail and personal services | 37,648 | 37,944 | +0.8 | 60,716 | 60,225 | −0.8 | 98,477 | 100,012 | +1.6 |
| Finance, insurance, real estate and business services | 38,944 | 40,560 | +4.1 | 56,622 | 57,998 | +2.4 | 66,775 | 70,440 | +5.5 |
| Government and community services | 13,568 | 14,854 | +9.5 | 47,822 | 52,034 | +8.8 | 67,896 | 70,977 | +4.5 |
| Total | 119,324 | 117,818 | −1.3 | 294,324 | 283,993 | −3.5 | 445,927 | 436,368 | −2.1 |

SOURCE: City of Toronto

*Note that the City of Toronto's employment estimates for 1960 vary slightly from those of Metropolitan Toronto (see Table 3.1).

TABLE 4.7 *Employment by place of work and by major land use, Central Planning Area, Toronto, 1970*

| Land use | Downtown area No. | % | North sector No. | % | East sector No. | % | West sector No. | % | South sector No. | % | Central area No. | % |
|---|---|---|---|---|---|---|---|---|---|---|---|---|
| Office | 91,239 | 56.1 | 42,108 | 54.5 | 1,438 | 10.7 | 2,173 | 4.5 | 2,038 | 11.7 | 138,996 | 43.6 |
| % of Central Area | (65.6) | | (30.3) | | (1.0) | | (1.6) | | (1.5) | | (100.0) | |
| Retail | 25,065 | 15.4 | 6,325 | 8.2 | 682 | 5.1 | 2,053 | 4.2 | 1,299 | 7.5 | 35,424 | 11.1 |
| % of Central Area | (70.8) | | (17.8) | | (1.9) | | (5.8) | | (3.7) | | (100.0) | |
| Manufacturing, warehousing | 13,602 | 8.4 | 1,275 | 1.7 | 7,949 | 59.0 | 34,871 | 72.2 | 12,032 | 69.4 | 69,729 | 21.9 |
| % of Central Area | (19.5) | | (1.8) | | (11.4) | | (50.0) | | (17.3) | | (100.0) | |
| Other | 32,706 | 20.1 | 27,530 | 35.6 | 3,391 | 25.2 | 9,210 | 19.1 | 1,985 | 11.4 | 74,822 | 23.4 |
| % of Central Area | (43.7) | | (36.8) | | (4.5) | | (12.3) | | (2.7) | | (100.0) | |
| Total | 162,612 | 100.0 | 77,238 | 100.0 | 13,460 | 100.0 | 48,307 | 100.0 | 17,354 | 100.0 | 318,971 | 100.0 |
| % of Central Area | (51.0) | | (24.2) | | (4.2) | | (15.1) | | (5.5) | | (100.0) | |

SOURCE: Metropolitan Toronto Planning Board

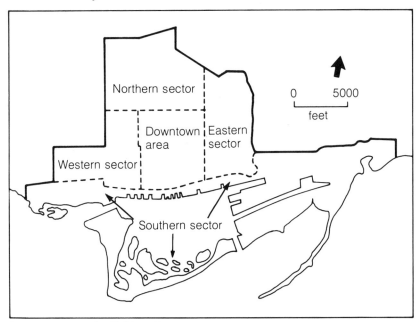

Reference map for Table 4.7

tation industries), rising employment in office and other service functions (e.g., financial and government services) and the stabilization of retail employment.

Table 4.7 illustrates the generalized spatial distribution of employment within the central area. The downtown area (slightly larger than the downtown core) is primarily given over to office and retail functions; manufacturing-warehousing activities are relatively more important in the eastern, western and southern sectors; and the northern sector is particularly important for office employment. In the case of Toronto there is clear evidence of a redistribution of jobs within the central city (Figure 4.3); declining employment in the goods-handling industries is mainly responsible for the loss of jobs in the eastern, western and southern parts of the central area (zones of discard) while employment within the downtown core and its northern extension (zone of assimilation) has recently increased as a result of the construction of the Yonge Street subway (opened in 1954) and the consequent expansion of office functions.

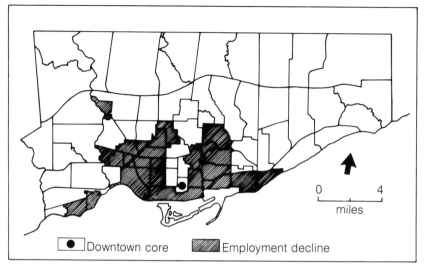

FIGURE 4.3   Minor planning districts which experienced an absolute decline in employment between 1956 and 1970, Metro Toronto (Municipality of Metroplitan Toronto).

*Source:* Metropolitan Toronto Planning Board.

Figure 4.4 illustrates at a more detailed level the geographical shift of employment between 1960 and 1970. Within the downtown core (University Avenue and Simcoe, Front, Jarvis and College streets), employment growth has been almost entirely concentrated within the office district, bounded by Yonge, Queen, Simcoe and Front streets. Within the latter area the number employed increased from 55,600 to 69,700 during the ten-year period compared to only a slight increase from 63,800 to 64,300 in the rest of the downtown core. Employment in the southern, western and eastern sectors declined, while substantial growth occurred in the northern midtown districts centred on the Yonge-Bloor intersection; the latter location became especially attractive as a result of the opening in 1966 of the Bloor Street subway and it is actually more accessible to the metropolitan population than is the downtown core, particularly when public transportation is used. The growth of employment in the northwestern zone bounded by Bloor Street, University Avenue, College Street and Spadina Avenue is mainly attributable to

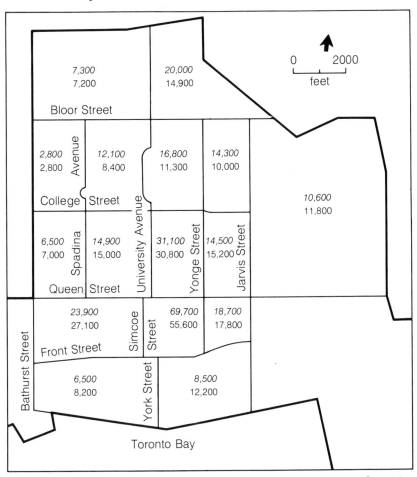

FIGURE 4.4  Changes in the distribution of employment within the Central Planning Area (CPA) of Toronto, 1960-1970. In the rest of the CPA employment increased from 38,900 to 40,900 while total CPA employment grew from 294,300 to 319,000 during the same period.

*Source:*  Metropolitan Toronto Planning Board and City of Toronto Planning Board.

Note: *Figures in italic represent 1970 employment.*

the expansion of the University of Toronto. As Table 4.7 illustrates, the downtown and midtown employment profiles are very similar and Toronto's downtown is rapidly developing a bi-nodal structure—a pattern which can also be seen traced in many large metropolitan centres (e.g., New York and Montreal).

TABLE 4.8 *Percentage distribution of land use, downtown core and fringe districts, Toronto, 1958-1971*

| Land use | Downtown core | | Northern fringe | | Western fringe | | Eastern fringe | | Southern fringe | | All districts | |
|---|---|---|---|---|---|---|---|---|---|---|---|---|
| | 1958 | 1971 | 1958 | 1971 | 1958 | 1971 | 1958 | 1971 | 1958 | 1971 | 1958 | 1971 |
| Commercial | 62.5 | 59.7 | 33.3 | 38.9 | 17.0 | 18.7 | 8.0 | 8.7 | 7.4 | 7.6 | 18.0 | 18.6 |
| Industrial | 9.5 | 5.6 | 2.7 | 1.2 | 3.9 | 2.5 | 5.8 | 4.8 | 40.6 | 35.6 | 20.4 | 17.6 |
| Institutional | 18.7 | 22.9 | 19.5 | 20.4 | 28.8 | 34.4 | 8.2 | 11.4 | 13.9 | 14.5 | 16.6 | 18.9 |
| Transportation & utilities | 1.0 | 1.1 | 1.6 | 1.9 | 0.8 | 0.8 | 3.0 | 3.1 | 22.8 | 27.0 | 10.7 | 12.8 |
| Residential | 6.3 | 3.7 | 35.1 | 26.9 | 43.2 | 33.5 | 54.9 | 46.8 | 5.8 | 4.5 | 24.4 | 19.3 |
| Open space | 1.2 | 1.9 | 6.6 | 6.6 | 5.3 | 5.5 | 19.2 | 19.9 | 7.0 | 7.0 | 8.3 | 8.4 |
| Vacant | 0.8 | 5.1 | 1.2 | 4.1 | 1.0 | 4.6 | 0.9 | 5.3 | 2.5 | 3.8 | 1.6 | 4.4 |
| Total (%) | 100.0 | 100.0 | 100.0 | 100.0 | 100.0 | 100.0 | 100.0 | 100.0 | 100.0 | 100.0 | 100.0 | 100.0 |
| Total (acres) | 469 | 469 | 499 | 499 | 758 | 758 | 793 | 793 | 1885 | 1962 | 4404 | 4481 |

SOURCE: Metropolitan Toronto Planning Board

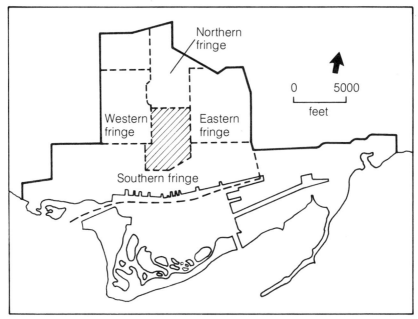

Reference map for Table 4.8. Hatched area indicates the downtown core.

Although there are clear differences in terms of both employment and land use between the CBD's advancing front (zone of assimilation) and its area of abandonment (zone of discard) all zones within Toronto's central area have recently experienced very similar types of change (Table 4.8). The advance of CBD functions into the northern sector (midtown) initiated land use changes similar to those which occurred in all the declining districts and in the central area as a whole; indeed, the sole exception to the general direction of change was a decrease in the area devoted to commercial uses *within* the downtown core. Of particular interest is the increasing amount of vacant land within all districts; in other words, the rate at which land was released by former activities exceeded the rate of absorption by new users. This is largely accounted for by two related factors: the higher density of new developments (i.e., the replacement of an equivalent amount of floorspace required less land) and the increased holding of land by both speculators and developers. The relationship between these two factors demonstrates an important land use principle which applies to all urban areas undergoing change: the higher

TABLE 4.9 Floor space ('000 sq. ft.) by land use and sub-area, Montreal's city centre, 1949 and 1962

| Land Use | Core | | Frame | | Total CBD | | Periphery | | Total city centre | |
|---|---|---|---|---|---|---|---|---|---|---|
| | 1949 | 1962 | 1949 | 1962 | 1949 | 1962 | 1949 | 1962 | 1949 | 1962 |
| Office | 7,174.4 | 13,960.8 | 4,186.2 | 6,191.3 | 11,360.6 | 20,152.1 | 497.7 | 861.3 | 11,858.3 | 21,013.4 |
| Retail | 3,744.8 | 3,751.8 | 3,860.6 | 3,676.1 | 7,605.4 | 7,427.9 | 2,703.5 | 2,307.8 | 10,308.9 | 9,735.7 |
| Manufacturing | 838.7 | 324.2 | 4,397.1 | 3,995.3 | 5,235.8 | 4,319.5 | 6,060.0 | 6,230.2 | 11,295.8 | 10,549.7 |
| Wholesale | 161.9 | 144.7 | 4,417.9 | 3,949.3 | 4,579.8 | 4,094.0 | 2,392.6 | 2,677.6 | 6,972.4 | 6,771.6 |
| Public and institutional | 602.3 | 468.5 | 4,259.9 | 5,376.9 | 4,862.2 | 5,845.4 | 4,745.5 | 6,128.8 | 9,607.7 | 11,974.2 |
| Residential | 400.8 | 211.8 | 4,740.9 | 3,083.5 | 5,141.7 | 3,295.3 | 16,783.4 | 16,490.0 | 21,925.1 | 19,785.3 |
| Other | 1,790.2 | 3,588.1 | 2,338.2 | 2,507.4 | 4,128.4 | 6,095.5 | 1,755.2 | 2,023.6 | 5,883.6 | 8,119.1 |
| Total | 14,713.1 | 22,449.9 | 28,200.8 | 28,779.8 | 42,913.9 | 51,229.7 | 34,937.9 | 36,719.3 | 77,851.8 | 87,949.0 |
| Floor space index* | 4.3 | 6.9 | 1.9 | 2.0 | 2.3 | 2.9 | 1.5 | 1.7 | 1.9 | 2.2 |

SOURCE: City of Montreal

*Floor space index (F.S.I.) equals total floor space divided by buildable area (i.e. excluding streets)

Reference map for Table 4.9

the rent-paying ability of the new use (and generally the higher the development density the higher is the land rent), the longer is the period for which land can be economically held by speculators, either vacant or at a sub-optimal use. As a result of the operation of the land market it was therefore inevitable that the amount of vacant land in Toronto's city centre should increase, and this trend may be expected to continue as long as redevelopment to a higher density continues to be the norm.

Floorspace data are not available for Toronto but changes in Montreal's city centre between 1949 and 1962 corroborate the con-

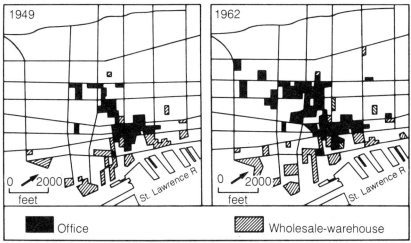

FIGURE 4.5   Changes in the distribution of office and wholesale-warehouse uses, Montreal's city centre, 1949 and 1962.

*Source:* City of Montreal, *Le Centre-Ville* (Montreal, 1964).

clusions which have been drawn from the above analysis. Offices accounted for the bulk of the floorspace increase in the city centre as a whole. Within the CBD, office floorspace increased by 8,700,000 square feet compared to a net addition of only 8,300,000 square feet in the total floorspace; within the core, offices accounted for 88 per cent of the total addition and increased their share of the total floorspace from 49 to 62 per cent, while within the frame, office space grew by an amount greater than the total addition and increased its share of the total floorspace from 15 to 22 per cent. In the periphery the expansion of office space was relatively small. Manufacturing and wholesaling declined throughout the CBD but increased slightly in the periphery. Retailing remained stable within the core but declined marginally in the frame and in the periphery. Public and institutional uses increased in all areas with the exception of the core. The floorspace index remained highest in the core, where it also showed the greatest proportionate increase (i.e., the tallest structures added during this period were concentrated here). As a result of these changes the core-frame-periphery differences were sharp-

TABLE 4.10 *Employment and floorspace, downtown peninsula, Vancouver, 1970 and 1985*

| Land use | Existing 1970 | | Forecast 1985 | | | |
| | | | Low forecast | | High forecast | |
| | Employment (No.) | Floorspace ('000 sq. ft.) | Employment (No.) | Floorspace ('000 sq. ft.) | Employment (No.) | Floorspace ('000 sq. ft.) |
|---|---|---|---|---|---|---|
| Office | 48,000 | 7,800 | 82,000 | 13,100 | 105,000 | 16,600 |
| Retail | 18,000 | 6,100 | 20,000 | 7,200 | 25,000 | 8,600 |
| Service and warehousing | 14,000 | 7,700 | 12,000 | 8,200 | 15,000 | 8,300 |
| Public and institutional | 6,000 | 1,700 | 9,000 | 2,600 | 15,000 | 3,700 |
| Hotel | 4,000 | 3,100 | 9,000 | 7,800 | 12,000 | 10,400 |
| Residential | 1,000 | 23,300 | 1,000 | 28,700 | 1,000 | 32,200 |
| Total | 91,000 | 49,700 | 133,000 | 67,600 | 173,000 | 79,800 |

SOURCE: City of Vancouver

ened; the core increased its share of office (60 to 66 per cent) and retail (36 to 39 per cent) floorspace, while the periphery increased its share of manufacturing, wholesaling, public-institutional and residential floorspace. The spatial changes which resulted are illustrated by Figure 4.5; office floorspace, a growing use, expanded to the northwest (the zone of assimilation), while wholesaling and warehousing, declining uses, remained rooted in the port-industrial district (the zone of discard).

## The Future City Centre

Clearly, the future of the city centre will depend largely on its ability to retain its present importance for office employment, in which case it may well become primarily an office district with only sufficient retailing and other services to serve the needs of the downtown work force. Table 4.10 indicates the current strength of office employment in downtown Vancouver and its anticipated share of future growth; 70-80 per cent of the net increase in employment by 1985 is expected to be in office functions. It is not, however, certain whether this particular preeminence can be maintained much longer, and it is already evident that advances in communications technology have begun to erode the CBD's near-monopoly of this function. Many inter-office trips are now being replaced by some form of telecommunications, which has the effect of weakening the horizontal linkages that have hitherto encouraged office firms to cluster in the centres of cities. Although office functions remain communication-intensive activities, the proportion of information being relayed by face-to-face contact is declining (see also pages 84 to 88) and correspondingly, the proportion of offices located downtown is decreasing in most cities (see, for example, Table 4.11).

The principal problems of the city centre stem directly from its essential function, which is to serve as the location of first-order activities. As a result of population growth and changes in both technology and consumer demand many first-order functions in time become lower-order functions, i.e., they can be profitably supplied to trading areas which are less extensive than the metropolitan area. Throughout its history the city centre has continually delegated lower-order functions to suburban areas while replacing them with new first-order functions, and as a result has undergone continuous redevelopment. In the past the redevelopment process

TABLE 4.11 *Office space\* by district, Metro Toronto, 1962-1973*

| District | 1962 | | 1973 | |
|---|---|---|---|---|
| | Sq. ft. | % | sq. ft. | % |
| Downtown core | 7,488,470 | 40.0 | 14,396,429 | 34.5 |
| Rest of downtown | 5,040,534 | 26.8 | 8,618,695 | 20.6 |
| Midtown district | 4,687,574 | 25.0 | 10,138,683 | 24.3 |
| Suburban district | 1,551,858 | 8.2 | 8,629,752 | 20.6 |
| Total | 18,768,436 | 100.0 | 41,783,559 | 100.0 |

SOURCE: A.E. LePage Limited

*Excludes buildings of less than 20,000 square feet.

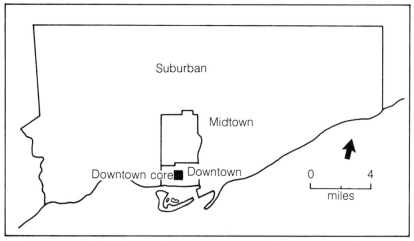

Reference map for Table 4.11

resulted in net gains in overall importance but since about 1950 stability or even decline has increasingly characterized the history of the city centre; in only a few cities, mainly those which perform a supra-regional or national role, has downtown employment shown any recent increases.

Because of their age and fully developed state, downtown areas are inelastic and unresponsive to change in comparison with suburban

*Courtesy Canadian Imperial Bank of Commerce*

*Commerce Court, Toronto.*

areas, where the most modern technological designs are relatively easily accommodated in the conversion of open land to urban uses. The city centre is therefore becoming increasingly unsuitable for a growing number of existing users and at the same time frustrates the efforts of redevelopers; its major problems, dilapidation and traffic congestion, are both the result and the cause of its lack of redevelopment. The private redevelopment that does take place is generally restricted to small areas within the city centre. Consumer preference for centrality and window space, combined with the high cost of land and construction economics, has, for example, encouraged the almost universal appearance of slim towers of glass with a central elevator shaft (rents within high-rise buildings generally increase in proportion to the height above ground level). As a result of the high density of such new developments, the geographical incidence of renewal is being restricted to smaller areas than ever before, which in turn accounts for the simultaneous increase in the number of luxury skyscrapers and of dilapidated or vacant areas.

PART TWO
# Canadian Urban Development

# 5.
# Selected Aspects of Canadian Development to 1867

Until 1867 the Canadian economy was dominated by the production of successive export staples—fish, furs, timber and wheat—and the evolution of the urban system during this period (and, indeed, until the First World War) is therefore best explained in terms of the staple theory of economic growth. At first, settlements were established solely in order to facilitate the exploitation of easily procured natural resources such as fish and furs. Accordingly, fishing bases, fur-trading posts and forts were the first pre-urban settlements. These were merely outposts of European commercial enterprises, and their production functions were oriented to export rather than self-sufficiency.

## Staple Theory, Mercantilism and Reciprocity

A staple may be defined as a commodity which is derived from the primary industries (fishing, hunting, lumbering, agriculture and mining) and which requires little processing before being exported. A staple-dominated, commercial economy is generally characterized by a low population density, an abundance of land, a low level of development, and a high dependence on foreign trade. In the Canadian context the early emphasis on staples did little to stimulate settlement; it was only after some two hundred years that permanent settlements began to assume any significance in the fishing industry, while with a few notable exceptions the fur trade remained basically incompatible with settlement throughout its history. Of the later staple industries the square timber trade did little to encourage the growth of permanent settlements, while wheat cultivation, although requiring the presence of a resident population, did not encourage high-density development.

According to the staple theory of growth, the first stages of economic development can be best explained in terms of the prevailing external demands for the country's primary products. Viewed in this light, staple exports function as the principal generators of economic growth and the income derived from export-oriented activities provides the base or support for growth in other sectors of the economy. In short, there is a multiplier effect: support industries emerge to cater to those engaged in staple activities; investment in transportation, the growth of urban centres, and other by-products of the staple industries create external economies (savings to other producers) which make feasible the development of other industries; finally, capital accumulated in the staple industries can be used to exploit other resources which might not otherwise have been utilized. Accordingly, Canada's early economic history can be explained more adequately in terms of the external demands for the country's staples than in terms of internal or domestic demands. Canada has in fact remained very dependent on foreign trade, and high proportions of national production and consumption are today sold and bought on the international market.

In addition to the staple theory of economic development the mercantilistic principles of the European trading nations explain much of Canada's economic growth and the structure of the urban system prior to 1850. British mercantile policy was at first rigidly applied in the regulation of colonial trade. In 1651, the first English Navigation Acts were passed, and with modifications these remained in force until 1849. In the Canadian context, mercantilism meant the exchange of primary products (staples) for British manufactured goods. Britain was legally the exclusive source of almost all manufactured goods, while the primary products of the colonies entered Britain at preferential rates. Trade between a colony and a foreign country was not generally tolerated by Britain and all goods had to be carried in British ships. Mercantilism was undermined after 1821 and was finally ended in the 1840s when Britain adopted a free trade policy. The abolition of the Corn Laws in 1846 represented the end of the system of preferential or differential duties on the importation of colonial goods into Britain. In 1847 the colonies were permitted to impose their own tariffs on imported goods, and in

1849 the repeal of the Navigation Laws made unrestricted foreign trade possible by removing the requirement that British ships be employed as carriers.

The end of British mercantilism as a formative force in the development of the Canadian economy marked the beginning of a major reorientation of the colonial economies towards the United States. The new trading emphasis was foreshadowed in 1847 when the Province of Canada abolished the imperial preference and adopted the same rates of duty for both British and American imports. Three choices had emerged by 1849: a) annexation to the United States, which was favoured by Montreal merchants in their Annexation Manifesto, published in the Montreal *Gazette* and supported by the other English newspapers in the city; b) confederation of the British North American colonies, which was proposed by the British American League at its meeting in Kingston; and c) a reciprocity trade treaty with the United States, which was supported by the governments of all the colonies. It was generally believed that some wider economic alliance was necessary to take the place of the imperial trading system. Reciprocity with the United States was perhaps the most favoured alternative and in 1854 a reciprocal trade agreement was signed between the United States and the British North American colonies allowing the duty-free movement of "natural products of the earth."

The Reciprocity Treaty was the formal expression of a trend which had begun two decades earlier. Although it is certain that trade with the United States would have increased in any case, it is equally clear that the agreement was instrumental in increasing this trade and in accelerating the re-orientation of the Canadian economy towards the United States. During the term of the treaty Canadian trade with the United States increased to between two and three times the level of the early 1850s. The special advantages conferred by the treaty are illustrated by the fact that more than 90 per cent of Canadian exports to the United States during this period consisted of duty-free products. Further benefits were gained from the resumption of American wheat exports through the St. Lawrence, although these were largely offset by the diversion of Upper Canadian wheat through New York. After 1866, when the treaty was terminated at the request of the United States, there was a sharp drop in trade; but this lasted only a few years, and by the early 1880s the United States had replaced Britain as Canada's chief trading partner for both exports and imports.

## St. Lawrence Fur Trade

In the late sixteenth century beaver hats were considered the height of fashion in Europe, and as a result the fur trade became an increasingly profitable sideline for fishermen along the Acadian coast. The number of merchant ships engaged full-time in the fur trade increased rapidly until France instituted a fur-trade monopoly, primarily in order to ensure that permanent settlement would follow. Without a monopoly, the costs of bringing out settlers, of securing their safety, and of financing their supplies during the first years would have been far beyond the means of individual merchants in competition with each other. Accordingly, from the time of the first fur-trading monopoly, which was granted in 1588 (but revoked four months later), responsibility for colonization was one of the obligations stated in the charter of each company.

The first trading colony to be successfully established was Quebec, founded in 1608 by Samuel de Champlain under a monopoly charter granted to Sieur de Monts. Prior to this, unsuccessful attempts had been made to implement the fur-trade monopoly in several areas: in 1600 at Tadoussac at the mouth of the Saguenay River; in 1604 on an island at the mouth of the St. Croix River on the Bay of Fundy; and in 1605 at Port Royal (now Annapolis Royal). The transfer to Quebec was largely due to the difficulty of enforcing a fur-trading monopoly in Acadia. Not only did French fishing ships continue to trade with Indians at numerous sites along the coast, but their complaints when they were prevented from doing so led in 1607 to the cancellation of de Monts' monopoly in Acadia.

Quebec, however, had a number of advantages as a base from which to control a fur-trade monopoly. It was a natural fortress, with a steep escarpment which afforded a commanding prospect of the St. Lawrence at the strategic point where the river narrows from a wide estuary. Furthermore, the St. Lawrence was of vital importance in the fur trade; besides providing a major route into the interior it marked the dividing line between the hunting Indians of the cold northern areas on the Canadian Shield and the semi-sedentary agricultural Indians to the south. From the record of Cartier's voyages it is clear that Quebec was one of the meeting places at which the northern Indians traded furs for the agricultural products of the southern Indians. At first, the French obtained furs exclusively at the annual trade fairs which were established at Quebec, Montreal and Trois-Rivières; the Algonquins and the Hurons, both semi-agriculturists from the Georgian Bay-Lake Simcoe area, were the first Indian tribes to act as middlemen between the French and the fur-hunting tribes of the west.

In 1645, the Company of New France (also known as the Company of One Hundred Associates) leased its exclusive fur-trading rights to the Company of Habitants, a small group of traders in New France, and in 1647 the French king permitted all settlers (*habitants*) to participate in the trade providing that all the furs collected were sold to the Company. As a result the French entered more directly into the trade and *coureurs de bois* began to travel into the interior to peddle manufactured goods in exchange for furs. This became increasingly necessary after 1649 when the Iroquois effectively ended the Algonquin and Huron alliances with the French by nearly annihilating the Hurons; whereupon the Algonquins retreated from the St. Lawrence region and ceased to trade with the French. The attempts in the 1650s to substitute the Ottawa Indians as middlemen were thwarted by repeated Iroquois attacks, and in order to continue the fur trade it became essential to suppress the Iroquois—a goal which could be achieved only by the use of military force.

The failure of the attempt to establish the Ottawa Indians as middlemen in the fur trade made it necessary for the French to obtain furs directly from the hunting Indians of the west. Because of the constant threat of Iroquois attack the presence of a military force was required to safeguard the transportation of furs, and the arrival of 1,200 regular troops in 1665 marked the beginning of an expansionist phase in the history of the fur trade. In 1666 the Iroquois suffered a major defeat which temporarily ended their attempts at intimidation and opened the western routes; hostilities were resumed, however, in 1689 and were not finally terminated until the signing of a peace treaty in 1701.

Between 1666 and 1701 two features characterized the expansion of the fur trade: the establishment of fortified trading posts on the Great Lakes, and the extension of the fur empire into the Mississippi basin. Soon after the Iroquois had been defeated French traders began using the St. Lawrence–Lower Great Lakes route to inaugurate the profitable southwest trade, while continuing to use the Ottawa route to the northwestern tribes. Military stations and fur-trading posts were established together at a number of important points, as a defence against both the Iroquois and the English. Fort

Frontenac (also known as Fort Cataraqui) and Fort Niagara were built in 1673 and 1678 respectively at the extreme ends of Lake Ontario at the termini of portage routes; in 1679 Fort Michilimackinac was built near the meeting-point of lakes Superior, Michigan and Huron; in 1701 a post was established at Detroit to guard the narrow stretch of water (the Detroit River) between lakes Huron and Erie. The French were by this time in conflict with the English on two fronts. In 1664 the English had captured New York and replaced the Dutch as competitors from the south, and in 1670 the Hudson's Bay Company began its operations in the north. Of these the competition from the Albany-based traders was the more intense, particularly since the French were unable to match the cheaper and better English goods which were being offered to the Indians in exchange for furs.

Major French explorations of the continent began in 1669, the year after the signing of the first peace treaty with the Iroquois. In that year Dollier de Casson explored the Great Lakes as far as Sault Ste. Marie, while La Salle journeyed to the southwest towards the Ohio River. They were followed in the early 1670s by Jolliet and Marquette who discovered the easy portages between Lake Michigan and the Mississippi River; in the early 1680s La Salle travelled to the mouth of the Mississippi and explored the Gulf of Mexico. In 1672 a French expedition from Tadoussac travelled overland to Hudson Bay via the Saguenay River, thus initiating the long conflict with the Hudson's Bay Company; and in 1697, after more than a decade of intermittent clashes, the French captured all the English trading posts on Hudson Bay with the exception of Fort Albany. By 1700 the area covered by the French fur trade had grown tremendously. The two major river basins in North America, the St. Lawrence and Mississippi, had been joined into a single economic system based on fur, and the commercial empire of the St. Lawrence extended from Hudson Bay to the Gulf of Mexico and as far west as the Lake of the Woods.

The territorial expansion of this period was characteristic of the St. Lawrence fur trade throughout its history. Because of competition and the depletion of fur-bearing animals, continuous expansion was imperative. As the French became more directly involved in the trade with Indians, the need for the annual trade fairs at Quebec, Montreal and Trois-Rivières diminished, and they soon ceased altogether, as increasingly distant points were utilized as meeting places for the French traders and Indian trappers. At strategic points depots were established as outfitting centres for traders who travelled to the Indian tribes; one of the most important of these was Fort Michilimackinac which was ideally located to serve both the southwest trade via Lake Michigan and the northwest trade via Lake Superior.

The demise of the trade fair and the growing importance of *voyageurs* and *coureurs de bois* required a different form of financing for the fur trade. Since a trading expedition could be away for as long as three years, the time that elapsed between the outlay of capital for the purchase of trade goods and provisions and its repayment after the furs were sold could be as much as five years. The long-term financing which became an integral part of the fur trade was shared primarily by Quebec and Montreal. The former acted as the intermediary between local merchants and French financiers, while the latter was the operational base and its merchants were engaged in the provision of supplies and credit to trading expeditions in exchange for furs. In 1729, for example, of the furs obtained by the French West India Company, 78 per cent were received at Montreal and only 17 per cent and 5 per cent at Quebec and Trois-Rivières respectively.

The terms of the Treaty of Utrecht in 1713 officially recognized British territorial rights on Hudson Bay while rights over the region south of the Great Lakes, which included the Ohio Valley, were left ambiguous. Competition from traders to the south increased sharply and culminated in the establishment of Fort Oswego by the English in 1722. The English traders had by this time begun to follow the example of the French in trading directly with the hunting tribes and as a result relied less on the Iroquois to act as middlemen. The intrusion of the English had prompted the French to build a fortified trading post at Toronto in 1720 in order to safeguard the Toronto Passage, an Indian route between Lake Ontario and Lake Huron, and six years later they also reconstructed Fort Niagara in order to protect the portage route between lakes Ontario and Erie.

Between 1731 and 1743 the French fur trade was extended to the northwest as far as Lake Winnipeg and the Saskatchewan River, under the vigorous leadership of Pierre de La Vérendrye and his sons. There were two principal reasons for this expansion: the better quality of the furs and the French desire to intercept the trade between the Indians and the Hudson's Bay Company, which operated exclusively from its forts on the Bay, particularly York Factory at the mouth of the Nelson River. More than half a dozen forts were established under La Vérendrye's direction, including Fort Rouge (Winnipeg) and Fort La Reine (Portage la Prairie) in 1738. By establishing trading posts along the major rivers leading to Hudson Bay, the French were able to obtain a substantial share of the region's furs, since the Indian hunters generally preferred to trade with French pedlars instead of journeying down to the trading posts on the Bay.

By 1743 the French fur trade had reached its maximum territorial extent; although the northwest trade had brought in rich and abundant furs, the technology of the time, the prevailing prices for furs and the resources of the colony would not support further expansion. While there was a certain amount of decentralization, Montreal remained the heart of the commercial system and territorial expansions were costly; already, because of the considerable distance to Montreal only the best and lightest furs were acquired by traders in the northwest. Further, the colony had only 45,000 people and, although able to supply its own needs quite adequately, the small agricultural population could hardly produce enough food or supply enough military backing to support traders scattered over such an extensive area for any length of time.

There was little disruption of the St. Lawrence fur trade after control had been transferred from French to British merchants. For a few years after the Conquest trade was restricted to the posts but in 1768 pedlars were once more permitted to travel into the bush to trade directly with the Indians. The trading posts, forts and transportation routes developed during the French regime remained in operation, and the bulk of the trading continued to be in the hands of the French. In many respects the fur trade was stronger than before; the availability of lower-priced English trade goods, including rum, was perhaps the principal reason. The southwest trade (Ohio-Mississippi region) continued to surpass the northwest trade in importance as it had during the French regime; the importance of the former was recognized in the Quebec Act of 1774 which extended the boundaries of the province as far as the Ohio and Mississippi rivers. The inclusion of this natural hinterland of the St. Lawrence was, however, one of the factors which contributed to the American Revolutionary War (1775-1783), and the area was later granted to the United States by the Treaty of Paris (1783).

Partly as a result of the American Revolution the St. Lawrence fur trade expanded rapidly after 1775 when a number of Scottish-American merchants, mainly based in Albany, transferred their operations to Montreal. At the same time trade began to grow more quickly in the northwest than in the southwest. In 1776 a group of merchants engaged in the northwest trade pooled their resources in a loose association which they called the North West Company; this was a one-year agreement and was followed by several such short-term partnerships. The creation of a monopoly organization had always been characteristic of the fur trade but it was particularly important in the northwest trade because of the considerable distances involved and increasing competition from the Hudson's Bay Company, which had established its first inland post in 1774. The cession of the Ohio-Mississippi region to the United States rendered imperative some degree of cooperation among the growing number of merchants who were already trading in the northwest or who had intentions of doing so. Accordingly, in the winter of 1783-84 the North West Company drew up a more permanent agreement under the leadership of Simon McTavish, a former Albany merchant. It was still not a company in the usual sense of the word and was never incorporated; the firms in the company retained their separate identity and merely pooled their resources, while profits were divided annually on the basis of the shares held by each firm. Although at first a very satisfactory arrangement, the looseness of the association proved a crippling handicap in the company's struggles against the Hudson's Bay Company.

The southwest trade did not decline immediately after the region was granted to the United States. Instead, there was a slow withdrawal from the area, and the Montreal merchants continued to trade from Detroit, Michilimackinac, Niagara, Oswego and other military posts which were still held by Britain in American territory. The formal retreat from the southwest began in 1796 when British military forces were withdrawn from all posts in American territory in accordance with the terms of Jay's Treaty (1794). Until this treaty was signed the southwest trade was still the more important but its subsequent decline was rapid as operations were transferred to the northwest. In 1795 a new fur trading organization, the XY Company, was formed by a few Montreal merchants trading in the northwest; it rapidly emerged as a strong rival of the North West Company, particularly after it was joined by Alexander Mackenzie, a former "Nor'Wester." In 1804 the two companies were amalgamated. Montreal merchants, including the North West Company, did not entirely abandon the southwest trade, and continued to press for the re-annexation of the region by Britain. In the War of 1812 Fort Michilimackinac, then a key American trading post, was captured by a British force and was once more used as a base for Montreal traders. Despite the protestations of Montreal merchants, however, the fort and the surrounding territory were returned to the United States by the Treaty of Ghent (1814), and hopes of regaining the natural hinterland of the St. Lawrence were finally crushed in 1815 when the American government prohibited all Canadian trading in the southwest region.

The progressive transfer of Montreal-based fur trading operations to the northwest after 1775 coincided with the active expansionist policy of the Hudson's Bay Company, which began to establish trading posts in the interior instead of relying solely on its posts on Hudson Bay, as it had in the past. The early competition of the Bay was matched by a vigorous extension of the Montreal-based fur empire undertaken by a number of well-known Nor'Westers. In 1779 Peter Pond explored the Athabasca – Peace River country; in 1789 Alexander Mackenzie reached the Arctic Ocean via the Mackenzie River and in 1793 travelled overland to Bella Coola on the Pacific Ocean. After the merger of the XY and North West companies renewed efforts were made to expand the fur trading area, which at that time extended as far west as the Rocky Mountains, and as far north as the Arctic Ocean, and included the Saskatchewan, Peace, Athabasca and Mackenzie river basins. The expansion to the Pacific Coast was led by Simon Fraser (1806-8) and David Thompson (1807-11), the two principal explorers. The steep canyon of the Fraser River made it unsuitable as a canoe route and no trading posts were established there. David Thompson travelled down the Columbia River with the specific intention of establishing a trading post on the Pacific Coast but found on his arrival at the mouth of the river in 1811 that Fort Astoria had been built a few weeks before by a rival organization, the American Fur Company, owned by John Jacob Astor. Two years later, during the War of 1812, the North West Company purchased Fort Astoria. This transaction marked the achievement of the maximum extent of the Montreal-based fur trading empire, the apex of the North West Company's fortunes, and the establishment of Canada's first transcontinental economic system, albeit one which was far in advance of settlement and which lacked any formal political control.

In 1815 the complete exclusion of the North West Company from the southwest trade and the renewed competition from the revivified Hudson's Bay Company (which had paid no dividends from 1809 to 1814) signalled the beginning of a difficult period which for various reasons proved fatal for the Montreal-based company. The collapse of the North West Company was due to a combination of factors which cumulatively placed the company at a disadvantage in its struggle with the Bay rather than to any single cause. An important factor was the higher transportation cost of the long overland haul from Montreal compared to the relatively short distances to the ocean ports on Hudson Bay. This became increasingly important as more Indians were persuaded to become full-time trappers, thus increasing their demand for a variety of goods to replace those articles which they formerly supplied for themselves; some of these goods—woollen blankets, for example—were bulky and therefore costly to transport from Montreal. The intense competition also meant that higher prices (i.e., more trade goods) were offered in exchange for furs, and additional strain was thereby placed on the overland transportation system. Another factor was the duty placed on furs exported from the St. Lawrence which did not, however, apply to the Bay; in 1814 this payment was considered to be three times as heavy as the additional cost of the overland haul to Montreal. Further losses were suffered by both companies because of the excessive number of trading posts which were maintained; in about twenty instances the two companies operated adjacent posts and the profits of both were consequently reduced. However, the additional costs of operation were probably not significant factors in the failure of the North West Company, since they were largely offset by the latter's superior communications system which operated between Montreal and London for marketing, financing and other purposes, and between the wintering partners in the northwest and the proprietors in Montreal (including their annual meeting at Fort William) for the relaying of information. Although it is probable that the reduction in profits was greater for the Hudson's Bay Company during this period, it was more damaging to the North West Company because of the nature of its organization.

The structure of the North West Company was particularly un-suited to surviving a long period of low profitability. The renowned morale and efficiency of the Nor'Westers had developed during a period of continuous expansion when the opening up of new areas permitted rapid promotion through the ranks; the stability of the trade area after 1815 and the declining profits which resulted were not conducive to the maintenance of the celebrated *esprit de corps*. Decentralization of authority to the wintering partners and pedlars, formerly one of the most important assets of the company, proved to be a disadvantage during the period of intense competition with the Hudson's Bay Company; effective cost-cutting measures required a more centralized authority. Another, and perhaps the most important factor, was the looseness of the bond among the associated firms of the North West Company. The emphasis on the annual accumulation of capital made it difficult for the company to accommodate long periods of low profitability or loss, and it was consequently unable to build up the reserves necessary for a prolonged competitive war. Prior to 1815 there had been no problem in obtaining the necessary financing but in the following years, as the result of renewed competition and low profitability it became increasingly difficult. Finally, the North West Company contract was due to be re-negotiated in 1822, and there was considerable support among the constituent firms for union with the Hudson's Bay Company. This was finally achieved in 1821 when the two companies amalgamated under the name of the Hudson's Bay Company in order to retain the advantages of the original charter.

This union brought an abrupt end to the St. Lawrence fur trade, to Montreal's western empire, and to Canada's first transcontinental economy. The Hudson's Bay Company had its headquarters in London, and, with a virtual monopoly of the fur trade, it chose to operate out of Hudson Bay where operating costs were lower. As a result, the overland route to Montreal fell into disuse and the flow of furs through the city became negligible.

## Timber Trade

The export of square timber from British North America began in the 1790s as a result of the almost continuous wars in Europe between 1793 and 1815 (the Napoleonic Wars). British North America's importance as a source of timber received official recognition when preferential duties were placed on the import of colonial timber, a standard practice in the implementation of mercantile principles. The procedure used was to place duties on the import of foreign timber while allowing colonial timber to enter Britain duty-free or at a nominal rate. In 1795 a duty of 10 shillings a load was placed on foreign timber but because of the uncertainty of long-term prospects this low tariff did not at first encourage the commercial development of the industry. As a result, the duty on foreign timber was raised in 1805 to 25 shillings, but of greater importance was the establishment in 1807 of Napoleon's "continental system" which made trade between England and the rest of Europe virtually impossible. This produced a marked decline in the amount of Baltic timber reaching Britain and led to a sharp rise in timber prices, an increase in the duty on foreign timber, and an acceleration of Canadian exports. The timber duty was raised in 1807, in 1810, in 1812 and in 1814, when it reached the record level of 65 shillings per load. This level obtained until 1821 when it was moderately reduced to 55 shillings. It was not until 1842 that any substantial reduction was made and not until 1860 that it was finally abolished.

ST. LAWRENCE VALLEY

The timber trade in the St. Lawrence Valley did not assume significant proportions until the first decade of the nineteenth century, although a small trade in the export of masts had been carried on during the French regime. The first preferential tariffs had little impact on the development of the St. Lawrence timber industry, which did not begin to grow until 1804. At that time Britain was critically short of masts as a result of its war operations and a large naval contract was given to a British firm in the St. Lawrence, thus shifting the centre of the naval mast trade from New Brunswick, which had been the principal supplier since the 1780s.

This encouraged the rapid exploitation of the forest resources of the St. Lawrence and Ottawa valleys and the greatest beneficiary of this trade was Quebec, which functioned as the terminus for transatlantic shipping and the headquarters of the major timber firms. After 1800 a number of British firms were encouraged by their government to transfer operations from the Baltic to Canada; few of them became directly involved in the timber-cutting operations and most therefore remained in Quebec where a steady stream of timber rafts arrived during the summer. In many cases expeditions were financed in much of the same way as in the fur trade; teams of lumberjacks, consisting in many cases of farmers, would be outfitted by Quebec merchants to whom the timber would be sold under contract. Improvements to the timber raft by the first decade of the nineteenth century made possible the inexpensive transportation of square timber from as far afield as Kingston and Ottawa, more than three hundred miles distant from Quebec. In 1807, when the first shipment of Ottawa Valley timber arrived in Quebec, it was only one of more than three hundred rafts, and between 1807 and 1810 the export of square timber from Quebec City was more than trebled.

Because of its strategic position Quebec remained the unrivalled centre of the St. Lawrence square timber trade until the decline of the industry in the last decades of the nineteenth century. The reduction of the preferential duties in the 1840s did not appreciably weaken the trade, which continued to grow until 1864. From the 1820s to the early 1840s forest products of various kinds accounted for more than half the total value of exports from Canada, but after 1840 the export of wheat and flour increased and the importance of forest products declined steadily as a result. The eventual demise of the square timber industry was due to the decreasing market for wood in Britain, a drop in the demand for wooden ships, an increase in the more profitable export of lumber to the United States, and the exhaustion of the more accessible timber stands by over sixty years of exploitation. The cost of timber at Quebec had risen in proportion to the greater distances over which timber was being carried. The construction in 1829 of timber slides around the Chaudière Falls enabled timber to be brought down the Ottawa River from as far afield as Lake Timiskaming, and by 1850 the square timber trade had also extended to the southern end of Lake Huron. The higher cost of Quebec timber and the removal of the preferential tariffs favoured Baltic exports to Britain after 1850, and by 1860 the latter had increased their share to the point where they outweighed the total exports from British North America.

After 1830 the lumber industry began to capture a significant share of the Canadian export trade and square timber was gradually replaced in importance by sawn lumber which found a profitable market in Britain. Around 1850 Canadian lumber exports to Britain began to decline relative to those from the Baltic, but this fortunately coincided with the expansion of the market in the United States. The first recorded lumber export to the United States was in 1835 but the major increase took place in the 1840s, when the rising urban popula-

*Timber rafts on the Ottawa River, looking west from the*
*Parliament Buildings, circa 1870.*

tion and the diminishing forest resources of the United States
created a considerable demand for Canadian lumber—the first
Canadian staple to be in great demand in the American market;
between 1840 and 1850, for example, the export of Canadian lumber
to Oswego increased from 2 million to 60 million board feet. Also, in
the 1850s exports of sawn lumber to the United States increased
tremendously, stimulated by the Reciprocity Treaty and the construction of American railways to lakes Ontario and Erie. Large
amounts of American capital were consequently invested in the
Canadian sawmilling industry.

In the lumber industry, as in the square timber industry, the
Ottawa Valley became one of the most productive areas, and in the
1850s a number of Americans including Booth, Bronson, Eddy and
Perley built sawmills in the Ottawa Valley, especially in the
Ottawa-Hull area. The timber slides around the Chaudière Falls

enabled the Ottawa-Hull mills to utilize the abundant water power of the site, while drawing upon the timber resources of areas far upstream. The Rideau Canal was the first route to be used for the export of Ottawa lumber to the United States market, via Oswego and the Erie Canal. In 1854, partly financed by American capital, the Bytown and Prescott Railway was built to transport lumber from the Ottawa mills to the American railhead at Ogdensburg (opposite Prescott), which in 1850 was the first American railroad to link the St. Lawrence with the Atlantic coast.

The growth of the United States market was instrumental in the development of the lumber industry of the north shore of Lake Ontario in the 1840s. After 1850 the industry was given a considerable boost by the construction of railways from ports on Lake Ontario, some of which were deliberately designed to tap the forest resources of the Canadian Shield. The Northern Railway from Toronto to Collingwood (1855), for example, was directly responsible for the mushrooming of the lumber industry in Simcoe County. Other lumber railways originated from Port Hope and Cobourg on Lake Ontario.

The growth of the lumber industry did not, however, benefit Quebec to the same extent as had the square timber trade. This was principally because lumber exports to the United States were not generally channelled through Quebec, and by the late 1860s the United States had replaced Britain as the chief market for Canadian forest products. The lumber industry was also more dispersed than the square timber industry; steam sawmills were set up close to the forest belt, wherever feeder railroads permitted easy transport to the lake ports, from which lumber was shipped to the United States by steamer. By the late 1870s the replacement of sailing ships by steamships, the decline of the square timber trade and the rise of the lumber industry, the transportation of lumber by rail, and the dredging of the St. Lawrence Ship Channel enabled Montreal to oust Quebec from its position as the commercial-transportation centre of the forest industry.

THE MARITIMES

The timber trade of the Maritime colonies began with the export of masts for the Royal Navy; the first exports were made from Port Royal in 1710, the year of its capture, and after Halifax was established as a naval centre in 1749 the export of masts was supplemented by the demands of the local dockyard. Until the American Revolution, the Canadian trade was restricted to Nova Scotia, which possessed extensive resources of pine timber suitable for masts, but the province remained second in importance to New England, the traditional and principal source of naval masts. This was changed by the outbreak of war, which increased the demand for masts from the Maritimes and encouraged the industry to develop its operations along the St. John River. New England exports continued to exceed those from New Brunswick and Nova Scotia for a few years after 1783, however, until major naval contracts were granted to firms operating in the Maritimes.

The first naval contract for masts from the St. John Valley was drawn up in 1779, and after the American Revolutionary War this was followed by several major contracts. As a result of the European wars the New Brunswick mast trade expanded considerably after 1795 and until 1803 the province was the principal source of masts for the Royal Navy. The export of masts from New Brunswick fell sharply in the following year as a result of the transfer of the naval contracts to the St. Lawrence but recovered rapidly after Napoleon's blockade of Baltic supplies in 1807 and reached a record of just over 3,000 in 1811 although this compared poorly with the 19,000 exported from the St. Lawrence in the same year.

New Brunswick's commercial timber trade did not assume any significance until Britain's supplies from the Baltic were interrupted. The export of timber doubled within a year to 27,000 tons in 1807 and by 1810 had risen to 88,000 tons; by 1815 timber exports had once more doubled. Although the province began to export deals, staves and other forms of sawn lumber to the West Indies, it was the trade in square timber which continued to be its principal support; the latter was unaffected by the end of the Napoleonic Wars, and exports increased to 247,000 tons in 1819, 266,000 tons in 1822 and 321,000 tons in 1824.

The timber industry was largely concentrated in New Brunswick, where it was the dominant economic activity. In 1806, when the Maritime square timber trade was of little consequence, New Brunswick's timber exports barely exceeded those of Nova Scotia. Within five years both provinces had significantly increased their exports but New Brunswick's were almost four times greater than Nova Scotia's. By 1815 New Brunswick's economy was almost entirely based on the timber trade—at least four-fifths of the population were estimated to be dependent on it at that time. Forest products continued to dominate the province's economy for almost half a century, although during and after the 1830s the emphasis shifted from square timber to lumber. The Crimean War, the Reciprocity Treaty, and the American Civil War gave the industry its final opportunities for expansion; lumber exports to the United States had by this time grown considerably in importance, and were almost trebled during the term of the Reciprocity Treaty. During the heyday of the timber trade both fishing and agriculture were of secondary importance but agriculture began to improve its relative economic position after 1850. In the early 1860s, when the timber trade had reached its apex, agricultural products accounted for just under 10 per cent of New Brunswick's exports.

## Shipbuilding

The shipbuilding industry in the St. Lawrence Valley was closely related to the square timber trade. The industry had its beginnings in the 1660s when Jean Talon attempted to introduce it on the St. Charles River in Quebec, and in 1732 the French made a further attempt to encourage the industry by granting bounties for ships built in the colony. It was not until the 1790s, however, that the commercial shipbuilding industry began in earnest, stimulated by Britain's shipping needs during the Napoleonic Wars and by the growing importance of the square timber trade. Ships were often built specifically for the timber carrying-trade; a Quebec-built ship would frequently carry a cargo of square timber to Britain where both cargo and ship would be sold. This arrangement was ideally suited to the square timber trade since the heavy, bulky exports to Britain far out-weighed the manufactured goods which predominated in the import trade. It was only after 1825 that the problem was partially solved when ships began to carry immigrants on the return journey. The St. Lawrence shipbuilding industry, which specialized in wooden ships, lasted as long as the square timber trade remained viable; it began to decline in the 1860s after the end of the American Civil War, and finally petered out into insignificance in the 1880s.

Quebec was by far the most important shipbuilding centre, followed by Montreal. In 1809 the first Canadian-built steamship was launched at Montreal, which subsequently maintained its preeminence in the manufacture of steam engines. The *Royal William*, the first steamship to cross the Atlantic by steam alone, was built in Quebec in 1831 but towed to Montreal to have its engine installed. Lake Ontario had many shipbuilding centres, of which Kingston was both the oldest and the most important.

In the Atlantic region shipbuilding was first associated with the fishing industry. Local ships were built for both the inshore and bank fisheries, and Nova Scotia, which was the principal base for the fisheries, became the centre for the shipbuilding industry. Ships were built at a number of widely dispersed centres, since the majority of vessels were small and were used only in coastal waters. Yarmouth and Lunenburg were two of the most important centres outside Halifax, but nearly every fishing port had a shipyard. The extensive forests of good timber, the lack of effective control over the forest resources and the preponderant demand for small fishing boats encouraged the dispersal of the industry in Nova Scotia. After 1783 the growing importance of the West Indian trade in Nova Scotia encouraged the building of larger ships, and the consequent development of an impressive mercantile navy.

In New Brunswick the shipbuilding industry was from the beginning closely tied to the timber trade; the first ship was built on the St. John River in 1769 but it was not until the Napoleonic Wars that shipbuilding became economically important. The early New Brunswick ships had a very bad reputation; this was due in part to the poor quality of local wood but mostly to the fact that the ships were built for the timber carrying-trade, which generally utilized the poorest vessels. After 1840 the quality of New Brunswick ships had improved considerably, and they were increasingly employed in the general cargo trade. The shipbuilding industry continued to grow until 1874 but the burgeoning ascendancy of the iron steamship in oceanic trade led to the eventual collapse of the New Brunswick industry.

## Communications and Transportation

Prior to 1763 few improvements had been made to the natural waterways which constituted the principal means of inland transportation. Apart from an unsuccessful attempt to construct a canal around the Lachine Rapids on the St. Lawrence in 1700, no efforts were made to improve navigation on the waterways. In 1734 the first trunk road was completed along the north bank of the St. Lawrence between Montreal and Quebec; the corresponding road along the south bank was still unfinished when the French regime ended. In the Atlantic colonies, settlement was restricted to the coastal area except for a few small settlements along the St. John River; inland transportation was therefore of minor importance in the region.

The transfer of New France to Britain did not prompt any immediate improvements in transportation, since the fur trade continued to be the dominant economic activity. Ocean shipping was confined to Quebec, and goods bound for Montreal were carried in flat-bottomed boats called *bateaux*, which could be adapted for use with either oar or sail. Beyond Montreal the birchbark canoe was the principal means of transportation since it was light enough to be easily portaged.

There were two major routes employed in the fur trade: the Ottawa route and the lower Great Lakes. The shorter and quicker passage to Lake Huron was the Ottawa River – Lake Nipissing-French River route to Georgian Bay; its main disadvantages were the thirty-six portages which lay along the route and which meant that only light canoes could be used. The longer route via the upper St. Lawrence and lakes Ontario and Erie had fewer portages and was more suitable for the transport of heavier goods; the only major portage was at Niagara Falls, and the use of larger vessels was therefore feasible. Because of this difference the two routes developed complementary roles in the fur trade; on the outward journey from Montreal the lake route was generally preferred for the bulky trade goods and provisions, while for the in-bound cargo of fur the Ottawa route was favoured. Besides the advantage of speeding the delivery of furs to Montreal, the Ottawa route was preferred because it was considered some insurance against accidental loss to transport the valuable furs in many small canoes rather than in one large boat. In the northwest fur trade, cargo was carried from Montreal to Grand Portage (after 1803 to Fort Kaministiquia, renamed Fort William in 1807) in large canoes known as *canots du maître*, while west of Lake Superior the lighter *canots du nord* were used for travel into the interior.

After 1800 much attention was devoted to improving the available methods of transportation. In 1809 the Durham boat was introduced on the St. Lawrence; it was propelled by oars, poles or sail, and was capable of carrying up to ten times the cargo of a *bateau*, although employing about the same number of men. Also in 1809, the first steamer, the *Accommodation*, was introduced on the river route between Montreal and Quebec. It was so successful that it was replaced within two years by a larger vessel, and by 1819 there were seven vessels operating between the two centres. With the introduction of steamers and tugboats, cargo transportation between Montreal and Quebec had become far more efficient. In 1816 the first steamship the *Frontenac*, was launched on Lake Ontario, and two years later the American-owned *Walk-on-the-Water* was launched on Lake Erie. By 1819 a regular steamship service had begun operating on Lake Ontario between Kingston, the transshipment point for river and lake transportation, and the communities of Niagara, Toronto and those in the Bay of Quinte region.

The need for extensive canal construction became increasingly urgent, since it was evident that steamships would in future dominate the internal carrying-trade. The Lachine Canal, opened in 1825, was the first to be completed on the St. Lawrence. By the mid-1830s, after the completion of the Welland Canal (1824-1829) between lakes Erie and Ontario, and the opening of the Rideau Canal (1826-1832) between Kingston and Ottawa, a rudimentary canal system, offering safe transportation between Montreal and the upper Great Lakes was more or less complete. It was not an economically satisfactory route, however, particularly since the 126-mile Rideau Canal, which had been built primarily for military reasons, provided only a very roundabout passage between Montreal and Kingston. As a result, the Ottawa River-Rideau Canal route was used primarily for upstream traffic and Durham boats continued to travel downstream from Kingston to Montreal along the still unimproved St. Lawrence. The construction of an integrated canal system on the St. Lawrence was not undertaken until the early 1840s, partly because the two provinces of Upper and Lower Canada (united in 1841) were unable to agree on a joint program. In 1848, the completion of a 9-foot-deep canal system allowed unimpeded transportation between Montreal and Lake Superior. By this time the St. Lawrence canals, though valuable, were clearly inadequate and it became obvious that a trunk railway system would have to be constructed if the competition from the United States for the lake carrying-trade was to be matched.

By the mid-1830s railways were being widely projected and many companies were chartered as a result. Very little came of these early plans, but a number of the railway companies were reorganized in the more prosperous 1840s, and construction eventually began during the 1850s. The first railways were mainly designed to connect important waterways. In 1836 the 16-mile Champlain and St. Lawrence Railway, the first in Canada, began operating between La Prairie, opposite Montreal on the south bank of the St. Lawrence, and St. Jean, above the Chambly Rapids on the Richelieu River; the Montreal-New York route via the Richelieu and Hudson rivers was considerably shortened as a result. Other portage routes included the eight-mile horse-drawn Erie and Ontario Railway, from Queenston to Chippawa around Niagara Falls, which was opened in 1839, and the eight-mile Montreal and Champlain Railway between Montreal and Lachine, inaugurated in 1847. In the Maritimes the first railway, a private line, was opened in 1839 and ran six miles from the Albion coal mines to Pictou Harbour. Construction of the first long-distance or trunk railway, the St. Lawrence and Atlantic, began in 1848 and was completed between Montreal and Portland, Maine, in 1853. By 1840 only 16 miles of steam railway had been completed in British North America, compared to 2,800 in the United States; by 1850 the respective figures were 66 and 9,000.

In Canada the construction of the St. Lawrence canals had consumed most of the available public capital and it was not until their completion that financing could be made available for the major railway systems. As a result, Canada experienced a railway boom in the 1850s. The most important railway company at this time was the Grand Trunk, chartered in 1853. After acquiring the Montreal-Portland railway in 1853, the company embarked on its plan to capture the American and Canadian lake trade. In 1856 its line from Montreal was extended to Toronto and in 1859 to Sarnia on Lake Huron; in the east it had reached Lévis, opposite Quebec, by 1854 and Rivière-du-Loup by 1860; and in the latter year the opening of the 9,000-foot Victoria Bridge across the St. Lawrence at Montreal linked the hitherto separate sections of the Grand Trunk Railway Company to form a network which included more than 1,000 miles of track. It was not the only important railway in central Canada, however. By 1855 the Great Western Railway had linked Hamilton to Niagara, London, Windsor and Toronto; the Northern Railway was opened from Toronto to Collingwood on Georgian Bay in 1855; the St. Lawrence and Ottawa Railway operated between Prescott and Ottawa in 1854; and the Buffalo and Lake Huron Railway, linking Buffalo to Goderich on Lake Huron, was opened in 1858. The lines to Sarnia, Windsor, Collingwood and Goderich were deliberately designed to capture the American midwest trade.

In the Maritimes there were ambitious plans to link the major ice-free Atlantic ports and the populated centres of central Canada. Three schemes were initiated but not completely realized: from Halifax a line was completed as far as Truro in 1857; the 108-mile line from Saint John to Shediac on the Gulf of St. Lawrence was completed in 1860; and, the earliest and most ambitious of the three, the St. Andrews and Quebec Railway, which was chartered in 1836, was abandoned in 1868 after only 126 miles of line had been built between the small port of St. Andrews and Woodstock on the St. John River. Despite the boom of the 1850s, railway construction in Canada still lagged far behind that of the United States, even allowing for the population difference; in Canada the railway mileage had increased to 2,065 by 1860 and 2,617 by 1870 compared to 31,000 and 53,000 respectively in the United States.

As well as the construction of the St. Lawrence canals and the trunk railways, long-distance communications were greatly improved by the development of a telegraphic system. In 1846, Hamilton and Toronto became the first cities to be connected by telegraph; a year later the system covered more than 500 miles and included Montreal, Quebec, Toronto and Hamilton, with connections to New York.

The 1850s also marked the beginning of the final program of improvements designed to make the St. Lawrence a more useful link with the continental interior. With the completion of an adequate canal system above Montreal it became imperative to improve the river channel above Quebec in order to bring ocean and inland shipping closer together. From 1850 the St. Lawrence Ship Channel between Montreal and Quebec was dredged at repeated intervals from a natural depth of 10 1/2 feet to 20 feet by 1865 (later increased to 25 feet by 1882, to 30 feet by 1907 and to its present depth of 35 feet in 1952). As well as being deepened the Ship Channel was progressively widened and marked with buoys, beacons, lighthouses and other navigational aids; the telegraphic system was also used to provide advance meteorological and other navigational information to ships. The aim of these undertakings, which was in effect to divert traffic from Quebec to Montreal in order to increase the competitive position of the St. Lawrence in relation to New York, was not, however, achieved until iron steamships had replaced wooden sailing ships in the transatlantic service. In oceanic trade the sailing ship was queen until the mid-1860s when steamships began to dominate the mail and passenger trade; by the late 1870s they were also carrying the bulk of the cargo trade. In 1860 the ocean shipping tonnage in Montreal was just under one-tenth of Quebec's, a proportion which had remained constant since at least the 1820s. By the early 1880s, however, Montreal's port activity had grown considerably as a result of the increased use of iron steamships and its shipping tonnage exceeded that of Quebec, which had begun to show an absolute decline during the 1870s.

MONTREAL V. NEW YORK

Of considerable importance for much of this period was the rivalry between Montreal and New York, both of which vied for the trade of the Great Lakes region, and it was within the context of this struggle that the fortunes of many of Canada's major cities were determined. Until the opening of the Erie Canal in 1825 Montreal had exercised unchallenged dominance over this vast area and as a result had emerged as the financial-commercial capital of Canada. After its fur trade empire had come to an end in 1821, Montreal's primary economic function became its entrepôt role in the foreign trade of Upper Canada and the American midwest, and the maintenance of its commercial importance therefore depended on the continued movement of western trade through the St. Lawrence. Although Quebec was the ocean terminus it was the Montreal merchants who controlled the import-export trade and who had most at stake in the future of the St. Lawrence as the transportation artery for the growing western settlements. Montreal's vital role as a transshipment centre had been initiated by the presence of the Lachine Rapids, but it was also encouraged by the British Navigation Laws which until 1849 prohibited American vessels from proceeding downstream past Montreal.

New York's bid for the lake trade began in 1817 with the construction of the state-financed 350-mile Erie Canal from Buffalo on Lake Erie to the Mohawk River—a deliberate attempt to extend the Hudson-Mohawk water route from New York to the centre of the continent. The four-foot barge canal was completed in 1825 and, by means of feeder canals, it soon achieved an extensive catchment area. In 1822 the Champlain Canal had joined Lake Champlain to the

Hudson River, effectively diverting the Vermont trade from Quebec to New York, and in 1828, the 38-mile Oswego feeder provided an important outlet to eastern Lake Ontario. The Welland Canal, completed in 1829, functioned more or less as an auxiliary of the Erie Canal and the greater part of the tonnage passing downstream through it was destined for Oswego, thus saving a long haul from Buffalo on the Erie Canal.

The success of the Erie Canal was instantaneous. The trade of the American midwest was abruptly diverted to New York, restricting Montreal's commercial hinterland to Upper Canada and thus reducing it by half. Even the Upper Canadian trade would have been captured by New York were it not for the British import tariffs which imposed lower duties on goods shipped from colonial ports, and American tariffs, which would have added to the cost of shipping goods to Britain via New York. Indeed, when both these restrictions were removed in 1846 the bulk of Upper Canada's trade did pass through New York. Within a few years of the opening of the Erie Canal the toll revenue had completely recovered the costs of its construction, and the competitiveness of the canal was later maintained by exempting some goods from toll charges. By 1830 the region from Vermont to the Mississippi was within the commercial hinterland of New York, which had subdued its old rivals, Philadelphia and Boston, and in the process encroached on Montreal's protected dominion over Upper Canada. For the first time New York was the undisputed commercial capital of North America.

In many respects Montreal suffered in comparison with New York. Although the costs of transporting goods to Montreal from the west were lower than to New York, the costs thereafter were higher. Although Montreal was closer to Europe than New York its transatlantic freight and insurance rates were higher because of the degree to which outgoing cargo exceeded incoming shipments, the handicap of seasonal navigation (the river was ice-bound for five to six months), the delays in obtaining cargo, the slow and hazardous nature of navigation because of ice, fog and the constrictions of the river, and the additional expenses of towing and pilotage. On the other hand, the port of New York was open all year round and, as a focal point for international shipping, it offered lower freight insurance rates, superior banking and shipping services, and faster, more reliable conveyance.

If Montreal's natural hinterland were to be regained, improvements to the St. Lawrence waterway were imperative. Although the canoe and the *bateau* were adequate for the transportation of furs, they were definitely unsuitable for the transportation of timber and wheat, the new commercial products of the west. Sailing ships, still the principal vessels in oceanic trade, were also reluctant to travel up as far as Montreal because of the slow and hazardous nature of the passage above Quebec; with unfavourable winds the 180-mile journey from Quebec could take up to two months and ships had been known to wait weeks at the bottom of the St. Mary's Current at Montreal for a favourable wind. Above Montreal the undertaking of transportation improvements had been delayed by the failure of the two Canadas to agree on joint financing of canals. The divided nature of Canada's political jurisdictions at this time was in contrast to the political unity of the state of New York, which stretched from the Atlantic to Lake Erie. Upper Canada, which lacked a seaport, favoured a publicly-supported canalization program while Lower Canada, with the exception of Montreal, opposed any transportation improvements. The need for a political solution was evidenced by the vigorous campaigning of Montreal merchants in the early 1820s for the union of the two provinces and by the fact that Upper Canada officially favoured the annexation of Montreal. That Montreal was situated in Lower Canada was unfortunate from the point of view of developing the potential of the St. Lawrence as a transportation artery; at this crucial time in its history the city suffered from both its subordinate role in the rural-dominated Lower Canada Parliament and its political separation from its commercial hinterland of Upper Canada. The St. Lawrence rapids straddled the border between the two provinces so that neither could do much on its own. In 1841, the union of the two provinces was finally accomplished and in the following year the St. Lawrence canalization program began in earnest. In 1848, twenty-three years after the opening of the Erie Canal, a St. Lawrence canal system was completed. Unfortunately the most opportune moment had already passed and tariff changes in the 1840s cancelled most of the benefits which had been anticipated.

In purely economic terms the increased traffic on the St. Lawrence did not justify the expenditure on canal improvements; the volume of traffic had increased but the St. Lawrence failed to recapture its former hinterland, although it was better able to hold its own in competition with New York. The coincidence of measures adopted by Britain and the United States robbed the St. Lawrence of one of its most important advantages over New York, the preferred entry of its exports into Britain. In 1848 the British Corn Laws were repealed and Canadian wheat lost its tariff privileges in Britain. The U.S. Drawback Acts of 1845-46 permitted the duty-free or "in bond" passage of goods shipped between Canada and any other country through the United States. This was a deliberate attempt to capture some of Upper Canada's trade from Montreal and was prompted by the imminent completion of the St. Lawrence canal system. Together, the British and American acts diverted a considerable amount of Upper Canada's trade to New York. Further factors encouraging New York's continued dominance were the high ocean freight rates from the St. Lawrence ports (estimated to be twice as high as New York's in the 1850s), which were unaffected by canal improvements, and the building of American railroads to the Great Lakes, which were completed by 1850 in advance of Canadian railways. In 1850 less than 10 per cent of Upper Canada's wheat exports were sent via the St. Lawrence and by the end of the 1850s only 10-15 per cent of the total lake trade was channelled through Montreal and the St. Lawrence.

By mid-century, however, Montreal had entered upon a period of slow recovery, first wresting control over the oceanic trade from Quebec and later extending its port hinterland by means of its railway system and the dredging of the St. Lawrence Ship Channel.

# 6.
## Canadian Urban Development to 1867

Canada's economic history began with fishing, and the first settlement nuclei were the sheltered harbours where European ships put in for periodic repairs, to obtain wood and water, and to dry their catch. Within five years of Cabot's discovery of Newfoundland and Cape Breton in 1497 English, French, Spanish and Portuguese vessels had begun to fish regularly in summer along the coast and by 1540 on the Grand Banks as well. Initially, fishing did not lead to settlement and no formal colonies were established in Canada during the sixteenth century.

The English fishery differed from that of the other European countries, and led to the establishment of the first fishing stations in Canada. The French, who constituted the largest group of fishermen, were engaged in wet or green fishing (i.e., the fish were heavily salted and stored on board) and did not require any on-shore facilities. The English, on the other hand, because of their lack of salt, were almost from the start engaged in dry fishing (i.e., the fish were lightly salted and dried on shore before being stored on board), and they therefore needed to maintain both men and equipment on shore. Since smaller fish were more suitable for drying, the English engaged predominantly in in-shore rather than deep-sea fishing. With the construction of warehouses and houses for land-based workers, the fishing stations gradually acquired a degree of permanence. In time, some of the men engaged in the drying process were left to winter at these depots in order to repair equipment and to prepare for the following fishing season.

The English fishing bases were almost entirely concentrated along the southeastern coast of Newfoundland in the Avalon Peninsula, and the excellent harbour of St. John's soon became the most important of these. In the sixteenth century St. John's itself was probably more frequented by French and Portuguese fishermen than by the English. In 1527, for example, an English captain named John Rut noted that of the sixteen vessels in St. John's harbour (which was already known by its present name) eleven were Norman, one Breton, two Portuguese and two English; in 1583, the year in which the first claim to English sovereignty in Newfoundland was made by Sir Humphrey Gilbert, twenty of the thirty-six ships in St. John's harbour were Portuguese or Spanish. In contrast to the English, the French vessels fished along a considerable length of coast as well as on the off-shore banks. When the French also took up dry fishing they located their shore bases principally in the Gaspé Peninsula, because the English had already appropriated the most accessible area in Newfoundland for their own curing operations.

French exploration and contact between Indians and fishermen at fishing stations led initially to the occasional exchange of furs for manufactured goods and eventually to the organized fur trade and colonization. Jacques Cartier, the first explorer to penetrate the Canadian interior, had himself fished for some years on the off-shore banks before undertaking his initial voyage of exploration in 1534. On this voyage Cartier noted in his journal that he had acquired some furs from the Indians at Chaleur Bay; although this was the first time such an exchange had been put on record it is certain that similar transactions were quite common at the various harbours frequented by fishermen. In 1535, on his second voyage, Cartier travelled up the St. Lawrence River as far as Hochelaga (the site of present-day Montreal) in his search for a passage to China, and wintered on the bank of the St. Charles River, on the present site of Quebec City. On his final voyage, in 1541, Cartier wintered at Cap-Rouge near Quebec, as did Sieur de Roberval (France's first viceroy in Canada) and about two hundred colonists in the following year. Both attempts were part of a single colonization program, but they were unsuccessful and no further efforts were made by the French in the sixteenth century, except for the ill-fated and unintentional settlement by the Marquis de la Roche of some of his crew of prisoners on Sable Island in 1598. The establishment of a wintering fur depot or trading post (not a colony) at Tadoussac in 1600 was the first step towards eventual colonization, and marked the beginning of a division in function between the fur-based St. Lawrence economy, and that of Acadia (the Maritime provinces) and Newfoundland where fishing remained the principal economic activity.

## New France

The adoption of a monopoly system in the fur trade had not had the desired effect of encouraging colonization and by 1663 when the colony was created a royal province and thus brought under the direct control of the French king, its population numbered only 2,500, half of whom lived in the three settlements of Quebec, Montreal and Trois-Rivières. Champlain had considered these to be strategic sites on the St. Lawrence, and annual trade fairs were consequently established by the Quebec-based company at Trois-Rivières in 1610 and at Montreal in the following year. These were not very successful (Montreal's was abandoned in 1618), and settlements were not founded until 1634 at Trois-Rivières and 1642 at Montreal; the latter was initially the mission colony of Ville-Marie, one of several missions established in the St. Lawrence Valley during the seventeenth-century religious revival in France. In the 1650s, because of its strategic location at the head of navigation on the St. Lawrence and at the mouth of the Ottawa River, Montreal became the outfitting centre for the fur-trading expeditions into the northern country. Quebec, however, remained the terminus for ocean shipping and the chief commercial centre, as well as being the site of the governor's seat.

After 1663 the French began deliberate attempts to create a colony rather than just a fur-trading preserve, however there was no end to the colony's preoccupation with the fur trade. The appointment of an intendant was the first measure to be adopted after the assumption of direct control over the colony's commercial affairs, including the regulation of the fur trade, the granting of seigneuries, and the transportation of settlers from France. During the term of the first intendant, Jean Talon, from 1663 to 1672, the population of New France increased appreciably from 2,500 to 6,700. This growth was encouraged by a series of measures introduced by Talon, including the officially subsidized immigration of marriageable girls, (known as *les filles du roi*), the granting of bonuses to large families, and the penalties imposed on single men, who were frequently refused fur-trading licences. After Talon's return to France little immigration took place (except in the 1740s) and the colony grew mainly by natural increase from 8,000 in 1675 to 15,000 in 1700, 18,000 in 1713 and 65,000 in 1763.

The early efforts to stimulate agriculture, domestic industry, and trade with the West Indies met with only limited success. The fur trade and defence needs absorbed such a large proportion of the available resources that the colony's agricultural efforts rarely produced enough for its own needs, while Talon's attempts to stimulate shipbuilding, tanning, shoemaking and other industries failed in part because of the colony's small population and the official restriction on the importation of manufactured goods into France. The colony was also unable to participate in the French West Indian trade in the way that New England shared in the trade of the British West Indian islands; besides the lack of food surpluses in the colony, the port of Quebec was blocked with ice for five months of the year and its ships were unable to maintain a competitive schedule. New France therefore developed largely in isolation from the other French colonies and furs constituted its sole export to France. The colony's internal development was directed towards the westward expansion of the fur trade and the establishment of military stations intended to protect its interests against both the Iroquois and the English. The growth of the St. Lawrence commercial empire was not accompanied by any commensurate extension of political and military control. The extensions of French influence to the southwest and northwest of the Great Lakes were purely commercial undertakings, and the land could not be described as occupied or settled. All that existed was a rudimentary transportation system, consisting of natural waterways and portage routes linking a widely dispersed network of forts and trading posts.

As the commercial importance of the fur trade grew, the populations of Quebec and Montreal expanded. Throughout the period of French domination Quebec retained the ascendant position; it was both the political, cultural, institutional and military capital of a colony in which there was a highly centralized bureaucracy, and the entrepôt between the colony and France in all matters, including trade. Because of Montreal's strategic location at the Lachine Rapids (the terminus for river shipping) it was here that goods were transshipped to canoes for travel into the interior, and the city accordingly emerged as the outfitting centre for fur traders. The complementary roles of Quebec and Montreal which thus developed, persisted throughout the French regime. The third urban centre was Trois-Rivières, which lay halfway between Quebec and Montreal, and which gradually declined in commercial importance relative to the other two. These three settlements were the administrative capitals of the three judicial districts into which the colony was divided. In 1665, the colony's small population of 3,215 was mainly located near Quebec and the other two centres were merely outposts. In 1698 the populations of the three towns (excluding neighbouring settlements) were 1,988 for Quebec, 1,185 for Montreal and about 250 for Trois-Rivières; together the three towns accounted for 22 per cent of the total population of 15,355 in New France. The Quebec administrative district was the most important at that time and contained 60 per cent of the cultivated land, compared to 28 per cent and 12 per cent respectively for the Montreal and Trois-Rivières districts; all the land on both banks of the St. Lawrence between Montreal and Quebec had by this time been granted in seigneuries.

In 1754, at the outbreak of the hostilities between the French and the English in North America which led eventually to the declaration of war in 1756 and to the conquest of New France, the population of the St. Lawrence colony was only 55,000. In general, the fur trade had discouraged the development of other activities, including agriculture, and had kept the colony in a state of weak economic health. Its balance of trade with France was generally unfavourable and consequently there was little local accumulation of capital. This was partly because of the nature of the French economy, which tended to be more self-contained than that of England, and therefore offered less potential for the development of trade with and between its colonies. Under these conditions fur was an ideal staple; it was a luxury item, easily transported and valuable. France was thus able to extend its influence over a vast territory without the need for settlement; there was in fact, little official support for colonization. Because of its economic *raison d'être* the development of New France was in sharp contrast to that of the British colonies on the Atlantic seaboard: the former was a trading colony, and its extensive territory was more or less a fur-trading preserve, while the latter were intensively developed, stimulated by the enormous volume of trade within the English empire. Thus, while the total population of New France numbered only 65,000 in 1763, the combined population of the English colonies at that time approached 1.5 million.

At the close of the French era in 1763 settlement was largely restricted to a strip of land only a few miles along the banks of the St. Lawrence River, the "main street" of New France. In 1734 the three urban centres, Quebec, Montreal and Trois-Rivières, were joined by road. This was the only major transportation improvement introduced by the French, and was intended merely to complement the river route by providing a winter road. Urban development was markedly polarized in Montreal and Quebec which lay at the extremities of the settled portion of the colony; this was encouraged by the centralization of political and economic controls, the small population of the colony, the absence of secondary industries, and the preponderence of subsistence agriculture. The ascendancy of Quebec over Montreal was very marked at this time; the former's population had grown from 2,300 in 1716 to 4,600 in 1739, 5,500 in 1744, and 8,000 in 1754, while Montreal's population had reached only 4,000 by 1754. Constricted by its intermediate location between the two urban poles, Trois-Rivières never assumed much significance. It played a minor role in the fur trade, the nearby St. Maurice forges were of little importance and it was the administrative centre of the smallest judicial district; in 1754 its population was only 800.

## Upper and Lower Canada

The area covered by the modern provinces of Ontario and Quebec continued to function as a single economic system as it had done during the French regime, but there were some important differences, mainly due to the influx of English-speaking settlers in the early 1780s. The settlement of United Empire Loyalists in the western half of the province led to the political division of the colony into Upper Canada (Ontario) and Lower Canada (Quebec).

The development of the urban system may be divided into four periods. The arrival of the Loyalists altered the economic and political structure of the region. In 1821 the Montreal-based fur trade ended, and a major re-adjustment of the regional economy took place as a result. The 1820s marked, moreover, the beginning of the first large-scale immigration of British settlers into Canada and the emergence of agricultural communities. In 1849 the British mercantile system came to a formal end; the great wave of immigration was almost over and the reorientation of the region's economy towards the United States had begun to make itself evident.

1763-1783

Montreal was the chief beneficiary of the influx of English-speaking merchants into the fur trade, which was at that time the principal commercial activity. As official regulations governing internal trade were relaxed under the British regime, a larger proportion of the fur trade was concentrated in Montreal and correspondingly less in Quebec. Quebec's former links with French financiers were now redundant and new alliances were forged directly between Montreal merchants and London firms; in many cases the Scottish-American merchants who transferred their operations to Montreal merely retained their old associations.

By 1783 Montreal and Quebec each had a population of about 8,000, and were the only important urban centres in the region; Trois-Rivières, the third largest settlement, had about 1,000 people. Montreal was the most important commercial centre while Quebec, which had remained the terminus for ocean-going ships, had increased its port functions and had managed to double its port tonnage during the twenty-year period. Quebec's shipbuilding industry lay dormant and its other historically important functions — governmental, military and institutional—were not as highly centralized in the city as they had been during the French regime. In the region which later became Upper Canada there were no urban centres at all.

1783-1821

Throughout this period the Montreal fur trade was of primary economic importance, closely followed by the Quebec-based timber trade; agriculture played a relatively minor economic role. Although the arrival of the Loyalists led to the political reorganization of the colony into Upper and Lower Canada in 1791, the impact on the commercial system was less immediate. The number of Loyalists who entered the St. Lawrence Valley was quite small compared to the influx into the Maritimes; about 6,000 Loyalists settled in Upper Canada (Ontario) and about 1,000 in Lower Canada (Quebec). At the end of the period the principal commercial activities were still centred in Lower Canada. Upper Canada remained a frontier society and the colony's sparse population was concentrated in a thin band along the shores of lakes Ontario and Erie. Agriculture in the colony was of little commercial importance although some wheat had been exported before 1800. Of greater significance at this time were square timber, potash and pearl-ash—pioneer products which were in many cases obtained during the process of clearing land for agricultural use. By 1821 the population of Upper Canada was only one-third as large as Lower Canada's.

Montreal and Quebec were the only major urban centres in the Canadas at this time; each dominated some sphere of the region's economy, and both functioned as nerve centres of the vast commercial network based on the St. Lawrence. Montreal's importance had been substantially increased by the success of the North West Company, the city's chief employer, and as a result its population had grown to about 9,000 (almost the same size as Quebec) by 1800. The city's population increased steadily during the next twenty years whereas Quebec, which grew rapidly during the first decade of the nineteenth century increased more slowly between 1812 and 1819 because of the depression of its timber trade. By 1820, Quebec's population was approaching 16,000 while Montreal's was closer to 19,000. Trois-Rivières had only about 2,500 inhabitants at that time. In Upper Canada the largest urban centres in 1820 were Kingston and York (Toronto) with 2,336 and 1,240 inhabitants respectively.

Montreal was the market place of Canada; it was the location of the principal wholesalers and importers for both the fur trade and the growing agricultural settlements in Upper Canada and the Eastern Townships, in addition to its role as the country's financial-commercial capital. Its capitalists and entrepreneurs, unlike those engaged in Quebec's timber industry, were local men and, although the fur trade took the greater part of available capital prior to 1821, its merchants were ready to switch to any more lucrative investment which presented itself. The growth of commercial agriculture in Upper Canada offered just such an opportunity. Although Quebec was the seaport, goods had to be transshipped at Montreal and it was therefore in the latter city that wholesaling was concentrated. Thus it was convenient, if not strictly necessary, for Upper Canadian merchants to deal with wholesale houses in Montreal, and it was almost inevitable that the city would adopt the role of broker in the colony's external trade. This was particularly the case prior to 1825, when there were no feasible alternatives to the St. Lawrence route in external trade. The growing importance of the city's commerce was evinced by the establishment of a merchants' exchange and, in 1817, Canada's first bank, the Bank of Montreal.

Because of both the hazardous nature of the river passage above

TABLE 6.1 *Population distribution by administrative district, Lower Canada, 1784 and 1822*

| | Population | | | |
| | 1784 | | 1822 | |
| District | No. | % | No. | % |
| --- | --- | --- | --- | --- |
| Quebec | 44,760 | 39.6 | 133,674 | 31.4 |
| Trois-Rivières | 12,618 | 11.2 | 47,856 | 11.3 |
| Montreal | 55,634 | 49.2 | 243,986 | 57.3 |
| Total | 113,012 | 100.0 | 425,516 | 100.0 |

SOURCE: Census of Canada, 1871

the city, and the enforcement of the Navigation Laws, which prohibited foreign vessels from sailing as far as Montreal, Quebec was able to maintain a near monopoly of the St. Lawrence foreign trade. In 1824 less than one-tenth of the ocean shipping which entered the St. Lawrence went as far as Montreal. On the other hand, Quebec's overall commercial importance had declined relative to Montreal's because of the progressive shift of the colony's population westward (Table 6.1); by the 1820s three-quarters of the people in Upper and Lower Canada lived closer to Montreal than Quebec. Despite the fact that Quebec lacked the large indigenous capital market possessed by its rival, its commercial importance was considerable, based on its dominance in the square timber, shipbuilding and foreign trades. To facilitate these trades the Quebec Exchange and Quebec Bank were established in 1817 and 1818, respectively.

In Upper Canada the evolution of an embryonic urban system was apparent soon after the arrival of the first Loyalists, who settled mainly in the Niagara peninsula, the Bay of Quinte and the upper St. Lawrence River. These were pioneer settlements in what had hitherto been designated an Indian preserve. Niagara (now Niagara-on-the-Lake), at the mouth of the Niagara River, was chosen as the site for a Loyalist settlement in 1780, since it was a major point of entry for settlers going to the Niagara peninsula. At the other end of Lake Ontario, Fort Cataraqui was chosen as a base for organizing the settlement of Loyalists after the end of the American Revolutionary War, and the British naval base for Lake Ontario was transferred to it from nearby Carleton Island, which had been ceded to the United States by the Treaty of Paris (1783). In 1788 a town was laid out on the site and the settlement was renamed Kingston. A number of other settlements were founded in the upper St. Lawrence and Bay of Quinte regions, including Bath, Brockville, Cornwall, Napanee and Picton, all of which were established by 1784; Belleville (1790) and Port Hope (1793) were established shortly afterwards.

The most critical factor in the subsequent development of the Upper Canadian urban system was undoubtedly the area's designation as a province in 1791. The choice of the administrative capital and the military base for Lake Ontario were the two most important decisions to be made at that time in the largely uninhabited (15-20,000 people) province. Niagara was both longer-established and larger than Kingston, and also contained the majority of the colony's small elite. In 1792 the first Parliament met at Niagara (then called Newark) but its future as the provincial capital remained in doubt since it was felt that its situation, so close to the United States, made it vulnerable to attack. The first lieutenant-governor, John Graves Simcoe, favoured the site of the present city of London as the capital, and proposed that York (renamed Toronto in 1834 when it was incorporated as a city) should be developed as a commercial-military centre. York had many advantages: its excellent harbour, which was reported to be the best on Lake Ontario, its remoteness from the United States, and its strategic position at the mouth of the Humber River, the terminus of the Toronto Passage (or Toronto Carrying-Place), which was an old Indian route to Georgian Bay and the shortest course between lakes Ontario and Huron. The Toronto Passage, which had never in fact been of much significance in the fur trade, was considered to have great potential as a commercial route to the upper Great Lakes, and York was accordingly envisaged as one of the future commercial centres of the province. London was Simcoe's choice for the capital both because of the advantages of an inland location for defence against the United States, and because it would afford a way of settling a hitherto uninhabited district. Lord Dorchester, the governor of Canada, had actually favoured the thriving Loyalist settlement of Kingston, but like Niagara, this was considered to be unsuitable because of its vulnerability to American attack. In 1794 York was selected as the temporary capital, a choice which represented a compromise between the alternatives of London and Kingston; for another twenty years this temporary status remained unaltered.

Until 1814, at the conclusion of the War of 1812, progress in Upper Canada had been slow. The population had increased to 95,000 but little urban development had taken place. York had grown very slowly, with a population in 1814 of only 691, and it ranked behind both Kingston and Niagara in terms of commercial importance. Except for the transfer of the government to York in 1796, the capital had been largely neglected. Its anticipated military role did not materialize since the naval base had remained at Kingston, and the Toronto Passage, which was still largely avoided by the fur traders, had not achieved any commercial significance. Contributing to the uncertainty of York's position was its capture by the Americans in 1813, when the Parliament Building and garrison were burned. As a result of its proven vulnerability the British government decided in 1815 to transfer the capital to Kingston, but (principally through the efforts of government officials who were reluctant to bear the personal costs entailed in such a move) the lieutenant-governor was persuaded to seek a reversal of this decision and in the end York remained the capital.

York's early growth was much impeded by the absence of a commercial hinterland, which the early road-building program in the province did little to remedy. In 1796 Yonge Street, parallelling the Toronto Passage, was completed as far as Holland Landing and was later extended to Penetanguishene on Georgian Bay. By the turn of the century the lakeshore road was opened; this was an extension of the Montreal-Kingston road to York, Dundas and Niagara. Dundas Street itself was begun in 1793 and opened for some distance towards London but was not completed until the late 1820s. By 1820 York's hinterland was still only thinly settled and largely undeveloped. Administrative functions provided its principal economic base and, although the wealthier-than-average residents supported a wide range of commercial activities, the town remained of secondary importance as a trading centre. The political leverage conferred by its capital status was, however, very much in evidence in York's struggle with Kingston for the charter of the Bank of Upper Canada, the province's first bank. In 1817 Kingston merchants petitioned for the bank charter, and this was followed a few days later by a similar petition from York. In 1819 the Kingston group began a private banking association which failed shortly after the charter for the Bank of Upper Canada was granted to the York group in 1821. York's victory was primarily achieved through the political influence of its oligarchy. Nearly all the bank's directors were either members of the government or were connected with the "Family Compact" (the term commonly used to describe the small group of people who had a stranglehold on the government); indeed the government appointed four of the fifteen directors and held one-quarter of the stock.

In spite of its inferior political status, Kingston functioned in fact if not in name as the commercial and cultural capital of Upper Canada. It was an outpost for Montreal merchants; its most important asset was its location at the east end of Lake Ontario, the junction of lake and river shipping, and transshipment functions were the town's principal economic support. Kingston was in short a gateway city, and through it was channelled the trade of both Upper Canada and the American midwest. It benefited considerably from the superiority of the St. Lawrence over other routes in the trade of the Great Lakes region. Goods were carried in *bateaux* and Durham boats from Montreal to Kingston, where they were transferred to lake vessels. Kingston had also benefited considerably from the War of 1812, in contrast to its two rivals, York and Niagara, whose progress was forcibly checked by their capture and destruction by the Americans. Niagara's prospects for growth were crushed by this demonstration of its susceptibility to American attack, and although its commercial importance remained it was gradually superseded by York.

In addition to Kingston, York and Niagara, the only centres with more than 1,000 inhabitants by 1820, there were a number of incipient urban settlements, none of which were as yet much more than hamlets. In 1813 the townsite of Hamilton was laid out and in 1816 it was designated as the administrative centre for the extensive District of Gore. In spite of this its growth was very slow; at first it was eclipsed by Dundas, which was longer-established, and which had easier access through the Dundas Valley to the growing agricultural communities beyond the Niagara Escarpment. Hamilton was handicapped both by poor connections beyond the escarpment and by a sand bar, which blocked the entrance to its otherwise excellent harbour. Outside the Lake Ontario-Niagara peninsula region, settlement was restricted to the upper St. Lawrence River, where the small villages of Brockville and Prescott were situated, and to the southwest of the province where the extensive Talbot Settlement, begun in 1803, had as yet generated no major centres. Port Talbot, which was itself founded in 1803, had failed to develop into a centre of any importance, although it was for some time the sole port of entry for both goods and settlers. Amherstburg on the Detroit River had been founded in 1796 as a fortified post after the evacuation of British troops from Fort Detroit but was relatively unimportant.

## 1821-1849

The most significant development during this period was the growth of settlement as a result of large-scale immigration between 1825 and 1850. For the first time in Canadian history there was a spontaneous migration of large numbers of British citizens into the country. A major contributing factor was the reduction in transatlantic fares for immigrants. During the fur-trade era ships had carried light, valuable cargo on the outward journey to Britain and returned with heavy, manufactured goods. Because of the growth of the timber trade, the outgoing cargo became heavy and bulky, and many ships were forced to make the return journey either in ballast or with a small load; this imbalance meant that fares for west-bound passengers were low and immigration increased considerably as a result. Although a number of the immigrants on timber ships were actually bound for the United States, many stayed in Canada and measures were therefore taken to encourage agricultural development in the colony; in particular, the bulk of the clergy and crown reserves, the size of which had begun to hinder settlement, were transferred to land companies or otherwise disposed of between 1825 and 1834. By 1850 nearly all the good agricultural land had been settled.

Between 1825 and 1851 the population of Upper and Lower Canada almost tripled from 637,000 to 1,842,000; the bulk of the increase occurred in Upper Canada and the urban areas had a more than proportionate share. From 158,000 in 1825 the population of Upper Canada approximately doubled every ten years as a result of its greater appeal to immigrants; it reached 213,000 in 1830, 348,000 in 1835, 432,000 in 1840 and 952,000 in 1851. Lower Canada grew at a much slower rate and its population less than doubled between 1825 (479,000) and 1851 (890,000). The urban population in the two provinces increased appreciably during this period, both in absolute numbers and as a proportion of the total population. The number of settlements with more than 1,000 inhabitants increased from 6 to 49 between 1821 and 1851, and their total population rose from about 45,000 in 1821 to 264,000 in 1851 (i.e., from about 8 per cent to 14.5 per cent of the total population).

The period was distinguished by two struggles for urban dominance, between Montreal and Quebec, and between Toronto and Kingston. The two contests were largely similar in nature. Both

Quebec and Kingston had an initial advantage over their rivals since they were the first settlements in their respective provinces and each acted as the gateway for its region; Quebec was the transshipment point for ocean and river shipping, while Kingston was the meeting point for lake and river navigation. Their gateway functions derived from the supremacy of the St. Lawrence as a transportation route which meant that the entry and exit of goods were necessarily channelled through them. Montreal and Quebec were the corner-stones of the St. Lawrence commercial empire and their struggle was for "national" supremacy. Kingston and Toronto were subordinate to these two cities, particularly Montreal, and their contest was more regional in scope.

The amalgamation of the North West Company with the Hudson's Bay Company in 1821 brought an abrupt end to Montreal's far-flung trading empire; thereafter the flow of furs through Montreal dwindled rapidly and the city's influence was reduced to a strictly local sphere. Though slowed, its commercial growth was not checked altogether and the capital accumulated from the fur trade was increasingly used to finance the new staples, timber and agriculture, the growth of which accelerated during the following decades. But the attention of the Montreal merchants was now directed towards the control of economic development within the St. Lawrence-Great Lakes region. They were no longer prepared to accept the officially regulated division of functions between Montreal and Quebec, which had remained almost unchanged since the French regime. As a result, the long-standing rivalry between the two cities intensified in the 1820s and, although commercial in nature, the battle was largely fought in the political arena.

From the late 1820s, when the influx of migrants into Upper Canada began, Montreal's advantages over Quebec became gradually more obvious as its centrality for the bulk of the Canadian population increased. Montreal was the financial metropolis of Canada and no other city could match it in terms of access to capital and entrepreneurial endeavour. Its banks and its merchants exercised a hegemony in nearly all economic spheres with the notable exception of the timber trade. Unlike Montreal, Quebec was not a headquarters city; the majority of its timber and shipbuilding firms were branches of London-based companies, and when the city's timber trade began to decline their capital was transferred else-where. The Montreal merchants attempted to capitalize on these advantages by pressing for public support of measures which included the canalization of the upper St. Lawrence and the dredging of the lower stretches of the river, in order to erode Quebec's previously unchallenged transportation functions.

The turning point in Montreal's struggle for economic sovereignty took the form of a political victory. In 1830 the Montreal Harbour Commission was created—a signal triumph for Montreal merchants in their struggle against the vested interests in Quebec. Until then its harbour had been entirely under the jurisdiction of the Board of Trinity House in Quebec, and practically no improvements had been made except for the building of a few private wharves. Between 1830 and 1833 a small sum of money which had been granted by the Legislative Assembly was used to improve harbour facilities.

By 1831 Montreal and Quebec had derived approximately equal benefits from the growth of the St. Lawrence economy, and each had about 28,000 inhabitants; in the succeeding years of the decade Montreal began to outstrip its rival. The city's growing political autonomy was a major factor; the establishment of the harbour commission and the city's incorporation (1832) allowed Montreal to assume some of the responsibility for its own local improvements which had previously belonged to the authorities in Quebec. The most important reason for Montreal's increasing ascendancy, however, was the continued westward shift of the centre of population gravity as a result of the rapid settlement of both Upper Canada and the Eastern Townships. The division of functions between the two cities did not change appreciably, and the difference in the size of their population was primarily because agricultural produce had begun to replace timber as the primary export and because commercial services to communities had risen considerably in importance. Montreal's greater importance as a regional metropolis was indicated by the higher value of goods imported in 1829— £1,714,000 against £836,000 for Quebec.

Despite its ascendancy, Montreal did not grow as fast during this period as might have been expected of Canada's primate city, and its growth rate was actually below that for the population as a whole. From a population of 22,000 in 1825 it increased to 36,000 in 1834, to 40,000 in 1840 and to 58,000 in 1851. This was no match for Toronto, whose population numbered 1,700, 9,300, 13,000, and 31,000 at the same dates. Montreal had experienced a number of setbacks in the second quarter of the nineteenth century: the opening

TABLE 6.2 *Urban population\* by size group, Upper and Lower Canada, 1851*

| Population | Upper Canada | | | Lower Canada | | | Total | | |
|---|---|---|---|---|---|---|---|---|---|
| | No. of centres | Population | % | No. of centres | Population | % | No. of centres | Population | % |
| 100,000 and over | — | — | — | — | — | — | — | — | — |
| 25,000–99,999 | 1 | 30,775 | 23.2 | 2 | 99,767 | 76.0 | 3 | 130,542 | 49.4 |
| 10,000–24,999 | 2 | 25,697 | 19.3 | — | — | — | 2 | 25,697 | 9.7 |
| 5,000–9,999 | 2 | 14,795 | 11.1 | — | — | — | 2 | 14,795 | 5.6 |
| 2,500–4,999 | 7 | 26,788 | 20.2 | 6 | 20,981 | 16.0 | 13 | 47,769 | 18.1 |
| 1,000–2,499 | 21 | 34,872 | 26.2 | 8 | 10,531 | 8.0 | 29 | 45,403 | 17.2 |
| Total urban | 33 | 132,927 | 100.0 | 16 | 131,279 | 100.0 | 49 | 264,206 | 100.0 |

SOURCE: Census of Canada, 1851
*Incorporated centres with a population of 1,000 or over.

of the Erie Canal in 1825; the long delay in constructing the St. Lawrence canal system and in dredging the river channel; the need for improvements to its harbour facilities; the abolition of the British Corn Laws; the U.S. Drawback Acts; the British Navigation Laws which barred foreign ships from the St. Lawrence River above Quebec. The coincidence of these impediments in the late 1840s precipitated one of the most serious depressions in the city's history.

The depression in Montreal reached its economic and emotional nadir in 1849. In that year the governor general, Lord Elgin, wrote that "property in most of the Canadian towns, and more especially in the Capital (Montreal), has fallen 50 per cent in value within the last three years. Three-fourths of the commercial men are bankrupt." In the same year the frustrations of the city's merchantocracy became painfully obvious when the Parliament Building was burned (a move provoked by the passage of the Rebellion Losses Bill which was intended to compensate the rebels of 1837) and when the Annexation Manifesto was published shortly afterwards. In this document, 325 prominent Montrealers, mainly merchants, with considerable backing from the English-language newspapers, expressed their support for union with the United States. The city's traditional resilience and entrepreneurial adroitness proved equal to the crisis, however, and by the following year its economy was once more on the upswing, despite the transfer of the capital to Toronto in 1849, only five years after it had been moved to Montreal.

In the second quarter of the nineteenth century Upper Canada developed from an agricultural frontier into a moderately prosperous province based on commercial agriculture (mainly wheat production) and lumbering. The shift to a more commercial emphasis after 1825 was mainly the result of the massive influx of people, and the major transportation improvements, which included the Erie Canal and the St. Lawrence canals. The development of Upper Canada was in marked contrast to that of the lower province, which remained an urban-centred community throughout the French regime and only developed a substantial rural population in the last quarter of the eighteenth century. The three communities of Quebec, Montreal and Trois-Rivières accounted for between 20 and 25 per cent of New France's population from the 1660s to the end of the French era; the three centres contained 20 per cent of the colony's population in 1685, 22 per cent in 1698, and 23 per cent in 1754. After 1763 the three urban centres accounted for a decreasing pro-

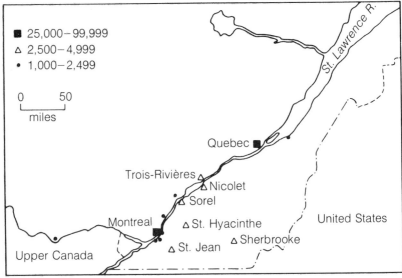

FIGURE 6.1   Distribution of urban centres, Lower Canada, 1851.

*Source: Census of Canada, 1851.*

portion of the total population and by 1825 they contained only about 10 per cent of Lower Canada's population. In Upper Canada urban development had barely begun by 1825 and the three urban centres of Kingston, Toronto and Niagara together accounted for under 4 per cent of the Upper Canadian population. By 1851 there was clear evidence of a developed urban system in Upper Canada (Table 6.2 and Figure 6.1) and thirty-three of its incorporated communities had more than 1,000 inhabitants, compared to only three in 1825. Toronto was the dominant centre with 30,775 inhabitants, followed by Hamilton (14,112), Kingston (11,585), Ottawa (7,760) and London (7,035). The proportion of the provincial population in urban centres (i.e., more than 1,000 inhabitants) had risen to 14 per cent.

The second quarter of the nineteenth century was a critical period in the development of the Upper Canadian urban system; during this time administrative and port functions were the two most important economic factors encouraging urban growth. The performance of these two functions generally supported a wider range of commercial activities, and in places such as Toronto, Hamilton and Kingston where both functions were important, growth was substantial. Inland centres with administrative functions, such as London, also grew rapidly, while strategically located ports, such as St. Catharines on the Welland Canal, were able to rise in the hierarchy even though they lacked the advantages of an administrative centre.

One of the most interesting changes within the urban system after 1825 was the growth of Toronto's ascendancy in Upper Canada, particularly since until this time Kingston's dominance had been unchallenged. Three developments in the second half of the 1820s were instrumental in encouraging Toronto's emergence as the primate city: after the charter of the Bank of Upper Canada was granted to Toronto legislation prevented any further establishment of banks within the province and a virtual monopoly was thus maintained for some time; the Erie Canal was opened; and the back country was settled as a result of the influx of colonists. It was not until 1831, when the Commercial Bank of the Midland District was incorporated, that Kingston merchants were able to obtain a chartered bank to replace the private banking association which had failed ten years before. The opening of the Erie Canal and the settlement of the American midwest increased Upper Canada's trade with the United States and, although Kingston continued to be the most important port on Lake Ontario, trade was widely dispersed to Toronto, Hamilton and a number of other smaller ports such as Port Hope and Cobourg. Trade with the United States was not channelled through any particular port and Kingston's gateway function in the St. Lawrence trade was not duplicated. In these circumstances entrepôt functions were related to the size of the port's hinterland and in this respect Kingston's position continued to deteriorate as more and more of the province's unoccupied land was settled. The rapid growth of settlement in the western half of the province caused the centre of population gravity to shift farther west of Kingston. Toronto's hinterland, potentially a rich agricultural region, was largely unsettled before 1830; Kingston, on the other hand, lay at the edge of the Canadian Shield and its hinterland, which had very limited agricultural potential, had already been almost fully settled. The conjunction of the westward shift of population and the relative decline of the St. Lawrence reduced Kingston's transshipment and forwarding functions, and in turn its commercial importance.

During the 1830s Toronto's battle with Kingston was finally won. In 1830 the respective populations of Kingston and Toronto were 3,587 and 2,860. By the following year the positions had been

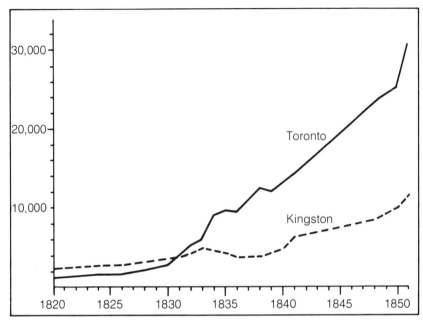

FIGURE 6.2   Growth of population, Kingston and Toronto, 1820–1851.

*Sources: Census of Canada*, 1851, and Provincial Archives (Ontario)

reversed; Toronto had 3,969 inhabitants compared to its rival's 3,820. Throughout the 1830s Toronto consolidated its supremacy, and the population of Kingston actually declined between 1833 and 1840 (Figure 6.2). With the growth of settlement in both its own hinterland and in the rest of the province, Toronto's commercial functions assumed significant proportions for the first time. In 1841 the commercial dominance of the city was already too firmly established to be much affected by the transfer of the administrative capital of the united province of Canada to Kingston. Ironically Kingston was chosen as the capital at the very time when its long history of dominance in Upper Canada was at an end; in 1840, the year before its selection, Kingston's population of 4,828 was already far below that of Toronto (13,092). By mid-century Toronto was the dominant centre in Upper Canada for wholesaling, banking and industry, and from 1849 the alternating capital (with Quebec) of the province of Canada.

Kingston's economic fortunes were closely connected with those of Montreal, and the declining importance of the St. Lawrence route both reduced the strength of the Montreal-Kingston alliance and contributed to the rise of Toronto as an independent metropolitan centre. Perhaps the single most important factor which contributed to Toronto's rise to metropolitan preeminence was the growth of trade with New York. As long as Upper Canada's external trade remained channelled through the St. Lawrence, Toronto's growth was inevitably frustrated by the natural advantages of Montreal and Kingston. Various events in the late 1840s accelerated Upper Canada's trade with and through the United States. Besides the abolition of the British Corn Laws and the passage of the Drawback Acts, the province of Canada abolished the imperial preference in 1847 and the same import duties were applied to American and British goods. In the same year Toronto was connected to New York by telegraph, making possible efficient communication between Toronto wholesalers and New York shipping companies. Moreover, in the 1840s there was a marked rise in the export of Upper Canadian lumber to the United States. Toronto's benefits were mainly in the import trade, since the export trade was shared by a number of ports on Lake Ontario; by the middle of the century Toronto was the most important importation centre in Upper Canada for foreign goods (mainly American), a reflection of its wholesale distribution function, while Kingston remained more important in the export trade, principally as a result of the growth of lumber exports via the Rideau Canal.

After the mid-1830s Hamilton grew rapidly and by the middle of the century it had emerged as the second largest centre in Upper Canada. The completion in 1832 of the Burlington Canal through the sand bar which blocked its harbour shifted the commercial advantage to Hamilton from Dundas, its principal rival. As a result Hamilton grew from less than 1,000 inhabitants in that year, to 2,155 in 1835 and to 3,413 in 1841. The 1837 opening of the Desjardins Canal from Hamilton Harbour to Dundas did little to improve the latter's position and in 1851 its population was only 3,517. In contrast, Hamilton's growth was accelerated during the late 1840s. The opening of the deepened Welland Canal in 1845 gave the city access to low-cost coal from Pennsylvania and contributed to its growth as an industrial centre; in 1846 the first dock was com-

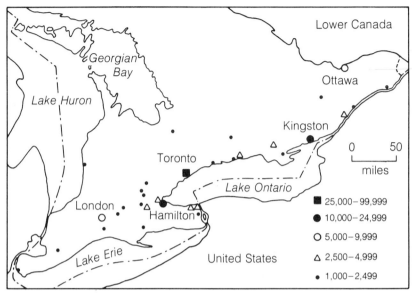

FIGURE 6.3   Distribution of urban centres, Upper Canada, 1851.

*Source: Census of Canada,* 1851.

pleted, and in 1850 the Great Western Railway, headquartered in the city, built a grain elevator on the waterfront in anticipation of the completion (1854) of its Niagara-Windsor railway. By 1846 Hamilton's population had risen to 6,832, and by 1851 this had increased to 14,112.

The remaining centres in Upper Canada with more than 5,000 inhabitants in 1851 were Ottawa and London, which were both founded in 1826 but which developed quite different economic functions. The Ottawa townsite was laid out by Colonel By, the engineer in charge of the construction of the Rideau Canal, which was begun in the same year and the settlement was known as Bytown until its incorporation as a city in 1855. The town grew rapidly after the completion of the canal in 1832 and by the late 1830s its population had reached 2,500; it had already outstripped the older settlement of Hull (then Wright's Village) which had been founded in 1800 on the opposite bank of the river. Ottawa's early growth was almost entirely the result of the rising demand for lumber in the United States, and sawmills had been established in the 1830s on both sides of the river below the Chaudière Falls. In 1842 Ottawa was chosen as the administrative centre for the District of Dalhousie but it was the lumbering industry which was mainly responsible for its growth to 6,275 in 1848 and to 7,760 in 1851.

Although the townsite of London had been surveyed and reserved as the proposed site of the provincial capital in 1793, no settlement had taken place until 1826 when it was re-surveyed and chosen as the administrative centre for the London District. Its growth was slow at first, reaching 1,000 inhabitants in 1835 and 2,000 in 1841; with the growth of settlement in its region and its central location on the proposed Great Western Railway (construction began in 1851) the town grew more rapidly thereafter to 4,688 in 1848 and 7,035 in 1851.

Of note during this period was the decline of Niagara, from third to eleventh place in the Upper Canadian urban hierarchy. This was due mainly to the completion of the first Welland Canal (1829) which bypassed the town and instead encouraged the growth of St. Catharines. Niagara, at the mouth of the Niagara River, ceased to function as a transshipment point between lake and river shipping. The town's population history reflected its changed status: 1,376 in 1825, 1,148 in 1830, 2,086 in 1840 and 3,340 in 1851. In contrast, St. Catharines had grown to 4,368 by 1851. Although founded in 1790, the size of St. Catharines was negligible until the construction of the Welland Canal; the town grew particularly rapidly after the deepening of the canal in 1845.

1849-1867

The final phase of Montreal's struggle for supremacy over Quebec began in 1850 with the dredging of the river channel. The success of the early dredging operations was minor; between 1850 and 1860 the ocean shipping cleared from the port of Montreal increased from 47,000 tons to 77,000 tons, but it remained only one-tenth as large as the corresponding volume cleared from Quebec. Montreal's potential as a major seaport could not be fulfilled until the advent of the iron steamship. During the 1850s sailing ships still dominated the ocean carrying-trade and Quebec remained the popular turnaround point on the St. Lawrence. In 1853 the first ocean steamer arrived at Montreal and three years later a regular steamship service was inaugurated between Liverpool and Montreal (Portland in winter).

After 1860 Montreal's port activity increased rapidly as the iron screw steamship began to dominate the transatlantic carrying-trade. This growth was almost entirely at the expense of Quebec, since

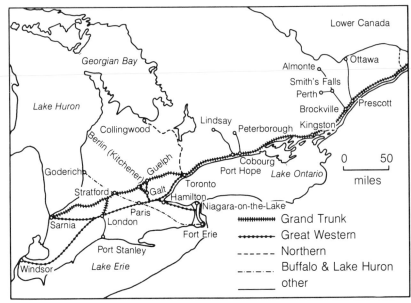

FIGURE 6.4   Railways of Upper Canada, 1860.

*Source:* G.P. deT. Glazebrook, *A History of Transportation in Canada* (Toronto: Ryerson, 1938).

until the 1880s the St. Lawrence continued to attract only a minor share of the lake trade compared to New York. By the end of the 1860s Montreal's ocean shipping tonnage had increased to 260,000 tons or two-fifths of Quebec's, by 1875 it had risen to 400,000 tons or two-thirds of Quebec's, and by 1880 to 600,000 tons or slightly more than Quebec's.

After a decade of vigorous growth Quebec City experienced a series of setbacks in the 1860s and entered a long period of economic stagnation. All its economic supports had prospered in the 1850s—timber exports, shipbuilding, port activity and even administration, as it shared with Toronto the responsibilities of being Canada's capital. In the 1860s its economic fortunes changed. The square timber and shipbuilding industries began to decline after 1865; the Canadian government was permanently transferred to Ottawa in 1865; many ships began to bypass the city in favour of Montreal; a serious fire in 1866 destroyed 3,000 houses and rendered more than 20,000 people homeless; and in 1870 British military forces were completely withdrawn from the city. A further factor was the exclusion of the city, until 1879, from the increasingly important railway system. The city's selection in 1867 as the capital of the province of Quebec and the growth of the shoemaking industry were the only important gains. Quebec's declining economic importance during this period was indicated by the ocean shipping tonnage entering its port; from 775,000 tons in 1861 port activity declined to 670,000 tons by the end of the decade, to 615,000 in 1875, 555,000 in 1880, 295,000 in 1885 and 240,000 in 1889, the year before the opening of a modern harbour which led to a revival of its port.

Montreal's struggle with Quebec for national supremacy had reached its conclusion by the end of the 1860s, at about the time when Toronto began to emerge as a national metropolitan centre. By mid-century Toronto was clearly the dominant centre in Upper Canada, but its influence was still largely restricted to an immediate hinterland. This was changed with startling rapidity in the 1850s by the advent of the railway; by 1860 railways radiated from Toronto in almost every direction (Figure 6.4) and the city was able to consolidate its position vis-à-vis its rivals by gaining domination over a region large enough to support its rise to national metropolitan status. Particularly important to Toronto's development was the Northern Railway, which was completed as far as Collingwood in 1855. It was intended to achieve two objectives: to exploit the timber and agricultural resources of the land to the north of the city; and, on a more ambitious scale, to lure western trade to Toronto via the Toronto Passage. The Northern Railway was successful in attracting a substantial amount of American midwestern grain and Toronto accordingly became the largest wheat exporter on Lake Ontario. The more important and lasting benefit of the railway was, however, its effect on the development of Toronto's hinterland; besides agriculture, the railway gave rise to a large lumber industry in Simcoe County. As a result of its preeminence as a railway centre, Toronto was able to strengthen its control over Upper Canada's financial, commercial and cultural affairs, and in 1867 the city was chosen as the capital of the newly created province of Ontario.

Kingston continued to decline in importance within the urban system and by 1871 was only the fifth largest centre in Ontario. Although the city remained a transshipment point until the end of the nineteenth century, the importance of this function declined steadily as a result of the canalization of the St. Lawrence. (After 1901, when the St. Lawrence canals were deepened to fourteen feet, the city was almost completely bypassed as larger lake vessels proceeded directly to Montreal.) Although a relative decline had begun as early as the second quarter of the nineteenth century, the city continued to grow at a modest rate until the 1850s. The closing of the British naval dockyard and the partial withdrawal of military forces from the city in 1853 as a result of the Crimean War foreshadowed the complete evacuation of British troops in 1870. The demise of its military function was a severe blow to the city, which lost 10 per cent of its population between 1861 and 1871. The city's other main function as a wholesale centre continued to decline relative to other Ontario ports.

Three other cities in Ontario had more than 10,000 inhabitants in 1871: Hamilton (26,716), Ottawa (21,545) and London (15,826). Hamilton developed into a major industrial centre, complementing its established position as a wholesale-distribution centre. By 1855 the Great Western Railway had linked the city to Toronto, Niagara-Buffalo, London and Windsor-Detroit, and greatly extended its commercial hinterland, while in 1859 the company located its shops in the city to manufacture the rails and other equipment which had been previously imported from England. Nevertheless, Hamilton's population declined between 1858 and 1864 (from 27,500 to 17,000) after which it began to increase steadily. In 1858 Ottawa was selected as the permanent capital of the province of Canada but the government was not actually transferred to the city until 1865 and two years later the city was named as the capital of the Dominion of Canada. Until 1867 its growth was almost entirely dependent on the lumber industry, which was greatly stimulated in the 1850s by the rising American demand for sawn lumber. London had grown appreciably as a result of its location in the middle of a rich agricultural region and its selection as the focus of the railway network of southwestern Ontario, and it subsequently became the regional capital of an extensive district for which it performed wholesale, marketing and processing functions.

## The Atlantic Region

Until 1763 the Atlantic economy was based almost exclusively on fishing, and although increasing numbers of French and English fishermen visited the banks and coastal waters of Acadia and New-foundland, few settlements were established. The French were largely indifferent to colonization since their fishery had little need for permanent settlements while the English fishermen were generally hostile to colonization, which they regarded as a possible threat to the pursuit of their livelihood. The generally infertile soils of the region were a further deterrent to settlement. Consequently the population of the Atlantic region grew slowly. In 1713, more than one hundred years after the founding of the first colony at Port Royal, the resident population numbered less than 5,000 and fifty years later it was still only about 25,000.

By 1763 the whole of the Atlantic region was under British control, with the exception of the small islands of St. Pierre and Miquelon and fishing rights on the north shore of Newfoundland, which were retained by France. After the influx of United Empire Loyalists in 1783 there was a major reorientation of some regional economies and each colony developed distinctive economic characteristics. Prince Edward Island became predominantly agricultural but continued to rely heavily on fishing. New Brunswick exploited its vast forest resources and specialized in the timber and shipbuilding industries. Nova Scotia developed the most diversified economic structure and here fishing, shipbuilding, lumbering, agriculture and trade were all of substantial importance. Newfoundland, which received no Loyalists because it was not officially recognized as a colony, remained almost completely dependent on fishing.

The total population of the four Atlantic colonies grew to about 140,000 by 1806. The population continued to increase rapidly, although not as fast as in the central provinces of Upper and Lower Canada. In 1851 the Atlantic population was about 640,000 and by 1871 this had increased to about 920,000. Because of the economic and geographical characteristics of the region, its inhabitants continued to settle mainly along the coast, with the exception of a few major river valleys.

ACADIA TO 1713

The first settlement in Acadia was an offshoot of the fur trade. In 1603 Sieur de Monts was granted a fur-trading monopoly in Acadia, Gaspé and the St. Lawrence. The company was also responsible for colonization and Port Royal was selected as a possible site during the first trading expedition made in the following year. The first winter was, however, spent on an island at the mouth of the St. Croix River on the other side of the Bay of Fundy. In 1605 the St. Croix settlers were transferred to Port Royal and the colony was officially founded. In 1607, as a result of protests from unlicensed fur-trading merchants, de Monts' monopoly was withdrawn and the Port Royal colonists returned to France. In 1608 the second fur-trade monopoly acquired by de Monts was limited to the area of the St. Lawrence, and Acadia remained without a monopoly fur-trading company, which was at that time France's only instrument of colonization.

In 1610 a colony was again established at Port Royal by Sieur de Poutrincourt, to whom the area had been granted by de Monts in 1604. Since it was the most important settlement in Acadia, the colony became the focus of hostilities between England and France during the next hundred years. In 1613 the settlement was captured and destroyed by a small English force from Virginia; in 1621, 1654 and 1690 the settlement was again captured and held for varying lengths of time before coming permanently under English domination in 1710.

The semi-agricultural colony of Port Royal developed slowly, and largely in isolation from France. After 1632 it came under the effective commercial control of New England, even though such trade had been considered illegal by both France and England. New England merchants felt a proprietary interest in the colony, and were the instigators of its capture and retention between 1654 and 1670 and between 1690 and 1697. The settlement's small population had grown slowly, from 363 in 1671 to 456 in 1701 and to 570 in 1707. Other French settlements had sprung up after Acadia had been returned to France in 1670 and these had grown appreciably; for example, Beaubassin (Chignecto Bay), founded in 1671, and Minas, founded in 1682, had populations of 271 and 585 respectively in 1707. The total Acadian population at that time was just over 1,500.

THE MARITIMES: 1713-1763

The Treaty of Utrecht (1713) partially settled the question of the ownership of the various Atlantic territories: England secured Nova Scotia (Acadian peninsula) and Newfoundland; France retained Cape Breton (Isle Royale) and Prince Edward Island (Isle St. Jean). New Brunswick (Acadian Mainland) remained under French control although its ownership was disputed by England. The focus of French settlement in the Atlantic region after 1713 was shifted from

Nova Scotia to Cape Breton, while the English colonization of Nova Scotia was delayed until 1749.

In 1714 the French established Louisbourg on Cape Breton. Although the port had for a long time been used by French fishermen, no settlement had preceded its designation as France's administrative and military centre in the Atlantic region. In 1720 the construction of fortifications began; it was to continue for over twenty years, by which time the fort was the strongest military station in North America, providing both a defence for the St. Lawrence colony and a base from which to attack the English colonies in Newfoundland and New England. Apart from its military function, Louisbourg was the base for a substantial residential and summer fishery, and this encouraged its development as the main French commercial and shipping centre on the Atlantic. From the time of its founding in 1714 to its final capture in 1758, Louisbourg was the largest French settlement in Cape Breton. From a total of 637 inhabitants in 1716, the population of Louisbourg grew to 952 in 1726, 1,126 in 1734 and 2,460 in 1752; the latter figure represented more than half of Cape Breton's 4,122 inhabitants. The military importance of Louisbourg was reflected in the size of its garrison: about 1,500 men (not included in estimates of the resident population) were stationed there in 1752. Apart from Louisbourg, the Cape Breton population was dispersed among a number of small ports; in only a dozen or so of these did the population exceed one hundred.

Prince Edward Island was little more than a summer fishing station during most of the French regime, and its population was accordingly small. In 1720 the island's population was only about 100 although it increased steadily thereafter. In 1728 it had reached 330; the two largest settlements were Port La Joie on the south coast and St. Pierre on the north coast with 67 and 138 inhabitants respectively. By 1735 the island population had reached 541 and by 1752 it numbered about 2,000. Thereafter it rose sharply, since some of the Acadians expelled from Nova Scotia in 1755 settled on the island; by 1763 the population had reached about 4,000. After the transfer of the island to England by the Treaty of Paris (1763) many Acadians were driven from the island and their land was reserved for English proprietors; as a result the French population had declined to about 1,400 by 1765.

The first British town to be established in Nova Scotia was Halifax, founded in 1749 as a naval and military centre to counterbalance the French fortress at Louisbourg, to secure the safety of

English naval and commercial vessels, and to protect the small fishing settlements along the coast. The deep harbour at Halifax was easily defended and offered safe anchorage; it had been used by French fishermen in the seventeenth century (when it was known as Chebucto) but had never been the site of a permanent settlement.

The growing commercial importance of New England in the Atlantic region was a principal reason for the establishment of a settlement at Halifax. The New England merchants traded illegally with nearly all the French settlements; in fact they were Louisbourg's major suppliers while its fortifications were being built. As the fortress neared completion, however, New England ships suffered from increased harassment and losses, and in 1744 the nearby port of Canso, a popular base for New England and English fishermen, was captured by a Louisbourg force. In retaliation a New England party travelled overland and captured Louisbourg in 1745. After it was returned to France in accordance with the terms of the Treaty of Aix-la-Chapelle in 1748, the establishment of a strong naval base in Nova Scotia was demanded as some protection against a possible renewal of French hostilities. The establishment of the Halifax settlement was regarded as one step towards greater security for English interests, while the expulsion of Acadians in 1755 was another.

In 1749, the year of its founding, 2,576 people arrived in Halifax, including Lord Cornwallis, the governor of Nova Scotia. Right from the outset Halifax had taken its place as the political and commercial capital of the province, in addition to its role as a military centre. Until 1749 Annapolis Royal (formerly Port Royal) had functioned as the centre of government and defence. Despite attempts to encourage British immigration to Halifax, the number of arrivals at first failed to match the number of departures; in part this was due to the thin and infertile nature of the soil which made farming extremely difficult. As the British colonists moved out New Englanders moved in and by 1762 the latter constituted about half of the population of 2,500.

Only one other major settlement, Lunenburg, had been established in Nova Scotia during the 1750s. A large number of Germans had been brought to Halifax between 1750 and 1752 and about 1,500 were subsequently resettled in Lunenburg. This was the only fertile district along the Atlantic coast and it had the added advantages of an excellent harbour and considerable potential as a fishing base. After an indifferent start the settlement proved to be very successful in agriculture, fishing and shipbuilding, and by 1762, with a population of 1,400 it was the second largest settlement in the province.

NOVA SCOTIA

At the outbreak of the American Revolution Halifax was still the largest and most important settlement in the Maritimes. Its superiority at this time was not so much dependent on its economic advantages as on its naval, military and political importance. From the outset it was regarded as the bastion of British naval power and its fortunes fluctuated according to whether war or peace prevailed. As the foremost British citadel and naval base in North America the city benefited immensely from the stationing of troops during the American Revolution, although it suffered as a result of the cessation of trade with New England. The city's preeminence was less marked in the economic sphere. The insular nature and poor agricultural potential of the Nova Scotian peninsula meant that many settlements shared substantially in the major economic functions of fishing, lumbering, shipbuilding and trade. The city was nevertheless the wealthiest, most advanced urban centre in the Maritimes and, though possessing few natural advantages, it was able in time to extend its economic influence over the whole region. The ubiquity of natural advantages was itself a factor discouraging the rise of competitors; instead there developed a pattern of many small, coastal settlements and only a small number of medium-sized towns. While many centres shared in the external trade, no area was too remote from Halifax to be brought within its sphere of influence, thus denying any of its competitors a protected hinterland. After the introduction of larger ships with a greater load capacity, many marginal centres declined, and Halifax was able to consolidate its position as the entrepôt for the region.

At the conclusion of the American War of Independence Halifax was able to extend its financial-commercial orbit to include all of the Atlantic provinces, and also to gain entry to an extensive trading system which included Britain, the United States and the West Indies. After 1783 Halifax was the chief beneficiary of Britain's attempts to encourage the British North American colonies to supplant New England in the West Indian trade. Although these plans were not wholly successful, the West Indian trade remained an important element of the city's economy for the following fifty years. As early as 1791 American ships were for a time allowed to trade with the West Indies, while between 1815 and 1830 a series of retaliatory acts were legislated by both the United States and Britain over access to the West Indian trade; finally, in 1831 the legal war ended when American ships were freely permitted to trade with the islands. Nevertheless, the West Indian trade was quite substantial during those periods when American ships were prohibited from trading with the British islands; in 1828, for example, the volume of Nova Scotian shipping engaged in trade with the West Indies (27,700 tons) was approximately equal to that engaged in trade with Great Britain (27,200) and much more than that currently trading with the United States (16,100) and other countries (3,200).

Halifax prospered as a result of its participation in the West Indian trade, and the long period of war (between 1793 and 1815) in Europe and North America. The War of 1812 was particularly profitable for the city; on occasion as many as 10,000 troops were stationed in Halifax, doubling its population. The entrepôt functions which Halifax undertook during the War of 1812 were of considerable economic importance, since a substantial amount of the United States' foreign trade was channelled through its port; American foodstuffs were re-exported to Europe and the West Indies while British manufactured goods were imported by Halifax merchants for sale to American merchants. The prosperity fostered by the wars lasted for only two years after the treaty of 1815. The city's population had increased substantially from 4,900 in 1791 to 11,200 in 1817; thereafter it grew to 14,000 by 1822. Between 1822 and 1839 Halifax experienced a period of economic stagnation initiated by the slow-down of military activity and exacerbated by the fact that American ships were once more permitted to trade with the British West Indies in most commodities (all restrictions were lifted in 1830). By 1838 its population was only 14,400.

After 1840 Halifax experienced a period of renewed growth which was stimulated by the expansion of world trade and the development of the city as the mercantile centre for the Maritimes. In 1840 the Cunard Line was inaugurated and provided a regular transatlantic steamship service; although Halifax was the first port of call out from Liverpool, most of the passengers and the bulk of the cargo were destined for Boston, the terminal point of the service. Nevertheless, Halifax benefited greatly from the Cunard Line and enjoyed a general prosperity in maritime trade. By 1851 its population had reached 20,749.

This prosperity continued until Confederation. Trade with the United States increased as a result of the Reciprocity Treaty and the American Civil War while within the province railway construction strengthened the Halifax economy. The city was connected by rail to Truro in 1857, to Windsor on the Bay of Fundy in 1858, and to Pictou on the north shore in 1867. Its population increased to 25,026 in 1861 and 29,582 in 1871. Its growth was proportionate to the general increase in provincial population; between 1851 and 1871 Halifax grew by 42.6 per cent and Nova Scotia by 40.1 per cent. As had always been the case, in time of peace Halifax was dominant but not preeminent among Nova Scotian towns. Fishing, shipbuilding and maritime trade continued to be the main economic activities, and the open coast of Nova Scotia encouraged a dispersal of these functions among a number of ports.

NEW BRUNSWICK

Little settlement had occurred on the Acadian Mainland (New Brunswick) prior to its transfer to Britain in 1763. The first French settlement at the mouth of the St. Croix River in 1604 had been abandoned in the following year. Fort La Tour, a fur-trading post, was established in 1631 on the site of the modern city of Saint John, and although a succession of forts was built in the area there was practically no settlement prior to 1758 when the fort was captured by the English, and re-named Fort Frederick. Higher up the St. John River, at the limit of navigation, the French had established the mission settlement of St. Anne's (later Fredericton) shortly after the Treaty of Utrecht (1713). The population of the Acadian Mainland had increased appreciably after 1755 as a result of the immigration of Acadians from Nova Scotia, and in 1763 the population, which was almost entirely French, numbered about 6,000.

Between 1763 and 1783 very little settlement occurred in the province but its subsequent economic specializations were already evident. Following the capture of Fort La Tour in 1758, New England colonists were encouraged to settle in the region and the first settlements were made in 1762 at Maugerville, near Fredericton on the St. John River, and in 1764 at Portland Point, which subsequently became a suburb of Saint John. In 1779 a contract was made with the Royal Navy for the supply of masts from the St. John Valley, and in the following year the first shipment was sent to Halifax, thus initiating the development of the timber industry, which was to dominate the provincial economy for the next hundred years.

The St. John River was a natural highway for the transportation of timber and because of its abundant resources of white pine it became the most important Maritime centre for both the timber and ship-building industries. Between 1812 and 1825 it seemed possible that the Miramichi River in the northern half of the province might oust Saint John from its paramount position; by 1824 it was already exporting more square timber than the latter. In 1825, however, a disastrous fire in the Miramichi district destroyed several thousand square miles of forest and effectively curtailed the threat to the St. John Valley.

Saint John was founded in 1783 after the arrival of some 4,200 Loyalists, many of whom settled in the two adjacent townsites of Parrtown and Carleton, which subsequently amalgamated in 1785 to form the city of Saint John. Most of the other Loyalists who entered New Brunswick settled along the St. John River, on land formerly occupied by the Acadians. Although no reliable data are available prior to 1824, the year of the first provincial census, it is certain that the city's population had declined to about 1,000 by 1785, when it became Canada's first incorporated city. In the same year Fredericton, 85 miles upriver, was selected as the capital of New Brunswick, thus denying Saint John the political-cultural status enjoyed by the major city of each of the other Atlantic colonies. An inland location for the capital was chosen primarily for military reasons, but also with the intention of encouraging agricultural settlement. As a result, from its earliest days New Brunswick had two capitals, political and commercial, and inevitably a considerable rivalry arose between them.

In 1824 the city of Saint John had 8,488 inhabitants (about 12,000 if the adjoining suburbs were included) and was by far the most important settlement in New Brunswick. There were only two other urban settlements at this time: St. Andrews, at the mouth of the St. Croix River, and Fredericton. Although the timber trade of the province was equally divided between the north shore (Miramichi Valley) and the Bay of Fundy, the former was concerned almost entirely with the export of square timber and masts and consequently there were no settlements of any significance in the area. Although square timber and masts figured prominently in the export trade of Saint John and St. Andrews, shipbuilding and sawmilling were also important. The ships were generally sold in Britain while much of the sawn lumber was exported to the West Indies. Saint John and St. Andrews had been actively involved in the West Indian trade since at least 1808, when they were designated free ports in order to facilitate the import of goods from the United States destined for the West Indian islands. St. Andrews, located on the boundary with the United States, was also the centre of a thriving smuggling trade. In 1827 Saint John's principal export market was Britain (£187,000), but the West Indies (£74,000), and other North American colonies (£72,000) were also important.

The northern half of the province fronting on the Gulf of St. Lawrence was not within Saint John's sphere of influence. Indeed, in so far as the region was dependent on an outside metropolitan centre, it was served by Halifax. Saint John's influence was restricted to its own river valley and the Bay of Fundy, including some of the Nova Scotian communities; in 1827, for example, a regular steamship service was inaugurated between Saint John and Digby, Nova Scotia. Because of the commercial effects of this limitation, Saint John merchants strongly supported the construction of a canal through the isthmus of Chignecto. This proposal was first made in 1800 and revived in the 1840s, but was finally blocked both by the practical difficulties of construction and by the opposition of Halifax, which feared competition in the area which had hitherto been its hinterland. Consequently it was not until 1860, when the Saint John–Shediac railway was completed, that the city was able to enjoy adequate communications with this region. Although Saint John was the foremost commercial, financial and industrial centre in New Brunswick, it did not exercise over the other communities the formative influence which is the hallmark of a metropolis. Its size belied the strength of its control over the provincial economy and it could be more accurately described as the largest commercial-industrial centre than as the commercial capital.

Between 1825 and the mid-1860s the city experienced a moderately fast rate of growth, primarily as a result of the increasing importance of shipbuilding, square timber and, more recently, sawmilling. In the early 1860s the city achieved its peak of prosperity and was very much the New Brunswick metropolis; about one-fifth of the provincial population lived within Greater Saint John, and the city's port accounted for four-fifths of the shipping registered in the province as well as three-fifths of the tonnage cleared from New Brunswick ports.

There were very few urban centres in New Brunswick apart from Saint John. Fredericton, the second largest city, had a population of 4,458 in 1851 and by 1871 this had risen to 6,006. St. Andrews had already begun to decline as a port and its population in 1871 was less than 1,000. Moncton, which later became the province's second largest city, had only 600 people in 1871. It had been an important port on the Petitcodiac River during the French era but its rise to major urban status was as a railway transportation centre; it was linked to the Saint John–Shediac railway in 1860 but it was not until after it became an important junction on the Intercolonial Railway (1876) that its rapid growth took place.

PRINCE EDWARD ISLAND

The population of the island (known as the Island of St. John until 1799) grew slowly for the first few decades after its designation as a province in 1769, at which time its population was only about 300. The province's early development was greatly hampered by the large number of absentee landlords, many of whom were the proprietors of the 67 lots of 20,000 acres each into which the island was divided in 1769. By 1797 the population was still only 4,500, and about one-half of the island lots remained uninhabited. Thereafter the population grew steadily, to 24,600 in 1822, 47,000 in 1841, 62,700 in 1848, 80,900 in 1861 and 94,000 in 1871. The economic base of the province was initially fishing, but the importance of agriculture increased during the first quarter of the nineteenth century, and thereafter it remained the principal economic activity.

The agricultural orientation of the small island did not support a large urban population and the only centre of any significance was Charlottetown, founded in 1768 on the site of the French settlement of Port La Joie (begun in 1722 as Fort La Joie on the opposite side of the river). In 1841 the provincial capital of Charlottetown had 3,896 inhabitants and was the only settlement which could be considered urban; Georgetown and Princetown, with 556 and 387 inhabitants respectively, were the only other centres of any size at all. The population of Charlottetown grew to 4,717 in 1848, 6,706 in 1861 and 7,872 in 1871. Even at this late date the only other settlement of more than 1,000 inhabitants was Georgetown, with 1,056.

NEWFOUNDLAND

Until the last decade of the eighteenth century the establishment of permanent settlements in Newfoundland was inhibited by the opposition of England's West Country fishermen. The purpose of the various laws against settlement was to treat the island as a fishing station rather than a colony and to make Newfoundland "a great English ship moored near the Grand Banks," in order to facilitate English fishing and to serve as a training ground for the Royal Navy. It was imperative, therefore, that colonists not interfere with the summer fishery and that the "green" sailors (those who were taken for the first time as crew members) be returned to England where the navy could put their experience to good use. Newfoundland was considered by Britain to be second in value only to the West Indian islands and every effort was made to preserve its barrenness in order to protect the summer fishery from the competition of a resident fishery.

The first of the repressive laws was enacted in 1633; it provided that in the case of each harbour the first captain to arrive for the fishing season was to be designated as the Fishing Admiral and that for the duration of that season he should function as the governor of his harbour, meting out justice as he saw fit. After 1660 colonization became the specific target of a number of laws governing the Newfoundland fishery; ships were forbidden to carry settlers and penalities were imposed if any crew members were left on the island. In 1675 new and more drastic regulations were enacted, reiterating the ban on the building of residences within six miles of the shore (first instituted in 1637), with the intention of forcing the settlers either to return to England or to remove themselves to the New England colonies. Although a temporary reprieve was granted in 1677 to those colonists already settled in Newfoundland, the repressive laws continued. In 1698 strong measures were again invoked for the benefit of the summer fishery, including the re-establishment of the iniquitous rule of the Fishing Admirals. The lot of the settlers was somewhat improved in 1729 when the system of government by Fishing Admirals was replaced by the appointment of a naval governor; the settlers were still legally unrecognized, however, and the naval governors returned to England each winter. In 1775 (Palliser's Act) many of the earlier prohibitions against settlement were once more legislated in a final attempt to uproot the island's residents. The establishment of a Supreme Court of Judicature in 1793 ended the arbitary judicial rule of the fishing admirals and naval governors and marked the first step towards the recognition of Newfoundland as a British colony.

Despite the formidable weight of legal deterrents, the number of settlers increased steadily from the early seventeenth century when English colonies were first chartered. Between 1610 and 1623, six English colonies were chartered and established in the Avalon Peninsula of Newfoundland. None of them was particularly successful, and in 1637 all the charters were cancelled and the whole island was granted to a group which included Sir David Kirke, the conqueror of Quebec. The charter of 1637 did little to encourage colonization; colonists were forbidden to either cut wood or to build within six miles of the sea in the area between Cape Race and Cape Bonavista, where nearly all the English fishing stations were located. In the case of Newfoundland such prohibitions negated any chance of establishing a successful colony since fishing, the only viable occupation, could not be carried on under these conditions. By the 1650s the resident English population of Newfoundland was still less than 1,000, while the number of English summer fishermen sometimes rose as high as 12,000.

Although St. John's in the first quarter of the sixteenth century was one of the most important rendezvous for fishermen, no attempt was made to establish a colony there; its importance as a base for the summer fishery was in itself a principal reason for its avoidance by the early settlers. It is certain, however, that the practice of leaving men behind each year to prepare for the following season's fishery was well established before 1600.

As dry fishing increased in popularity the French also sought bases in Newfoundland, and in 1635 they were granted permission by the King of England to dry their fish on shore in exchange for a duty of 5 per cent levied on the value of their catch. In 1662 Placentia, on the south coast of Newfoundland, was founded by the French as a fishing base. The site was fortified and settlement was encouraged. In 1675 the payment of duty was abolished by Charles II and Placentia's importance increased rapidly at a time when strong measures were being taken to curb the growth of the English settlements. The Placentia-based French fishery expanded faster than its English rivals and by the first decade of the eighteenth century the settlement had grown to over 300 inhabitants. The increasing importance of Placentia was implicit in its choice as the base for a strong military force which subsequently launched a number of attacks against the English settlements on the east coast of the Avalon Peninsula. In 1696, 1705 and 1708 St. John's was captured and destroyed by Placentia-based forces. In 1713, the French territories in Newfoundland were transferred to Britain, and France retained only fishing rights along the north shore of the island.

In the second half of the seventeenth century St. John's was clearly the largest and most important British settlement on the island, and by 1696 it contained about 350 of the island's 2,300 winter residents. There were only two other settlements of any size, Bonavista and Carbonear, and all estimates around this time confirmed the primary rank of St. John's, whose small population was clearly related to the enactment of the repressive laws against settlement.

After 1720 English fishermen increasingly favoured the Grand Banks, about one hundred miles east of St. John's, while the resources of the inshore fishing grounds were made available to the resident population. The increased activity on the Banks was of considerable benefit to St. John's, since fishing operations tended to concentrate at fewer and larger bases as a result. It was the nearest established centre to the Banks, and possessed the best harbour on the east coast of the Avalon Peninsula. As the resident fishing population increased, a commercial system emerged to finance its operations, and St. John's was transformed from a fishing station into a commercial capital whose merchants largely controlled the resident fishery through the granting of credit and the provision of supplies to the fishermen. In the outports (a term which is commonly applied to all settlements in Newfoundland outside St. John's) middlemen acted on behalf of the St. John's merchants in the distribution of supplies to the fishermen and in the collection of fish and oil as payment, frequently in accordance with prices determined by the merchants themselves.

Complementing its role within the island, St. John's was involved in a profitable external trade. Many English ships had by this time abandoned fishing, and instead concentrated on trade with the resident fishermen and fish merchants; St. John's was the centre of this trade. In addition, the St. John's merchants were involved in the illicit trade organized by New England merchants, whereby fish acquired in St. John's were traded to the French and Dutch colonies in the West Indies. According to the Navigation Acts such trade was illegal but merchants in St. John's, as in almost every port in the Atlantic region, carried on a very profitable contraband traffic.

Newfoundland's population began to grow steadily in the last decades of the eighteenth century and increased from about 12,000 in 1765 to 17,000 in 1792. By the 1790s the catch of the resident fishery had surpassed that of the visiting fishermen and the island's population grew at a correspondingly faster rate and had reached 26,500 by 1806 and 52,700 by 1816. It was patent by then that settlement in Newfoundland could neither be restrained nor uprooted and in the same year the first resident governor was appointed. In 1824 the island was recognized as a British colony and in 1832 representative government was granted to Newfoundland, whose population then numbered 59,300.

After 1763 St. John's continued to enlarge its control over almost every facet of the island's economy. In 1783 its population was estimated to be close to 3,000, or one-fifth of the island's population, and the number of its merchants engaged in the fishing trade had grown appreciably from perhaps half a dozen in 1763. In 1811 St. John's residents were for the first time permitted to own waterfront property, which had been formerly reserved for the use of summer fishermen; this was in recognition of the growth of the resident fishery and of the vital role which St. John's played in its preservation.

## The Prairies

The prairies were first brought into the European trading system when the Montreal-based French fur trade was extended into the region in the 1730s. Although the English had been operating from Hudson Bay since 1670 and had encouraged the Indians to trade furs at York Factory and other posts, their impact on the region was less than that of the French, who traded directly with the Indian tribes. The Hudson's Bay Company post at Cumberland House, established in 1774, was the first of their inland posts and was built in response to the increasing competition of the pedlars from Montreal. In the 1790s the competition between the Hudson's Bay Company and the North West Company intensified, and as a result most of the northwest was brought within the fur-trading system. The commercial organization of the territory by means of a dense network of trading posts was not accompanied by settlement, although a small amount of farming was undertaken in the vicinity of some of the posts.

In 1811 the Earl of Selkirk, a major shareholder in the Hudson's Bay Company, obtained a grant of 116,000 square miles for the establishment of an agricultural colony to be settled by impoverished Scottish crofters. The company regarded the colony as a fulfilment of its obligation to encourage settlement, a labour pool for its supply brigades, a source of provisions for the growing number of people stationed at its trading posts, and a convenient retirement centre for its employees. Officially, the North West Company disputed the right of the Hudson's Bay Company to grant title to the land, and sought to bring about the downfall of the colony, which was regarded as a possible threat to its trading activities.

The first Selkirk settlers, about one hundred in number, arrived in 1812 to found the Red River Colony. The settlement was established at Point Douglas (which later became part of the city of Winnipeg) about a mile north of the North West Company's Fort Gibraltar, which had been built in 1805 at the confluence of the Assiniboine and Red rivers. The colony did not prosper for the first few years and was a source of contention between the two fur companies. In 1816, in the "battle" of Seven Oaks, the governor and twenty-one colonists were killed by a group of Métis associated with the North West Company. In 1817 and 1819 the colony's crops were all but destroyed by frost and grasshopper plagues, and in 1826 disaster struck in the shape of the highest flood in Winnipeg's history; as a result of the flood the Hudson's Bay Company transferred its operations to a new site, Lower Fort Garry, twenty miles north of the confluence of the two rivers.

Despite the early setbacks the Red River colony grew; in 1831 there were 2,100 settlers, but still only 1,880 acres under cultivation. Agriculture was not, however, the sole occupation of the colonists, and a considerable amount of illegal trade in furs took place between the colony and several American companies. The Hudson's Bay Company had by this time recognized the vital role of the settlement in the fur trade and, in particular, the importance of its site at the confluence of the two rivers. In 1835 the company rebuilt the Fort Garry trading post at the junction of the rivers and in the following year repurchased all the rights of the colony from Selkirk's heirs. At this time the population of the colony was about 3,000. The main policies pursued by the company after this date were to contain agricultural expansion, to tie the colony more closely to the company

*Red River cart, circa 1874.*

both economically and politically, and to discourage the formation of ties with the United States.

The company was never able to control the illegal trade in furs, which increased considerably during the 1840s when Red River carts travelled regularly to St. Paul, Minnesota. In 1849 the company discontinued its attempts to restrict the trade in furs between the colonists and the American traders who operated from St. Paul, Pembina and other centres across the border. In that year the population of the colony numbered 5,400.

During the 1840s Fort Garry began to demonstrate the advantages which eventually earned it a dominant position in the western fur trade. In the 1830s the York boat, which was capable of handling larger and bulkier cargoes than the canoe, was the principal means of transportation in the west but was restricted to the major rivers leading to York Factory on Hudson Bay. The growing bulkiness of goods and the hazards of boat travel prompted the use of carts and land transportation. The Red River carts quickly came into their own during the 1840s and cart brigades left Fort Garry for points as

Courtesy Glenbow-Alberta Institute

*Klondikers with York boat on the Peace River, circa 1899.*

far away as Fort Carlton and Fort Edmonton. Fort Garry's importance increased after 1859, when the first steamboat went into
service on the Red River; a short portage was the only barrier
between the Red and Mississippi rivers. In the 1860s St. Paul was
connected by rail to the Atlantic ports and henceforth the advantages
of Fort Garry as a communications centre considerably outweighed
those of York Factory. Even the Hudson's Bay Company had already begun to trade through St. Paul, and York Factory was
gradually abandoned. In 1872 the (U.S.) Northern Pacific Railway
reached Fargo on the Red River, thus providing a direct connection
between rail and steamboat services, and the Hudson Bay route was
completely abandoned as a result.

In 1870 Rupert's Land was transferred to Canada and in the same
year Manitoba became a province. A large proportion of the
province's 12,000 people lived within the area which is now the city
of Winnipeg. Winnipeg Parish had 241 inhabitants in 1870 but the
population contained within the modern city of Winnipeg was 2,950
or 24 per cent of the provincial total. The city's trading links were at
this time almost exclusively with the United States, but its commercial development was hampered by the monopoly control of the
Hudson's Bay Company.

## The Pacific Region

Although Captain Cook in 1778 and Captain Vancouver in 1792 had explored the Pacific coast by sea and Alexander Mackenzie had travelled overland to the coast in 1793, England had no immediate interest in exploiting the resources of the area. Initially, what little commerce existed was in the hands of New England merchants, who until 1800 dominated the small but profitable trade in sea-otter skins, which were sold in China. The English trading system was introduced to the region by Montreal's North West Company, which in 1805 began to pursue its policy of expanding the fur trade as far as the Pacific coast.

In 1813 the North West Company purchased Fort Astoria (renamed Fort George) and thus gained entry to the Pacific trade. The company's Pacific operations were never very successful, however, and, after the amalgamation of the two fur companies, the Hudson's Bay Company did not prosecute this trade on a very large scale.

In 1825 Fort George on the south bank of the Columbia River was abandoned in favour of Fort Vancouver on the north bank, and the British retreat from Oregon began; the Columbia River was proposed by Britain as the international boundary but this was not acceptable to the United States. As a result of the failure to resolve the deadlock between the two countries the Convention of 1818 had allowed the joint occupancy of the Pacific region by British and American citizens as a temporary measure, which was initially intended to last for ten years. During the early 1840s, when the American influx into the Columbia region was considerable, it became clear that the area would ultimately be annexed by the United States. The Hudson's Bay Company accordingly formulated plans to abandon Fort Vancouver in favour of a new site that could be expected to remain British after the resolution of the boundary question. In 1842 the company surveyed the south end of Vancouver Island and chose the site of Victoria, where Fort Camosun (later Fort Victoria) was erected in the following year—the first British settlement in the province of British Columbia. In 1846 the 49th parallel was chosen as the international boundary and Fort Victoria became the headquarters of the company's Pacific trade.

In order to maintain British control over the region, Vancouver Island was created a colony in 1849 and ceded to the Hudson's Bay Company on the condition that settlers be brought to the island. The mainland was not designated as the colony of British Columbia until 1859, when its establishment was precipitated by the gold rush of the previous year, following the discovery of placer gold on the lower Fraser River in 1856. The two colonies were united in 1866 as an economy measure, when declining revenues from gold mining increased the per capita public debt; the latter was considerably increased by the construction of the Cariboo road which ran from Yale, the terminus of steamboat navigation on the Fraser River, to Barkerville in the Cariboo country.

The union of the two colonies was not a final solution and the continued decline in population and gold mining rendered the public debt increasingly burdensome. There was an urgent need for integration into a larger economic system and the choice was either the United States or Canada. The economic links at this time were almost entirely with the United States, and after the completion in 1869 of the first transcontinental railroad (Union Pacific) to San Francisco, British Columbia became part of the American commercial empire. Victoria, the political and commercial capital of the province, was itself an outpost of San Francisco, from which it received the bulk of its imported goods on the regular steamship service which connected the two cities. In spite of this, agreement was reached with Canada in 1870 and in the following year British Columbia entered Confederation.

In 1870 the population of British Columbia was little more than 10,000 and only one settlement, Victoria, could by any stretch of the imagination be described as urban. Victoria, which had the advantage of being the first settlement in the province, benefited enormously from the gold rush to the mainland as well as from being designated capital of the united province in 1868. It was also the gateway or entrepôt for the external trade of the whole colony; the only adequate means of transportation in the region was by sea and the routes to Europe were via Cape Horn and San Francisco. Its location at the southern tip of the province made it the obvious choice for a trading centre. Goods were imported into Victoria and distributed to the many coastal settlements; and in turn their exports were assembled in the city before being transported elsewhere. Victoria had also become a regular port of call for ships sailing between England and the Orient via Cape Horn. In 1870 the city's population was 3,270 with a further 140 in the adjacent community of Esquimalt.

Apart from Victoria, urban or pre-urban settlements were to be found at New Westminster, Nanaimo, Yale and along Burrard Inlet. New Westminster had been founded in 1859 as the capital of the mainland colony and in the 1860s it became one of the principal centres of the lumber industry. Yale's growth dated from the Cariboo gold rush, when it functioned as a transshipment point between river and land transportation. By 1870 Burrard Inlet had become the centre of the sawmilling industry; in 1870 the town of Granville (later Vancouver) was laid out to the west of the mill at Hastings, while further up the inlet lay Moody's mill (now Port Moody). Commercial logging, which began along the east coast of Vancouver Island during the 1850s, was the principal commercial activity throughout the province; the most important markets in the pre-railway era were San Francisco, South America, Australia and the Orient. On Vancouver Island Nanaimo was the largest settlement outside Victoria, having been established in 1852 by the Hudson's Bay Company as a coal-mining centre.

# 7.

# Canadian Urban Development Since 1867

No "national" urban system existed at the time of Confederation; intercolonial trade was insignificant, as were inter-urban linkages. The nearest approach to an extensive urban system was found in Upper and Lower Canada; although politically separate between 1791 and 1841, the two provinces had remained united in a single economic system centred on the St. Lawrence. In the Atlantic region both geographical and political factors militated against the evolution of an integrated urban-economic system, although a number of large urban centres emerged in spite of this handicap. The size of an urban centre at this time was more or less a function of its local importance and the ranking of urban centres in British North America by population or any other index would therefore be misleading.

During the first few decades after Confederation efforts were made to create a viable national economic unit out of a transcontinental political union. In effect, it was intended to promote an east-west flow of trade in opposition to the strong, natural north-south flow; this was to be achieved by the construction of a transcontinental railway, the imposition of tariff barriers against imported manufactured goods, and the settlement of the west. All three strategies were integral parts of the National Policy, although this term is often restricted to the protective tariff structure which was imposed in 1879.

It may be said that a national economy has been achieved when the various regions of a country have developed complementary economies and when interregional exchanges have developed to a significant degree. At the time of Confederation the British North American colonies traded very little with each other, and shared a common orientation to Great Britain and the United States. Dependence on trade with the United States was especially important in the cases of Manitoba and British Columbia. A national or transcontinental economy was not achieved until the turn of the century, and a nationally integrated urban system was not established until about 1920.

## The National Policy

RAILWAYS

As a condition of union Nova Scotia and New Brunswick demanded that they be linked by railway to central Canada. The federal government's Intercolonial Railway was completed in 1876 from Rivière-du-Loup, the terminus of the Grand Trunk Railway, to Moncton and Truro, thus affording equal access to both Saint John and Halifax. For military reasons the Intercolonial was built as far from the U.S. border as possible, thus bypassing the St. John Valley, which would have afforded the most direct all-Canadian route and which was the most populous area of New Brunswick. Because of its circuitous route and the considerable construction costs, the Intercolonial was an unprofitable line from its inception and offered no serious competition to the Grand Trunk line which ran from Montreal to Portland.

The Pacific railway was the more ambitious undertaking. According to the terms of union in 1871, British Columbia was to be connected by rail to eastern Canada within ten years. The Canadian Pacific Railway was completed from Montreal to Vancouver in 1885, and five years later was extended to Saint John, partly by leasing already constructed lines. The completion of the transcontinental railway did not lead immediately to the settling of the west, and more than a decade elapsed before the hoped-for migration began.

After the initial influx of immigrants at the turn of the century, construction began on two more transcontinental railways, with the assistance of all levels of government. The first of these was the Canadian Northern which began in 1897 as a local line in Manitoba, and which was completed from Quebec to Vancouver in 1915. The third transcontinental railway was the Grand Trunk Pacific, which had agreed to construct a line from Prince Rupert to Winnipeg (completed in 1914) which would link up with the National Trans-continental Railway (completed in 1913) to be built by the federal government from Winnipeg to Quebec (later extended to Moncton). Both the Canadian Northern and the Grand Trunk Pacific subsequently ran into financial difficulties; they were taken over by the federal government between 1917 and 1923, and formed into the Canadian National Railways, which also included the National Transcontinental, the Grand Trunk and the Intercolonial railways.

The railway network was greatly expanded during the first fifty years after Confederation. From 2,278 miles in 1867 the railway mileage increased to 6,858 in 1880, to 13,151 in 1890 and to 17,657 in 1900. After the turn of the century railway construction increased rapidly, reaching a peak in the five years before the outbreak of the First World War. From 24,730 miles in 1910 the railway mileage had increased to 38,369 by 1917. Railway mileage in the prairie provinces alone accounted for about half of the national increase; from 4,000 miles in 1901 the prairie total grew to 6,000 in 1906, 8,000 in 1911 and 14,000 in 1916. Branch line construction was the main goal of prairie railway builders during the 1920s, and by 1929 the region's mileage had increased to 18,000.

TARIFFS

The first blatantly protectionist tariff system in Canada was imposed in 1879; unlike previous tariff structures it was a deliberate attempt to encourage domestic manufacturing production through the protection of the home market. As early as 1847, after the abandonment of the British mercantile system, the British North American colonies were permitted to set their own tariffs on imported goods and until 1859 the import tariffs in the Province of Canada (Ontario and Quebec) were designed mainly to produce revenue. In 1847 the tariff rate was 10 per cent, and this was subsequently increased to 12$^{1}/_{2}$ per cent in 1849 and to 15 per cent in 1856. The tariff of 1859 imposed a system of varying rates for the first time; the general rate on most products was raised to 20 per cent and on selected items rates of more than 20 per cent were applied (for example, 25 per cent on shoes). Although ostensibly for the production of revenue, the 1859 tariffs were intended to protect domestic industry, a policy which was frowned on by the British government. Officially the tariffs were regarded as offering "incidental protection"; in fact, the rates were far below those of the United States and were too low to be termed protectionist at all. In 1866 the Canadian tariffs were reduced to the lower levels prevailing in the Maritime provinces and at the time of Confederation their protectionist function was negligible.

The 1879 tariff structure (National Policy) was overtly protectionist. It was proposed that tariffs be used not only to produce government revenue but also to encourage the development of a domestic manufacturing industry through the creation of a sheltered home market for those products which could be manufactured in Canada at reasonable cost. Accordingly, a complex tariff system was drawn up after the Conservative victory in the 1878 federal election. The general rate on unspecified items was raised to 20 per cent, and on particular items rates were determined by the amount of protection required to ensure that domestic products could compete with imported goods. For existing industries such as shoemaking, rates were raised in order to maintain their competitive standing, while for potential industries such as primary iron production, rates were set at the level required to support the establishment of new plants. Despite the sharp increases, Canadian tariffs were still below those of the United States. The 1879 tariff system was not significantly altered until the 1930s when reciprocal preferential rates were given to Britain and other Commonwealth countries.

The impact of the 1879 tariff system was not immediately apparent, although it was undoubtedly one of the most important factors in the development of a modern manufacturing industry in central Canada at the end of the nineteenth century. The principal reason for its initial lack of success was the slow rate of settlement in the west before 1900, even after the completion of the transcontinental railway in 1885. The rate of population growth in Canada actually declined during the 1880s and 1890s, and failed to match the rate of natural increase (i.e., there was a net out-migration of people). Thus, despite the extensive efforts of the federal government, the period before 1895 was one of only minor achievement in the development and integration of the component regional economies.

WESTERN SETTLEMENT

In 1896 the vigorous immigration policy of the federal government for the first time coincided with circumstances which favoured the settlement of western Canada. A sharp rise in the price of wheat, a decline in ocean freight rates, and the exhaustion of the more accessible free land in the United States made Canada the natural outlet for settlers who would formerly have been lost to the United States. Part of the federal government's advertising campaign was actually aimed at the United States and as a result most of the first immigrants were Americans, many of whom were familiar with dry-farming techniques. Agriculture in the prairies was also encouraged by the Crow's Nest Pass agreement of 1897, which reduced the eastbound railway rates on wheat and flour destined for the head of navigation on Lake Superior. (In 1926 this reduction was extended to westbound grain shipments.) The first wave of settlement lasted from 1896 to 1914; during this period more than three million immigrants entered Canada, including a record 400,000 in 1913.

The production of wheat in the prairie provinces was the principal stimulus to the development of the Canadian economy between 1896 and 1930. The population of the prairie provinces increased from 420,000 in 1901 to 2,354,000 in 1931 or from 8 per cent to 23 per cent of the national total, and the area of occupied farm land in the prairies increased from 15.4 million acres to 109.7 million acres during the same period. From less than 5 per cent of the total value of Canadian exports at the turn of the century, wheat increased to 16 per cent in 1911 and by the end of the First World War it was the single most important export commodity. During the 1920s wheat generally accounted for more than one-quarter of total exports, peaking at about 40 per cent in 1928. Increasing wheat production was an important factor in development, both in the prairies and in Canada as a whole. The wheat boom encouraged a rapid extension of the railway network and together they functioned as the major supports of the Canadian economy in the decade before the First World War.

The production of wheat in the prairies stimulated the first important interregional movement of goods within Canada and was the basis for the economic integration of the various regions and colonies which had been politically united in Confederation. The out-movement of wheat from the prairies was matched by the in-movement of people, machinery, capital, consumer goods and building material. The National Policy, which was designed to forge a transcontinental economy and to create interregional interdependence or complementarity, was finally achieved, based mainly on the strength of wheat as an export staple. The enlarged and integrated Canadian economy made it possible for manufacturing firms to take advantage of scale economies in production and also to cater

TABLE 7.1 *Per cent of population urban,* * Canada and provinces, 1851-1971*

| | 1851 | 1861 | 1871 | 1881 | 1891 | 1901 | 1911 | 1921 | 1931 | 1941 | 1951 | 1961 | 1971 |
|---|---|---|---|---|---|---|---|---|---|---|---|---|---|
| Newfoundland | ... | ... | ... | ... | ... | ... | ... | ... | ... | ... | 43.3 | 50.7 | 57.2 |
| Prince Edward Island | — | 9.3 | 9.4 | 10.5 | 13.1 | 14.5 | 16.0 | 18.8 | 19.5 | 22.1 | 25.1 | 32.4 | 38.3 |
| Nova Scotia | 7.5 | 7.6 | 8.3 | 14.7 | 19.4 | 27.7 | 36.7 | 44.8 | 46.6 | 52.0 | 54.5 | 54.3 | 56.7 |
| New Brunswick | 14.0 | 13.1 | 17.6 | 17.6 | 19.9 | 23.1 | 26.7 | 35.2 | 35.4 | 38.7 | 42.8 | 46.5 | 56.9 |
| Quebec | 14.9 | 16.6 | 19.9 | 23.8 | 28.6 | 36.1 | 44.5 | 51.8 | 59.5 | 61.2 | 66.8 | 74.3 | 80.6 |
| Ontario | 14.0 | 18.5 | 20.6 | 27.1 | 35.0 | 40.3 | 49.5 | 58.8 | 63.1 | 67.5 | 72.5 | 77.3 | 82.4 |
| Manitoba | | | — | 14.9 | 23.3 | 24.9 | 39.3 | 41.5 | 45.2 | 45.7 | 56.0 | 63.9 | 69.5 |
| Saskatchewan | | | | | | 6.1 | 16.1 | 16.8 | 20.3 | 21.3 | 30.4 | 43.0 | 53.0 |
| Alberta | | | | | | 16.2 | 29.4 | 30.7 | 31.8 | 31.9 | 47.6 | 63.3 | 73.5 |
| British Columbia | — | | 9.0 | 18.3 | 42.6 | 46.4 | 50.9 | 50.9 | 62.3 | 64.0 | 68.6 | 72.6 | 75.7 |
| Canada (incl. Newfoundland) | ... | ... | ... | ... | ... | ... | ... | ... | ... | ... | 62.4 | 69.7 | 76.1 |
| Canada (excl. Newfoundland) | 13.1 | 15.8 | 18.3 | 23.3 | 29.8 | 34.9 | 41.8 | 47.4 | 52.5 | 55.7 | 62.9 | 70.2 | 76.6 |

SOURCE: L.O. Stone, *Urban Development in Canada;* and Census of Canada, 1971

*From 1851 to 1911 the urban population figures refer to incorporated cities, towns and villages of 1,000 and over only. From 1921 to 1951 the percentages are estimates of the percentages which would have been reported in the respective censuses had the 1961 census definition and procedures been used. For 1961 and 1971 the figures are those published in the respective censuses.

to the national market. This was particularly important in central Canada, where external economies (such as market accessibility, transportation advantages, and a diversified industrial base) contributed to the region's evolution as the industrial heartland. The financial and commercial firms of Toronto and Montreal also established branches in Winnipeg and other western cities, thus organizing, directing and integrating western development in a manner that complemented the established economic system of central Canada.

MANUFACTURING: 1870-1971

One of the most important goals of national economic policy was the development of a substantial domestic manufacturing industry. In 1870, when the first manufacturing census was taken, the principal industries were of a simple nature and consisted mainly of primary processing activities such as flour-milling, and traditional handicrafts such as shoemaking. In 1870 sawmilling, flour-milling, shoemaking and clothing manufacture accounted for almost half of the total value of manufactured goods. The iron and steel industry, which was also quite important, depended entirely on the importation of pig iron from the United States and Britain; the first blast furnace in Canada for the production of iron was not operational until 1895.

The period from 1870 to 1900 was one of steady, though unspectacular, expansion in manufacturing, during which the industry was characterized by increasing specialization in production at the level of the firm, a growth in the average size of firms, a diversification in terms of the variety of products, and the further localization or concentration of production in urban centres, particularly those in central Canada. During this period Ontario and Quebec increased their per capita share of national production while that of the Maritime provinces declined. The concentration of manufacturing in urban centres was one of the principal reasons for the rapid growth of the urban population, which increased from 18.3 per cent of the Canadian population in 1871 to 34.9 per cent in 1901.

After 1900, the settling of the west, the boom in railway construction, and the growth of the Canadian population greatly stimulated the manufacturing industry and confirmed its localization in the industrial heartland of Ontario-Quebec. The period from 1900 to 1910 was one of the most vigorous periods of industrial growth in

TABLE 7.2 *Interprovincial shipments of manufactured goods, 1967*

Destination (millions of dollars)

| Origin | Newfoundland | Prince Edward Island | Nova Scotia | New Brunswick | Quebec | Ontario | Manitoba | Saskatchewan | Alberta | British Columbia | Yukon and N.W.T. |
|---|---|---|---|---|---|---|---|---|---|---|---|
| Newfoundland | | — | 2.2 | 0.1 | * | 0.4 | — | * | * | * | * |
| Prince Edward Island | 2.3 | | 8.9 | 4.1 | * | 1.4 | — | * | * | — | — |
| Nova Scotia | 21.8 | 17.0 | | 42.5 | 59.1 | 46.2 | 6.2 | 2.3 | 7.4 | 6.0 | — |
| New Brunswick | 10.3 | 9.9 | 34.7 | | 49.1 | 72.0 | 4.2 | 1.5 | 2.8 | * | * |
| Quebec | 89.6 | 27.0 | 145.5 | 147.1 | | 2,098.2 | 180.8 | 113.0 | 201.0 | 281.7 | 5.0 |
| Ontario | 137.1 | 34.2 | 259.8 | 237.4 | 2,644.9 | | 502.7 | 342.9 | 620.7 | 747.4 | 20.6 |
| Manitoba | 3.4 | 0.6 | 7.3 | 5.6 | 53.1 | 149.2 | | 77.9 | 66.9 | 33.4 | 0.3 |
| Saskatchewan | 0.5 | 0.1 | 5.9 | 3.0 | 20.7 | 22.4 | 24.2 | | 22.0 | 7.3 | — |
| Alberta | 1.8 | 0.5 | 1.1 | 2.2 | 114.1 | 79.3 | 45.6 | 97.6 | | 158.7 | 13.0 |
| British Columbia | 4.4 | 1.2 | 8.3 | 5.0 | 63.5 | 121.4 | 50.4 | 52.9 | 163.1 | | 5.7 |

SOURCE: Dominion Bureau of Statistics, *Destination of Shipments of Manufacturers, 1967*

*confidential

—less than $100,000

Canadian history; the value of manufactured goods doubled from $556 million to $1,152 million. Of special note was the increasing number of large corporations and the decline of individual ownerships and partnerships. One of the most notable of the many industrial mergers of this period was that of the five Ontario and Quebec firms which combined to form the Steel Company of Canada, headquartered in Hamilton. Two of the fastest growing industries of this period were the transportation equipment and iron and steel industries, both of which were spurred by the railway boom.

The growth of the pulp and paper industry was particularly vigorous. The first mill to manufacture paper from wood was opened in Valleyfield, Quebec in 1866 but until the 1890s the industry grew slowly; in 1881 only five pulp mills were operating in Canada, but by 1891 the number had increased to twenty-four. After 1900 the industry grew rapidly; the development of hydroelectric power, the increased American market for newsprint which had been stimulated by the introduction of modern advertising, and the restrictions placed on the export of unprocessed wood by certain provinces, all contributed to its expansion. In 1891 British Columbia placed an embargo on the export of pulpwood cut from crown land in order to encourage the establishment of paper plants in the province; similar restrictions on the export of pulpwood were also imposed by Quebec in 1900 and by Ontario in 1902. The tremendous demand for newsprint in the United States led to the establishment of American pulp and paper plants in Canada, a trend which was accelerated after the removal of American duties on imported newsprint in 1909. As a result the pulp and paper industry enjoyed a period of sustained growth from 1910 to 1929.

Mineral discoveries in the Canadian Shield after 1900, the generation of hydro-electric power at Niagara Falls (1895) and at various sites on the Canadian Shield, the growth of pulp and paper exports to the United States, and the establishment of new industries such as automobiles and electrical products furthered the concentration of industry in central Canada, a trend which was consistent with the goals of the National Policy. The development of hydro-electric power was especially important, since the region had no coal resources. Southern Ontario benefited most because of its proximity to the American industrial heartland and particularly to the region west of the Appalachians, which had been rapidly developed since the 1870s. Accordingly, southern Ontario was able to capture the largest share of American capital and technology which were transferred to Canada in the form of branch plants after 1900. After the First World War the United States increasingly displaced the United Kingdom as a source of foreign capital and by 1922 it was the more important of the two. By 1920 the manufacturing industry had overtaken agriculture in terms of the value of production and Canada was on the point of becoming an industrial nation.

Since the First World War just over 80 per cent of the national manufacturing industry, in terms of both employment and value of production, has been accounted for by Ontario and Quebec, and in 1971 the nine metropolitan centres along the Quebec-Windsor industrial axis (Quebec, Montreal, Ottawa-Hull, Toronto, Hamilton, St. Catharines-Niagara, Kitchener, London and Windsor) together accounted for 55 per cent of the national manufacturing employment. One of the main reasons for the concentration and persistence of manufacturing in this region is the proximity of the American industrial heartland: in 1971 Ontario accounted for 49.1 per cent of the national manufacturing employment but for 58.2 per cent (1965-1968) of the foreign-owned firms in terms of taxable income, and for 61.7 per cent of foreign-owned plants established in Canada between 1961 and 1970.

The current interprovincial trade in manufactured goods exemplifies the success of the national tariff policy. In its trade with the rest of Canada, Ontario exported $5,550 million of manufactured goods in 1967 and imported only $2,590 million; the corresponding figures for Quebec were $3,290 million and $3,010 million. All the other provinces exported less than they imported. Table 7.2 illustrates the dominant position of Ontario in the interprovincial trade in manufactured goods.

Apart from the benefits derived from the high protectionist tariffs, the increasing importance of fully manufactured goods (i.e., end products) in Canadian exports has been to the advantage of the Quebec-Windsor industrial heartland. Between 1961 and 1971 end products increased as a proportion of Canadian exports from 12 per cent to 38 per cent, primarily as a result of expansion in the automobile industry, which is almost entirely concentrated in Ontario and Quebec. Correspondingly, there was a proportionate decline in the export of semi-manufactured goods and primary products.

*The National Urban System*

It was not until the 1920s that a truly national urban system emerged. Nearly all the good agricultural land was occupied by this time and a strong manufacturing industry had been established. The demand for urban services had expanded considerably and communicational advances had provided a means of integrating the widely scattered metropolitan centres. By 1921 47.4 per cent of the Canadian population lived in urban centres and by 1931 this had risen to 52.5 per cent. After the Second World War the rate of urbanization increased, and by 1971 76.1 per cent of the Canadian population was classified as urban (Table 7.1).

The reorganization of the Canadian economy into a metropolitan-dominated system was assisted by improved communications. After 1900 the telephone emerged as an important means of long-distance communications and its increasingly widespread use furthered the growth of both large individual business organizations and the urban centres which supported them. The concentration of head office functions in the largest urban centres encouraged the expansion of the national metropolitan centres, although all metropolitan areas were able to enlarge their spheres of influence to some extent and consequently began to emerge as the foci of more extensive economic systems. The growth of metropolitan economic regions was also promoted by the use of the automobile, which, although it had been introduced before the turn of the century, did not begin to play a significant role in inter-city transportation until around 1920. Canada's first highway, from Toronto to Hamilton, was opened in 1918, and in the following year the Canada Highway Act provided a per capita grant to each province for a program of highway construction. The number of motor vehicles registered in Canada rose from 9,000 in 1910 to 409,000 in 1920 and to 1,233,000 in 1930. Air transportation was of little significance prior to 1920 but its importance increased appreciably during the late 1920s and in the following decade. In 1937 the Trans-Canada Air Lines (now Air Canada) was formed as a crown corporation to provide a regular air service across the country. As with other advances in communications, air transportation enhanced the importance of the metropolitan centre, both within its own region and within the national economy.

Although metropolitanism has always been a formative force in Canadian urban history, metropolitan dominance has never been so pervasive as it is at present. Metropolitanism implies the focusing of extensive economic regions upon large urban centres which act as decision-making centres. The metropolis performs a clearing-house

TABLE 7.3 Rank of selected metropolitan areas (1971 limits) by size of population, 1921-1971*

| Rank | 1921 | 1931 | 1941 | 1951 | 1961 | 1971 |
|---|---|---|---|---|---|---|
| 1 | Montreal | Montreal | Montreal | Montreal | Montreal | Montreal |
| 2 | Toronto | Toronto | Toronto | Toronto | Toronto | Toronto |
| 3 | Vancouver | Vancouver | Vancouver | Vancouver | Vancouver | Vancouver |
| 4 | Winnipeg | Winnipeg | Winnipeg | Winnipeg | Winnipeg | Ottawa |
| 5 | Ottawa | Ottawa | Ottawa | Ottawa | Ottawa | Winnipeg |
| 6 | Quebec | Quebec | Quebec | Quebec | Hamilton | Hamilton |
| 7 | Hamilton | Hamilton | Hamilton | Hamilton | Quebec | *Edmonton* |
| 8 | Halifax | Windsor | Windsor | *Edmonton* | *Edmonton* | Quebec |
| 9 | London | London | *Edmonton* | Windsor | Calgary | Calgary |
| 10 | Windsor | Calgary | Halifax | London | London | London |
| 11 | Calgary | *Edmonton* | London | Calgary | Windsor | Windsor |
| 12 | *Edmonton* | Halifax | Calgary | Halifax | Halifax | Kitchener |
| 13 | Victoria | Kitchener | Kitchener | Victoria | Victoria | Halifax |
| 14 | *Saint John* | Victoria | Victoria | *Saint John* | Kitchener | Victoria |
| 15 | Kitchener | *Saint John* | *Saint John* | Sudbury | Sudbury | Sudbury |
| 16 | *Thunder Bay* | *Thunder Bay* | *Thunder Bay* | Sudbury | Regina | Regina |
| 17 | Regina | Regina | Regina | *Thunder Bay* | Thunder Bay | Saskatoon |
| 18 | Saskatoon | Saskatoon | Sudbury | Regina | *Saint John* | *Thunder Bay* |
| 19 | Sudbury | Sudbury | Saskatoon | Saskatoon | Saskatoon | *Saint John* |

SOURCE: Census of Canada (1921-1941) and Statistics Canada (1951-1971)
* From 1921 to 1941 the populations are in some cases estimated.

function for its region by acting as a forum for the regional viewpoint (e.g., through its newspapers), by organizing the regional economy through control over the allocation of resources (e.g., through its financial institutions and head offices), and by acting as an intermediary agent between its region and other metropolitan centres (e.g., through its superior communications facilities). In addition, the metropolitan centre is itself the site of a large proportion of the region's economic activities. In numerical terms Canada's twenty-two metropolitan centres (census metropolitan areas) accounted in 1971 for the larger part of almost every major index of economic importance; this was particularly evident in the manufacturing industry, where 66.2 per cent of national employment was located within these centres.

The metropolitan system is the principal spatial framework within which the modern Canadian economy operates, and growth can be expected to occur primarily within these centres and their regions. From 45.7 per cent in 1951 the twenty-two census metropolitan areas (1971 limits) increased their share of the Canadian population to 51.0 per cent by 1971. Between 1966 and 1971, the twenty-two metropolitan areas grew by 11.1 per cent compared to 3.9 per cent for the rest of Canada; together they accounted for 76.6 per cent of the total increase in the Canadian population. The growth of these centres has not, however, been even, and markedly different rates of change have been experienced. Such variations are accounted for by technological factors, by changes in the sectoral structure of the national economy, and by a variety of non-economic factors such as amenity considerations and cultural attractions. Discoveries of natural resources, such as oil in Alberta, have also had beneficial effects on particular centres. The appearance of stability in the metropolitan system is deceptive; between 1921 and 1971 only three centres, Montreal, Toronto and Vancouver, maintained their rank (as measured by population) among nineteen metropolitan areas (Table 7.3). In terms of percentage growth the variations among metropolitan centres have been particularly marked since 1951 (Table 1.3).

The metropolitan system, like all other urban systems, displays an hierarchical pattern. Only three centres, Montreal, Toronto and Vancouver, exercise a national influence and may be termed national metropolitan centres; although Vancouver functions in many respects as a national metropolis it is not quite as strong as its eastern counterparts. Below these there are about a dozen centres with essentially regional influences; of these, Winnipeg and Quebec once enjoyed a degree of metropolitan dominance over an extensive area when they performed a gateway function. A number of other metropolitan centres exercise a financial-commercial influence, the hallmark of a metropolis, over a very limited area and instead derive their status from the performance of lower-order or governmental functions; Victoria and Ottawa are the best examples but Hamilton may also be included in this category. Finally, many specialized urban centres have been designated as census metropolitan areas by virtue of their size (over 100,000 people) although they do not perform hinterland functions that are typically metropolitan; included in this group are the mining settlement of Sudbury and the specialized manufacturing centre of Chicoutimi-Jonquière which includes pulp and paper plants at Jonquière and the aluminum plant at Arvida.

Except for a few centres, the industrial structure of metropolitan areas is generally diversified, but they nevertheless exhibit recognizable functional specializations (Table 1.1). The most common differentiating characteristics are associated with heartland-periphery contrasts; in Canada the economic heartland lies along the Quebec-Windsor axis. The heartland metropolis is typically a production centre for the national market and often specializes in manufacturing (Montreal, Toronto, Kitchener, Hamilton, St. Catharines-Niagara, Windsor and London). The heartland also includes the national metropolis and the foremost financial centres. Metropolitan areas in the periphery generally act as regional centres and tend to specialize in transportation, trade and community services (e.g. the five prairie centres). Apart from the industrial specializations associated with the heartland-periphery division there are specialized metropolitan areas such as the mining community of Sudbury and the three government centres of Ottawa and (including defence functions) Victoria and Halifax.

TORONTO AND MONTREAL:
THE STRUGGLE FOR NATIONAL ECONOMIC LEADERSHIP

The most obvious characteristic of a national metropolis is its financial strength, and its essential function is the mobilization of capital: bringing together the capital resources of the country, reallocating these to the various regions, and acting as a centre for the international exchange of capital. Economic decisions which are made in the national metropolitan centres actuate impulses which permeate the national space economy and have differential impacts on the constituent regions. These vital decisions are made in the stock exchanges, the headquarters of large corporations, and the head offices of the financial houses.

The Canada Bank Act of 1871 was directly instrumental in concentrating economic power in a few national metropolitan centres. The Act adopted a branch-banking system (i.e., one where a few major banks each establish a number of branches) as used in Britain, in preference to the unit-banking system (i.e., one where each bank is independent) as employed in the United States. The branch-banking system encouraged the growth of fewer and larger banks and ultimately promoted a more centralized control over the spatial allocation of financial resources. The number of banks in Canada was reduced from fifty-one in 1875 to thirty-six in 1900 and thereafter a steady rate of amalgamation reduced the number to eleven by 1926, while the number of branches increased from 230 in 1874, to 708 in 1900 and to 3,840 in 1925. As the banks declined in number Montreal and Toronto increased their share of the national banking assets in terms of the location of head offices; by 1890 almost three-quarters of national banking assets were headquartered in the two cities.

By 1871 Toronto had emerged as a strong regional metropolis but still lacked the other accoutrements of mature metropolitan stature—manufacturing strength and financial power. After 1870 Toronto steadily improved its position vis-à-vis Montreal in manufacturing and by 1900 the differences between the two cities were relatively insignificant (Table 7.4). In finance, however, the gap was greater. Toronto's banking strength had been severely weakened by the collapse of the powerful Bank of Upper Canada in 1866 (partly related to the Canadian government's decision to transfer its account to the Bank of Montreal) and, despite the subsequent growth of its banks after 1870, by 1890 the city's banking assets were well below those of Montreal ($74.3 against $107.1 million). It was not until after 1900 that Toronto seriously threatened Montreal's metropolitan supremacy and it was only during the interwar period that the two centres emerged with approximately equal, though largely complementary, shares of the national market.

TABLE 7.4 *Employment and value of production in manufacturing, Montreal and Toronto, 1870-1920*

| Year | No. of employees | | Value of production ($'000) | |
|---|---|---|---|---|
| | Montreal | Toronto | Montreal | Toronto |
| 1870 | 22,955 | 9,400 | 35,935 | 13,686 |
| 1880 | 33,355 | 13,245 | 52,510 | 19,563 |
| 1890 | 38,135 | 26,242 | 67,654 | 44,964 |
| 1900 | 44,633 | 42,515 | 71,100 | 58,415 |
| 1910 | 67,841 | 65,274 | 166,297 | 154,307 |
| 1920 | 106,630 | 113,078 | 593,882 | 588,970 |

SOURCE: Census of Canada (1871, 1901 and 1911) and *Canada Year Book* 1922/23

One of the most useful indices of national metropolitan status is the presence of a strong stock exchange. The Toronto Stock Exchange was established in 1852 primarily as a grain or agricultural exchange and was incorporated in 1878; the Montreal Stock Exchange had been incorporated four years earlier in 1874. Two mining stock exchanges were started in Toronto in the 1890s and were merged in 1899 into the Standard Stock and Mining Exchange. It was because of the mining industry that Toronto was first able to achieve a degree of financial ascendancy over Montreal. The early involvement of Toronto interests in mining ventures in southeastern British Columbia, which dated from the mid-1890s, paid off at the turn of the century when several major mineral discoveries were made in northern Ontario: silver at Cobalt in 1903 and gold at Porcupine in 1911 and Kirkland Lake in 1912. These discoveries were made during the construction of the Temiskaming and Northern Ontario Railway (now the Ontario Northland Railway) fron. North Bay on the CPR's transcontinental line. The International Nickel Company was also formed at this time (1916) to develop the large nickel-copper ore deposits which had been discovered at Sudbury in 1883 during the construction of the CPR. Mining operations began in 1887 but the full exploitation of these resources awaited the development of a satisfactory process for separating the nickel from the copper. In the first decade of the twentieth century Ontario had become the most important province for mining and this helped to establish Toronto's subsequent dominance of the non-petroleum mining industry in Canada.

Whereas Montreal derived much of its importance from its position as the entrepôt for a national hinterland, Toronto's increasing prominence was based largely on the wealth of its regional hinterland, the richest commercial farming region in Canada. During the 1870s the Toronto region was developed more intensively; in agriculture, for example, there was a shift from wheat to mixed farming with a special emphasis on the production of beef and dairy products. South-central Ontario also developed rapidly as an industrial region, and by the end of the nineteenth century it constituted the single most important manufacturing area in Canada. On the basis of its strength as a regional service centre Toronto was able to extend its influence to much of the nation and by the time the west was being rapidly settled it was ready to challenge Montreal for economic sovereignty over this frontier also. Although Toronto had no direct link with a transcontinental railway until the Canadian Northern Railway (backed by Toronto interests) was completed in 1915, the city's commercial interests in the west were as strong as those of Montreal by the outbreak of the First World War.

It was in the field of finance that Toronto was best equipped to challenge Montreal for national economic leadership. Toronto's rise to financial preeminence dated from its involvement in the mining industry in the 1890s but it was not until the 1930s that it first achieved the ascendancy over Montreal. The general depression of the decade had a differential impact on the two centres. Toronto had the advantage of a richer, more diversified regional market for general financial-commercial services, and a more sustained demand for shares, especially gold, on its stock exchange. The value of cheques cashed (usually regarded as a general measure of financial strength) in Toronto exceeded the Montreal figure consistently during the 1930s and the gap has widened significantly since the Second World War (Figure 7.1). In the 1930s the value of shares on the Toronto Stock Exchange (amalgamated with the Standard Stock and Mining Exchange in 1934) exceeded for the first time the combined value of shares traded on the two Montreal exchanges (the Montreal Stock Exchange and the Canadian Stock Exchange which were merged in 1974 as the Montreal Stock Exchange). Although the exchanges of both cities were severely affected by the 1929 stock market collapse, the Toronto exchange was able to make a faster recovery because of its greater strength in mining shares. The Montreal exchanges never regained their former preeminence after the depression and the

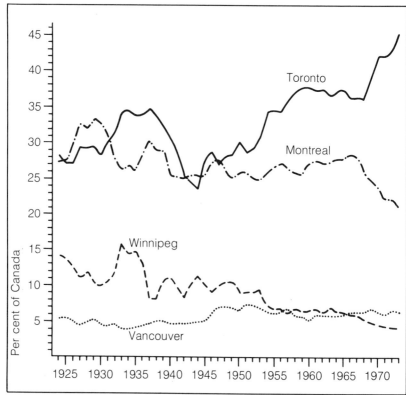

FIGURE 7.1 Relative importance (per cent of Canadian total) of the value of cheques cashed in the clearing centres of Montreal, Toronto, Winnipeg and Vancouver, 1924-1973.

*Source:* Statistics Canada, *Cheques Cashed in Clearing Centres* (various years).

Toronto Stock Exchange assumed an increasingly dominant position (Figures 7.2 and 7.3). Historically, Toronto's achievement of a primate position may be explained by the increasing amount of American investment in Canada; Montreal was the early focus of financial institutions because of its relationship to Britain, the principal source of foreign capital until the First World War. When the United States became the major source of investment (by the early 1920s) Toronto was the more natural funnel, since the Canadian

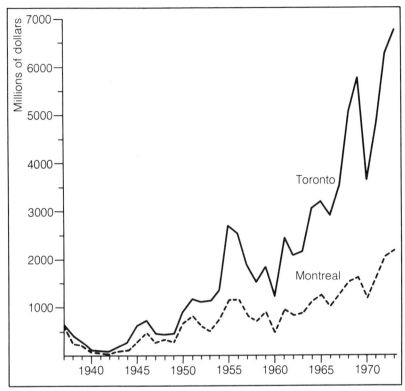

FIGURE 7.2   Value of stock exchange transactions, Montreal and Toronto Stock Exchanges, 1937-1973.

*Source:* Montreal and Toronto Stock Exchanges.

plants and head offices would thus be closer to their parent companies.

The two cities have recently entered a new phase in their continuing struggle for national economic leadership, and Montreal is definitely at a disadvantage. Montreal's relative decline may be seen from such diverse indices as the value of building permits (Table 7.5) and the destination of immigrants (Table 7.6). Since 1951 the population of Toronto has increased at a consistently faster rate than that of Montreal (Table 1.3), and if present trends continue it will be the

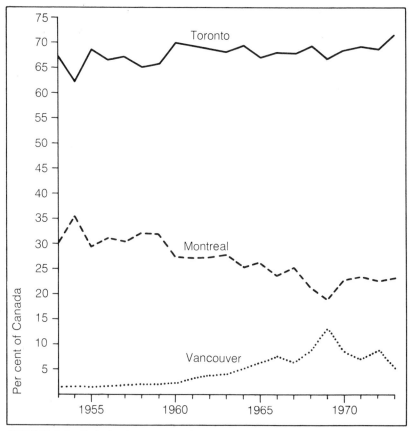

FIGURE 7.3   Relative importance (per cent of the Canadian total) of the value of transactions on the Montreal, Toronto and Vancouver Stock Exchanges, 1953-1973. (In 1953 the other two Canadian stock exchanges, Calgary and Winnipeg, together accounted for 1.5% of the national total; in every other year their combined transactions accounted for less than 1% and in 1973 for less than 0.1%.)

*Source:*   Montreal, Toronto, Winnipeg, Calgary and Vancouver Stock Exchanges.

larger of the two by 1980. Toronto is now dominant or imminently dominant according to almost every index of metropolitan stature. Its ascendancy is particularly evident from its growing importance as a head office for financial institutions, national retail firms, indus-

TABLE 7.5 *Building permits (valued in millions of dollars) issued in Toronto and Montreal metropolitan areas, 1966-1973*

|          | 1966  | 1967  | 1968  | 1969  | 1970  | 1971   | 1972   | 1973   |
|----------|-------|-------|-------|-------|-------|--------|--------|--------|
| Toronto  | 720.8 | 813.2 | 955.8 | 907.4 | 926.8 | 1141.4 | 1328.8 | 1924.6 |
| Montreal | 486.7 | 500.7 | 559.1 | 480.5 | 430.3 | 516.8  | 640.2  | 886.6  |

SOURCE: Statistics Canada, *Building Permits*

trial corporations, and other firms which are oriented to the national or international market (for example, Figure 7.4); moreover in 1973 the Toronto Stock Exchange accounted for 71.7 per cent of the national value of stock exchange transactions compared to 23.1 per cent for the combined Montreal exchanges. Even Montreal's traditional superiority in manufacturing was eroded during the 1960s and by 1971 its manufacturing work force was well below that of Toronto (297,000 against 334,000).

Toronto's ascendancy can be explained in part by the circumstances which have slowed Montreal's growth; recent advances in transportation technology, for example, have rarely benefited Montreal as much as other centres. The city's port traffic has remained relatively stable since the opening of the St. Lawrence Seaway in 1959; the latter's depth is 27 feet compared to the old 14-foot canal system, and Montreal has lost some of its traditional transshipment functions, since many ocean freighters now bypass the city and proceed as far inland as Lake Superior. The depth of the river channel below Montreal is only 35 feet, which is not much more than that of the Seaway and too shallow for a growing number of the large ships engaged in the transportation of bulk commodities such as petroleum, wheat and coal. Moreover, the expense involved in the provision of the specialized harbour facilities needed for the handling of containers and other cargo has encouraged their year-round use and ice-free ports have therefore been favoured. (Although winter navigation as far as Montreal has been possible since 1962, the amount of usage has been small because very few ships have ice-strengthened hulls.) The advantages of deep-water facilities for the handling of bulk commodities are reflected in the substantial growth of Port Cartier's and Baie Comeau's wheat exports, both of which now exceed those from Montreal, traditionally the most

TABLE 7.6 *Immigrants destined for major metropolitan centres, percentage of Canadian total, 1961-1973*

| Destination | 1961 % | 1962 % | 1963 % | 1964 % | 1965 % | 1966 % | 1967 % | 1968 % | 1969 % | 1970 % | 1971 % | 1972 % | 1973 % |
|---|---|---|---|---|---|---|---|---|---|---|---|---|---|
| Toronto | 26.2 | 26.2 | 30.0 | 31.3 | 30.0 | 30.3 | 29.7 | 29.2 | 28.4 | 30.2 | 29.4 | 28.8 | 34.9 |
| Montreal | 19.5 | 18.7 | 21.1 | 19.5 | 17.1 | 16.7 | 16.5 | 15.7 | 13.5 | 12.2 | 11.9 | 11.3 | 12.3 |
| Vancouver | 5.1 | 5.1 | 5.3 | 6.3 | 7.7 | 7.8 | 7.4 | 7.3 | 7.6 | 8.2 | 8.0 | 9.8 | 8.9 |
| Total | 50.8 | 50.0 | 56.4 | 57.1 | 54.8 | 54.8 | 53.6 | 52.2 | 49.5 | 50.6 | 49.3 | 49.9 | 56.1 |

SOURCE: Department of Manpower and Immigration

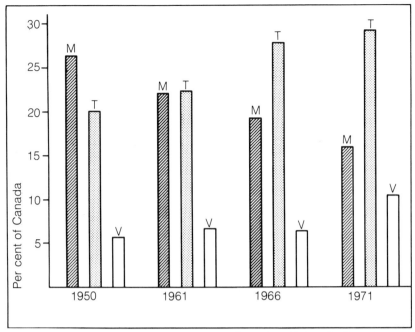

FIGURE 7.4   Percentage of major firms in Canada with head offices in Montreal (M), Toronto (T) and Vancouver (V), 1950–1971. The data are taken from the *Financial Post Survey of Industrials*; the survey includes only those companies in which there is a public investment interest, in either shares or debt securities.

*Source:* Financial Post *Survey of Industrials* (Toronto, annual).

important east coast port. In general the city's importance as a transshipment point for inland shipping has diminished, and at the same time it has failed to increase its maritime traffic.

Montreal's depreciated role in ocean transportation has adversely affected a variety of auxiliary industries: shipping services, manufacturing, wholesaling and others. As a result, it is beginning to exhibit the classic symptoms of a declining gateway city and may eventually replicate the history of Quebec, Kingston and Winnipeg. The recent unfavourable changes in the city's economic well-being have been difficult to measure, since they have coincided with political events that have brought into question the advisability of private investment in the province of Quebec, and in particular the location of head offices.

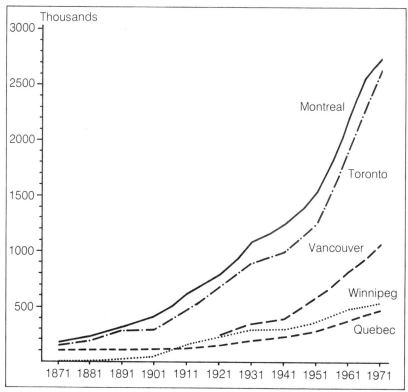

FIGURE 7.5   Population growth of the census metropolitan areas (1971 limits) of Quebec, Montreal, Toronto, Winnipeg and Vancouver, 1871–1971.

*Source: Census of Canada*, 1871 to 1971.

## Central Canada

At the time of Confederation the central provinces of Ontario and Quebec constituted Canada's dominant region in terms of population, economic wealth and political power. The area's commercial-industrial strength was derived in part from the influence of its major urban centres; in 1871 the three largest cities in Canada were Montreal (pop. 107,000), Quebec (60,000) and Toronto (56,000). The Maritime cities of Saint John and Halifax ranked next in terms of population, but neither possessed a hinterland which was large or rich enough to be used as a springboard to national economic significance. Political regulation of the economy (i.e., the National Policy) worked to the aggrandizement of the central Canadian metropolitan centres, in particular Montreal and Toronto (see Figure 7.5) where economic decision-making became increasingly concentrated.

Within the province of Quebec Montreal's ascendancy was unchallenged, and by 1921 its metropolitan population was more than five times that of Quebec (Figure 7.5). The difference in population reflected the changed roles of the two cities. Montreal had risen to a primate position in the national urban system while Quebec had retreated from the position of national significance which it had enjoyed during the pre-Confederation era to a purely provincial role. Montreal's superiority was most evident in finance, commerce and industry, the private sectors of the economy, while Quebec's strength was in government administration, education and a variety of institutional services. The divergent roles of the two cities were evidenced by the changes in their ethnic composition. At Confederation the French-English ratio was approximately the same for the two cities (49 per cent of the population in Montreal and 56 per cent in Quebec had been French in 1861), but in 1901 Quebec's population was predominantly French (83 per cent) while the corresponding proportion in Monteal (56 per cent) was much lower.

Between 1871 and 1921 the population of Quebec City increased by just under 60 per cent, a rate of growth which was exceeded by every major city in Canada with the exception of Saint John. Between 1871 (60,000) and 1891 (63,000) its growth was negligible as the city entered a transitional phase during which its government function, its timber and shipbuilding industries, and its port operations were severely reduced. The city's population was, however, stabilized by the growth of manufacturing, principally the production of shoes and clothes; its manufacturing employment grew from 7,250 in 1871 to 10,367 in 1891. In the following twenty years manufacturing employment declined, and other functions began to assume greater significance. After 1890 its transportation function revived as modern port facilities were completed. The first railway did not reach Quebec until 1879 and the city's growth was severely impaired by the delay. As a result of its improved railway access Quebec's port and wholesale functions began to grow, although they were far from rivalling those of Montreal. In 1905 the federal government began the construction of the National Transcontinental

TABLE 7.7 Urban population* by size group, Quebec and Ontario, 1881 and 1921

**1881**

| Population | Quebec | | | Ontario | | | Total | | |
|---|---|---|---|---|---|---|---|---|---|
| | No. of centres | Population | % | No of centres | Population | % | No. of centres | Population | % |
| 100,000 and over | 1 | 140,747 | 45.9 | — | — | — | 1 | 140,747 | 17.1 |
| 25,000–99,999 | 1 | 62,446 | 20.4 | 3 | 149,788 | 29.0 | 4 | 212,234 | 25.8 |
| 10,000–24,999 | — | — | — | 3 | 46,351 | 9.0 | 3 | 46,351 | 5.6 |
| 5,000–9,999 | 6 | 41,496 | 13.5 | 12 | 89,857 | 17.4 | 18 | 131,353 | 16.0 |
| 2,500–4,999 | 6 | 21,490 | 7.0 | 34 | 118,890 | 23.1 | 40 | 140,380 | 17.1 |
| 1,000–2,499 | 26 | 40,396 | 13.2 | 72 | 111,093 | 21.5 | 98 | 151,489 | 18.4 |
| Total urban | 40 | 306,575 | 100.0 | 124 | 515,979 | 100.0 | 164 | 822,554 | 100.0 |

**1921**

| Population | Quebec | | | Ontario | | | Total | | |
|---|---|---|---|---|---|---|---|---|---|
| | No. of centres | Population | % | No. of centres | Population | % | No of centres | Population | % |
| 100,000 and over | 1 | 618,506 | 51.4 | 3 | 743,887 | 45.6 | 4 | 1,362,393 | 48.1 |
| 25,000–99,999 | 2 | 120,194 | 10.0 | 3 | 128,990 | 7.9 | 5 | 249,184 | 8.8 |
| 10,000–24,999 | 9 | 148,199 | 12.3 | 19 | 304,342 | 18.7 | 28 | 452,541 | 15.9 |
| 5,000–9,999 | 13 | 96,169 | 8.0 | 21 | 142,411 | 8.7 | 34 | 238,580 | 8.4 |
| 2,500–4,999 | 26 | 88,137 | 7.3 | 48 | 169,120 | 10.4 | 74 | 257,257 | 9.1 |
| 1,000–2,499 | 83 | 132,493 | 11.0 | 93 | 142,050 | 8.7 | 176 | 274,543 | 9.7 |
| Total urban | 134 | 1,203,698 | 100.0 | 187 | 1,630,800 | 100.0 | 321 | 2,834,498 | 100.0 |

SOURCE: Census of Canada, 1881 and 1921.
*Incorporated centres with a population of 1000 or over.

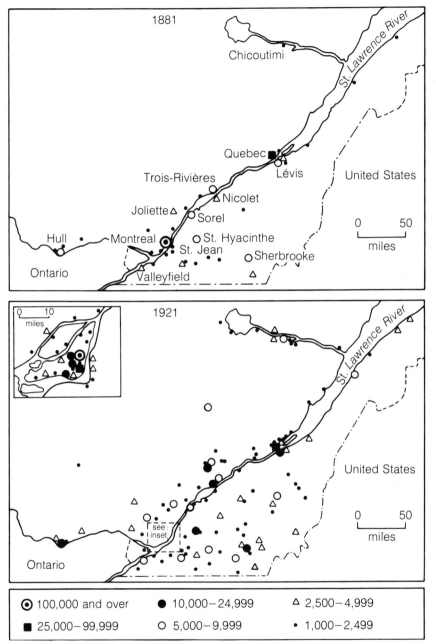

FIGURE 7.6 Distribution of urban centres, Quebec, 1881 and 1921

*Source*: *Census of Canada*, 1881 and 1921.

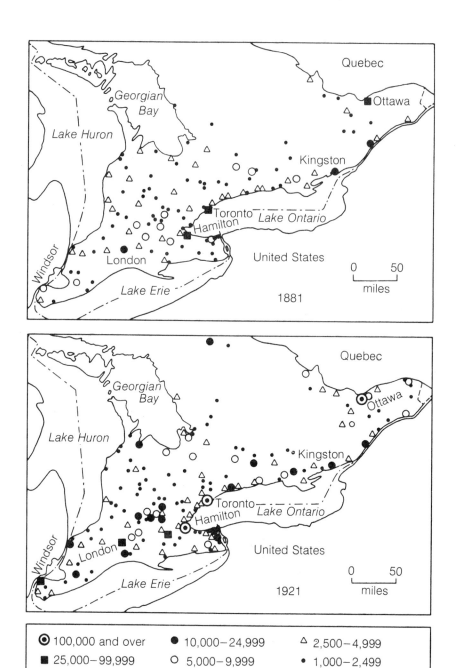

FIGURE 7.7  Distribution of urban centres, Ontario, 1881 and 1921.

Source: Census of Canada, 1881 and 1921.

Railway from Winnipeg through Quebec to Moncton; by 1913 the railway was completed and in 1917 the Maritime and western portions were joined by the Quebec Bridge over the St. Lawrence. The population of Quebec rose to 79,000 in 1911 and to 95,000 in 1921.

By 1921 51.8 per cent of the province of Quebec's population lived in urban centres (Table 7.1). Although 51 per cent of the urban population was accounted for by Montreal, the provincial urban system had become considerably more balanced in terms of both numerical size and spatial distribution; Montreal had increased its share of the urban population since 1851 (44 per cent) and 1881 (46 per cent) but the total number of urban centres had also increased, from 16 in 1851 to 40 in 1881 and to 134 by 1921, and a more normal distribution by class size had been achieved (Table 7.7). The greater geographical spread of urban centres (Figure 7.6) was, however, accompanied by a numerical concentration of the urban population in and around the cities of Montreal and Quebec; based on their 1971 Census Metropolitan Areas these two centres accounted for 41 per cent of the total provincial population in 1921.

Immediately following Confederation Toronto emerged as a full-fledged metropolis and the unrivalled primate centre in Ontario, and by 1921 the population of Toronto was more than four times that of Hamilton, the next largest centre. Its preeminence was especially evident in the import trade (the size of which is generally an indication of commercial importance), and by 1880 more than half the direct imports into Ontario were being channelled through Toronto. Manufacturing importance is also a valid measure of metropolitan stature, and in this sphere Toronto's growth was impressive. From 12 per cent of Ontario's manufacturing output in 1870, Toronto's share increased to 24 per cent in 1900 and to 29 per cent in 1920. The city's progress as a financial centre was slow in the first part of this period but accelerated after 1900.

Toronto had never been as dominant as Montreal within its own province and in 1921 it accounted for only 32 per cent of Ontario's urban population. In 1921 Ontario, with 58 per cent of its population living in urban centres, was Canada's most urbanized province and, compared to Quebec, its urban system was characterized by a larger number of centres and a more even distribution in terms of both spatial arrangement (Figure 7.7) and numerical size (Table 7.7). Although centres with less than 5,000 people showed the greatest

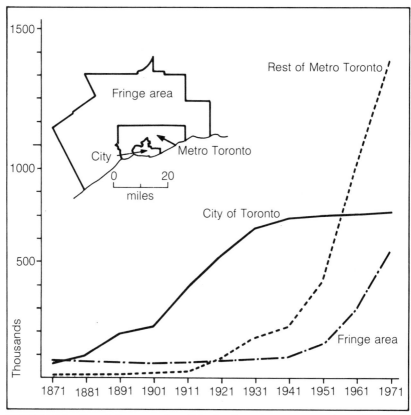

FIGURE 7.8 Population growth within the Toronto census metropolitan area (1971 limits), 1871–1971.

*Source: Census of Canada,* 1871 to 1971.

numerical increase (from 28 in 1851 to 141 in 1921) they decreased in importance as a percentage of the total urban population as a result of the localization of manufacturing and other functions in the largest cities.

Since 1921 the evolution of the central Canadian urban system, particularly in the southern regions of Quebec and Ontario, has been characterized by the numerical and spatial dominance of metropolitan centres. From Confederation until the First World War the movement of population within most of the present-day metropolitan areas in the region was generally centripetal; the major cities

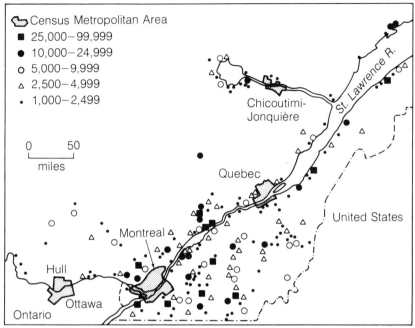

FIGURE 7.9   Distribution of urban centres, Quebec, 1971.

*Source: Census of Canada, 1971.*

absorbed large population increases while surrounding areas remained rural-oriented and often lost population. Primarily as a result of the construction of inter-city electric railways some decentralization began around 1900, but the horizontal spread of the metropolis was mainly due to the use of the automobile, the impact of which was not much felt before the First World War. The area which could be integrated into a single urban system was thus greatly expanded, while the construction of modern highways and freeways after the Second World War further encouraged the low-density spread of urbanization. The growth of population within the Toronto census metropolitan area (1971 limits) since 1871 is illustrative of a pattern characteristic of major metropolitan centres in central Canada (Figure 7.8). Between 1871 and 1911 the City of Toronto (37 square miles) absorbed the total net increase in the metropolitan area population and grew from 61,000 to 385,000; the population in the rest of Metro Toronto (204 square miles) increased modestly from 15,000 to

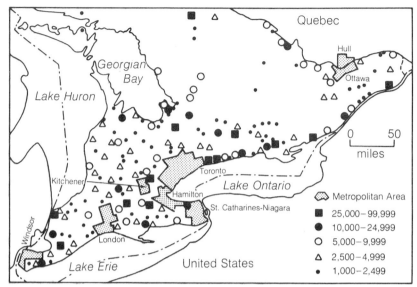

FIGURE 7.10   Distribution of urban centres, Ontario, 1971.

*Source: Census of Canada, 1971.*

25,000, while that of the fringe area (1,159 square miles) declined from 76,000 to 66,000. By 1921 large decennial increases in population were being experienced in the rest of Metro Toronto, and the post-Second World War period has been marked by a sharp acceleration in the rate of urbanization in the fringe area. The enormous horizontal spread of metropolitan centres is nowhere more evident in Canada than in the area commonly referred to as the Golden Horseshoe.

THE GOLDEN HORSESHOE

From Oshawa to Niagara Falls there is an almost continuously urbanized area which extends for 115 miles along the western shore of Lake Ontario, commonly referred to as the Golden Horseshoe. This region is the richest and most industrialized in Canada and is an excellent example of the modern trend towards a linear expansion of urbanized areas; where a number of metropolitan areas have merged (see, for example, Figure 7.10), the word megalopolis ("gigantic city") has been accepted as the appropriate technical term. Most such agglomerations have come about because of the historical concentration of urban centres along a transportation corridor; often a natural route such as a river, lake or coast. The automobile has also contributed directly to the megalopolitan phenomenon in two related ways: it has encouraged the horizontal spread of cities at very low densities and has thus caused formerly separate communities to coalesce and the use of trucks in both local and long-distance transportation has led to a fairly even spread of industries along inter-city highways in contrast to the former tendency to concentrate near railway terminals.

The Golden Horseshoe has the highest concentration of population in Canada. Included within the region are three metropolitan areas (as defined in the 1971 census): Toronto (population: 2,628,000 in 1971), Hamilton (499,000) and St. Catharines-Niagara (303,000); in addition the Oshawa-Whitby urban agglomeration contains 120,000 people. In 1971 the Golden Horseshoe included all but a small proportion of the following administrative divisions: the four counties of Ontario, Peel, Halton and Wentworth; Metro Toronto and the two regional municipalities of Niagara and York. The metropolitan areas of Toronto, Hamilton and St. Catharines-Niagara and the Oshawa-Whitby urban agglomeration together contained 3,550,000 people in 1971 or 97 per cent of the seven administrative divisions; moreover, 95.5 per cent of the region was classified as urban in 1971. In order to facilitate historical comparison the seven administrative divisions may therefore be considered synonymous with the present-day extent of the Golden Horseshoe (Figure 7.11).

In 1971, the Golden Horseshoe accounted for 47.4 per cent of Ontario's population and 16.9 per cent of Canada's. The dominant position of the region dates from the first decade of the twentieth century when the region experienced a period of accelerated growth in response to the rapid expansion of the Canadian manufacturing industry, and, with the exception of the 1930s, this faster-than-average rate of growth has persisted to the present day (Table 7.8).

The size of the consumer-industrial market of the Golden Horseshoe, the largest in Canada, is one of the most important reasons for the persistence and concentration of the manufacturing industry in the region, and in 1971, 30 per cent of the total value of goods manufactured in Canada was produced within the region. Within this area a diversified industrial base has developed, and a number of major industrial complexes have been established. Although there are a few specialized manufacturing centres within the region—for

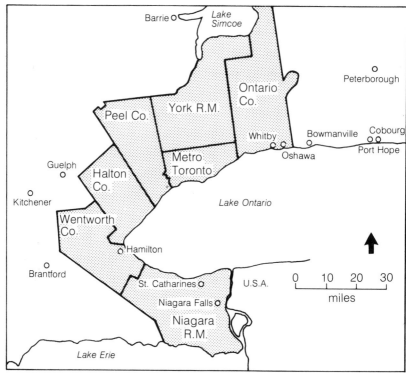

FIGURE 7.11   The delineation of the Golden Horseshoe, 1971.

example, Hamilton (steel) and Oshawa (automobiles)—its overall industrial structure is the most diversified in Canada. The Golden Horseshoe offers incomparable advantages in terms of scale and agglomeration economies; the size of the consumer-industrial market allows economies of scale, while specialization in production is facilitated by the ease with which inter-industry linkages can be established.

## The Maritime Provinces

Immediately following Confederation the Maritime provinces entered a period of economic depression which, while not related to their union with the central provinces, was nevertheless a foretaste of the region's long-term stagnation relative to central Canada. In the decades before 1867 the Maritimes had enjoyed unprecedented

TABLE 7.8 *Growth of population, Golden Horseshoe, 1871-1971*

| Year | Population | Decennial increase % | % of Ontario | % of Canada |
|------|-----------|---------------------|-------------|------------|
| 1871 | 323,387 | — | 19.9 | 8.8 |
| 1881 | 380,315 | 17.6 | 19.7 | 8.8 |
| 1891 | 475,043 | 24.9 | 22.5 | 9.8 |
| 1901 | 495,683 | 4.3 | 22.7 | 9.2 |
| 1911 | 718,848 | 45.0 | 28.4 | 10.0 |
| 1921 | 1,011,814 | 40.8 | 34.5 | 11.5 |
| 1931 | 1,298,285 | 28.3 | 37.8 | 12.5 |
| 1941 | 1,442,944 | 11.1 | 38.1 | 12.5 |
| 1951 | 1,842,068 | 27.7 | 40.1 | 13.1 |
| 1961 | 2,737,797 | 48.6 | 43.9 | 15.0 |
| 1971 | 3,647,425 | 33.2 | 47.4 | 16.9 |

SOURCE: Census of Canada

prosperity based on fishing, lumbering, shipbuilding and trade; this was the "golden age of wind, wood and water" or, as it has been alternatively phrased, "wooden ships and iron men." Within a decade of Confederation the shipbuilding industry had almost disappeared, the timber industry had collapsed, and the increasing use of steamships had sharply reduced the carrying-trade of the Maritime provinces, which only a decade before had had one of the largest shipping registries in the world. In 1867, for example, the Cunard Line's transatlantic service stopped calling at Halifax and did not resume until the boom in European immigration into Canada during the decade before the First World War. Only fishing continued to grow in importance.

The effects of economic integration with central Canada were generally negative for the Maritime provinces. National economic policies, such as the protectionist tariffs of 1879, largely favoured the commercial, manufacturing and financial interests of central Canada, reinforcing its position as the national heartland and relegating the peripheral regions to subordinate roles of primary production. The attempt to produce regional integration through the fostering of economic complementarity among the regions did not result in regional equality, and the economic stagnation of the Maritime provinces was evinced by the out-migration of people to central Canada and New England as well as by the persistence of the lowest per capita income rates in Canada. The Maritimes did not profit from the subsequent waves of immigration into Canada, and the region's population increased by only 16 per cent between 1881 and 1931 compared to a growth rate of 140 per cent for the national population.

Clearly, however, the effect of Confederation was only to exacerbate a decline which was caused principally by technological change. The Maritimes did not possess any significant natural resources except the sea, and the environment proved unresponsive to the new economic stimuli and the evolving industrial base of the national economy. Isolated as they were from the populated areas of central Canada the Maritime provinces receded into an economic backwater as the Canadian frontier pushed westward; they were increasingly excluded from maritime trade, and the dispersed nature of their meagre populations hampered the development of an industrial base. The distance of the Maritimes from central Canada and the lack of a natural hinterland frustrated the ambitions of Halifax and Saint John, which had hoped to develop viable roles as winter ports. Confederation did accelerate the decline of the region's economy, however, and has periodically been used as a scapegoat during periods of severe economic depression.

With the exception of shipbuilding and sawmilling, manufacturing had never been very important in the Maritimes but what there was declined rapidly after Confederation. In 1880 the region accounted for only 13.1 per cent of the gross value of Canadian manufactured products although it had 20.1 per cent of the national population. The high Canadian tariffs of 1879 encouraged the introduction of increased scales of production at the level of the plant and produced a sharp decline in the region's manufacturing industry. In line with the rest of the country many small industrial establishments went out of business, but they were not replaced by larger factories—as was the case in Ontario and Quebec. Consequently manufacturing employment in the Maritimes actually declined on a per capita basis as a result of the competition from the new, larger and more efficient establishments in central Canada. By 1920 the Maritime share of the national manufacturing industry by value of production was only 7.5 per cent. Perhaps the only major beneficiary of the national tariff policy was the Sydney iron and steel industry which developed in the late 1890s. The availability of local coal (first mined in 1732) and of iron ore deposits on Bell Island,

Newfoundland, as well as the protection afforded by the high tariffs encouraged the opening of an iron and steel plant at Sydney in 1901. (The plant is now owned by the government of Nova Scotia and is known as the Sydney Steel Corporation.)

The anticipated increase in trade as a result of improved communications between the Maritime ports and central Canada failed to materialize. Instead, the Intercolonial (1876), the Canadian Pacific (1890) and the National Transcontinental (1913) railways served only to bring the region more effectively under the dominance of the metropolitan centres of Ontario and Quebec. The federal government's attempts to stimulate the development of Halifax and Saint John as winter ports—for example, the subsidizing of a transatlantic mail service to Saint John in 1895—were half-hearted and generally unsuccessful, and as a result the region's economy became increasingly tributary to Montreal and Toronto.

The introduction of the iron steamship went some way towards maintaining the position of Halifax and Saint John as metropolitan centres because of the concentration of shipping in fewer ports. The more diversified economy of Halifax and its lesser dependence on lumbering and shipbuilding favoured it, rather than Saint John, as the regional metropolis. In 1871 Halifax was still smaller than Saint John but continued to grow slowly while the latter stagnated (Figure 7.12). The disastrous fire of 1877 which destroyed its business district was particularly damaging to Saint John since it coincided with an abrupt decline in the two principal supports of the city, shipbuilding and the timber trade. Many of the city's firms were bankrupted and not replaced, and since it lacked the stabilizing influence of government administration which was enjoyed by Halifax, its population declined slightly during the 1880s after which it remained relatively stable until the First World War.

Apart from Saint John, Moncton was the only centre in New Brunswick with more than 10,000 inhabitants in 1921. The latter grew rapidly after the completion of the Intercolonial Railway in 1876, and its population increased from 600 in 1871 to 5,032 in 1881 and to 9,026 in 1901. The completion of the National Transcontinental Railway enhanced the town's advantages as a distribution centre for the Maritimes and its population increased from 11,345 in 1911 to 17,488 in 1921. Fredericton, the next largest centre, continued to rely heavily on its role as the provincial capital and grew slowly from 6,006 in 1871 to 8,114 in 1921.

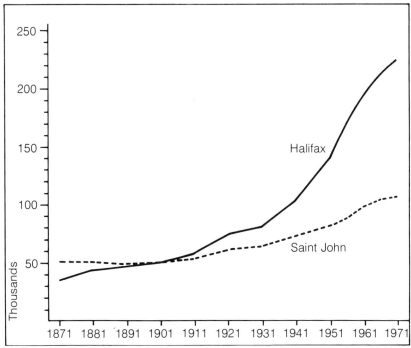

FIGURE 7.12    Population growth of Halifax and Saint John Census Metropolitan Areas (1971 limits), 1871-1971.

*Source: Census of Canada*, 1871 to 1971.

In Nova Scotia, the population of the Sydney urban region increased rapidly after 1890 in association with the growth of coal mining and the establishment of an iron and steel industry. The Sydney urban region (including Sydney Mines, North Sydney, Dominion, New Waterford and Glace Bay) grew from 7,400 in 1891 to 25,000 in 1901, to 50,000 in 1911 and to 63,000 in 1921. The largest of these settlements were Sydney, which grew from 2,427 to 22,545 between 1891 and 1921, and Glace Bay, which grew from 2,459 to 17,007 in the same period.

In Prince Edward Island, Charlottetown maintained its preeminence but it, too, felt the effects of the slow growth of its provincial economy. The population of the island increased from 94,000 in 1871 to 109,000 in 1881, and Charlottetown grew from 7,872 to 10,345. The provincial population remained at 109,000 in 1891 and

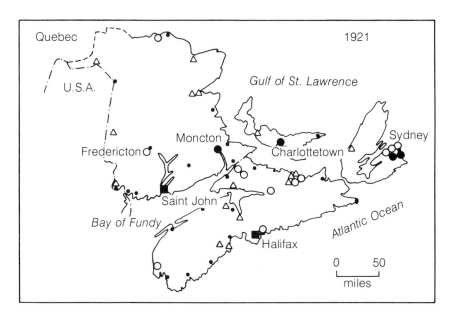

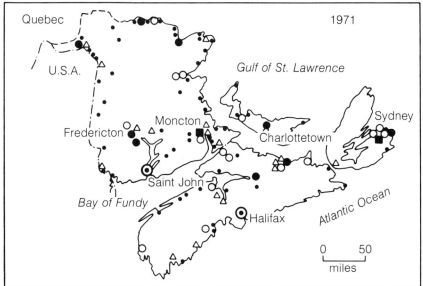

| ◉ 100,000 and over | ● 10,000−24,999 | △ 2,500−4,999 |
| ■ 25,000−99,999 | ○ 5,000−9,999 | • 1,000−2,499 |

FIGURE 7.13 Distribution of urban centres, Maritime Provinces, 1921 and 1971. (For 1971 the Halifax and Saint John populations are those of their census metropolitan areas.)

*Source*: *Census of Canada*, 1921 and 1971

TABLE 7.9 *Urban population* by size group, Maritime Provinces, 1921*

| Population | Nova Scotia | | New Brunswick | | Pr. Edward Island | | Total | | |
|---|---|---|---|---|---|---|---|---|---|
| | No. of centres | Population | No. of centres | Population | No. of centres | Population | No. of centres | Population | % |
| 100,00 and over | — | — | — | — | — | — | — | — | — |
| 25,000-99,999 | 1 | 58,372 | 1 | 47,166 | — | — | 2 | 105,538 | 29.6 |
| 10,000-24,999 | 2 | 39,552 | 1 | 17,488 | 1 | 12,347 | 4 | 69,387 | 19.5 |
| 5,000-9,999 | 10 | 73,026 | 2 | 13,684 | — | — | 12 | 86,710 | 24.3 |
| 2,500-4,999 | 9 | 28,340 | 6 | 22,207 | 1 | 3,228 | 16 | 53,775 | 15.1 |
| 1,000-2,499 | 13 | 20,362 | 12 | 19,647 | 1 | 1,094 | 26 | 41,103 | 11.5 |
| Total urban | 35 | 219,652 | 22 | 120,192 | 3 | 16,669 | 60 | 356,513 | 100.0 |

SOURCE: Census of Canada, 1921
*Incorporated centres with a population of 1,000 or over.

declined thereafter to 103,000 in 1901, to 94,000 in 1911 and to 89,000 in 1921. Charlottetown's growth was severely checked by migration from the province and its population declined to 10,098 by 1891 and to 9,883 by 1911, after which it rose again to 10,814 in 1921—only slightly larger than its size in 1881. Summerside, with 2,678 inhabitants in 1911 and 3,228 in 1921, was the only other urban area, and acted as a regional service centre for the western half of the island. Charlottetown and Summerside, with populations of 19,000 and 9,000 respectively in 1971, have remained the only urban centres of any significance.

By 1921 all the Maritime provinces had a lower proportion of their population in urban centres than the national average (Table 7.1); the largest centre (Halifax) had only 58,372 people, and metropolitan dominance was less evident in the region than anywhere else in Canada. No city exercised any significant degree of influence over the whole region; instead, the area was divided into a number of jurisdictions which were served by a variety of small to medium-sized cities while metropolitan functions, if available at all, were generally performed by central Canadian centres.

By and large the Atlantic provinces have not benefited greatly from the implementation of recent national policies nor from the operation of the free market within the older, politically-regulated national economic system. Distance from the central Canadian market has been one of the principal reasons for the Atlantic region's continued failure to capture a proportionate share of the national economy, and as a result it is characterized by slow-growth industries and high unemployment rates. Moreover, national transportation policies have worked largely to the disadvantage of the two Maritime ports of Saint John and Halifax; for example, the opening of the St. Lawrence Seaway in 1959 permitted ocean-going ships with a maximum draught of 27 feet to travel into the centre of the continent and adversely affected the entrepôt role of the Maritime ports. As winter ports they have been recently disadvantaged by the introduction in 1962 of an ice-breaker service designed to enable ice-strengthened ships to reach Montreal throughout the winter. The success of the service has been modest since the majority of ships do not have ice-strengthened hulls but the increase in the St. Lawrence activity has nevertheless been enough to deprive the Maritime ports of a substantial share of the winter traffic.

More recently, the increasing use of containerized shipping and larger ocean-going vessels have offered an opportunity for the two

Maritime cities to assume a significant share of the eastern Canadian port activity. Furthermore, the construction of deep-water facilities, such as Lorneville in Saint John, offer some promise of further growth in port activity by catering to super-tankers and other large ships. It is likely, however, that in the long run technological difficulties will be overcome in order to make St. Lawrence ports accessible to larger ships on a year-round basis; the completion of deep-water ports at Quebec, Port Cartier and Baie Comeau is only a beginning.

Saint John has continued to be handicapped by its political, institutional and cultural subservience to Fredericton, and its non-central location with respect to both its own provincial population and that of the Atlantic region. Its metropolitan functions within New Brunswick are in fact shared with Fredericton, the provincial capital, and with Moncton, the most important railway centre in the Maritimes. It was only in 1964, for example, that the University of New Brunswick in Saint John was established as a two-year institution; and the third year of a degree program must still be completed at Fredericton. Moncton has replaced Saint John as a major wholesale-distribution centre for much of the province, and has established itself as the supply centre for Prince Edward Island, much of Nova Scotia and even for Newfoundland. In 1971 its population numbered 48,000 while its wholesale trade was almost equal to that of Saint John. In New Brunswick there were only five other centres with more than 10,000 people in 1971: Fredericton (24,254), Bathurst (16,674), Edmundston (12,365), Oromocto (11,427) and Campbellton (10,335). The Saint John metropolitan area had 106,744 people in 1971.

Since the Second World War Halifax has emerged as the regional metropolis for the Atlantic provinces. Increasingly the city has been selected as the headquarters for federal agencies operating in the Atlantic region, although its attraction as a regional centre for private organizations is less evident. Besides being the largest and most culturally advanced metropolitan centre in the Atlantic region, Halifax has benefited from its geographically central location by air with respect to the major centres in the region. It has no commercial competitors within Nova Scotia. The second largest urban concentration is actually the mining-industrial area of Sydney where the urbanized region had a population of 125,000 in 1971; Truro (pop.

13,000) was the only other centre with a population of more than 10,000.

## Newfoundland

In 1867 Newfoundland was in the midst of an economic depression which had begun in 1861 and which was particularly severe in St. John's, the chief mercantile city. The city's population had declined from 25,000 in 1857 to 22,500 in 1869, when the depression ended and the anti-Confederation party won a resounding victory. The province's subsequent prosperity was maintained for almost two decades and the population of St. John's grew to 24,000 in 1874 and to 32,000 in 1884. The 1880s saw a recurrence of the depression, this time worldwide; large numbers of people left Newfoundland and by 1891 the St. John's population had declined to 29,000.

St. John's experienced further setbacks during the 1890s. In 1892 the most disastrous fire in the city's history destroyed three-quarters of the built-up area, including the whole of the business section. Only a fraction of this loss was covered by insurance and there was much bankruptcy among the city's merchant houses. In 1894-95 the province experienced a financial crisis when its two St. John's-based banks, the Commercial and the Union, suspended payment; it was also during this period (1895) that a further unsuccessful effort was made to negotiate Newfoundland's entry into Canada. The financial crisis was partially solved at this time by the establishment of Canadian branch banks, led by the Bank of Nova Scotia and the Bank of Montreal. The trans-island railway, which was begun in 1881 and completed in 1896, had also run into difficulties when in 1898 a new and controversial contract was drawn up for the operation of the 540-mile line between St. John's and Port-aux-Basques. By 1900, however, the railway was operational. In 1901, the population of St. John's reached 29,594 —still over 2,000 below its size in 1884. Only 13.4 per cent of the total population of Newfoundland lived in the city in 1901 compared to 20.0 per cent in 1857.

The railway had given rise to the first inland communities in Newfoundland. The first settlement developed around a sawmill which was built in 1893 on the Exploits River shortly after the railway reached the area. The lumbering industry was the chief beneficiary of the trans-island railway as sawmills sprang up at several places along the line. By 1901 the timber industry, although still small, was second in importance to the fisheries. The greatest boost to the island's forestry industry, however, was the 1909 opening of the first pulp and paper plant at Grand Falls on the Exploits River. In 1921, Grand Falls had a population of 3,800 and was the third largest urban centre in Newfoundland.

Of the urban settlements existing in 1921 only St. John's, with 36,444 inhabitants, had more than 5,000 people. The urban population (that is, towns with more than 1,000 inhabitants) at this date formed 28 per cent of the colony's population compared to 47 per cent for Canada as a whole and 39 per cent for the Maritime provinces. Metropolitan St. John's had about 48,000 inhabitants and accounted for 19 per cent of Newfoundland's population. All of the remaining 18 urban settlements, with the exception of Grand Falls, were situated along the coast. No large centres were to be found on the northern and western coast from Cape St. John to Cape Ray, where French fishing rights (which were first granted in 1713) were not abrogated until 1904.

St. John's has steadily increased its dominance of the Newfoundland economy and in 1971 accounted for 131,814 (or 25.2 per cent) of the provincial population. Only two other urban areas had more than 10,000 people: Corner Brook (26,000), and Grand Falls-Windsor (14,000), the two pulp and paper centres. St. John's has maintained its traditional commercial importance within Newfoundland despite its location at the southeastern extremity of the island. Newfoundland's entry into Confederation in 1949 did not have the adverse effects on the city which its commercial element had feared. The city's economy has, in fact, been strengthened by the growing involvement of the senior governments in the provincial economy.

## The Prairie Provinces

In the prairies very little settlement had preceded the construction of the first transcontinental railway and in general the distribution of fur-trading posts did not markedly influence the subsequent urban pattern. Towns which grew from trading posts, such as Winnipeg, Edmonton and Portage La Prairie, were exceptions rather than the rule. Settlements grew up along the railway and major cities developed at divisional points where car-repair shops and other

FIGURE 7.14   The alphabetically named towns along the CNR, formerly the Grand Trunk Railway, in Saskatchewan. (The gaps in the diagram represent subsequently established towns which do not conform to the alphabetical pattern.)

*Source*:  R. Rees, "Small towns of Saskatchewan," *Landscape*, 18 (1969), 29-33.

maintenance facilities were located. A curious reminder of the critical influence of the railway on the spatial urban system is Saskatchewan's "alphabet line" (part of the original Grand Trunk Pacific), along which the settlements were named by the railway company in alphabetical order (Figure 7.14). By 1931 about 80 per cent of farmers in the wheat province of Saskatchewan lived within ten miles of a railway station.

When it built the first transcontinental railway the CPR favoured the establishment of towns on vacant sites, preferably on the odd-numbered sections of land to which the company was entitled. As a result, completely new towns were established in most cases (Moose Jaw, Regina and Brandon, for example) while in others, such as Calgary, the actual townsite was shifted away from the original nucleus to the CPR's land. In the case of Winnipeg it was originally intended to route the railway through Selkirk, about twenty miles to the north, but the company was induced to change its plan in 1881 when the city offered it a number of concessions, including free land for a station, a cash bonus of $200,000 and exemption from municipal taxation in perpetuity.

In 1891 there were only four settlements in the prairies with more than 1,000 inhabitants; Winnipeg (30,000), Calgary (4,000), Brandon (3,800) and Portage La Prairie (3,400). Winnipeg and Calgary had assumed the major metropolitan functions in the pre-1920 era and had benefited from their strategic locations at the extremities of the prairies—Winnipeg at the edge of the Canadian Shield and Calgary near the foothills of the Rocky Mountains. Calgary was founded as a North West Mounted Police fort in 1875 and became a CPR divisional point when the transcontinental railway reached the settlement in 1883.

Edmonton, Regina and Saskatoon had made little progress by 1890. Edmonton had been an important centre for the western fur trade, and the first post had been built on the site of the city in 1802. The city was on the original route of the transcontinental railway to the Pacific via the Yellowhead Pass but in 1881 it was decided to build the railway through Calgary and the Kicking Horse Pass. However, its isolation was somewhat ameliorated when in 1891 a branch line was completed from Calgary to the south bank of the Saskatchewan River at Edmonton, which at that time had a population of less than 1,000. No settlement had existed at the site of Regina prior to its selection in 1882 as the capital of the Northwest Territories. In the same year the CPR reached Regina and in the following year it became the headquarters of the North West Mounted Police. Its growth was restricted by the absence of a regional population and by the CPR's decision to locate its divisional point at Moose Jaw, forty miles to the west; by 1891 Regina's population was still less than 1,000. Saskatoon was founded in 1882 as a temperance colony and remained isolated until it was connected to Regina by a branch line in 1890. Its population at that time was probably less than a hundred.

Winnipeg was the only urban centre in the prairies prior to the construction of the Canadian Pacific Railway, and its size was entirely due to its transportation links with the United States. In 1876 the first export of wheat (860 bushels) from western Canada travelled by steamboat down the Red River, by rail to Duluth and thence to eastern Canada, and in 1878 the federal government built a railway line from Winnipeg to the United States border in order to connect with a through line to St. Paul. The completion of the CPR line from Fort William (now Thunder Bay) in 1883 strengthened Winnipeg's links with eastern Canada, and the southern route quickly fell into disuse. Because of its location at the eastern edge of the prairies (which enabled it to perform a gateway function), its initial advantage as an established urban centre, and its selection as a major railway divisional point, the city seemed destined for preeminence in the prairies, particularly since its advantages were reinforced by a blatantly discriminatory freight rate structure which made it cheaper to send goods from eastern Canada via Winnipeg than directly to other western cities. The city's transshipment function would have emerged without the aid of the discriminatory freight rates, but they undoubtedly strengthened its wholesale-warehouse functions. By 1914, when most of the rail privileges had been removed and Winnipeg no longer monopolized transshipment functions, its position as the prairie metropolis was already assured.

Although in the history of the prairie provinces the first decade of the twentieth century is associated with a massive immigration of farmers, the period was also one of rapid urbanization; the urban proportion of the prairie population increased from 19.3 per cent to 27.9 per cent between 1901 and 1911. Spectacular growth rates were experienced by the five largest cities. Since the principal objective of prairie agriculture was the production of wheat for export, a form of metropolitan organization characterized the urban system from the very beginning. In 1911, 20 per cent of the prairie population lived in the five principal cities and their contiguous suburbs; there were only six other centres with more than 5,000 inhabitants. Metropolitan Winnipeg, with 11.7 per cent of the total population of the prairie provinces, was unrivalled; at that time it was the third largest urban centre in Canada.

Each of the five major prairie cities experienced a real-estate boom between 1908 and 1913. Not only land speculators but municipalities were carried away by the feverish activity of the period. In 1913, at the peak of the boom, the Saskatoon Board of Trade advertised the city as displaying "a record of progress and development that has never yet been approached within the British Empire or throughout the entire world"; at that time it was expected that Saskatoon would have a population of 400,000 by 1940 and enough land was subdivided by 1913 to accommodate such a number. Equally unrealistic expectations were rife in the other cities, and in many cases municipal services, such as sewers, waterpipes and even street-car lines, were built well in advance of development; consequently, the burden of the public debt for such services was overwhelming when the forecasted developments failed to materialize.

TABLE 7.10 Urban population* by size group, Prairie Provinces, 1911-1931

## 1911

| Population | Manitoba No. of centres | Manitoba Population | Saskatchewan No. of centres | Saskatchewan Population | Alberta No. of centres | Alberta Population | Total 1911 No. of centres | Total 1911 Population | % |
|---|---|---|---|---|---|---|---|---|---|
| 100,000 and over | 1 | 136,035 | — | — | — | — | 1 | 136,035 | 36.7 |
| 25,000-99,999 | — | — | 1 | 30,213 | 1 | 43,704 | 2 | 73,917 | 20.0 |
| 10,000-24,999 | 1 | 13,839 | 2 | 25,827 | 1 | 24,900 | 4 | 64,566 | 17.4 |
| 5,000-9,999 | 2 | 13,375 | 1 | 6,254 | 3 | 19,237 | 6 | 38,866 | 10.5 |
| 2,500-4,999 | 2 | 5,792 | — | — | — | — | 2 | 5,792 | 1.5 |
| 1,000-2,499 | 9 | 12,210 | 10 | 17,208 | 15 | 22,095 | 34 | 51,513 | 13.9 |
| Total urban | 15 | 181,251 | 14 | 79,502 | 20 | 109,936 | 49 | 370,869 | 100.0 |

## 1931

| Population | Manitoba No. of centres | Manitoba Population | Saskatchewan No. of centres | Saskatchewan Population | Alberta No. of centres | Alberta Population | Total 1931 No. of centres | Total 1931 Population | % |
|---|---|---|---|---|---|---|---|---|---|
| 100,000 and over | 1 | 218,785 | — | — | — | — | 1 | 218,785 | 30.9 |
| 25,000-99,999 | — | — | 2 | 96,428 | 2 | 162,958 | 4 | 259,386 | 36.6 |
| 10,000-24,999 | 2 | 33,387 | 1 | 21,299 | 2 | 23,789 | 5 | 78,475 | 11.1 |
| 5,000-9,999 | 2 | 12,344 | 5 | 31,216 | — | — | 7 | 43,560 | 6.1 |
| 2,500-4,999 | 3 | 12,487 | 2 | 6,827 | — | — | 5 | 19,314 | 2.7 |
| 1,000-2,499 | 12 | 17,488 | 22 | 31,818 | 27 | 40,076 | 61 | 89,382 | 12.6 |
| Total urban | 20 | 294,491 | 32 | 187,588 | 31 | 226,823 | 83 | 708,902 | 100.0 |

SOURCE: Census of Canada, 1911 and 1931
*Incorporated centres with a population of 1,000 or over.

Most of the prairie cities actually declined in terms of population after 1914. For example, Edmonton's population of 72,500 in 1914 was not equalled again until 1929.

The collapse of the pre-1914 speculative boom led inevitably to financial difficulties for all municipalities and to the forfeiture of much land as a result of tax default. Initially the large public land holdings were a burden, since the city collected no taxes on the land (some of it serviced) and reasonable sales were often impossible. In the long run, however, cities such as Saskatoon, Calgary and Edmonton were able to use their land holdings to plan suburban growth after the Second World War in an orderly and efficient manner. The economic depression of the 1930s added substantially to these municipal land banks; in metropolitan Winnipeg, for example, the amount of tax-forfeited land in 1945 was equivalent to 87 per cent of the then developed urban area. Most of the prairie cities abandoned public land ownership after disposing of their tax-forfeited lands by the early 1950s, with the notable exception of Saskatoon, which retained a permanent bank of municipally-owned land.

The prairie provinces have never been as metropolitan-dominated as the rest of Canada (with the exception of the Atlantic provinces) and in 1971 the five metropolitan areas (Winnipeg, Saskatoon, Regina, Edmonton and Calgary) together accounted for only 48.2 per cent of the population. The proportion of the regional population concentrated in these five centres increased from 13 per cent in 1901 to 24 per cent in 1941, and increased rapidly after the Second World War to 41 per cent in 1961. The relatively low incidence of metropolitan dominance in the prairie provinces is a function of the structure of the regional economy and its role within the national economy. From the beginning the prairie provinces were relegated to a colonial status within the national economy—they were intended to be producers of primary products for sale on the competitive international market and were to purchase the bulk of their manufactured goods from the tariff-protected industries of central Canada. The region's dependence on primary production would have emerged naturally from the operation of the free market but had nevertheless been encouraged by the national economic policies with respect to tariffs and railway freight rates. The railway freight rate structure has been a source of considerable grievance in the prairie provinces; by rail it is cheaper, for example, to ship many products from central Canada to Calgary via Vancouver than direct. The persistence of a high concentration of industry in central Canada is to be expected because of the presence there of the largest consumer-industrial market; firms are therefore able to achieve scale economies that are unobtainable elsewhere in Canada. In addition, however, the maintenance of high tariffs, the periodic adjustments to the tariff structure, and specific trade agreements (such as the automobile trade pact with the United States) have favoured the continued growth of the central Canadian manufacturing industry, and little decentralization may be expected in the near future. The role of the prairie provinces within the national economy has encouraged its metropolitan centres to specialize in regional service functions (see Table 1.1).

As a result of changes in the freight rate structure and the growing importance of Vancouver, manufacturing replaced commerce as the chief economic *raison d'être* in Winnipeg during the inter-war years. This is not to underestimate the firm grip which the city exercised over the prairie provinces in the financial-commercial sphere; besides the Winnipeg Grain Exchange (1887), the Winnipeg Stock Exchange (1903) and the Canadian Wheat Board (1934), the city contained a wide variety of important financial and insurance companies. Winnipeg developed a diversified manufacturing industry with special emphases which were related to its regional role: the manufacture of railway equipment, the processing of agricultural produce (e.g., flour-milling and meat-packing), the production of a wide range of consumer goods such as clothing, and the manufacture of farm machinery. By the late 1930s Vancouver's manufacturing industry was larger than Winnipeg's but the latter had retained a more diversified structure, a characteristic which has persisted to the present day. In 1971 Winnipeg had the largest and most diversified manufacturing industry in the prairie provinces; despite the rapid growth of Edmonton and Calgary after 1950, Winnipeg's manufacturing employment has remained larger than the combined total for these two metropolitan areas.

Between 1921 and 1971 Winnipeg had one of the slowest growth rates among western Canadian cities. Between 1921 and 1941 its metropolitan population (based on the 1971 census definition) increased from 229,000 to 302,000. The city was particularly affected by the 1930s depression and grew by only 2 per cent between 1931 and 1941, the smallest increase of all Canadian metropolitan areas with the exception of Saskatoon, which declined slightly during the

TABLE 7.11 *Labour force engaged in wholesale trade, and finance, insurance and real estate per 10,000 population, Prairie Provinces and Canada, 1941-1971*

| | Wholesale Trade | | | | Finance, Insurance & Real Estate | | | |
|---|---|---|---|---|---|---|---|---|
| | 1941 | 1951 | 1961 | 1971 | 1941 | 1951 | 1961 | 1971 |
| Manitoba | 158 | 232 | 219 | 203 | 85 | 114 | 133 | 160 |
| Saskatchewan | 86 | 149 | 154 | 150 | 40 | 57 | 77 | 114 |
| Alberta | 110 | 194 | 206 | 187 | 50 | 85 | 110 | 155 |
| Prairie Provinces | 116 | 191 | 195 | 182 | 57 | 84 | 107 | 146 |
| Canada | 107 | 157 | 159 | 162 | 78 | 103 | 126 | 166 |

SOURCE: Census of Canada, 1961 (Bulletin SL-1) and 1971

same period. Between 1951 and 1971 Winnipeg's growth continued to be slow. In addition to the loss of its economic functions to other cities, Winnipeg has suffered from the slow growth of the Manitoba economy, on which the city has become increasingly dependent. The Winnipeg metropolitan population increased from 38 per cent of the Manitoba population in 1921 to 41 per cent in 1941, to 46 per cent in 1951, to 52 per cent in 1961 and to 55 per cent in 1971. In no other province does a single metropolitan area account for such a high proportion of its provincial population: Vancouver had 50 per cent of the British Columbia population and Montreal had 46 per cent of Quebec's in 1971.

During the inter-war period Edmonton and Calgary grew to moderate-sized communities and in 1941 had metropolitan populations of 120,000 and 95,000 respectively. Calgary had grown more quickly prior to the 1930s as a result of the initial advantage of being selected as a divisional point along the first transcontinental railway. Despite the fact that Edmonton was named as the provincial capital in 1905 and had been chosen as the site of the University of Alberta in 1906, Calgary continued to enjoy economic superiority in Alberta. Its choice in 1911 as the location for the CPR's major western Canadian repair shops, the discovery in 1914 of oil in Turner Valley, twenty-five miles southwest of the city, and the establishment of western Canada's first oil refinery in 1921 were important stimuli to

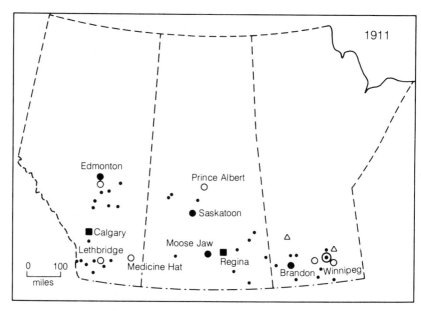

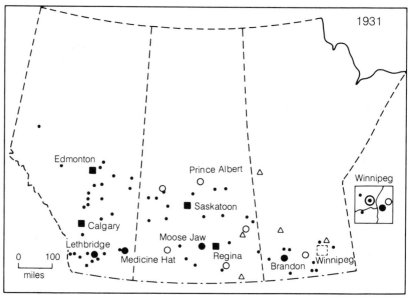

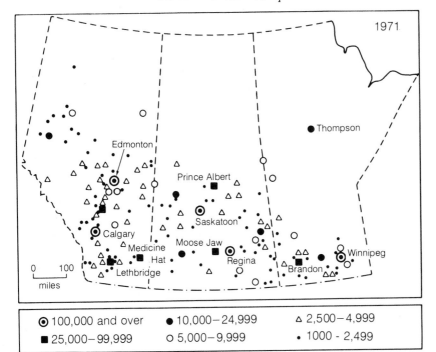

FIGURE 7.15   Distribution of urban centres, Prairie Provinces, 1911, 1931 and 1971. (For 1971 the five urban centres of over 100,000 represent the census metropolitan areas of Winnipeg, Regina, Saskatoon, Calgary and Edmonton.)

*Source: Census of Canada, 1911, 1931 and 1971.*

Calgary's growth, but the city remained dependent mainly on its transportation function and its role as a marketing, processing and distribution centre for the farming population of southern Alberta. During the 1930s Edmonton's growth was maintained by the stability of its governmental-institutional functions, its richer farming hinterland, and the growth of settlement in the Peace River country, while Calgary's population actually declined between 1931 and 1936.

Between 1921 and 1941 Saskatchewan had the largest total population but the smallest urban population of the three prairie provinces; in 1941 its two principal cities, Regina and Saskatoon, had only 58,000 and 43,000 inhabitants respectively. The single most important reason for the slow growth of both centres was their location within the effective sphere of influence of Winnipeg. Most of Saskatchewan was within overnight travelling distance, by truck or rail, of Winnipeg and with the available level of communications (telephone and telegraph) was well served by that city. The preeminence of Winnipeg in Saskatchewan is well illustrated by the per capita distribution of employment in wholesaling and finance in the prairie provinces (Table 7.11).

After the Second World War Edmonton, Calgary, Regina and Saskatoon experienced rates of growth that were well above the national average for metropolitan areas (Table 1.3). All four cities benefited from a strong rural-urban migration which was partly a result of the depressed urbanization rates between 1931 and 1941 but which was mainly due to the increasing size of farms and the growing popularity of "suitcase farming" (i.e., farmers who live in urban centres and commute to their farms). Calgary and Edmonton also benefited from the tremendous expansion of the Alberta economy as a result of the boom in oil and gas production after the Leduc oil discovery in 1947. In 1941 the latter two metropolitan areas accounted for 25 per cent of their provincial population; by 1971 this had increased to 55 per cent. In contrast Regina and Saskatoon together contained only 29 per cent of their provincial population in 1971. Both Saskatoon and Regina suffer from Saskatchewan's lack of economic diversification, and they experienced very low growth rates between 1966 and 1971. Indeed, Saskatoon's population actually declined between 1969 and 1971 as a result of a depression in the province's agricultural industry and a consequent population exodus which was matched only by that of the 1930's. By 1974, when the economic recession had ended. Saskatchewan's population had declined to an estimated 906,000—below the level of 1931.

Recently, the most significant changes in the prairie urban system have undoubtedly stemmed from the growth of the oil and gas industry in Alberta. Edmonton and Calgary have both gained from the resulting expansion of the provincial economy and have developed complementary roles in the petroleum industry. Calgary is the financial-management centre and contains the head offices of about half of the petroleum and related companies with head offices in Canada. Edmonton is the field-supply and refining centre for the petroleum industry; its oil refining operations have expanded considerably and in 1974 the city contained 29 per cent of the total crude refining capacity in western Canada. With the anticipated completion of Imperial Oil's 140,000-barrel-a-day refinery in Edmonton in 1975 and the scheduled phasing out of the company's existing refineries in Winnipeg, Regina and Calgary, Edmonton's share of western Canada's refinery capacity will be about 46 per cent.[1] As a by-product of oil refining Edmonton has developed one of the largest petro-chemical industrial complexes in Canada.

Despite their rapid growth in the twenty-five years since the Leduc discovery, Edmonton and Calgary have undergone little change in their industrial structure. The two cities have made little progress towards reduced dependence on regional resources; the processing of primary products and the performance of marketing-distribution functions for their regional hinterland have not diminished in proportionate importance. The growth of manufacturing employment in the two cities has recently been at a less-than-proportionate rate to the growth of their work force. Edmonton, which has benefited more from the growth of manufacturing, has attracted capital-intensive plants, particularly within the petro-chemical industry. Secondary manufacturing has continued to be of minor importance in both cities.

## British Columbia

Until the completion of the transcontinental railway British Columbia, and particularly Victoria, remained firmly within the economic orbit of San Francisco. When Vancouver was selected as the terminus of the CPR Victoria was rapidly supplanted as the commercial capital of the province. It had been originally intended that Esquimalt, adjacent to Victoria, would be the terminus of the railway, but in 1879 it was officially decided to abandon the route via Bute Inlet (where a bridge could be built to Vancouver Island) in favour of the Fraser Valley route, and this eliminated Esquimalt as the terminus of the railway. At that time the population of Victoria was already close to 6,000; in 1881 when New Westminster and

1 Information supplied by Business Development Department, City of Edmonton.

Nanaimo were the only other centres with more than 1,000 people in the province, Victoria was both an established port of call for steamships and the site of a naval dockyard (at Esquimalt) on which construction had begun in the 1870s.

Within two months of its selection as CPR terminus in 1886 Vancouver had grown from a settlement of only a few hundred people to a city of 2,000 inhabitants; even its complete destruction by fire at this time (June 1886) had little effect on its subsequent growth. In 1887 the first train arrived in Vancouver, and the first CPR ship arrived from Yokohama, exemplifying the city's function as the meeting place of transcontinental and trans-Pacific routes and the inevitability of its evolution as the commercial capital of the province. Vancouver's rapid growth testified to its future prosperity; by 1887 its population had reached 5,000, in 1891 it was 14,000 and in 1901 it had grown to 27,000, which made it the largest urban centre in the province. Victoria had been surpassed in terms of population during the 1890s, and in the following decade it was eclipsed in commerce, finance and industry, although it continued to grow in importance both as the provincial capital and as a naval centre. In 1921 Vancouver's population was 117,000 compared to Victoria's 39,000.

The coming of the railway did little to alter the character of the provincial economy, which remained almost entirely dependent on the exploitation of mineral, fish and forest resources. Coastal sawmills on Vancouver Island and Burrard Inlet continued to supply the pre-railway markets in the Pacific Rim countries, while inland mills were established in the 1890s to serve the growing prairie market. The lumber industry expanded considerably after 1900 as a result of the rapid settlement in the prairie provinces and the boom in railway construction. In the 1890s mining became important in southeastern British Columbia and gave rise to urban centres, which included Trail, Rossland, Nelson and Kimberley.

The dramatic growth of Vancouver after 1900 was in line with the boom in western Canadian cities, but in Vancouver's case there was the additional incentive of the Panama Canal (completed in 1914) which halved the distance to Europe by sea. As in most other western cities, the speculative bubble burst in 1913, but in the decade before the First World War the foundations for the city's rise to national metropolitan status were already laid. The freight rate

TABLE 7.12 *Wholesale trade (millions of dollars), western Canadian cities, 1930*

| Vancouver | Winnipeg | Calgary | Edmonton | Regina | Saskatoon | Victoria |
|-----------|----------|---------|----------|--------|-----------|----------|
| 78.4 | 72.9 | 30.5 | 24.7 | 17.6 | 17.3 | 8.1 |

SOURCE: Dominion Bureau of Statistics

structure which had discriminated in favour of Winnipeg was abolished and Vancouver was able to develop as the wholesale centre for British Columbia. In 1907 the Vancouver Stock Exchange was founded and became a vehicle for the city's control of the province's resource-based industries. By 1920 the city was on the threshold of national metropolitan stature.

By 1921 Vancouver had already overtaken Winnipeg in terms of population (231,000 against 229,000 based on the 1971 Census Metropolitan Area limit) and in the 1920s the latter was rapidly supplanted as the western Canadian metropolis. The impact of the Panama Canal was first felt around 1920 when ocean freight rates fell sharply as a result of the release of shipping tonnage at the end of the war. Consequently, Vancouver was able, for the first time, to compete with eastern Canadian ports in the exporting of prairie wheat. The first shipment of wheat to Europe via the Panama Canal was made in 1917 and regular shipments began in 1921. In 1926 Vancouver's competitive strength was increased by the extension of the low eastbound freight rates on wheat (Crow's Nest Pass Agreement, 1897) to westbound traffic, and by the end of the decade its wheat exports were already exceeding those of Montreal. The low ocean freight rates via the Panama Canal also caused the transcontinental rail rates to be reduced, thus increasing Vancouver's importance as a wholesale centre and by 1930 (excluding bulk commodities such as wheat) its wholesale trade was larger than Winnipeg's (Table 7.12). In many respects Vancouver had replaced Winnipeg as the gateway to the prairies; prior to 1914 practically all of western Canada's import-export trade was channelled through Winnipeg but by the 1920s Vancouver's competitive sphere of influence extended well into Saskatchewan. As a result Vancouver experienced a boom during the 1920s which was every bit as hectic as the one before the First World War; between 1921 and 1931 its metropolitan population increased by 50 per cent to 349,000.

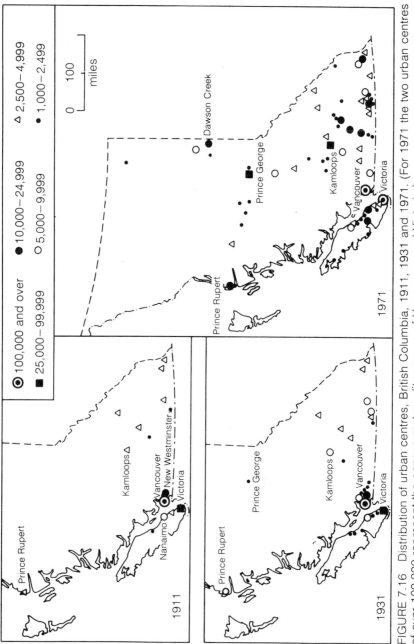

FIGURE 7.16 Distribution of urban centres, British Columbia, 1911, 1931 and 1971. (For 1971 the two urban centres of over 100,000 represent the census metropolitan areas of Vancouver and Victoria.)

Source: *Census of Canada*, 1911, 1931 and 1971.

TABLE 7.13 *Urban population\* by size group, British Columbia, 1911 and 1931*

| Population | 1911 | | | 1931 | | |
|---|---|---|---|---|---|---|
| | No. of centres | Population | % | No. of centres | Population | % |
| 100,000 and over | 1 | 100,401 | 50.2 | 1 | 246,593 | 64.0 |
| 25,000-99,999 | 1 | 31,660 | 15.8 | 1 | 39,082 | 10.1 |
| 10,000-24,999 | 1 | 13,199 | 6.6 | 1 | 17,524 | 4.6 |
| 5,000-9,999 | 2 | 16,502 | 8.3 | 6 | 41,337 | 10.7 |
| 2,500-4,999 | 9 | 30,477 | 15.3 | 6 | 19,975 | 5.2 |
| 1,000-2,499 | 5 | 7,594 | 3.8 | 12 | 20,652 | 5.4 |
| Total urban | 19 | 199,833 | 100.0 | 27 | 385,163 | 100.0 |

SOURCE: Census of Canada, 1911 and 1931
*Incorporated centres with a population of 1,000 or over.

The British Columbia economy continued to be metropolitan-dominated and the proportion of the provincial population in metropolitan Vancouver (1971 census definition) rose from 44.1 per cent in 1921 to 50.2 per cent in 1931; no other centre in Canada at that time enjoyed such a marked primacy within its own province as did Vancouver within British Columbia. In 1941 the Vancouver metropolitan area contained 410,000 people, while a further 85,000 lived in metropolitan Victoria; together the two metropolitan centres accounted for just over 60 per cent of the provincial population. In 1941, apart from these two metropolitan areas, there were no urban centres in the province with more than 10,000 people; the largest settlements were Trail (9,400), Prince Rupert (6,700), Nanaimo (6,600), Kamloops (6,000), Vernon (5,200) and Kelowna (5,100).

The functional roles performed by Vancouver and Victoria have become increasingly complementary; Vancouver is the decision-making centre for the private sphere of the economy while Victoria is the provincial government's legislative-executive centre. Victoria's growth since the First World War has been based on its functions as a government, tourist and retirement centre, while Vancouver is the headquarters of the province's financial and industrial corporations. It functions as the nerve centre for the provincial economy and increasingly as a supra-provincial or national decision-making centre. Although the city is not a head office centre for nationally oriented firms it is becoming an increasingly important centre for financial transactions, as exemplified by its importance as a head office location (Figure 7.4) and by the growth of the Vancouver Stock Exchange (Figure 7.3) which has greatly increased its share of the total value of national stock exchange transactions since 1960.

PART THREE
*Canadian Urban Prospects*

# 8.
# Urban Planning,
# Municipal Finance
# and Metropolitan Government

Current urban land use policy in Canada is by and large inadequate, and the achievement of an efficient and attractive environment will therefore depend very considerably on the continued reform of the institutional-governmental systems which largely direct the development of cities. In order that the public sector may intervene more intelligently in the process of urbanization it must be better informed about the functioning of the urban system. If public policy in the resolution of urban problems is to be effective, reform is particularly necessary in four main areas: the process of community goal-formulation must be improved through increased public participation in the planning process; the nature of public control over land use must be amended in order to conform more closely to the modern process of urbanization and to the current set of social values; the financial resources of municipalities must be expanded in order to match the growth of their functional responsibilities and to improve their effectiveness in dealing with urgent urban problems; and in metropolitan areas, the governmental system must be restructured if planning is to be effective.

## Urban Planning

Planning is an inescapable function of all urban governments; in most cities, for example, at least two-fifths of the land is public property, including roads, parks and schools. Although considerations of efficiency and utility are usually paramount in the provision of a wide range of public services, it is generally the case that such investments are (and should be) made in the light of their considerable influence on private development. The location of highways, subways and trunk sewers, for example, have long-term effects on the pattern of urban growth. Although public investments play a major part in shaping the direction and nature of urban development, they do not provide an adequate means of deriving the greatest communal benefits from the urbanization process, and a variety of direct public controls over private property are accordingly applied almost universally. In effect, the public regulation of urban development involves some interference with the operation of the private land market, and there are frequently compelling reasons for such action.

City planning is concerned with anticipating and regulating change in the physical environment in order to promote the orderly development of the city and to increase the social and economic benefits of urbanization. Cities exist essentially because of the advantages which spatial concentration affords to economic activities (producing, marketing and transferring goods) and to social interaction, whether between individuals or mediated by a variety of cultural institutions. These social and economic forces are in turn manifested in the physical organization of cities. The planner's concern with the physical elements of the city is therefore subordinate to the ultimate goal, which is the socio-economic well-being of the urban community. The aim of land use planning is to promote public welfare, and considerations of beauty, safety and health are therefore inseparable from the economic question of efficiency. Ultimately, the planner is concerned with people's happiness (for want of a better phrase, this is often called the "quality of life"), and it is his job to translate this intangible goal into physical form for the spiritual enrichment of the urban community.

Planning is an inexact science. It draws its theoretical knowledge from urban disciplines, including geography, economics, sociology and political science, but is itself a profession rather than a discipline. In the practice of planning, theoretical knowledge of the urban system must accommodate political expediency; the planner is as concerned with what can be done as he is with what should be done. This pragmatic and compromising approach derives from the inescapable link between planning and politics; planning decisions are political decisions and in a democracy must accordingly be made by politicians. It is also the result of the lack of knowledge concerning the urbanization process. The planner's partial knowledge of the intricate interdependencies which exist among urban activities makes it impossible for him to argue the case for what is "best"; it is more appropriate to promote that which is "better." In short, planning combines the weaknesses of social science theory with the pragmatism of politics. This is not to deny that planning has the potential to improve the urban environment but rather to point out its fundamental weakness. This is the reason for its acceptance *in principle* by almost everyone (according to their own conception of its aims) but the rejection *in practice* of almost every proposal by a substantial proportion of the community.

In keeping with his obligation to promote the well-being of people, it is the planner's job not only to adjust the physical urban environment in order to reflect the prevailing socio-economic values but also to propose new life styles. Because of the diversity of human life it is possible for the practice of planning to be seen on a total scale, covering every facet of cities, but by and large it is related to each country's culture, history and socio-economic development. In Canada there is some debate as to whether a planner's job is to be an effectuator or a visionary. As an effectuator the planner's primary responsibility is to introduce greater rationality into the urban land market through the dissemination of information, the detailing of the long-term strategy of public investment and the like. It is not his responsibility to alter the prevailing socio-economic system, and planning decisions are based more on what people would like to have than on what they ought to have. As a visionary, it is up to the planner to aim for better standards and to forward projects which would not otherwise be realized through the normal operation of the urban market. In practice, most planners adopt both principles but with a decided philosophical emphasis on one or the other. The debate on the role of planning has been focused on the question: is planning the art of the inevitable or the possible, or should market forces or ideology prevail in decision-making?

There are essentially four reasons for the public sector's involvement in the urban land market: to protect the public from the self-interest of private individuals (i.e., to maintain a balance between private gain and social cost in each development); to improve the working of the urban land market; to obtain socially desirable uses, such as parks, which cannot be adequately provided by the market; and to alter the balance between the social, economic and physical systems in order to achieve specified community objectives.

The presence of externalities is one of the principal reasons for the fact that market forces do not result in an optimal use of urban land, and it is, therefore, the major economic justification for government intervention in the market process. Urban uses are so closely located that they inevitably have negative or positive effects (externalities or spillovers) on neighbouring uses; the omnipresence of externalities accounts for the complex interdependency which prevails among urban activities. Even from the point of view of the private sector, the urban land market does not operate as efficiently as it might because of the presence of externalities, and one of the principal aims of planning is therefore to promote the optimal operation of the market.

There are two complementary ways in which public welfare may be increased through the control of externalities: by preventing developments where the private gain is less than the social loss (avoiding negative externalities) and by encouraging mutually beneficial uses to locate close together (harnessing positive externalities). A factory located in an established single-family residential area is likely to have negative effects on the neighbouring homes—a drop in house prices and a loss of amenity will probably result—and will create an unstable condition which will result in an out-movement of residents. If the gain resulting from the factory's presence (that is, its contribution to public welfare) is less than the combined losses of the affected homeowners, the location is sub-optimal and therefore contributes to a net loss of public welfare. Planning may therefore assist the private market in achieving its goal of maximizing the aggregate benefit to all property owners by prohibiting those uses which would cause neighbouring uses (where these are the "highest and best" uses) to depreciate in value. There are many other situations in urban areas where private and public benefits are not in equilibrium because of market imperfections; for example, the failure of individuals to maintain property standards commonly results in private gain being considerably less than the social or neighbourhood loss. By segregating incompatible uses it is possible for planning to avoid the social losses resulting from negative externalities. Government intervention may also perform the positive role of bringing together those uses which obtain maximum benefits by locating near each other.

In a perfect market, groupings of like or complementary uses would result naturally; but because of various defects the market never operates optimally and it is often possible to achieve a more efficient land use pattern through public control than through the unconstrained operation of the market. Imperfect knowledge, inertia, monopolistic competition and the like may lead to inefficiency or sub-optimality in the land use system. Private location decisions may, for example, be strongly conditioned by historical patterns rather than by considerations of optimal arrangements for the future. Where decisions are made in isolation by individuals (without certain knowledge of the locational preferences of others and without any one user having the ability to significantly influence the overall system) it is unlikely that the future land use pattern will deviate by much from the existing form, since location decisions tend to be incrementally cumulative rather than coordinated. Uncertainty of the future locations of other users (compatible and incompatible) may be as serious a limitation as imperfect knowledge of the optimal location. To the extent that planning can provide increased knowledge of and confidence in the future land use pattern, as expressed through official plans, zoning bylaws and the like, the probability of greater economic efficiency is enhanced. However, the urban system will not at any point in time necessarily conform to the optimal pattern, since the planner is unlikely to possess perfect knowledge of either present or future land use forces.

There are many urban goods which, because of scale economies or because non-paying consumers cannot be easily excluded, are best provided by the public sector. Highways, airports, sewage treatment plants, mass transit and electric generating stations are examples of goods which cannot ordinarily be supplied economically without public ownership or control. These public goods may be supplied to consumers at cost (user-charge), at a subsidized price, or free. In the case of any urban use for which a substantial proportion of its external benefits cannot be internalized and converted into profit, it is unlikely that a private entrepreneur will undertake its development. Most of these uses become public goods and are supplied to consumers at no cost; parks and other open spaces are examples of free urban goods.

Finally, public control of urban development is justified when the results of the market operation do not conform to community objectives. The role of the public sector is to maintain a balance among the various purposes for which cities exist; the achievement of maximum economic efficiency through the market may, for example, fail to coincide with a socially desirable allocation of resources. The importance of non-economic goals in planning is evident from the wording of most provincial planning acts, which empower municipalities to prepare programs, as in Ontario, "to secure the health, safety, convenience or welfare of the inhabitants of the area." In the process of promoting public welfare it is common for social goods to be augmented at the expense of economic goods; for example, by requiring 5 per cent of a residential subdivision to be allocated without charge as a public park a municipality raises the price of housing (an economic loss) while increasing the amount of open space (a social gain). Since the market's principal aim is economic efficiency, to the almost complete exclusion of non-economic considerations, it is commonly the case that any increase in social welfare will be accomplished by a decline in economic well-being. The choice between public and private transportation, for example, need not be based solely on economic arguments, but may include social preferences concerning such factors as atmospheric quality and noise tolerance.

PUBLIC PARTICIPATION

Growing public control over urban development has generated a need for some form of direct public participation in the planning process. In the early 1950s planning was essentially local and physical in nature; the house and the neighbourhood were the primary concerns. During the 1960s planning was expanded to include both metropolitan and regional forms, and began to involve all social science disciplines from the initial stage of goal formulation to the final implementation of plans. During this developmental process, Canadian planning moved away from its traditional emphasis on physical design (which accounted for the predominance of engineers and architects among early planners) to a more explicit concern with social goals and such intangibles as the quality of life. In essence, the planner has been asked to articulate community goals; as well as his traditional concern with the "how" of urban development, he is now being called upon to explain "why."

Citizens have in the past had opportunities to express their opinions in various referenda (for example, on money bylaws), but recently community input has been more direct and more closely linked to plan formulation. Calgary, Vancouver and Hamilton are among the first Canadian cities to recognize the direct involvement of the community in urban redevelopment. Of these, Hamilton's is the most advanced neighbourhood planning program; the city is divided into 114 neighbourhoods each of which is to have its own plan. In Toronto, on the other hand, local ratepayers associations have had to fight for a voice in the decision-making process; in 1971 their efforts resulted in the provincial government's cancellation of the partially completed Spadina Expressway and encouraged the reorientation of transportation planning in favour of public transit. The most prominent focus for public participation in Toronto is the Confederation of Resident and Ratepayer Associations (CORRA) which is an executive body representing thirty-six ratepayer groups. CORRA has been the vehicle for public participation in city-wide issues such as the $1-billion Metro Centre redevelopment, as well as local issues such as the rezoning of single-family housing areas for the development of apartments. In 1972 the community movement achieved a signal victory when "reform candidates" (those who were supported by neighbourhood associations) won a majority of seats on the Toronto city council.

One of the most important tasks in planning is the formulation of community goals. In a democracy political decisions must be acceptable to a majority of citizens, and one of the ways of ensuring this is through a process of consultation. It is therefore necessary for planners to seek the active cooperation of a wide spectrum of interests in the community when they are seeking to define the problems, expectations and aspirations which must be taken into account if the planning process is to be effective. It is especially important at the municipal level for citizens to be involved at every stage in the decision-making process. Higher levels of government are more likely to practise representative democracy (i.e., decisions are taken by representatives on behalf of but without consulting the people) than are municipal governments. There are two principal reasons for this. Municipal politicians are closer to the people because they each represent a smaller constituency; this is especially so in cases where municipal elections are based on the ward system. The second and more important reason is the local, territorial bias of municipal politics; practically all of its revenue (excluding grants from senior governments) is raised and spent within the municipality. Every decision made by a municipal council has direct repercussions on some or all of its citizens, and representative democracy is clearly inadequate for coping with such direct responsibilities.

Although essential in principle, public participation is bedevilled by problems in practice. Planning is commonly defined as the process of preparing programs for achieving approved objectives, and it is from its consequent inability to establish clear community goals that planning derives much of its characteristic fuzziness, vacillation and indecisiveness. Goal formulation is frustrated in part by the varying and conflicting interests of the many communities which exist within a city. It is the democratic responsibility of planning to protect minority rights in so far as these are consistent with public welfare, but in practice the protection of one usually works to the detriment of the other, and unfortunately there is often no scientific or objective way of resolving such legitimate conflicts of interest. Where consensus is not forthcoming and opposing views cannot be reconciled, compromise is essential and any decision made under these circumstances, based as it must be on value judgments, is contestable. Municipal politicians have accordingly been reluctant to involve the public directly in the decision-making process for fear of stirring up a hornet's nest over every issue. However, if an active program of public participation does not exist there is some danger that too much prominence may be given to the more vocal members of the community— ratepayers associations, developers and the like—who do not necessarily represent the views of the total or even the majority of the community. It remains the responsibility of the municipal council to protect the interests of those who do not involve themselves in public debate.

A further confounding problem in goal formulation is the difficulty of defining the appropriate community of interest in the case of a particular problem. There are essentially two dimensions to a community: its areal extent and its continuity over time. One of the paradoxes of urban planning is that it is concerned with the welfare of the future community yet its decisions are always subject to the approval of the existing community. This leads to a host of questions. Can the existing community be trusted to express unbiased judgments on the future directions of the community when, on the average, one household in five changes residence each year? Are the many conservative members of the community (including the poor and retired households whose incomes are relatively inflexible) sufficient in number to frustrate planning? Are people capable of understanding and expressing qualified opinions on the trade-off between present and future benefits? The territorial definition of a community is an equally difficult task, since the defined area is likely to influence the decision. For example, it is difficult to determine which community was the most involved in, and should therefore have decided upon, the fate of the now-cancelled Spadina Expressway in Toronto: the people in the northwestern suburbs which the expressway was principally designed to serve; the people in the path of the expressway, whose homes were either to be demolished or to be located within polluting range; or the people in Metro Toronto, who would derive some benefit from the completion of a network of expressways. It is unfortunately true that city-wide referenda frequently work to the disadvantage of minorities whose legitimate interests must therefore be protected by resolving the conflicting goals of the various communities involved, albeit in a less democratic manner.

The right of citizens to participate in the planning process is incontrovertible, but it is doubtful whether the present institutional system is capable of accommodating the degree of participation that is currently being demanded by various segments of the community. Traditionally, provinces have sought to provide for citizen input through the creation of a citizens advisory body called the planning board or planning commission. The board generally acts only in an advisory capacity to city council, and is normally given responsibility for the preliminary planning stages—survey, analysis and plan preparation. Although in some instances certain planning responsibilities are delegated to the board, the decision-making role is normally reserved for the municipal council.

In order to ensure that it is representative of the citizen body, the planning board's membership is to some extent controlled by the planning act, and in most provinces it is specified that municipal councillors may not constitute a majority on the board. Nevertheless, the board's political bias cannot be denied, since its members are nominated by the council and consist entirely of politicians, civic administrators and politician-appointed citizens. It is not possible to legislate the right people for membership and each municipal council chooses its own pot-pourri of local talents, such as specialists in some aspects of community planning, politically ambitious individuals and people with largely conservative views.

Broadly speaking, the planning board has been unable to accommodate direct public participation in the decision-making process; it has failed to represent the community's attitudes and aspirations and has often misinterpreted community goals as a result. The handful of "citizens" on the board cannot represent the many points of view in a community and the board has generally acted as a semi-political or semi-professional body. Because some members serve for many years, the board often takes the form of a standing commission and its policies become increasingly unresponsive to changes in community aspirations; semi-permanent members may become "professionalized" through their long association with planning principles, but nevertheless suffer from a lack of professional training and be technically incompetent to perform such duties.

There is a growing realization that plan formulation is an integral part of the political process and that it must be more closely associated with the municipal council, the decision-making authority. The adoption of a citizens advisory board was made at a time (1920s and 1930s) when the present complexity of city planning was not realized, and it was intended primarily as a protection against the abuse of political power. One solution is offered by the Ontario Planning Act which permits municipal councillors to constitute a majority of the members of the planning board, thus making it a committee of council. The citizens advisory function of the board may then be carried out by neighbourhood or ward working committees. In Ontario's newly created regional municipalities there is, for example, no provision for a citizens advisory board and the responsibility for plan preparation has been placed directly in the hands of the regional council. In Alberta, at least half the members of the planning commission of an incorporated city must be appointed officials of the city.

The growth of citizen activism in the late 1960s demonstrated above all else the increasing need for information as a prerequisite for meaningful and effective debate on major issues and planning principles. Planning, as a non-scientific profession, can ill-afford to work in secrecy. Planning decisions are always value judgments, often based on cost-benefit analysis which measures the costs in dollars but the benefits in social well-being. Further, planning should encourage innovation and the planner's primary responsibility should be to stimulate public debate through the articulation of alternative philosophies as well as through the publication of physical, social and economic analyses of the city.

Confrontations between municipal councils and citizen groups have often diverted attention from the true source of the problem: the absence or inadequacy of public policy formulation. One of the main sources of discontent is the non-partisan nature of city politics, which produces a fragmented policy-making system characterized by *ad hoc* decisions and susceptible to influences from private groups. A second problem is the lack of representation by wards in many cities. Both municipal party politics and ward-system representation are contentious issues; recent attempts to introduce party politics (excluding citizen organizations) into Canadian municipal elections have largely failed, but there is evidence of growing support for ward rather than city-wide elections to city council. Of note was the Ontario Municipal Board's decision in 1969 to order the City of Toronto to change its "strip" wards into "block" wards in order to represent community interests more adequately; this was a deliberate attempt to encourage citizen participation at an earlier stage in the decision-making process, and hopefully to avoid last-minute confrontations.

In the final analysis, public participation in city planning is subject to a fundamental limitation; citizen involvement is better suited to the protection of the *status quo* than to the task of directing change. The citizen is understandably concerned more about the local area and his own future than about the needs of the wider community. True neighbourhood planning works best when a community is trying to preserve something, not when it is trying to create something new; most "spontaneous" citizen groups (e.g., the many ratepayers associations) tend on the whole to represent the forces for preservation rather than for change. Unfortunately, fundamental changes are taking place in the social and economic systems of the modern city and it is consequently impracticable to maintain the *status quo* of much of the existing physical structure.

LAND USE CONTROLS

The public control of urban development consists of two successive stages: the adoption of an official plan (also known as a master plan or a general plan) and the exercise of regulatory powers. The official plan is a political document which formally states the community's goals and objectives, as well as detailing the planning policies which are designed to achieve them. The implementation of a municipality's official plan requires the exercise of legislative powers which are normally delegated by its province through a planning enabling act. Four principal methods are used by municipalities to regulate private land development: zoning, development control, subdivision control and building codes. A fifth method of control, which is normally employed by private developers, is the use of restrictive covenants.

The zoning bylaw is the method most commonly used to implement an official plan. So widespread is the use of zoning that in the mind of the public it represents planning; it is, however, essential to separate the two functions. Unlike the official plan, a zoning bylaw is a legal document, and it must specify precisely the uses which are permitted and prohibited within each of the districts or zones into which the municipality is divided for planning purposes. The official plan, on the other hand, designates only the general land use category for large areas of the city; for example, within an area designated as single-family housing in the official plan, there is frequently a neighbourhood shopping centre, a school, a park and a number of other uses which are permitted by the corresponding zoning bylaw.

Each landowner is entitled, according to the zoning enabling acts, to know precisely what he can do with his property. The zoning bylaw therefore, cannot allow any latitude in the interpretation of its regulations; for example, it is illegal to state that in a particular zone "any other use may be permitted with the approval of the municipality" since this would invest the municipality with discretionary power. Moreover, in order to avoid the abuse of power by municipal politicians and overt discrimination among individual landowners, provinces generally discourage the designation of very small zones (spot zoning) such as a typical building lot.

Traditionally, zoning bylaws have been concerned with the regulation of "the height, bulk and use of buildings, the use of land and the density of population." The bulk of a building is often expressed in terms of the floor area ratio (FAR) for high-density zones; the FAR is the ratio between the total floor area of the building and the lot it occupies. An FAR of 5, for example, would allow the construction of a

5-storey building which occupies 100 per cent of the lot or a 20-storey building which covers only 25 per cent of the lot. Generally similar is the floor space ratio (FSR) or floor space index (FSI) which refers to the net rather than the gross floor area (i.e., it excludes stairways, elevators and hallways).

Zoning is an indirect method of development control which suffers from two major defects; its emphasis on areal rather than individual control, and its inflexibility in the face of changes in the urban environment. Because of its areal emphasis and its stipulation of minimum/maximum standards for a variety of dimensions, the application of a zoning bylaw frequently produces a uniform and monotonous environment. Both because it is a legal document and because it establishes permitted uses in advance of applications for development, a zoning bylaw tends to be inflexible with regard to changes in the socio-economic system and is best suited to maintaining the *status quo*; consequently it is generally regarded as a tool for protecting property values rather than as a vehicle for effecting change. Its inability to guide development has led to the most serious and justified criticism of zoning; no planning document can remain unaltered over time, and changes in both social values and technology demand that community plans be periodically adjusted in order to accommodate the corresponding modifications to the physical environment. Zoning bylaws understandably incorporate the social values which prevail at the time of their formulation and tend therefore to perpetuate old land use patterns rather than to encourage new concepts and innovative development.

Development control (also known as direct development control) is a more flexible form of planning, since it permits each application for development to be judged on its own merits (for example, in terms of its contribution to public welfare) rather than on whether it conforms to a preconceived set of regulations. In short, it is a direct form of development control. Although guidelines or principles, often in the form of an official plan, are generally made available to the public, these are not legally binding on the municipality and therefore do not entitle the landowner to use his property in any specific way other than its existing use. The philosophical justification for development control is based on acceptance of the idea that all urban activities exist to serve the community, and an individual is not therefore entitled to use his land for any purpose which he desires, except at the discretion of the community. Although zoning may be justified in the same manner, development control differs from zoning in one fundamental way; the latter places a "development value" on the land before an application for development is made, while if the former is used the community reserves this privilege until a mutually acceptable agreement can be made with a developer.

Because of its discretionary nature development control has a number of drawbacks: it is open to abuse by the public officials responsible for its administration; the control procedure tends to be very time- consuming even for simple development applications and a fairly elaborate and expensive administrative structure is therefore required; and the changing philosophies of local politicians may result in gross inconsistencies which in turn hamper the development process. Despite these weaknesses there are many situations for which *ad hoc* development control is a superior method of land use regulation. In old urban areas which are undergoing redevelopment and in rural areas which are in the process of being urbanized, development control provides a flexible tool for the public control of future land use changes which cannot be predicted in detail and which cannot, therefore, be adequately incorporated into a zoning bylaw.

From a theoretical standpoint development control is superior to zoning as a means of directing urban development, but provincial governments have understandably been reluctant to grant such discretionary power to municipalities except on an interim basis prior to the adoption of an official plan. Alberta, Saskatchewan and Newfoundland are the three provinces which have permitted such development control procedures. In 1950 Alberta became the first province to allow development control and both Edmonton and Calgary have subsequently made extensive use of this type of control. In Edmonton, for example, about one-fifth of the city is under development control and, appropriately, these zones are mostly on the fringe of the built-up area, in the central area and in older strip-commercial areas (see Figure 8.1). In Ontario, where development control is not permitted by the Planning Act, there has recently been some progress towards the institution of such a method of control. The Niagara Escarpment Planning and Development Act, 1973 was the first to authorize the use of development control procedures within the province. The act allows the minister to designate any area of land within the Niagara Escarpment Planning

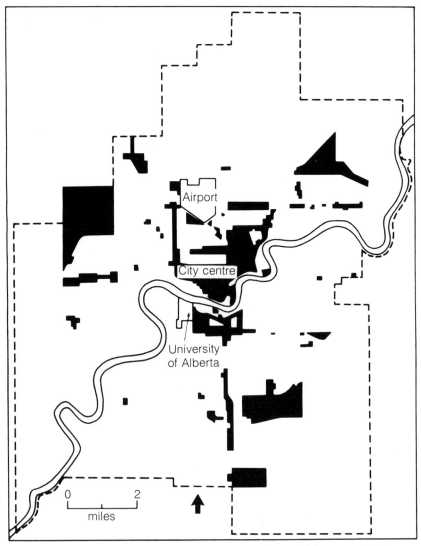

FIGURE 8.1   Areas under development control, City of Edmonton, 1974.

*Source*: Planning Department, City of Edmonton.

Area as a development control zone. This form of control will be used both during the preparation of the official plan and after its adoption. Within development control zones a permit will be required for each development proposal; permits will be obtained directly from the minister or from the appropriate body to which the authority is delegated. In provinces where such authority has not been legislated, municipalities have achieved approximate controls by employing a variety of zoning methods, including under-zoning land, freezing development by designating existing uses as the sole permitted uses, and deferral of the up-dating of zoning bylaws. None of these is entirely satisfactory but their growing use in Canada is indicative of the need for more direct control than is permitted by conventional zoning bylaws.

When land is deliberately zoned below its "highest and best" use (e.g., if an FSI of 2 is assigned to land in the central business district), it is frequently necessary for prospective developers to obtain rezoning permission, the terms of which are at the discretion of the municipality. In 1973, for example, the City of Toronto passed a zoning bylaw amendment (which is legally enforceable only after the approval of the Ontario Municipal Board) to restrict new downtown buildings to a height of 45 feet and a floor area of 40,000 square feet in an area where the existing zoning bylaw allowed an FSI of 12. The new bylaw amendments on height and density are so severe that they will in practice impose a freeze on downtown development, since it will generally not be economical to build within the legal restraints. The bylaw amendment is clearly designed to give the City complete control over all aspects of development, since a higher or larger building may be allowed only at the discretion of the city council. In effect, the City has attempted to institute development control procedures by means of a zoning bylaw. (In its application to the Ontario Municipal Board the City proposed that the *Restricted Area Bylaw* be approved as an interim measure for a two-year period until September 30, 1975. This would grant the City the power to review significant development proposals until the adoption of policies resulting from on-going planning studies of the central area.)

Most bonus schemes come into the under-zoning category and recently many Canadian cities have made extensive use of the bonus system, supplemented with rules and guidelines, in order to obtain a measure of direct development control over most high-density developments. Bonuses in the form of higher floor area ratios are used to encourage development standards which are above the minimum prescribed by zoning bylaws. Since the bonus criteria are not part of a zoning bylaw they may be changed from time to time without much difficulty. Moreover, the absence of the rigid set of land use regulations incorporated into each zoning bylaw permits the developer and the city to cooperate more closely on the design of developments. In general, bonuses are earned for the provision of on-site amenities, including the provision of open spaces around buildings, the placement of parking in underground or screened spaces, the orientation of buildings in particular ways in order to avoid "wind tunnels" and open spaces with only a northern exposure, and the integration of one development with neighbouring buildings through the inclusion of pedestrian walkways and the avoidance of shadows. In many downtown areas it is primarily through the bonus system that cities are hoping to remedy their lack of public open space, and the incorporation of plazas and mini-parks in private redevelopments is therefore one of the principal means of earning floor area bonuses. The under-zoning principle is also used to discourage the premature urbanization of rural land or to minimize the effects of such developments; a minimum lot size of forty acres may, for example, achieve both ends.

By zoning according to existing uses a municipality may obtain a measure of direct development control. This method of control, which normally takes the form of a restrictive zoning bylaw, was pioneered in London, Ontario. Under this system existing uses are zoned as permitted uses even when they do not conform to the official plan, and an amendment to the zoning bylaw is therefore required before any development proposal can be approved. In drafting a rezoning bylaw the municipal council has an opportunity to review the development proposal in terms of the particular merits of the scheme, its timing, its effect on surrounding uses and other planning considerations. When the zoning bylaw is subsequently amended to cover the proposed development, it is so worded with respect to building heights, building arrangements and other specifications that no other development scheme is legally permitted; consequently development control is built into the system, since any future changes (buildings or uses) will necessitate further amendments to the bylaw.

The restrictive zoning bylaw differs from conventional zoning in that it designates the precise uses permitted in each land use district or zoning category. Traditionally, zoning categories have been hierarchical or cumulative, based on the principle of intensity of land utilization; for example, a single-family house (a low-intensity use) may be built in an apartment district but an apartment (a high-intensity use) may not be built in a single-family housing district. This considerably reduces the possibility of controlling development effectively through the use of zoning bylaws since, as a result of cumulative zoning, most lower-intensity uses are generally over-zoned; problems frequently arise from the fact that commercial uses, such as shopping centres, are not only permitted in commercial districts but in industrial districts as well. Where it is intended to approximate direct development control the restrictive zoning bylaw frequently results in a proliferation of land use districts. In Peterborough, Ontario, the first restrictive zoning bylaw, adopted in 1972, lists twenty-three special (restrictive zoning) districts in addition to twenty-two land use zones of the more conventional type. The permitted uses in each special district are generally intended to conform exactly to the existing use; for example, in the case of Special District 14 the bylaw states that "no person shall...use any land, alter or use any building or part thereof for any purpose other than...manufacturing of injection moulded plastic products."

Given the character of the Canadian political system the most satisfactory form of planning is probably a combination of development control and zoning. The theoretical superiority of development control has to be weighed against its practical disadvantages, in particular the expense of its operation, the degree of competence required of public officials, the need for consistency in policy-making, and the need for trustworthiness in those responsible for the implementation of public policy. Ideally, the two methods should be used in combination, so that the bulk of the city may at any one time be covered by zoning bylaws while only a small proportion need be kept under development control. A newly developed suburban community may, for example, be best covered by a zoning bylaw; such an area is unlikely to change radically for at least a generation and development applications are generally minor in scope (building garages, adding rooms, installing a swimming pool and so on), and can easily be covered by standard zoning bylaws and easily administered by non-professional planning staff. In the city centre where redevelopment is taking place, and in the urban fringe where land is being actively converted from rural to urban uses, there is need for more direct planning control, since applications for development are not likely to be of a routine nature. Under these circumstances development control offers the flexibility required to deal with land use changes which are largely unpredictable except in the short term, and which cannot, therefore, be legislated far in advance.

Subdivision control may also be utilized by municipalities in order to direct land development, since municipal approval is normally required whenever a tract of land is to be subdivided into two or more lots. Subdivision control is designed to produce the same community benefits as zoning bylaws; that is, to promote "the health, safety, convenience and welfare of the future inhabitants" (the Planning Act, Ontario). In the case of residential areas, subdivision regulations generally include minimum standards for lots, roads, utilities and municipal services, as well as reservations for school sites and public open space. In setting subdivision standards the municipality may also include design elements such as pedestrian-vehicular separation, underground servicing and curvilinear roads. Finally, the municipality may decide if the proposed subdivision is premature or immediately desirable in the public interest, regardless of whether it conforms to zoning and subdivision regulations.

Every municipality has a building code—bylaws which specify minimum standards for construction materials, size of windows, essential services and other building features. The plans for a new structure must conform to these regulations before a building permit is issued, but a building code or, more correctly, a property standards bylaw, may also be used to force owners to upgrade existing buildings by prescribing minimum property standards. The building code is a particularly useful tool for maintaining or improving the quality of inner-city neighbourhoods.

Restrictive covenants are generally used by private developers to prevent individual owners frustrating the overall aim of a large, comprehensive project. These restrictions are added to, but cannot violate, the permitted uses of the zoning bylaw; for example, in a zone which permits two-unit houses purchasers of land may be restricted to the construction of detached houses. Private restrictions imposed as a condition of sale might extend to the minimum floor area or value of houses, the prohibition of front fences or even the colour of garage doors, as is the case in Kanata, near Ottawa. Although public caveats can also be used to restrict the rights of property owners, these are normally incorporated into the zoning bylaw.

## Municipal Finance

Local governments[1] in Canada are responsible for almost 25 per cent (23 per cent in 1972) of the total expenditure by all levels of governments, but their fiscal resources are much more limited than those of senior governments. Moreover, local government expenditure has recently been rising at a faster rate than that of higher levels of government. This rapid increase in expenditure has been partly offset by grants from senior governments, but the fiscal base of municipalities has remained inadequate. Basically the fiscal resources of Canadian municipalities are limited to the property tax base; of the revenue raised directly by municipalities between 85 and 90 per cent is ordinarily obtained from the property tax[2] and the remainder from licences, fines, amusement taxes and a variety of minor sources (Table 8.1). In Canada, the property tax accounts for a larger proportion of national revenue than in almost any other advanced industrial country, and its use as a major source of local revenue has had major repercussions on the ability of municipalities to participate effectively in the solution of the urgent problems which occur within their boundaries.

The property tax is a handicap to the efficient planning of cities and may itself be a principal cause of urban problems. Much criticism has been levelled at it, both as an anachronistic method of raising municipal revenue and because of its effect on the urban land use system. In terms of city planning two factors must be considered: whether the incidence of the tax conforms to generally accepted taxation principles such as ability-to-pay and benefit-received, since this affects its elasticity or flexibility as a source of revenue; and whether the tax has any undesirable effects on the social, economic, political and physical structure of cities.

The property tax is regressive; it takes a larger proportion of income from low-income than from high-income households (Figure 8.2). Its regressivity violates the ability-to-pay principle of taxation whereby individuals are taxed at progressively higher rates in accordance with the level of their income (as in the case of the progressive tax on personal income—see Table 8.7); but municipalities, unlike

1 Municipalities, local school boards and special-purpose boards of a local nature.
2 For a particular property the tax levy is the municipal mill rate on the assessed value of property (land and buildings). A municipal tax rate of 70 mills, for example, results in a tax levy of $70 for every $1,000 of assessed valuation.

TABLE 8.1 *Local government revenue by source, Canada, 1971 and 1972*

| | 1971 | | 1972 | |
|---|---|---|---|---|
| Item | Millions of dollars | % | Millions of dollars | % |
| Revenue from own sources | | | | |
|   Taxes[1] | 3,814.2 | 45.0 | 4,042.1 | 44.2 |
|   Grants-in-lieu of taxes[2] | 116.7 | 1.4 | 123.4 | 1.4 |
|   Sales of services[3] | 344.8 | 4.1 | 358.6 | 3.9 |
|   Other[4] | 306.5 | 3.7 | 317.0 | 3.5 |
| Transfers from senior governments[5] | | | | |
|   Conditional | 3,551.4 | 41.9 | 3,913.5 | 42.9 |
|   Unconditional | 307.6 | 3.6 | 350.2 | 3.8 |
| Transfers from own agencies | 27.9 | 0.3 | 28.1 | 0.3 |
| Total | 8,469.1 | 100.0 | 9,132.9 | 100.0 |

SOURCE: Statistics Canada, *Local Government Finance*, (Dec. 1973)
[1] Principally property and business taxes
[2] Principally federal and provincial government property
[3] Principally water charges
[4] Licences, permits, fines, penalties on taxes, etc.
[5] Transfers from the federal government amounted to $73.6 million and $120.8 million in 1971 and 1972 respectively

the federal and provincial governments, have no access to a progressive income tax. The property tax is actually a tax on fixed property assets, which are not directly related to the earning power of the owner. With respect to residences the tax tends to be regressive throughout the income range because housing accounts for a larger proportion of the income of low-income households than of high-income households. Table 8.7, for example, indicates that in Guelph, where houses had been assessed at their market value, the property tax (and therefore the value of the occupied house) varied little among households earning less than $8,000; in other words, the type of house occupied was not directly related to the gross income of the household's principal income recipient. The use of a uniform mill rate itself constitutes a further contribution to the regressiveness of the property tax when tax rates are increased; for example, if the existing mill rate in Calgary (Table 8.2) were raised from 47.5 to 52.5 mills, the increase would amount to 1.3 per cent of the income of households earning less than $2,000 but only 0.3 per cent of the income of those earning more than $15,000. For various reasons,

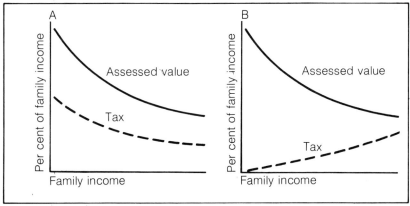

FIGURE 8.2   Property tax and the assessed value of residential property in relation to family income. A: A uniform mill rate normally results in a regressive tax. B: A graduated rate of taxation may be designed to produce a progressive tax.

including the greater administrative costs of operating a complex system, municipalities prefer a uniform rather than a graduated scale of property taxation.

Two principal arguments have been advanced against ascribing too much importance to the regressivity of the property tax. Firstly, although the property tax is itself regressive, the total burden of taxation is progressive (i.e., proportionately greater for higher-income households); the combined property and income taxes for Guelph households, for example, generally increase as a percentage of gross income in accordance with rising income levels (Table 8.7). The existence of progressivity within the total tax structure does not, however, alter the fact that local governments must raise almost all of their own revenue in a manner which places a disproportionate burden on poorer households; this has a fundamental influence on their fiscal capacity and in turn affects their ability to institute a variety of programs. Secondly, it should be noted that the benefits received from municipal expenditure form a larger part of the income of poorer households than of richer households, principally because of the disproportionate share of personal services (relative to tax contributions) received by low-income households; these include welfare, health, education and recreation. To some extent this redresses the regressivity of the property tax but is certainly not suffi-

TABLE 8.2 *Average property taxes by family income, Calgary, 1965*

| Average property tax | Family income (dollars) | | | | | | | |
|---|---|---|---|---|---|---|---|---|
| | Below 2,000 | 2000 to 3999 | 4000 to 5999 | 6000 to 7999 | 8000 to 9999 | 10000 to 11999 | 12000 to 14999 | 15000 and over |
| Dollars | 237 | 270 | 300 | 324 | 362 | 384 | 394 | 508 |
| % of income | 13.1 | 9.0 | 6.0 | 4.6 | 4.0 | 3.5 | 2.9 | 2.8 |

SOURCE: *Urban Crisis: Alberta Municipal Finance Study, 1968*

cient justification for its continued use, since similar disproportion-ate benefits accrue to low-income households from many programs of the senior governments whose revenue is largely derived from progressive taxations of income.

Property taxation does not generally conform to the benefit-received principle of taxation, and for some uses the costs of munici-pal services are much less than the amount of revenue received; if the property tax accorded well with benefits received, it might be re-garded as a user-charge. Table 8.3 illustrates the almost universal discrepancy between the cost-revenue ratios of two types of residen-tial use, single-family houses and high-rise apartments. The munici-pal profit on apartments derives from the generally smaller house-hold sizes, fewer school-age children, lower maintenance costs (fewer streets, for example), and the higher assessed value per per-son. Similarly favourable cost-revenue ratios (i.e., where revenue exceeds expenditure) are generally associated with most commercial and industrial uses, while low-density housing and all forms of public housing generate higher costs than revenues.

Favourable cost-revenue ratios may also be achieved by varying the proportion of the market value at which a particular class of property is assessed for tax purposes. Although attempts have been made to standardize assessment procedures, the method has re-mained largely subjective since the fair market value of land and/or improvements cannot always be accurately determined. This is particularly relevant in the case of the large number of buildings and lots which change hands only infrequently so that few actual market transactions are recorded. Because of the extremely varied nature of urban properties and the innumerable forces which determine their value, it is unlikely that assessment procedures could ever achieve a

TABLE 8.3 *Cost-revenue of providing public services, Calgary, 1968*

| Housing type | Services to property | Services to people | Cost by type of service (in dollars) | | Total cost | Total revenue | Balance |
| --- | --- | --- | --- | --- | --- | --- | --- |
| | | | Education | Other services | | | |
| Single-family house | 107.19 | 68.55 | 270.32 | 71.55 | 517.61 | 466.10 | -51.51 |
| Apartment unit | 41.69 | 34.27 | 10.72 | 44.73 | 131.41 | 302.98 | +171.57 |

SOURCE: City of Calgary

high degree of objectivity and uniformity. Since these qualities are frequently lacking, the valuation procedure often penalizes those members of the community (the poor, for example), who do not have the necessary resources or knowledge to appeal their assessment. The fairly common policy of assessing single-family houses at a smaller proportion of their market value than is the case for multi-family accommodation places a disproportionately high tax burden on renters, many of whom have relatively low incomes. In 1972, for example, the borough of York in Metro Toronto assessed single-family houses at an average of 17.9 per cent of their market value, townhouses (row housing) at 26.5 per cent, and multi-storey apartment buildings at 33.1 per cent. (Assessment in Ontario became a provincial responsibility in 1970 and it is anticipated that by 1977 all properties in the province will be assessed at their full market value.)

The fiscal resources of municipalities are further constrained by the fact that the property tax is generally used to support services for which it is not ideally suited and for which expenditure is largely outside the direct control of the municipality. As well as services to property (such as fire protection, garbage collection and sewage disposal) a number of services to people, including education, health, welfare and recreation, are being paid for in part by the property tax. The demand for these personal services has been accelerating at a much faster rate than the property tax base, since it is a function of rising personal and corporate incomes, which are liable only to federal and provincial taxes. Services to people account for more than half the total public expenditure at the local government level and are among the fastest rising budgetary items (see Table 8.4). In addition, municipal governments have little or no control over many of these services; education, for example, accounts for about one-half of the property tax revenue in most cities but a municipal council has no decision-making role in education and simply collects the taxes on behalf of the school board. When there are increases in education, health, welfare and other costs, which are largely outside its control, a municipality is often persuaded to hold the line on its own programs, frequently to the detriment of the urban environment.

The fiscal resources of municipalities are further limited by the large number of tax-exempt properties within their boundaries. Federal and provincial lands are exempted from municipal taxation by the terms of the British North America Act; grants-in-lieu of

TABLE 8.4 *Local government expenditure by type of service, Canada, 1971 and 1972*

| | 1971 | | 1972 | |
| --- | --- | --- | --- | --- |
| Type of service | Millions of dollars | % | Millions of dollars | % |
| General government | 366.0 | 4.1 | 422.6 | 4.3 |
| Protective | 639.6 | 7.1 | 706.3 | 7.0 |
| Transportation | 1,120.8 | 12.4 | 1,217.3 | 12.1 |
| Environmental health | 651.4 | 7.2 | 864.0 | 8.6 |
| Public health and welfare | 510.9 | 5.5 | 556.0 | 5.6 |
| Environmental development | 79.7 | 0.9 | 97.3 | 0.9 |
| Recreation and cultural | 359.0 | 4.0 | 441.1 | 4.4 |
| Education | 4,527.8 | 50.0 | 4,802.1 | 47.8 |
| Fiscal | 723.5 | 8.0 | 840.5 | 8.3 |
| Other | 79.0 | 0.8 | 98.6 | 1.0 |
| Total | 9,057.7 | 100.0 | 10,045.8 | 100.0 |

SOURCE: Statistics Canada, *Local Government Finance* (Dec. 1973)

taxes are paid by the federal and provincial governments on some of their properties and not on others. Some properties are exempted from municipal taxation altogether because of the benefits that citizens derive from their presence; places of worship, charitable institutions, hospitals and other non-profit organizations are generally considered to merit such public support. In some cities tax-exempt property may form a significant proportion of the total assessed value of property; in the cities of Kingston and Halifax, where there are many government properties and institutions, 35 per cent and 37 per cent respectively of assessed real property was tax-exempt in 1971. The grants-in-lieu of taxes for these properties are often well below the taxes paid by equivalent, non-exempted properties; thus the grants made by Queen's University (which accounted for 13 per cent of Kingston's total real property assessment) amounted to only 15 per cent of what a non-exempted property would have paid. Even though some properties may be reasonably exempted from taxation, it is doubtful whether an indirect subsidy through property tax exemption is appropriate. Exemptions narrow the municipal tax base and thereby increase the burden on owners of taxable property.

In addition, the property tax has a number of adverse effects on the land use structure of cities since it punishes owners who improve their property and rewards those who allow either their property to deteriorate or their land to remain vacant as a form of speculation.

Since the assessment is based on the property's market value, any improvements, even fire-proofing a building, will result in higher taxes; on the other hand, an owner who allows the condition of his property to deteriorate, perhaps to the point where it constitutes a fire hazard, is rewarded by lower taxes. Since property values are in part determined by the potential development of land, the property tax system contributes directly to land use problems when the existing use does not conform to the use prescribed in the zoning bylaw. Land is frequently zoned for a particular use well in advance of expected development (as part of a 20-year plan, for example), and as a result it may be impossible for existing or interim uses to function efficiently, and urban blight may ensue. This normally occurs when land has been zoned for a more intensive use and land values consequently rise above the economic rent which the existing use is capable of supporting; agriculture may be uneconomical where rural land has been zoned for urban use, or the maintenance of a single-family house may be impracticable if the land has been re-zoned for apartments.

By impairing the efficient working of the urban land market, the property tax system weakens municipal control of the development process. The property tax works against the public interest because of the types of development which it encourages. Property owners, acting in accordance with the tax structure, tend to use land less intensively and to maintain their buildings less adequately than is socially desirable; old buildings are favoured over new buildings, vacant land is held for long periods for speculative purposes, parking lots are preferred to parking structures, and so on. The existence of a property tax is of no particular benefit in the process of urbanizing land on the fringe of cities, and is a disincentive to redevelopment in the older parts of cities. Moreover, municipal decisions tend to be viewed largely in terms of their impact on the property tax base; the process of municipal decision-making is strongly influenced by the need to bolster the assessment rolls, and municipalities often approve development policies more because of the anticipated growth of their tax base than because they favour the social and economic consequences.

The fact that a municipality's revenues are largely determined by the way in which its land is used has been the direct causes of two of the major problems in metropolitan areas: inefficiency of the land use system and inequity of the intermunicipal tax burden.

Courtesy Photographic Branch — Government of Alberta

*Edmonton's petrochemical industrial complex located on the edge of the city.*

Land use planning often has as its primary objective municipal tax-base balance, and with few exceptions municipalities attempt to reduce their residential tax burden by attracting commercial-industrial development. In the pursuit of balanced assessment intermunicipal rivalry has been most apparent in the field of industrial promotion; suburban municipalities in particular have sought to attract industry by means of tax incentives, low-priced (at cost or less) serviced land, and less stringent zoning regulations, all of which frequently produce a less than optimal distribution of industrial activities. Firms are normally attracted to the metropolitan area for economic reasons, and property tax concessions and other municipal incentives that influence the intra-metropolitan locational decision can in the long run work only to the detriment of the metropolitan community. One of Canada's most glaring examples of the inequity of the property tax system is Edmonton's petrochemical industrial complex, which lies immediately outside the city. In this case, the industrial plants enjoy low tax rates by reason of their location in a rural municipality (whose residents also pay lower average taxes because of these plants), and as a result they pay no taxes to the City of Edmonton, with which they are functionally integrated and from which they benefit; for example, almost all of their workers live in the city.

Property taxation is clearly not the most potent force in the decentralization of economic activity in metropolitan areas but it is an important factor. Intermunicipal differences in assessment policy (for example, the proportion that the assessed value for tax purposes forms of the market value) and tax rates may be significant factors in the intra-metropolitan location decisions. It is understandable that each taxing jurisdiction should strive to strengthen its fiscal resources by encouraging some uses and discouraging others, but this generally leads to an inefficient land use arrangement; for example, since many urban activities benefit from the clustering of like or complementary uses, the scatter of interdependent land uses among a number of municipalities generally reduces socio-economic welfare. The property tax is itself a deterrent to redevelopment and thus to the orderly renewal of the central city's physical plant; the suburban cities have decided advantages both because of their lower tax rates and their supply of vacant land. In general, intermunicipal competition for real property assessment works to the disadvantage of fully developed municipalities, such as the central city.

Inequitable tax burdens within metropolitan areas are most apparent in comparisons between central cities and suburban municipalities. Although both groups have disproportionate shares of some expenditures (for example, education in the suburbs and welfare in the central city), the plight of the central city is of more serious concern since there is a common relationship between the per capita expenditure of the central city and the proportion of the metropolitan population which lies outside its boundaries. A variety of specialized services are normally supplied at no cost or subsidized prices to the entire metropolitan area by the central city because it is the only municipality which is large enough to support activities with high threshold requirements; these include, for example, zoos, rapid transit, museums and theatres. In the past it was generally the case that the revenue produced by the concentration of commerce and industry in the central city compensated for the costs of providing such services to the suburban population. Since the Second World War differentials in per capita assessment have been decreasing as a result of the decentralization of economic activities and the outward shift of high-income households, and in many cases suburban municipalities now have higher per capita assessments. The financial difficulties of central cities have also increased because of widespread suburban resistance to the entry of low-income housing; suburban municipalities have been reluctant to permit such developments since each new house means a certain tax increase for their existing residents. Although there are other elements involved, suburban municipalities zone out low-income housing primarily for fiscal reasons.

In some metropolitan areas the inequitability of the tax burden has been reduced by two principal means: the institution of many services on a metropolitan-wide basis, and the acceleration of municipal amalgamations. In the political reorganization of metropolitan areas uniform tax rates are applied throughout the region for metropolitan-wide services while local governments are permitted to levy supplementary taxes for purely local services. To the extent that metropolitan-wide services increase as a proportion of total services, the intermunicipal rivalry for particular land uses is decreased; for example, in most metropolitan or regional government districts in Ontario about three-quarters of the property tax is appropriated by the metropolitan authorities (including the school board) for the provision of uniform services. Municipal amalgamation has also reduced some of the disparities in the level of taxation.

No fiscal institution has been subjected to so much criticism as the real property tax. No serious student of the municipal tax system has ever concluded that it has more advantages than disadvantages, yet in Canada its present form is no different from that of a hundred years ago. The philosophical basis for the use of the property tax dates from the days when services to property— fire-fighting, street lighting, sidewalk construction, the supply of water and the like—were the principal responsibilities of municipalities. Education, welfare and a variety of services to people were either not provided by municipalities or were of minor importance. It should also be noted that at the time when the property tax was introduced in Canada there were no personal income taxes, which were first levied during the First World War.

Since the Second World War local government expenditures have

TABLE 8.5 *Surplus (+) or deficit (-) on a national accounts basis by level of government, Canada, 1970-1973 (millions of dollars)*

|  | 1970 | 1971 | 1972 | 1973 |
|---|---|---|---|---|
| Federal | +264 | − 95 | − 701 | −14 |
| Provincial | − 231 | − 458 | − 632 | − 411 |
| Local | − 462 | − 632 | − 755 | −1,215 |

SOURCE: Statistics Canada, *National Income and Expenditure Accounts*

generally exceeded the ability of municipalities to finance them solely by means of the property tax, and this in turn has contributed directly to their reluctance to initiate appropriate programs for the solution of urban problems. Table 8.5, for example, illustrates the disproportionately large deficits which have been incurred recently by local governments. The fiscal squeeze has arisen simply because the expansion of the property tax base of most cities has not kept pace with the growth in demand for municipal services. As a result, municipalities have been forced to follow a number of unfortunate courses: to raise their mill rates, thus aggravating the unfair burden which falls on certain segments of the population; to defer necessary long-term programs; to increase their dependence on conditional grants from senior governments, thus restricting their flexibility in dealing with their own problems; and to increase intermunicipal competition to the detriment of the larger community.

The present urban preoccupation with social goals has shifted the public debate from physical property services to the quality of urban life, and the excessive concern of municipal politicians with the physical urban plant is seen by citizens as largely irrelevant. It is, however, the property tax system which forces municipal councils to adopt these caretaking or housekeeping roles. Only a very small proportion of a typical municipality's revenue, perhaps as little as 1 per cent, is available for innovation, experimentation and all the other ingredients involved in the search for "the good life." Grants from senior governments, which now account for almost one-half of local government revenue (Table 8.1), are generally conditional, i.e., tied to specific, standardized programs; although municipalities usually share part of the expenditure, they normally have very little control over the content of such programs.

Municipalities are particularly restricted in their ability to finance large capital investments, and therefore in their commitment to rational planning. Because of the regressive nature of the property tax, municipalities ordinarily cannot finance many of the long-term capital programs, such as land banks, even though these may be essential to the orderly development of urban areas; for example, if Calgary were to finance its capital loans by means of the property tax, the debt charges would be proportionately (as a percentage of family income) five times as heavy for the lowest income group as for the highest (Table 8.2), clearly an inequitable burden. Services in advance of need generally cannot be financed by municipalities through the property tax; federal and provincial governments (both of which have access to progressive forms of taxation) must necessarily be involved in long-term investments such as trunk sewers, transit systems, expressways and land banks.

The property tax is clearly a deterrent to the involvement of municipalities in the formulation of an appropriate urban policy for Canada, and it must therefore be progressively decreased as a proportion of municipal revenue if cities are to participate actively in the urban decision-making process. There is a clear divergence in Canada between functional responsibility and financial resources in the management of urban areas: the federal government has the necessary financial resources (because of its unrestricted taxing powers), the provincial governments have the necessary legislative power (through the British North America Act), and the municipalities are left with the political-financial responsibility for controlling a complex, multi-governmental area without being in a position to wield commensurate legislative and taxation powers.

Because it is an available source of taxation, real property will in all probability continue to be taxed, and since it is easily administered and since many municipal services are tied to property, it will remain quite appropriately as a form of local government taxation. There are, however, many measures which are currently being used to reduce municipal dependence on property taxes, including the sharing of programs with senior governments, the transfer of some responsibilities from municipal to other levels of government, and provincial rebates to residential taxpayers.

Conditional grants from senior governments have the disadvantage of restricting a municipality's flexibility in dealing with the unique elements of those problems which occur within its bound-

TABLE 8.6 *Conditional transfers from federal and provincial governments to local governments by type of service, Canada, 1971 and 1972*

| Type of service | 1971 Millions of dollars | % | 1972 Millions of dollars | % |
|---|---|---|---|---|
| General government | 10.2 | 0.3 | 9.6 | 0.3 |
| Protective | 19.0 | 0.5 | 18.0 | 0.5 |
| Transportation | 354.2 | 10.0 | 352.9 | 9.0 |
| Environmental health | 63.8 | 1.8 | 93.7 | 2.4 |
| Public health and welfare | 252.2 | 7.1 | 282.1 | 7.2 |
| Environmental development | 36.3 | 1.0 | 55.3 | 1.4 |
| Recreation and cultural | 23.9 | 0.6 | 48.5 | 1.2 |
| Education | 2,775.9 | 78.2 | 3,036.4 | 77.6 |
| Other | 15.9 | 0.5 | 17.0 | 0.4 |
| Total | 3,551.4 | 100.0 | 3,913.5 | 100.0 |

SOURCE: Statistics Canada, *Local Government Finance* (Dec. 1973)

aries. There have been very few instances of local services which have either been entirely removed from the responsibility of municipalities for economic reasons or have been financed exclusively by sources other than the property tax. As Table 8.1 indicates, only a small proportion of transfers from senior governments are unconditional. Moreover, the bulk of these transfers are to education (Table 8.6). Higher levels of government are understandably reluctant to increase unconditional grants to municipalities, since it is politically undesirable for money raised by one government body to be spent by another without any control.

Rebates have for some time been used by provinces to alleviate the burden of the property tax on households. The common procedure has been to grant a flat rebate to homeowners for their principal place of residence; besides producing an overall reduction in the amount paid the rebate compensates to some extent, though not entirely, for the regressiveness of the tax, since it forms a higher proportion of the income of low-income than of high-income households. In 1972, Manitoba and Ontario took a further step towards a more equitable property tax system by relating the amount of the rebate to the income of each household and by including renters in the tax-rebate scheme. Although the rebates are graduated in favour of low-income households, the net property tax paid generally remains regressive throughout the income range (Table 8.7, for example).

TABLE 8.7 *Property and income taxes as a percentage of gross income,* *before and after property tax credit, Guelph, Ontario, 1972†*

| Income Class | Dollars Property Tax | | % of Gross Income Property Tax | | Income Tax | Combined Taxes | |
|---|---|---|---|---|---|---|---|
| | Before | After | Before | After | | Before | After |
| Below 2,500 | 291 | 168 | 19 | 12 | 2 | 21 | 14 |
| 2,500 - 2,999 | 317 | 197 | 11 | 7 | 4 | 15 | 11 |
| 3,000 - 3,499 | 300 | 186 | 9 | 6 | 7 | 16 | 13 |
| 3,500 - 3,999 | 292 | 183 | 8 | 6 | 8 | 16 | 14 |
| 4,000 - 4,499 | 294 | 192 | 7 | 5 | 11 | 18 | 16 |
| 4,500 - 4,999 | 296 | 199 | 6 | 4 | 12 | 18 | 16 |
| 5,000 - 5,499 | 308 | 213 | 6 | 4 | 12 | 18 | 16 |
| 5,500 - 5,999 | 302 | 213 | 5 | 4 | 13 | 18 | 17 |
| 6,000 - 6,499 | 300 | 215 | 5 | 4 | 14 | 19 | 18 |
| 6,500 - 6,999 | 308 | 228 | 5 | 4 | 15 | 20 | 19 |
| 7,000 - 7,499 | 310 | 234 | 4 | 3 | 15 | 19 | 18 |
| 7,500 - 7,999 | 329 | 256 | 4 | 3 | 16 | 20 | 19 |
| 8,000 - 8,499 | 340 | 270 | 4 | 3 | 16 | 20 | 19 |
| 8,500 - 8,999 | 352 | 286 | 4 | 3 | 17 | 21 | 20 |
| 9,000 - 9,499 | 350 | 289 | 4 | 3 | 17 | 21 | 20 |
| 9,500 - 9,999 | 357 | 302 | 4 | 4 | 18 | 22 | 22 |
| 10,000 - 11,999 | 393 | 343 | 4 | 4 | 19 | 23 | 23 |
| 12,000 - 14,999 | 463 | 430 | 4 | 4 | 21 | 25 | 25 |
| 15,000 - 19,999 | 534 | 523 | 3 | 3 | 24 | 27 | 27 |
| 20,000 - 24,999 | 639 | 637 | 3 | 3 | 27 | 30 | 30 |
| 25,000 - 49,999 | 689 | 689 | 2 | 2 | 34 | 36 | 36 |
| 50,000 & over | 873 | 873 | 1 | 1 | 44 | 45 | 45 |

SOURCE: Ministry of Treasury, Economics and Intergovernmental Affairs, *Analysis of Income and Property Taxes in Guelph* (Toronto: Government of Ontario, 1972)

* The gross income of the principal income recipient in each household.

† Derived from an extrapolation of 1968 data.

In the long run all the current attempts to alleviate the property tax burden by means of grants and shared programs are inadequate, since they do not eliminate the most fundamental problem—the fact that municipalities continue to raise almost 90 per cent of their own revenue from the property tax. The disproportionate share of municipal taxation which is borne by those who are least able to pay can be redressed only by access to new fiscal resources, and a widening of the financial base of municipalities through a redistribution of taxing powers among the three levels of government. Unless municipalities have a realistic fiscal source (a progressive tax on income, for example), they cannot participate fully in the resolution of urban problems. A municipality's expenditure (including school boards) is now mainly proportional to the composition of its population (in particular the number of children) although its revenue potential is directly related to the way in which its land is used. It is little wonder that municipalities have been accused of being anti-family, of preferring industries (which have no children) to houses.

Municipalities must eventually have access to revenue from personal and corporate income if they are to plan rationally for the welfare of people; many Canadian municipalities, including Montreal, Toronto and St. John's, actually collected an income tax before the Second World War but this was subsequently halted by federal-provincial tax agreements. Although a personal income tax system appears to be the most attractive source of potential revenue, it is in fact difficult to institute at the municipal level because of the small geographic areas covered by local governments. The fact that a municipality's revenue must be raised within its boundaries has led directly to a considerable amount of inter-municipal disparity, as businesses and households have taken advantage of varying tax rates by location within particular jurisdictions. One partial solution to this problem lies in the formation of larger local governments, since the degree of inter-municipal disparity is inversely related to the average size of municipalities (i.e., the smaller the size, the greater is the disparity).

Canadian municipalities need a sound fiscal base if they are to execute their legislative mandate to promote "the health, safety, convenience and welfare of the future inhabitants."

## Metropolitan Government

A large number of local government jurisdictions usually exist within each Canadian metropolitan area, and some of the most common metropolitan problems stem from this multiplicity of authorities in an area which functions as a socio-economic unit. Indeed, the term "metropolitan problem" is often reserved for those urban problems which require inter-governmental cooperation for their solution. It would take great faith in the democratic system of local government to believe that the end result of the competing and inconsistent actions of local authorities would be an efficient arrangement of metropolitan activities and the maximization of benefits for the metropolitan community. There is no instance in which metropolitan planning has been successfully achieved through the voluntary cooperation of municipalities, and the consequent reduction of inter-jurisdictional competition, through the reorganization of municipal government structure, is often a prerequisite for the proper control of development in metropolitan areas.

Since the metropolitan area functions as a single social and economic system, a metropolitan-wide political or decision-making authority is considered necessary if the urban developmental process is to be properly controlled. The constituent municipalities of metropolitan areas are so intimately bound together by economic, social and physical ties that attempts to plan any one of them without continuous reference to the larger area work inevitably to the detriment of either the metropolitan or the local community. It is now generally accepted that private property rights must be subordinate to community interests, and public controls are therefore exercised over the operation of the land market in order to promote social benefits. In metropolitan areas intermunicipal competition is analogous to the operation of the market, and regulatory powers are equally necessary if the metropolitan community is to be protected from the self-interests of its constituent municipalities. It is commonly the case that high-income suburban communities frustrate the efficiency of the housing market by excluding low-income families through the legislation of high minimum standards in their zoning bylaws. In metropolitan Winnipeg, for example, Tuxedo (which was incorporated in 1913 before urban development had taken place) excluded all but the wealthiest households by restricting house lots to a minimum frontage that was about twice that of the City of Winnipeg and by specifying a minimum housing floor area that was more than twice the average size of houses in the metropolitan area; consequently the average household income in Tuxedo is more than three times the metropolitan average. (In 1972, Tuxedo became part of the reorganized City of Winnipeg.)

In general, the existence of so many municipal and other local government jurisdictions within metropolitan areas leads to inefficiencies in the functioning of the urban system and to inequities in the tax burden of the constituent communities. Because of their functional interdependency and spatial proximity most urban activities within a metropolitan area affect each other, and this spillover is largely unaffected by the existence of political divisions. These external effects take various forms: air pollution from industrial plants may affect an area of several hundred square miles, trucks may be routed through residential areas of a neighbouring municipality, or a local municipality's parks and other recreational facilities may be used by people from other parts of the metropolitan region. Wherever there are spillovers from one municipality to another there is a possibility of some inequity in the sharing of costs and benefits; in metropolitan areas, where there is a high degree of spatial interaction, these inequities may be quite substantial. Disparities in tax rates between the central city and suburban municipalities do not necessarily indicate that the latter are bearing a less-than-proportionate share of metropolitan costs; many suburban communities do not, and often choose not to, have many urban services, and volunteer fire departments, unpaved streets, open storm sewers, poor street lighting and no sidewalks are common. Whereas these communities would choose to continue without many conveniences in order to maintain low tax rates, amalgamation into a larger political unit in which the costs of a number of these services are borne universally would result normally in a demand for similar levels of servicing and consequently an overall increase in taxes within the metropolitan area.

Historically, metropolitan control has generally been achieved either by annexation or by the creation of special-purpose boards. Annexation has, on the whole, been unsuccessful; suburban municipalities have often been reluctant to merge with a larger central city for a variety of social, political and economic reasons, while the central city itself has often preferred not to annex neighbouring areas because of the costs involved in extending unprofitable services such as public transit. Accordingly, both Montreal and Toronto had abandoned their policy of annexation by 1920. Instead special-purpose boards are usually established, often voluntarily, to administer services which will demonstrably benefit all the member municipalities; this is frequently the first step towards the establishment of a metropolitan authority.

Voluntary metropolitan-wide cooperation is normally possible in the case of municipal services which enjoy scale economies (since the cost to each municipality will be reduced as a result), which are fairly standardized, and for which each municipality's portion of the total cost may be easily determined on a user-charge basis. The retailing of water to municipalities is one of the first functions to be adopted by metropolitan authorities because of the standardized nature of the service and the ease with which equitable cost-sharing arrangements can be determined; for example, the Greater Winnipeg Water District was established as early as 1913, almost fifty years before the formation of a metropolitan government. Police, education, recreation and other personal services, which also enjoy scale economies, are less attractive prospects for intermunicipal cooperation because of the desire for local control over the quality of service. Metropolitan-wide cooperation is also difficult to achieve where costs cannot be easily allocated to member municipalities despite unanimous agreement on standards—for example, in the case of air pollution control and public transit.

Special-purpose boards, no matter how efficiently they execute their terms of reference, cannot handle the complex, multi-faceted problems of metropolitan areas; the formation of a number of such specific-purpose authorities obviously results in a multiplicity of independent agencies and thus in the further fragmentation of public administration. Single-purpose boards have three principal disadvantages: the lack of coordination among the special-purpose agencies; the lack of direct answerability to the people (since board members are normally appointed rather than elected); and the limited number of suitable services of a specific nature. Metropolitan planning is easily frustrated if each special-purpose agency pursues its own objectives within a limited area of jurisdiction. The basic requirement for the formulation and achievement of metropolitan-wide community goals is the creation of a multi-purpose agency or metropolitan government. Given the need for some form of metropolitan government there remain two problems to be resolved: its areal extent and the form of the political system.

Although the divisions are blurred in practice, it is conceptually possible to recognize two types of planning approaches at the sub-national level—physical (environmental) and economic—and two types of planning areas—local and regional. Physical planning problems tend to be local in nature, while at the regional level problems are largely economic. Provided that costs are borne locally and that there is no spillover into other municipalities, it is reasonable to allow local communities to assume the responsibility for many services; how frequently garbage is collected for instance, is a purely local matter and as such should be at the discretion of those who receive and pay for the service. In a democracy it is therefore inappropriate to centralize, and so standardize, many community services. At the regional level there are very few physical planning problems that need the attention of a centralized authority; for example, it is of little consequence to the rest of the metropolitan Toronto region whether the city of Barrie provides 8 or 12 acres of local parks per 1,000 people. The location of major industrial plants and public invest- ments in airports and highways are, however, of vital importance to regional economic growth. Although these developments have phys- ical implications, they are largely economic in nature, and economic tools are therefore most frequently used in determining their cost- benefit ratios. Between the two extremes of local (physical) and regional (economic) it is generally the practice to insert a middle tier, commonly called metropolitan, which is concerned with both physi- cal and economic planning.

The two types of planning control, physical and economic, and the two types of planning area, local and regional, actually combine to produce four types of planning jurisdiction: regional-economic, regional-physical, local-economic, and local-physical. Although there is an overlap or continuity among all four levels there are good reasons for maintaining these divisions in practice. The conventional distinctions between city, metropolitan and regional planning are mainly produced by the organizational need to break any complex human system into smaller, manageable sub-systems; in the case of the urban system, the spatial element requires a vertical-horizontal arrangement of government.

Each of the four planning jurisdictions is theoretically necessary for the effective implementation of national urban policies. Regional economic planning is the highest level of sub-national planning and is concerned principally with interregional resource allocation as a means of reducing regional disparities in socio-economic welfare or of increasing national welfare; this is also known as national regional planning. The territorial jurisdiction for regional economic planning in advanced countries is the "metropolitan region," which includes widely separated communities whose economies are integrated into a single economic system focused on a metropolitan centre. Regional

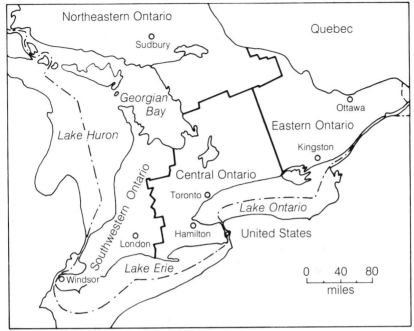

FIGURE 8.3   Southern Ontario Planning Regions.

*Source*:  Ministry of Treasury, Economics and Intergovernmental Affairs, Government of Ontario.

physical planning is also carried out at the level of the metropolitan region but its primary emphasis in this case is on the spatial arrangement of generalized land uses (urban, agricultural, recreational and so on) which will best facilitate the region's designated role in the national economy. Local economic planning is concerned with the determination of the optimal roles for communities within each of the local economies that make up the metropolitan region; its geographical jurisdiction is the "metropolitan area," which is often defined as the area within commuting distance of the central city and which embraces free-standing communities that on a day-to-day basis are closely integrated, both socially and economically, with a metropolitan centre. A metropolitan land use plan (indicating commercial, residential, industrial and other urban uses) and the provision of area-wide services (water supply, sewage disposal, public

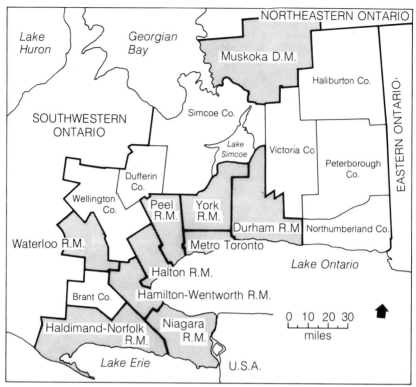

FIGURE 8.4  Regional municipalities (R.M.) within the Central Ontario Planning Region. (The municipal structure of the Muskoka District Municipality is virtually identical to that of a regional municipality and the municipality is unique primarily as a result of its substantially lower population.)

*Source:* Ministry of Treasury, Economics and Intergovernmental Affairs, Government of Ontario.

transit and so on) are the principal objectives of local economic planning. Local physical planning is the most localized level, and generally corresponds to what is conventionally understood as municipal, community or city planning; zoning bylaws, subdivision regulations, building codes and other legal devices are used to promote the orderly and socially acceptable development of the physical urban environment. Figure 8.3 illustrates the boundaries of the Southern Ontario Planning Regions (for regional-economic and regional-physical planning), while Figure 8.4 shows the regional municipalities (for local-economic planning) which have so far been created within the Central Ontario Region; below these levels municipalities retain their traditional responsibilities for local-physical planning.

Although some form of political or policy-making authority is necessary for each of the geographical zones into which the national urban system is divided, the appropriate administrative system will vary. The advantages of efficiency in large local governments must, for example, be balanced against the loss of the close relationship which exists between public officials and citizens in small local governments, and consequently the most popular solution has been a federal system.

In 1953 the two-tier or federal system of metropolitan government introduced in Toronto was the first of its kind in North America; until that time the only other attempt to create such a system in an English-speaking country had been the establishment in 1888 of the London County Council, which almost from its inception, had proved inadequate to cope with metropolitan problems. The two-tier model has been widely regarded as appropriate for metropolitan areas: at the lower level, communities retain exclusive or shared responsibilities for some services, through the operation of their local council, while surrendering jurisdiction over matters of area-wide concern to the metropolitan council, on which they are also re-presented. The federal system is especially advantageous for those metropolitan areas which include rural municipalities, since the latter may be more willing to enter a partnership if they can be self-determining and self-financing for purely local responsibilities; for example, they may be prepared to forego snow removal or regular garbage collection if these are locally financed operations and therefore optional. Area-wide functions are either paid for on a user-charge basis if costs can be assigned easily to each municipality (e.g., water supply) or shared according to some equitable formula (e.g., on a per capita basis or by a uniform levy on real property assessment) when costs cannot be apportioned on the basis of usage.

The creation of a metropolitan government in Toronto has served as a means of alleviating many of the problems which are commonly found in such areas, but has not entirely resolved them. In 1973 Metro Toronto had full or partial responsibility for forty-five functions while the local municipalities had exclusive jurisdiction over only twenty-seven functions; 73 per cent of the revenue raised from

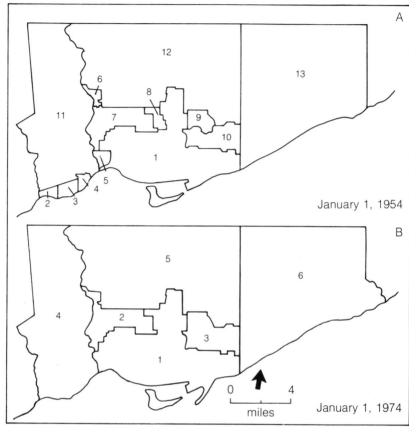

FIGURE 8.5  Municipal divisions within Metro Toronto (Municipality of Metropolitan Toronto). A: At the time when the metropolitan council assumed jurisdiction over the area on January 1, 1954. Municipalities: 1, City of Toronto; 2, Village of Long Branch; 3, Town of New Toronto; 4, Town of Mimico; 5, Village of Swansea; 6, Town of Weston; 7, Township of York; 8, Village of Forest Hill; 9, Town of Leaside; 10, Township of East York; 11, Township of Etobicoke; 12, Township of North York; 13, Township of Scarborough. B: On January 1, 1974. Municipalities: 1, City of Toronto; 2, Borough of York; 3, Borough of East York; 4, Borough of Etobicoke; 5, Borough of North York; 6, Borough of Scarborough.

*Source:* Metropolitan Toronto Planning Board

the property tax in 1971 was spent by the metropolitan authority. Although this has significantly reduced intermunicipal competition for certain high-revenue land uses it has not increased the willingness of suburban municipalities to permit low-income housing. Neither

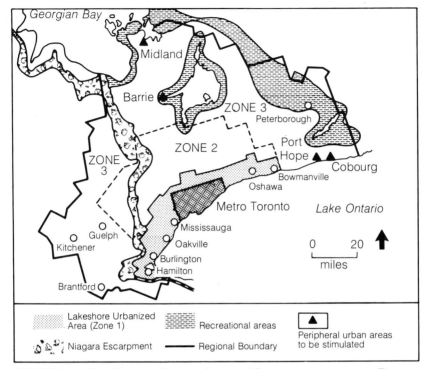

FIGURE 8.6    The Toronto-Centred Regional Development concept. The region has been divided into three zones: 1. The *Lakeshore Urbanized Area* (Zone 1), centred on Toronto, extends from Bowmanville to Hamilton and is expected to retain the large majority of the region's population. 2. The *Commutershed* (Zone 2) lies within easy daily commuting range of Toronto. As much land as possible will, however, be retained for recreational, agricultural and open space uses, while limited growth will be allowed within existing communities. 3. The *Peripheral Belt* (Zone 3) lies beyond the commutershed but is well within the orbit of Toronto's highly specialized functions. Much of the area, including the Niagara Escarpment, is to be maintained as recreation and open-space areas. However, Barrie and Midland in the north and Port Hope and Cobourg in the east are to be developed into large centres in order to decentralize some growth from metropolitan Toronto.

*Source*: Government of Ontario, *Design for Development: The Toronto-Centred Region* (Toronto: Queen's Printer, 1970).

has the formation of a metropolitan government led to any appreciable reduction in the number of special-purpose boards (there are about a hundred such bodies); their activities are, however, better coordinated. The reduction in the number of municipalities in 1967 from thirteen to six (see Figure 8.5) further diminished the inter-municipal disparities in the residential tax burden; in 1966, for example, Leaside (merged with East York in 1967) had the highest level of household income and the lowest tax rate in the metropolitan federation because its industrial plants drew their work force from neighbouring municipalities, which accordingly bore the costs of providing services.

Another aspect of metropolitan planning has been pioneered in Toronto. The adoption of an official plan for the metropolitan region (Figure 8.6) has in effect instituted a four-tier planning system: the provincial government has determined broadly defined goals for the 8,600-square mile Toronto-centred region (regional economic planning), and has prepared a generalized land use plan for the region (regional physical planning); Metro Toronto is responsible for the preparation and implementation of a land use plan for the 240-square mile metropolitan area (local economic planning); and direct control over the physical urban development process has been retained by municipalities (local physical planning). The preparation and implementation of the Toronto-centred regional plan are the responsibility of the provincial government; this arrangement is probably best since regional economic planning involves interregional discrimination in the allocation of public funds, and this can only be satisfactorily undertaken by a central agency, in this case, the provincial government. The loose associations among the constituent communities of the extensive metropolitan region militate against effective decision-making with respect to strategic land uses, such as airports and highways, and so regional physical planning is also appropriately a provincial responsibility. (The Nova Scotia Planning Act, 1970, also made that province responsible for regional planning.)

Ontario has recently instituted a number of regional governments which are in practice similar to the Metro Toronto model. The greatest concentration of regional government districts is in the Golden Horseshoe of western Lake Ontario: Durham, Toronto, York, Peel, Halton, Hamilton-Wentworth and Niagara, in addition to the contiguous regional municipalities of Waterloo and Haldimand-Norfolk (Figure 8.4). Outside this area regional municipalities have been formed in Ottawa and Sudbury but there are long-term plans to include practically the whole province. A notable departure from the two-tier system was the reorganization

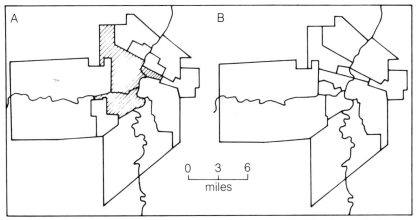

FIGURE 8.7   The reorganization of local government in Winnipeg. A: Municipal divisions which existed within the present-day City of Winnipeg (Unicity) immediately prior to the latter's incorporation on January 1, 1972. (The former city of Winnipeg is shown hatched.) B: Existing community committees within the present-day City of Winnipeg. The boundaries of the former Metropolitan Corporation of Greater Winnipeg corresponded almost exactly to those of the new city but excluded part of the western sector.

*Source:* City of Winnipeg.

of Port Arthur and Fort William into the single city of Thunder Bay which in 1971 accounted for 97 per cent of the census metropolitan area population of 112,093.

With the creation in 1960 of the Metropolitan Corporation of Greater Winnipeg, Manitoba became the second Canadian province to experiment with a two-tier system of metropolitan government; the only significant variation from the Toronto model was its provision for the direct election of metropolitan councillors from constituencies which in every case included parts of more than one municipality. In this case there was a deliberate attempt to foster a metropolitan consciousness rather than municipal self-interest among the metropolitan councillors. In practice, however, this division led to serious conflicts between the policies of the metro and local councils; these were not easily resolved because municipal councillors lacked the opportunity to participate directly in decision-making at the metro level. In Toronto the members of the Metro Council have always been chosen from among the elected members of the local council; for example, the City of Toronto's twelve metro members are the mayor and the senior alderman (based

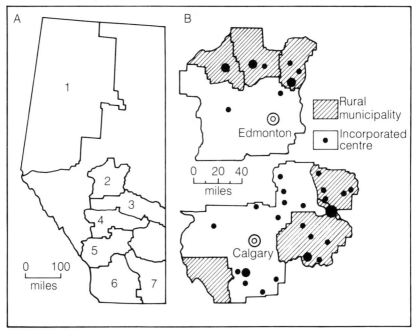

FIGURE 8.8 Regional Planning Commissions in Alberta. A: Regional Planning Commissions: 1 Peace River; 2 Edmonton; 3 Battle River; 4 Red Deer; 5 Calgary; 6 Oldman River; 7 Medicine Hat. B: Rural municipalities (hatched) and incorporated centres (three increasing sizes of circle representing village, town and city respectively) which are not yet members of the Edmonton and Calgary regional planning commissions.

on the number of votes received by the two elected aldermen) from each of the city's eleven wards. In 1972 Winnipeg's metropolitan municipality was reorganized into a single-tier city, but provision was made for some form of decentralized decision-making through the formation of thirteen "community committees." These local committees were created to serve primarily as communications channels between city council and citizens, but they have been given responsibility for some local functions (such as local parks and community centres) which were previously performed by local municipalities; indeed the territorial jurisdiction of the community committees correspond closely to the boundaries of the former municipalities (Figure 8.7). The creation of community committees to replace municipal councils is unprecedented, and makes the

Winnipeg scheme particularly interesting to students of local government.

British Columbia has the distinction of being both the first province to create a regional planning body and the first to institute a province-wide two-tier system of local government. In 1949 the 1,800-square mile Lower Mainland Regional Planning Board was established by the province at the request of municipalities within the Vancouver-centred region; this was the first metropolitan or regional planning organization in Canada. In 1951 the province also created the purely advisory Capital Region Planning Board in order to formulate a regional plan for the Victoria metropolitan area. During the late 1960s the whole province was divided into twenty-eight regional districts. Only one statutory function has actually been allocated to the regional tier—that of providing hospital services—but each council has been empowered to adopt any function which is approved by a voting majority of its members. (The number of a municipality's members and votes are related to its population.) The regional councillors were at first nominated by their local municipal council, but since 1973 councillors have been elected directly by voters, subject only to their concurrent election to their own local council. The Greater Vancouver Regional District is only slightly smaller than the census metropolitan area, while the Capital Regional District covers a much larger area than the Victoria census metropolitan area (934 against 189 square miles) although its population is only slightly larger (205,000 against 196,000 in 1971).

Alberta became the first province to formally institute regional planning, by amending the then Town and Rural Planning Act in 1950. The first regional planning commission (Edmonton) was established in the same year and the most recent (Battle River) in 1960; the seven existing commissions do not, however, cover the entire province (Figure 8.8). According to the act the province has the authority to establish regional planning commissions, but in practice these are normally formed when a number of adjacent municipalities request that the provincial government create such a commission; a subsequent order from the province establishes the commission and its regional planning area. Any municipality situated within a regional planning area is thereafter permitted to apply to the commission for membership. Although financial support of the commission has become obligatory membership has remained voluntary, and in each of the regional planning areas a number of municipalities have not applied for membership (see Figure 8.8). The regional planning commission is not a government body and does not wield political power; its primary responsibilities are to act as the approving authority for subdivision (excluding the cities of Calgary and Edmonton which are themselves approving authorities) and to advise member municipalities on zoning and development. The commission is also responsible for the preparation and implementation of a regional plan. The regional planning commissions have, for example, been quite successful in containing urban development on the fringes of both Edmonton and Calgary, through their adoption of preliminary regional plans.

In the other provinces a variety of approaches have been taken to the problem of metropolitan government. In the province of Quebec two-tier "urban communities" have been created for both Montreal and Quebec; similar in structure is the Regional Community of Outaouais, on the Quebec side of the Ottawa-Hull metropolitan area. The urban communities are equivalent to metropolitan governments, and although given some statutory functions, they are permitted to adopt further responsibilities by a majority decision of their members. In both Montreal and Quebec the urban community is smaller than the census metropolitan area; in Montreal, for example, the two areas cover 191 square miles and 1,032 square miles respectively. In the remaining provinces there are no metropolitan or regional governments, although in many cases annexation programs have enabled the central city to encompass practically the total metropolitan population; the city of Saskatoon, for example, contains its entire census metropolitan population, while in Regina and Saint John only a small proportion of the metropolitan population lies outside the central city.

Canadian municipalities are constitutionally controlled by their provincial governments, and consequently the forms of metropolitan government, their planning powers and the extent of their territorial jurisdictions vary from one part of the country to another. Despite the persistence of political fragmentation in most metropolitan areas, the present Canadian political system is probably better suited to the solution of the characteristic problems of the metropolis than is the case in many other countries; intermunicipal problems, for example, are nowhere as unmanageable as in most metropolitan areas of the United States. It should be noted that variations in size, function and land use problems would preclude any one governmental system from being adopted in all Canadian metropolitan areas.

# 9.
## Urban Problems and Public Policy

In order to determine what policies can be most appropriately used in the resolution of future urban problems it is clearly necessary to have at least some idea of the size and distribution of the future urban population; but forecasting is at best a very risky proposition. The many social, cultural, economic and technological factors which are necessarily involved in any attempt to forecast beyond the short term (less than five years) make the task extremely difficult; the assumption that past trends in demographic or economic structure will continue, for example, may well be invalid.

Despite variations in forecasts of the Canadian urban population for the year 2000 there are a number of features common to all. Urban centres will significantly increase their share of the national population; between 1951 and 1971 the proportion rose from 62.4 to 76.1 per cent, and by the end of the century it will probably be between 90 and 95 per cent. An increasing proportion of the national population will be found in the three national metropolitan centres, Montreal, Toronto and Vancouver; between 1951 and 1971 they increased their share of the national population from 24.2 to 29.9 per cent and by the year 2000 this will probably rise to between 35 and 40 per cent. The most common differences between forecasts stem from their varying estimations of the actual or absolute size of the urban population; this is largely due to variations in the assumed rate of natural increase (i.e., birth rate minus death rate). Except for a few metropolitan centres, the bulk of future population growth will result from the natural increase of the urban population, and rural-urban migration may be expected to decline in importance as the national population becomes increasingly urbanized. (It should be noted that the true rural population; i.e., the rural-farm population, accounted for only 6.6 per cent of the Canadian population in 1971, while 17.3 per cent was classified as rural non-farm.)

The Canadian population is already predominantly urban and the anticipated increase in the level of urbanization is not in itself a cause for anxiety. Urbanization has in the past been accompanied by net social and economic benefits, and there is no reason to suppose that future conditions will alter this. The primary concern of government should not be to limit urbanization, but rather to control the *process* of urbanization in order to increase its benefits and reduce its costs.

## Urban Problems

The high incidence of a particular problem in cities does not in itself mean that it is an urban problem; many such problems are basically societal in nature. In every advanced industrial country the great majority of the population is urban and it is therefore not surprising that most problems are concentrated in urban areas. In practice all the problems found in cities have societal and urban elements, and it is not always possible to separate them. Urban poverty, for example, stems partly from societal changes, such as the advent of modern technology and longer life spans, and partly from the urbanization process, which frequently encourages the dispersal of particular jobs to the point where most of them are beyond the reach of low-income households without cars.

Urban problems may be divided into two classes: those which are caused by the process of urbanization, and those which are caused by the institutional-governmental system. Although the two types are interrelated in any particular society, the former may be considered the true urban problems.

The process of urbanization is manifested in the development of three sub-systems, social, economic and physical, and changes in any one of these is capable of creating friction or disequilibrium. Socially defined, a city is a set of cultural institutions designed to provide a medium for a variety of human experiences and exchanges. Economically defined, a city is a system of activity nodes engaged in the assembly, production and distribution of goods. Physically defined, a city is a collection of buildings, outdoor spaces and communications networks and other man-made elements designed to facilitate social and economic exchanges. *An urban problem occurs when the rate of change of any of the three sub-systems is out of step with that of the others.* Modern construction technology, for example, has made it more economical to stack housing units vertically in high-rise structures than to arrange them horizontally. This new physical form is in advance of changes in social preferences and the friction or disequilibrium which results has created an urban problem which will ultimately be resolved by changes in life styles (social) and/or in the types of housing provided (physical). Similarly, in the manufacturing industry the preference for horizontal-line production systems (an economic change) has produced both physical and social problems: in the suburban fringe rural land has been converted to low-intensity industrial uses while in the inner city vacated loft buildings have created blighted areas; the shift of manufacturing to the suburbs has also created social problems by leaving the low-income inner-city inhabitants without adequate access to suitable jobs.

The chief source of the urban problem is therefore the *rate of change* — when a city grows quickly (usually the result of economic factors), when the urban environment is altered quickly (physical change), or when the goals of a community are changed quickly (social change). Friction or disequilibrium then results because the rates of change which can be accommodated by each sub-system will rarely coincide. In Canada, for example, the urban freeway systems (economic-physical) which were widely approved in the late 1950s and early 1960s were already incompatible with the social goals of the late 1960s (less pollution, more attractive environment) even before the proposed systems had been built; consequently, half-completed freeway systems can be found in almost every major city. In general it is the physical system which adjusts most slowly to change and consequently it is only when economic-social systems remain stable over a long period of time that the physical system is able to accommodate the renewal and replacement of buildings and other physical elements with relative ease. In the medieval era, for example, when the economic and social systems remained virtually unchanged for many centuries the physical urban environment remained in equilibrium with the other systems.

The operation of the three sub-systems, theoretically full of friction, is further complicated by the institutional-governmental or political system, the fourth dimension of the urban system. The majority of the decisions taken in Canadian cities are made by private individuals exercising free choice, but the nature of their decisions is largely moulded by the public framework. In Canada the governmental dimension consists of both a vertical or hierarchical arrangement (federal, provincial and municipal) and a horizontal or territorial arrangement. Variations in policy, goals and fiscal power among the various governmental units contribute to friction both among and within the social, economic and physical systems that make up the functional city (as opposed to the political city).

The solution to urban problems lies essentially in the ability of governments to intervene intelligently in the process of urbanization, and this requires first a clear understanding of how a city functions and second the development of an appropriate public policy for action. The modern city is one of the most complex of all human systems and simple intuitive solutions to urban problems are almost never right. Because of our limited knowledge of how the urban system functions, public programs have often been directed at the symptoms of urban problems rather than at their causes. Such programs have accordingly been either ineffective or, even worse, have aggravated problems through the effects of the altered environment on the rest of the urban system. The early slum clearance projects in the United States, for instance, concentrated on the mass removal of slum dwellings and therefore succeeded only in shifting slum dwellers (and slums) from one area to another. It has become increasingly clear that single-purpose agencies or programs are incapable of coping with complex urban problems; the housing problem, for example, cannot be solved without attention to transportation, the distribution of work places and other related elements. Action in any sphere has profound impact on others and the various programs must form part of one public policy whose aim must be that resolution of frictions among the social, economic and physical systems which maximizes public welfare.

Much of the inadequacy of public urban policy has resulted simply from a failure to comprehend the functioning of the urban system. The interdependency of urban activities is so strong and the urban system is accordingly so complex that it is impossible to trace all the repercussions or causal factors which result from the location of any activity. The complex nature of these interrelationships is due to the recursiveness of external effects, that is, the impact of one activity on another has a feedback effect. The urban environment is not conducive to laboratory experimentation since it is impossible to control the variables to the extent necessary for the precise relationships among activities to be identified. The lack of a laboratory-controlled environment is a serious constraint on our ability to understand the operation of the urban system, since particular forces do not work in isolation but are complexly interwoven with supporting and counteracting elements. Since he cannot effectively isolate the important variables, the urban scientist is only able to obtain insight into, and not answers about, the theoretical structure of urban problems, and consequently proposed solutions can be no more than informed guesses or value judgments. Herein lies the planning paradox: partial programs are unsuitable for the solution of urban problems yet, because of the impossibility of tracing the complex causal chain which links all urban activities to each other, a comprehensive program is unworkable. Even so, insight, when translated into action, can obviously improve the *status quo* and the knowledge of our ignorance is not an excuse for inaction.

As a rule, urban problems occur in areas undergoing change, where the physical environment is adjusting to changes in the social and economic systems. The wide variety of urban problems are concentrated primarily in two areas: the urban fringe, where rural land is being converted to the land-extensive urban uses of the modern socio-economic system, and the central city, where areas of physically deteriorated buildings belonging to a former economic system in which urban uses were mostly land-intensive are being subjected to redevelopment. Inner-city and suburban problems of congestion, blight and sprawl are, however, interdependent, and the solution of problems in one area frequently benefits the other; for example, if suburban housing could be made less costly and therefore accessible to low-income families this would be a major step in the solution of inner-city housing problems. Analytically, however, it is advantageous to separate these two frontiers of change since their characteristic problems, though interdependent, are quite different. At the same time planning programs for these two problem areas must be linked through the reorganization of the present institutional-governmental structure in metropolitan areas.

## The Urban Fringe

The urban fringe is here defined as existing outside the developed urban area and extending to the outer limit of the commuting range of a city. There are no well-defined breaks between rural and urban areas but rather an admixture, often haphazard, of urban and rural uses. Within this area two separate zones may be distinguished. The inner zone or suburban fringe is a fairly narrow belt of land which is being actively converted from rural to urban uses. The outer zone or

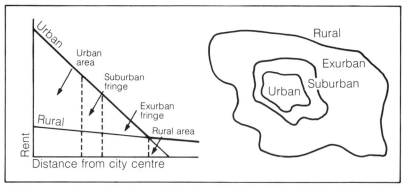

FIGURE 9.1 Hypothetical extent of the urban, suburban and exurban zones.

exurban* fringe covers a much wider area of land where urbanization is evident but not predominant. Some areas have already been converted to urban uses while others are still being used for rural activities; some urban-oriented uses (for example, vacation homes or cottages) are found, while much of the land remains idle in anticipation of future development. The hypothetical extent of the two zones is illustrated in Figure 9.1.

The process of development in the urban fringe is a critical area of concern, particularly since its results are frequently attacked on social, economic and aesthetic grounds. Public policy in this area has, however, been handicapped by the lack of knowledge about the process of converting rural land to urban uses; it is at best fragmentary and hypothetical and little is actually known about the effects of the private market process or about the present and potential impacts of various public controls. Nevertheless, the prevailing land use patterns in this area are generally considered to be unsatisfactory and it is therefore necessary that public policy be directed at bringing development more into line with social goals. Policies can, however, be successfully applied only after the process has been conceptually understood.

Urban fringe problems, like all other urban problems, result from an imbalance among and within the physical, social and economic

---

* It is convenient to use the now common term exurbia or exurban fringe to describe the wide urban-oriented zone which lies beyond the relatively narrow suburban zone.

systems. Specifically, urban fringe problems result from an imbalance between private and communal demands for urban land. In the urban fringe the amount of land which can be successfully urbanized (i.e., where the conversion from rural to urban uses would bring an *individual* resident net social and/or economic benefits) considerably exceeds the amount of land which needs to be urbanized in order to maximize the socio-economic welfare of the urban community. In the modern city much of this imbalance has resulted from the revolution in private transportation technology and in particular from the widespread use of the automobile. Assuming a walking speed of 3 m.p.h. and an average automobile speed of 30 m.p.h. the amount of land which can be urbanized in terms of time-distance will be one hundred times greater for automobile-based than for on-foot trips. The developable area has generally been extended even further than this direct comparison would suggest, since a significant decentralization of work places to the edge of the urbanized area has also taken place. Each radial extension of a city's sphere of influence also produces a geometric increase in area; for example, the expansion of a city's radius of influence from 10 to 11 miles would add 56 square miles to its developable zone but an expansion from 30 to 31 miles, which more closely approximates the situation around large metropolitan centres, would add 192 square miles.

THE SUBURBAN FRINGE

The modern suburban accretions of cities have been widely deprecated on aesthetic, social and economic grounds. The debate over the aesthetic and social qualities of suburbia is highly subjective and is inevitably concerned with life-style preferences; those who value privacy and spaciousness are generally satisfied with the suburban environment while the more gregarious prefer central-city living. Such debates are, of course, unavoidable in a society which has become increasingly concerned with the quality of urban life. There is, however, widespread agreement on certain aspects of the suburbanization process—usually those which involve costs and particularly the cost of land. Because of the interconnectedness of the urban system the high cost of suburban land has repercussions throughout the city.

A major problem which arises from low-density suburban development is the discrepancy between private benefits and social costs. Although the typical suburban homeowner (or renter) may appear to pay the full cost of development—land, services, house and so on—some costs cannot be internalized in the purchase of a house-and-lot and are therefore borne by the community as a whole. Some social costs, such as air pollution and highway construction, which result from the considerable dependence of suburban households on the automobile, cannot be easily charged to individuals. Also, many community services are provided at uniform cost (for example, public transit, garbage collection and snow removal) even though their costs are a direct function of the population density of a particular area. Since the costs of these services cannot be apportioned to each individual on a user-charge basis it is appropriate for the community to set density standards for suburban development in order to protect the public interest; unfortunately, the question of density is not the most fundamental problem within the suburban zone.

The most serious consequence of the present suburbanization process is the high cost of land; suburban land prices have recently increased more rapidly than the general rate of inflation (measured by the consumer price index) and this has had social, physical and economic repercussions throughout the city.) Between 1961 and 1973, the consumer price index rose by 50.4 per cent in Canada, while for single detached dwellings financed under the National Housing Act,[1] the cost of land increased by 79.5 per cent. The high cost of homes in the suburban area has directly affected the composition of its resident population, and therefore determined to some extent which groups of people will live elsewhere in the city. Because the homeowner buys a package (house and lot) it is reasonable to expect builders to construct expensive houses on high-cost land, if the consumer is to be satisfied. Accordingly, suburban houses in large cities are now priced well beyond the financial reach of all but the upper and middle income groups; the low-income families are forced to concentrate in the central city, exacerbating the problems of the inner city areas. This is nowhere more evident than in Toronto. Nationally, the average family income of purchasers of single-detached houses finance under the National Housing Act[2] was $12,856 in 1973 compared to $15,293 for purchasers in metropolitan Toronto; whereas 45.4 per cent of purchasers in Canada had family incomes below $12,000, the corresponding proportion

1 Central Mortgage and Housing Corporation, *Canadian Housing Statistics 1973* (Ottawa: 1974).
2 *Ibid.*

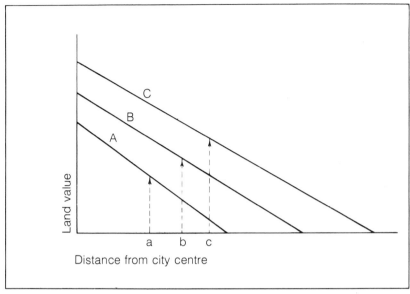

FIGURE 9.2    Urban land value curves of three cities. The distance of the suburban fringe (edge of the built-up area) from the city centre is shown by a, b and c for the respective cities.

for Toronto was only 13.0 per cent. The cost of land was a primary factor; in Toronto the average price of a lot was $13,261[3] compared to the national average of $4,673. Most of this difference is due to variations in the price of raw land, although some of it is the result of variations in the extent and method of financing municipal services. In 1972 a study commissioned by the Urban Development Institute of Ontario (a developers' association) estimated that only 4 per cent of families living in Toronto could afford to buy a new single-family house.

Suburban Land Costs

The price of suburban land is a function of two variables; the size of the urban population and the rate of urban growth. Together these two factors explain much of the variation in land prices from one city

3  This is not representative of the typical cost of a single-family lot in Toronto, which in 1973 was about $35,000-$40,000 for a privately developed suburban lot; only a small proportion of houses in metropolitan Toronto is financed under the National Housing Act.

to another. Figure 9.2 illustrates the effect of urban size on suburban land prices; theoretically the land at the suburban fringe of a large city has a higher price than that at the edge of a small city because of the larger population which is accessible to the user in the former case (land values are a function of accessibility). In a dynamic situation land prices also increase at a faster rate in faster growing cities. Assuming that the land value curves of City *B* and City *C* (Figure 9.2) refer to the expected distribution of City *A*'s land values at successively higher population levels, then the same curves may be used to represent different rates of growth for City *A*; for example, for the same period of time an annual growth rate of 1 per cent may result in a curve such as that of City *B* and one of 3 per cent may produce a curve such as that of City *C*. The higher the rate of growth, the faster will be the rate of increase of suburban land prices in a city.

Excessive increases in the price of suburban land can also result from the process by which the private market converts rural land to urban uses. This is often a long process and there may be many intermediaries between the two ends of the chain, the farmer and the homeowner. In their normal order of entry there are three types of intermediary: speculator, developer and builder. The speculator (not used in a moralistic sense) invests in raw land as a commodity and speculates on its future resale value. The developer is a "manufacturer" of urban land; he assembles raw land (perhaps by buying it from the speculator) and converts it into building lots by subdivision and the installation of services (water mains, sewers, streets and so on). The builder is the retailer; he purchases serviced lots and erects houses for sale or rent. Although all of these functions may at times be performed by one individual or company it is commonly the case that rural land passes through the hands of several intermediaries before being eventually urbanized.

One of the most important reasons for the high cost of suburban land is the length of time that elapses between the sale of land by the farmer (or other rural user) and its development for urban uses. Whether the land is held by speculator, developer or builder two things are commonly found: first, there is a low-equity capital invested and heavy use is made of credit; second, the land is either kept idle (unproductive) or used at a low level of intensity on a share-cropping basis. As a result, holding costs (total annual charges less returns), which include interest on loans, property taxes and administration, are generally high. Since the land does not produce any appreciable annual return to the non-farmer before it is urbanized the interest on borrowed capital must be calculated at a compound rate: at an interest rate of 10 per cent the cost of land will double every 7½ years, and at 12 per cent, which is common for such speculative investments, costs will double every 5½ years. The added costs of property taxes and payments for management, legal and other services may result in a doubling of the cost of speculatively held land every four or five years. It is perfectly reasonable, as a normal business practice, for developers and builders to acquire some land in advance of need since it is their basic raw material, but in large cities it is not unusual for rural land to be held fifteen years or more before any urban development is initiated. In metropolitan Toronto, for example, it has been estimated that the stock of developable land (as opposed to serviceable land which has access to trunk services), which is held by developers, speculators and builders, is four to five times the anticipated amount needed for a decade.

One of the best documented studies of land speculation in Canada was carried out in Montreal in 1964.[4] Within the metropolitan area 87,600 acres were classified as abandoned farm land, compared to only 113,300 acres of existing urbanized land. (Included in the abandoned category were 8,100 acres of recently subdivided land which had not yet been built up.) Based on the 1961-1964 rate of urbanization the abandoned lands alone were sufficient for expansion during a period of about fifteen years, or for a population increase of about 1.1 million; the metropolitan population was estimated to be 2.2 million in 1964. The abandoned lands were, however, only the most visible signs of speculation since they were generally the result of the speculators' failure to find a farmer interested in cultivating the land. In addition to the revenue to be derived directly from lease-farming, property taxes would have been lower on speculatively-held farmed acreages since these were legally assessed at a lower level (a ceiling of $100 an acre) than vacant land. In fact the total area under speculation was estimated to be 250,000 acres — more than twice the existing urbanized area.

The fact that virtually all the land which comes on the suburban market is in the hands of owners who have held it idle or near-idle for some time is the principal reason why higher prices due to holding

4 Service d'urbanisme, *Urbanization: A Study of Urban Expansion in the Montreal Region*, Technical Bulletin No. 5 (Montreal: City of Montreal, 1969).

costs can be so easily passed on to the consumer. The operation of the private land market in the urban fringe is closely related to the expected level of future land values, and so the larger the city and the faster its growth rate the longer will be the period during which the land is removed from productive use and held idle. If farm land is worth $500 per acre (that is, $500 is the capitalized annual bid-rent for farming) and suburban land, based on present values, is expected to be worth $2,000 in City A and $4,000 in City B, then land can be held idle for about ten years in the former case and about fifteen years in the latter (assuming a compound interest rate of 12 per cent in each case). In the operation of the private market, land should be removed from agriculture as soon as the future appreciation in land values would cover holding costs (ten and fifteen years in the above two cases), since the returns from future urban use would exceed the returns from farming; in other words speculation becomes the "highest and best use" from the point of view of the individual. Theoretically, therefore, at the point of urbanization land should be in the hands of non-farmers (with the exception of speculative farmers i.e., those who choose to farm while speculating on the enhanced urban value), and the base selling price (i.e., one which ensures that the seller does not make a loss) should be several times the value of farm land.

A second important reason for the high price of suburban land is the effect of municipal development policies at the point of urbanization. Minimum subdivision standards and municipal services account for a substantial proportion of the cost of a serviced lot; these commonly include 66-foot wide road allowances, 28-foot paved roads, 50-foot lot frontages, sidewalks on both sides of streets, buried utilities and so on. Many of these are considered to be neighbourhood amenities which presumably appeal to home buyers, but the consequent costs make it difficult for many families to purchase houses. Housing costs have also increased because municipalities are either unable or unwilling to incur long-term debts for the servicing of land, and therefore demand prepayment for services; alternatively these are built by developers to municipal specifications and turned over without charge to the municipality, which assumes responsibility for maintenance. Service costs are now commonly added to the initial purchase price of a house rather than being paid for over a long period of time in the form of a local improvement charge. Houses with prepaid services are pushed even further beyond the financial reach of many households since the down payment is related to the selling price. The length of time involved in getting municipal approval for subdivision and servicing has become quite lengthy (up to two years is common) and this adds to the developer's holding costs.

As a result of the property tax system it is actually in the self-interest of suburban municipalities to increase the cost of housing. Because of the relationship between assessment and market value, suburban municipalities have understandably been wary of attracting any type of single-family housing other than that which will be sought by the highest income groups, since these homes are the only ones which yield sufficient taxes to cover the costs of municipal services. In fact municipalities often appear to be anti-family—preferring commercial uses or apartments for childless couples and single people—because of the high costs of education. In 1973, for example, in the suburban municipalities of metropolitan Toronto the average cost of services alone was about $6,500 per lot, which was more than 50 per cent higher than the cost of a fully serviced lot (including land) in Saskatoon. Because of the prospects of increased education costs municipalities are also inclined to restrict the speed at which land is developed for housing in order to maintain a favourable ratio between commercial and residential assessment.

In Canada, several solutions to the problem of high suburban land prices have been repeatedly suggested: these include the assembly of land by government (public land banks), the use of special tax measures to discourage land speculation, the expansion of developable land beyond the immediate market demand through increased servicing programs, and reduction in subdivision and servicing standards. The last two measures have generally been proposed by land developers to counteract the escalation of land prices while the first two proposals are usually supported by government agencies. Solutions proposed by developers are intended to reduce costs at the point of urbanization while the governmental proposals are directed at the reduction of the profits made by holding land for speculative gain.

There is some justification for attributing a substantial proportion of increases in suburban land values to municipal servicing policies. The social amenities prescribed in subdivision regulations (e.g., buried utilities) have economic implications which are particularly detrimental in the case of low-income households, since they are often applied uniformly to all subdivisions within a municipality. (Often the high servicing standards demanded of developers are designed primarily to reduce the maintenance costs to the municipality rather than the cost to the consumer.) The second proposal commonly put forward by developers is to encourage the private land market to operate more efficiently through an over-supply of developable land; this is less practical. The construction of trunk sewers and water mains requires a considerable amount of capital and any extensive time-lag between the provision and use of these facilities is also likely to add to the cost of housing. This proposal is at best only a short-term solution in areas where there is a serious imbalance between supply and demand. It should also be noted that in many large Canadian cities the principle of perfect competition (i.e., where no producer owns a large enough share to affect the market price) does not obtain, since a few landowners share a very substantial proportion of the total developable land; in these circumstances an over-supply of serviceable land will not materially affect its selling price.

The public proposals are based on the belief that immoderate profits are being made by speculators in raw land. Public land banking (i.e., the acquisition, development and sale of land by a government agency in order to remove it from the open speculative market and so regulate land prices) is intended to eliminate private profits made by holding land for urban uses, while special tax measures are designed to reduce speculative profits. As well as the capital gains tax which already (since 1972) applies to profits from the sale of land, it is frequently proposed that an additional tax be levied on profits where land is sold without improvements; the latter would presumably discourage the speculator who simply holds raw land, but not the developer who subdivides and services land. Public land banking was significantly accelerated in 1972 by the adoption of a more deliberate program by the federal government which increased both its capital allocation and its share of acquisition costs (from 75 to 90 per cent). The federal-provincial land assembly program had until then been relatively insignificant; between 1948 (the year of the program's inception) and 1972 only 20,589 lots had been sold, or less than 1 per cent of the total number of dwelling units completed during the same period.

Public land banks which normally cater to long-range demand (fifteen or twenty years) have some of the same drawbacks as private land speculation, since land costs will also double every few years. One of the first federal-provincial land assemblies was the 1,600-acre (subsequently expanded to 1,700 acres) Malvern site in Scarborough (Metro Toronto); the land was acquired in 1953 and the first houses were not occupied until 1972. The principal advantages of public rather than private land speculation are that interest rates on borrowed capital are normally lower (for example, the federal government generally borrows money at the lowest interest rates) and that exorbitant profits will not be made. A further advantage of public land ownership is that development may be encouraged in areas where public ownership is predominant; since governments control development through planning regulations and investment in trunk services, they are in an advantageous position to speculate although they have in the past been politically reluctant to do so. Finally, since governments can better anticipate the time at which urbanization will take place it is more probable that the land will be used productively in the interim, thus reducing holding costs.

Neither the private nor public proposals discussed above are adequate, since they do not resolve the most fundamental reason for rising suburban land costs—the length of time that land is held idle or used at a low productivity level. The theoretical solution involves the elimination of the unproductive holding of land (between farmer and builder) and the transfer to the community of the urbanization or development value of land. Assuming that the non-urban value of land is related to its productivity for farming, the increased value generated by urbanizing the land should in principle accrue to the community which creates it and not to the private landowner. If the value of farm land is $500 per acre and the market value of suburban land is $2,500 per acre, then the development value is $2,000 (i.e., $2,500−500). If the development value were taxed, it would theoretically be the strongest possible disincentive to land speculation. Assuming that the development value were taxed at a rate of 50 per cent then the seller would receive $1,500 (i.e., $500 + $\frac{2,500 - 500}{2}$) instead of the selling price of $2,500. In the long-run the development value tax is superior to the capital gains tax because it maintains a constant base (except for the small rise in the price of *agricultural* land) for the calculation of taxes in all subsequent sales. If, for example, the above property were re-sold for $4,000 the seller's net price after a capital gains tax of 50 per cent would be $3,250 (i.e., $2,500 + $\frac{4,000 - 2,500}{2}$)or a profit of $750, but

after a development value tax the net price would be $2,250
(i.e., $500 + $\frac{4,000 - 500}{2}$) or a loss of $250. In short, a development value tax considerably reduces the marketability of raw land
except in the case of transactions between farmers at the going rate of
farm land (in which case there are no taxes paid) or between the
farmer and the final developer (in which case the development value
tax is approximately equal to the capital gains tax); the intervention
of intermediaries or speculators, however, clearly becomes unprofitable, and consequently there is a greater incentive for farmers to
retain land until the point of urbanization. In practice development
value taxation is difficult to administer for political and, in the
short-term, economic reasons; the latter are clearly the more fundamental and are primarily related to the withholding of speculatively
held land from the market, which produces inflated land prices. The
only western country to attempt development value taxation was the
United Kingdom between 1947 and 1953 and between 1967 and
1970 (Land Commission Act) but on both occasions there were
administrative as well as political reasons for its failure.

In 1974 Ontario became the first Canadian province to institute a
land speculation tax,[5] intended both to reduce the escalation of land
prices and to recover for the public a major share of the profit from
land speculation. Briefly, the Land Speculation Tax imposes a 50
per cent tax on the increase in value realized on the sale of designated
land; over and above this tax, normal personal and corporate income
taxes apply. Although the designated land includes all real property
in Ontario, the tax is designed to bear most heavily on owners of land
and property which are purchased and re-sold without real value
being added. Accordingly, a number of transactions are exempt
from the tax, including the disposition of one's principal residence
not exceeding ten acres of land, the disposition of property where
residential or commercial buildings have been constructed or reno-
vated and the disposition of a family farm to another member of the
family where the land remains in farming use. The Ontario Land
Speculation Tax is in fact a capital gains tax and not a development
value tax. The base price of land to be used in calculating the increase
in value for taxation purposes is the fair market value (which may

5 Hon. John White, *Ontario Budget 1974* (Toronto: Ministry of Treasury,
Economics and Intergrovernmental Affairs, 1974).

itself include a speculative element) on April 9, 1974, or the actual cost of the land if purchased after that date.

THE EXURBAN FRINGE

Exurbia is not simply a lower-density extension of suburbia, but is quite different in character. Most of these differences result from the spatial discontinuity of exurban development, which consequently causes widespread disruption of the rural economy while being itself much less economical and less aesthetically pleasing than suburban development.

The exurban fringe is often described as an urban shadow, the result of the blighting effect of the city on its surrounding region. All cities cast an economic shadow over their region in proportion to their size and importance. Cities actually generate positive benefits or externalities by enhancing the value of farm land before it is converted to urban use, and the blighting effect results simply from an over-supply of such developable land, which in turn leads to a variety of conflicting decisions being made by individual land owners. Because of the profits to be made from even the lowest-density urban development some rural land may be subdivided, while, because of the expectation of higher prices in the future, neighbouring land may be held idle. This process of random development wastes land and is costly to the community, since much land is leap-frogged in the haphazard spread of urbanization; the net result is that urban sprawl removes farm land from productive use far in advance of the time when it would have been urbanized if development had proceeded in an orderly manner. In summary, exurbia is typically neither city nor country and this semi-urban fringe development has been variously described as "urban sprawl" and "urban scatteration."

## Urban Sprawl

Urban sprawl suggests inelegance and wastefulness and is almost universally considered to be an unsatisfactory method of extending the urban area. The most distinctive characteristic of urban sprawl is not its low density (although this is typically much lower than in the suburbs) but the discontinuity and irregularity of development; small urbanized areas leap-frog over vacant or rural areas in an uncoordinated, haphazard manner. There are actually two types of urban sprawl: isolated pockets of urban dwellings that have leap-frogged rural or vacant land, and ribbon or strip developments along highways and country roads. It is this intermingling of urban, rural and vacant land which causes many of the social, economic and aesthetic problems of urban sprawl.)

One of its more serious consequences is the damage done to the rural economy. This is mainly due to the fact that land prices are bid past the economic limit for farming; but is also the result of differences in outlook and values between the established rural community and the urban-oriented newcomers. Ostensibly, exurbanites are disenchanted with the city environment and seek the charm of country living, but at the same time it is the high salary from urban employment which frequently supports the move to the countryside. The exurbanite does not adopt a rural life-style but rather tries to get the best of both worlds, rural and urban, and in the process becomes a source of friction for the rural community.

Rural activities frequently become uneconomic or illegal after the influx of exurbanites into a rural township. Demands for urban services soon follow the arrival of urban-oriented households. For example, snow-ploughing services must be extended because of the early departure of commuters for the city; country dirt roads have to be paved to cope with the increased traffic; piped water, sewers and garbage collection become necessary as density increases; police and fire protection services must be expanded; education costs increase because of the proportionately higher incidence of school-age children among the exurbanite families than among the farming families. In most cases these services have to be supported by the original inhabitants as well, even though they may not be users themselves, since costs cannot always be apportioned on a user-charge basis. Since the number of exurbanites may quickly increase to the point where they form the majority of the electorate in a rural township, there is often little difficulty in getting a number of urban services adopted by the municipal council. The rise in property taxes is one of the common reasons for rural activities becoming uneconomic in such areas; the spatial contiguity of farmer and exurbanite is a second source of conflict and a major reason for the abandonment of farming. In general, urban and rural uses are spatially incompatible, that is, there are negative externalities or spillovers from one to the other. Whether by court order or municipal regulation (where the majority of council members are exurbanites) many farmers in exurban townships have been legally forced to restrict the use of natural fertilizers (manure), or to discontinue certain types of intensive farming, such as large-scale poultry and livestock farming, because of complaints about waste disposal and disagreeable odours. Also, the use which is made of the urbanized land may result in direct costs to farmers; for example, many hobby farms of ten or twenty acres are overrun with weeds which quickly spread to neighbouring farms and which must then be removed, thus adding to the cost of farming.

Urban sprawl results in disproportionately high costs to the metropolitan-wide community; in other words, the private or market price of exurban land is too low to reflect the various social costs which its development would impose on the community-at-large. In terms of the individual consumer, a home in the exurban fringe may be socially or economically superior to one in the city primarily because the direct or private costs do not include many of the social costs which result from such development; for example, a location next to a highway provides the exurbanite with free and convenient access to a major road (as well as the benefits of free snow ploughing and road repair) while inconveniencing the general public through the use of the highway as a local service road. Irregular development also results in higher per capita costs in the case of those services which must be paid for on a uniform basis; these include water mains, fire and police protection, sewers, major roads and public transit. The disruptive effect of premature development is also evinced in the political fragmentation of metropolitan areas. Urban development in the exurban fringe leads typically to the incorporation of municipalities and results in a "scatteration" of public services and greater average costs (because of the absence of scale economies) than would be incurred by compact settlements. Finally, there are a variety of indirect social costs, such as air pollution, which result from the exurbanite's dependence on the automobile but which cannot be recovered in the form of user-charges.

Urban sprawl areas are widely condemned for their disproportionate cost to the rest of the community but it has become increasingly evident that they also work against the self-interest of their residents. One of the primary reasons for moving to exurbia is the low cost of housing, which generally prevails because of the low price of land and the lack of services. In the long run, as the sprawl development gradually merges with the city's built-up area and the density of population increases, residential costs rise above the average for the urban region. Typically, in the first stage of urban sprawl residential development takes place sporadically on unserviced lots;

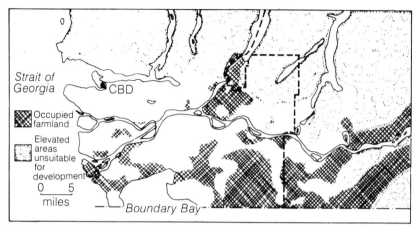

FIGURE 9.3 Occupied farmland in the Vancouver region. (Broken line indicates the eastern boundary of the Vancouver census metropolitan area, 1971.)

*Source*: Greater Vancouver Regional District, *A Report on Livability* (Vancouver, 1972).

in a later stage as density increases, these lots must be serviced for health or other reasons and the resulting cost per dwelling is normally much higher than that of pre-serviced developments. The period of time needed for sprawl developments to become suburbs may be surprisingly short; Surrey's urban sprawl of the late 1950s was being serviced and incorporated into the suburban fabric of metropolitan Vancouver within ten years. The per dwelling costs are high for post-development servicing for two principal reasons: the typical shapes of the lots (long relative to the width) increase the costs of servicing since there are usually fewer houses to the acre under these conditions, and the pre-existing development pattern often precludes an efficient infilling of large vacant land-locked areas with the result that the number of houses to the acre remain lower than in suburban subdivisions.

One of the easiest and most successful ways in which the public can control urban development in the exurban fringe is by the adoption of province-wide land use regulations to remove much land from speculation, and thus prevent premature development. For rural activities to function economically it is essential that the development value of the land (i.e., the difference between the market or urban value and the farming value) be artificially removed by the long-term prohibition of urban development through zoning, an official plan or some other legally enforceable system. Ideally, there should be two land markets —rural and urban. The most widely cited areas in need of land use planning to preserve agriculture are the Niagara Fruit Belt and the mixed-farming area of the lower Fraser Valley; the latter area produces about 65 per cent of the total value of agricultural production in British Columbia, and even within the Vancouver census metropolitan area there are more than 100,000 acres of occupied farmland (Figure 9.3). In 1973 the British Columbia government passed the Land Commission Act which requires each of the province's regional districts to formulate a land reserve plan setting out areas which should be designated as agricultural land; these plans are subject to approval by a government-appointed Provincial Land Commission. The principal aim is to preserve agricultural land, but the commission has been given much wider jurisdiction over land use throughout the province and has been specifically empowered by the act to purchase or acquire land for three major urban uses: *green belt land* —"the present condition or future potential of which merits preservation by reason of its aesthetic quality or its location in or around urban areas"; *land bank land*—"having desirable qualities for urban or industrial development or redevelopment"; *park land*—"having desirable qualities for, or future potential for, recreational use." It is the most radical land use legislation in Canada, but it illustrates the fact that each province must eventually adopt strong measures if farm land is to be preserved and the urbanization process controlled in the vicinity of large urban centres. In some instances where rural activities are either uneconomic or unimportant (as they are in areas of infertile soil, for example) it may still be in the public interest to prohibit urban development; thus, in areas where the social costs of development are high and where these cannot be recovered from a tax on the landowner (as in the case of ribbon developments along highways) it is appropriate to make urban development illegal.

Since individuals are capable of neither predicting nor controlling the urbanization process, it is the government's responsibility to ensure that as far as possible the transition from rural to urban use minimizes costs and maximizes welfare for each of its residents; invariably this requires the direct intervention of the provincial government in land use planning. Urban sprawl is largely due to the fact that subdivisions have been permitted in rural municipalities which cannot provide the full range of urban services and which are unaware of the long-term physical, economic and social consequences of urbanization. As a general rule, rural municipalities, which often lack professional planning staff, should not be responsible for subdivision approval. In Alberta subdivision authority is vested in regional planning commissions, while in Ontario it is now a provincial responsibility. (Ontario proposes to delegate this authority to those regional municipalities which are willing to assume the responsibility.) In 1970 the Ontario government assumed direct subdivision authority for the whole province specifically because of the widespread incidence of urban sprawl, and since then urban development has generally been prohibited in rural municipalities except where they have proven themselves capable of handling the consequences. The province's Toronto-centred regional plan is one example of the selective prohibition of urban developments in the urban fringe (Figure 8.6). Alternatively, it is possible to mitigate the effects of urban sprawl while to some extent accommodating the demand for exurban living. A frequently used method is to establish high minimum acreages for subdivisions—twenty or forty acres rather than the one-acre or five-acre lots which are generally preferred by exurbanites. The main advantage of larger acreages is that they can be easily integrated into the city's built-up area at a later date; the disadvantage, however, is that much more land is likely to be removed from agriculture.

Since many urban sprawl problems result from independent decisions made by a large number of suppliers with varying expectations about the future, one possible solution is the encouragement of large, comprehensive developments in the exurban fringe and the prohibition of piecemeal development, which would thus force small developers to cooperate with each other or sell to a large landowner. Exurban developments may, in fact, produce net social and economic benefits if they can combine the advantages of scale economies in the provision of urban services with those of cheap land in the exurban fringe. The consequent development of large-scale projects in approved areas separated by agricultural (green) belts is also likely to be more aesthetically pleasing and less disruptive of the rural economy. The successful development of a number of private new towns in North America since 1950 has demonstrated this and has paved the way for publicly developed new towns.

FIGURE 9.4  New towns under development within the Toronto metropolitan area.

New Towns

In Canada, metropolitan Toronto has been the location of the greatest number of private suburban new towns. Canada's first planned new town in a metropolitan area was Don Mills, which was begun in 1953 and which drew its inspiration from the publicly developed new towns in Britain. (There were also antecedents in Canada, even before the First World War, in large-scale, high-income suburban communities such as Oak Bay in Victoria, Shaughnessy Heights in Vancouver, Tuxedo in Winnipeg and Mount Royal in Montreal; these were single-purpose dormitory communities, however, and in no case was there any attempt to maintain a social or economic balance.) By the late 1960s Don Mills was already engulfed by Toronto's physical expansion and had matured to a well-designed inner suburb. Several new towns, each of more than 3,000 acres, are presently being developed in Toronto's fast-growing western sector, including Bramalea, Erin Mills and Meadowvale (Figure 9.4). Bramalea is the most advanced, with a population which rose from just over 2,000 in 1961 to 25,000 in 1971. Erin Mills, which is being developed by the builders of Don Mills, is a 7,000-acre scheme which is intended to house about 170,000 people by 1990; the 3,000-acre Meadowvale is immediately north of Erin Mills and is expected to cater to about 75,000 people by the same date. Although commercial and industrial uses are integral parts of all the new towns, the communities are designed to be neither self-contained in terms of supplying sufficient employment for their residents nor balanced in terms of the socio-economic composition of the population. Outside Toronto the best example of a private new town in a metropolitan area is Kanata, ten miles west of Ottawa.

Private new towns in Canada have been successful for three principal reasons: they achieve scale economies in the provision of services; they derive economic benefits from their location on the growing edge of established labour markets; and they take advantage of relatively low land prices. They are also able to achieve better aesthetic results than piecemeal developments since they can internalize within their boundaries (and thus make a profit from) many of the external benefits of public amenities. In private developments natural amenities such as ravine land are likely to be preserved as public open space only when the external benefits which they generate can be recovered in the form of higher prices for adjoining properties; where small-scale developments are the rule the owners of ravine property would probably choose to urbanize their land, since the benefits of preserving it in a natural state would accrue mainly to others. In the private new towns west of Toronto, municipalities have, for example, been able to obtain better development standards than in those areas where small developers predominated and where each developer tried to maximize the return from each parcel of land; the parkland donated by new-town developers has averaged about 10 per cent of the total area compared to the minimum of 5 per cent required by the Ontario Planning Act.

In Canada, as in the United States, new towns have so far been private large-scale schemes developed with the intention of making a profit, but there are signs of a movement towards wider acceptance of public involvement in order to ensure that public interests are fully served in the planning of such developments. The public new town is a logical extension of the public land bank, which has been accepted in practice by all provinces. In the United States the federal government enacted legislation in 1970 to promote the development of new towns and the program was launched in the following year. As early as 1956 the Alberta government passed an Act to Provide for the Development and Planning of New Towns (now the New Towns Act, 1969) but most new towns in Canada have been frontier or resource towns (the aluminum town of Kitimat and the government town of Inuvik are among the most noteworthy), and it is only recently that this device has been used in the planning of metropolitan areas. In 1972 the City of Edmonton began the development of the 5,600-acre Mill Woods community, which has a target population of 125,000; although it is only a few miles from the city centre it has been planned to create a balanced community, with a town centre and places of employment. In 1972 the province of Ontario (the Ontario Housing Corporation) began the development of the 1,600-acre Saltfleet community southeast of Hamilton, which has a projected population of 70,000; in the same year the Ontario government embarked on an extremely ambitious scheme, a 17,000-acre new town to be developed in North Pickering near the site of the proposed international airport, northeast of Toronto. In 1973 the federal government amended the National Housing Act to include a New Communities Program, which is specifically designed to counteract urban sprawl and to promote the development of growth centres; the new town program was inaugurated in the same year with the designation of a 9,000-acre site at Carlsbad Springs, ten miles southeast of Ottawa, which is to be developed in partnership with the Ontario government.

The new towns policy in Canada, as in the United States, has been influenced by the postwar experience in planning such communities in Britain. The British new towns policy, which began with the New Towns Act of 1946, has been generally adjudged a success; from the beginning it was regarded as an alternative to high-density, high-rise living in the central city, and was framed in the tradition of the Garden City movement which was initiated by the publication of Ebenezer Howard's *Tomorrow: A Peaceful Path to Real Reform* in 1898 (re-issued in 1902 as *Garden Cities of Tomorrow*). It was felt that the general preference for a house-and-garden could be most economically satisfied through the decentralization of people and jobs, while the concentration of development in new towns prevented urban sprawl and preserved much of the countryside. Fundamental to the British new town program was the creation of "self-contained and balanced communities for work and living." Stevenage, the first new town to be so designated in Britain, is an excellent example of self-containment; in 1966 only 15 per cent of the resident employed population worked outside the town while in terms of socio-economic composition it had a balanced population, except that it lacked the extremes of wealth and poverty.

The advantages of a public sector new town are both economic and social. Through public ownership the appreciated value of land which results from its urbanization can be retained by the community; although in principle this development value already belongs to the community, the most practicable way of capturing it is by outright ownership of pre-urban land. The profit which is made from the development of new towns can in turn be used to pay for community services and facilities and even to subsidize the redevelopment of inner city areas. The achievement of a socially, economically and demographically balanced community is also more likely under public rather than private ownership. Private new towns tend to be oriented only to the more profitable investments and often to short-term returns; private new towns in North America, for example, have catered almost exclusively to high-income groups. A balanced community can only be achieved where profit maximization is not the primary goal and where large amounts of capital are invested for a long time before any economic return is made; in both cases such enterprises are better suited to the public sector. In a public sector new town, for example, social balance may be achieved by using some of the profits from commercial-industrial development to subsidize low-income housing. The rapid growth of a private new town because of short-term profit-making may also lead to demographic imbalance; such a town will have a preponderance of young married couples with school-age children since these households are the most likely to buy suburban houses. Besides the social consequences there are economic reasons (e.g., school construction costs) for maintaining balanced demographic growth. The goal of self-contained employment is also more likely to be achieved by a public authority because of its control over the location of work places and its greater financial resources which make long-term planning more feasible; private developers may be tempted for economic reasons to allow an influx of either jobs or people, depending on market conditions.

The principal argument against the involvement of the public sector in new town development in Canada is a practical one and it is whether the current land use controls are adequate to ensure that the full benefits are achieved from such developments. In European countries, where public new towns have been most successfully developed, they have formed part of a national urban strategy, and because legislative and executive powers are more or less centralized at the national level it has been a relatively easy matter to guide development into predetermined locations. Since the Second World War, for example, virtually all new manufacturing plants (those covering more than 10,000 sq. ft. and including the physical expansion of existing buildings) in Britain have had to obtain an Industrial Development Certificate, which may be granted only at the discretion of the national government; a certificate has been easier to obtain for a site in a new town than for one in a highly congested area such as London. In Britain, as in Canada, there are special grants or incentives available to firms which locate in particular areas. In Canada there is no national urban policy, partly because of the constitutional division of power between the federal government and the provinces; moreover, the extent of current controls over the locations of commercial and industrial land uses in metropolitan regions make the success of new towns less certain. The stick-and-carrot approach, as used in Britain, would be essential to the successful development of public sector new towns; the Canadian approach of using incentives (carrot) to direct the location of industry would have to be accompanied by the prohibition (stick) of such development in other areas.

## The Central City

The problems of central cities are quite different in nature from those of suburban municipalities, and characteristically include blight, slums, poverty and traffic congestion. Consequently the planning approach must be modified and the main emphasis placed on redevelopment, rehabilitation and conservation. The central city's planning problems derive principally from three sources: changes in the technological-economic-social structure of cities, which have rendered many of its buildings and functions obsolete in addition to eroding its accessibility; the accommodation of the physical changes inherent in the process of urbanization, which is more complicated in the central, built-up areas than in the vacant urban fringe; the structure of municipal finance and the territorial fragmentation of local government, which also work more to the disadvantage of central than suburban municipalities.

In metropolitan areas recent technological, economic and social changes have typically produced striking contrasts in the spatial structure of cities. The central city is frequently the product of nineteenth-century technology while the suburbs are of the twentieth century; inner and outer zones are basically incompatible in functional structure and their physical contiguity may be regarded as little more than an historical accident. When the central city was developed technological conditions were such that the concentration of uses in a limited area was essential; the modern suburbs however, have developed under conditions (both technological and economic) which have made the dispersion of activities both possible and desirable. The market process, which does not always equate private and social costs, would, if allowed to operate without public restrictions, inevitably increase the incompatibility between central city and suburb. Although the redevelopment of the central city is capable of producing net social and economic benefits, in order to do so it must be undertaken by means of public investment and regulation. The functional-physical vitality of the central area can only be maintained by a public authority, since the coordination required cannot be achieved by individuals seeking to maximize their own profit.

The blighted conditions of central areas are the result of three interrelated factors: the physical deterioration of buildings, the functional obsolescence of buildings, and the decline in environmental quality. As a building ages, physical deterioration or a loss in serviceability will occur, primarily caused by wear and tear. Functional obsolescence is caused not only by physical deterioration but also by changes in tastes, fashion, design and technology. The physical life of a building is normally longer than the life of its original function. In the manufacturing industry the switch to horizontal-line processing is one of the principal reasons for the obsolescence of many loft buildings in the city centre, whereas in the case of residences it is often style and technological considerations, rather than physical deterioration, that cause high-income groups to choose new housing in the suburbs. Like buildings, the quality of the environment is impermanent and subject to deterioration. Except in the very early stages of development, environmental quality does not generally improve with time; this is due to both the obsolescence of buildings and shifts in the location of population and production.

Blight is also produced by the uncertainty of future land use changes. All major land uses, whether desirable or undesirable, cast

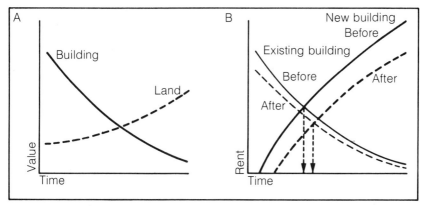

FIGURE 9.5    Impact of a property tax system on redevelopment. A: Changes in the value of building and land over time. B: The net potential rent of a new building compared to that of an existing building, before and after payment of property taxes. (The net rent of a new building is approximately equal to its expected rent minus the rent of the existing building.) Since at every period in time property taxes will be greater for the new building than for the existing one (assuming that the new building is at least as large as the old one), redevelopment will accordingly be delayed by the existence of a property tax system.

a shadow of uncertainty in proportion to their importance; blight occurs over a larger-than-necessary area when the expectation of spatial extension is combined with uncertainty about the direction of change. When the expanding use is considered beneficial (as in the case of central business uses), blight is caused by a wait-and-see attitude on the part of landowners. When the expanding use is undesirable (for example, a ghetto), blight may result from the lack of property maintenance because of the anticipated loss in market value.

A positive cause of physical change in central cities is the emergence of more intensive land uses. Typically, in a growing city the economic return from a building decreases over time because of physical and functional obsolescence, while the value of the site (land) increases (Figure 9.6), indicating that the site could be put to more profitable use. The theoretical termination of the economic life of a building is when the net income it (i.e., building and land) produces falls below the rent which could be realized by an alternative use of the site—in other words, when the building becomes a negative asset. The process of redevelopment for more intensive uses

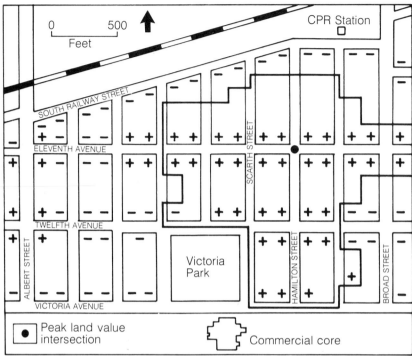

**FIGURE 9.6** Assessed land values for taxation purposes in relation to estimated market values within the CBD of Regina. Locations where land is assessed above (+) or below (−) the average percentage which assessed values form of market values within the CBD as a whole are shown in relation to the peak land value intersection and the commercial core (the latter is defined as the area where assessed land values exceed $500 per front foot).

*Source*: Planning Department, City of Regina.

is partly frustrated by the property tax system. Owners are discouraged from redeveloping their property since the increased revenue from the new buildings will be accompanied by higher taxes. The existence of a property tax system does not, of course, prevent redevelopment, but tends to postpone it (Figure 9.5). In some circumstances the highest economic return may actually be achieved by demolishing an existing building and leaving the land vacant (or used temporarily as a parking lot) for some time before redevelopment takes place. For example, on a site where the zoning bylaw permits construction of a 500,000-square foot office building (assumed to be its maximum potential development) it may be possible to construct a building of no more than 100,000 square feet in order to achieve an acceptable return on capital at the time when redevelopment first becomes feasible. If, however, demand is expected to increase at a fast rate it may then be more profitable to demolish the existing building (assuming that the rent which could be obtained is less than operational costs, including maintenance charges and property taxes) but to delay construction until the development value of the site approaches its maximum potential. In such a situation the annual increase in the development value of the land (expressed in terms of additional floor space) will exceed the loss of potential rent from a smaller building. (In many cases buildings are demolished and the land is held vacant not solely because of the above argument but because the previous owner may have "written off" the total value of the building for tax purposes. As part of the agreement for sale to a redeveloper such an owner may insist that the building, which may still have an economic life, be demolished immediately in order that it may be clearly seen that the purchase price was determined solely by the value of the land.) Moreover, variations in assessment policy often contribute directly to the maintenance of sub-standard structures and to land speculation; Figure 9.6 illustrates for Regina's downtown a phenomenon which is common to many cities—that the assessed value of land for taxation purposes forms a higher proportion of the true market value within the commercial core than is the case on the periphery.

Two major modifications of the property tax system have been proposed in order to encourage redevelopment in central areas: a graduated time-scale of taxation, and site-value taxation. Time-scale taxation means that taxes would be increased in proportion to the age of the building, which would have the effect of discouraging the retention of old buildings. (From a municipality's point of view this may be sound since the costs of municipal services, such as fire, health and welfare, are generally higher for old than for new buildings.) A variant of this method is the freezing of assessment values for buildings at pre-improvement levels for a contracted period of time; this method has been commonly used in the rehabilitation of residential areas but has also been applied to commercial redevelopment. In Halifax, for example, property tax concessions are granted to new commercial buildings (excluding land) and to improvements of existing buildings on a decreasing scale for five years—a 25 per cent rebate in the first year, 20 per cent in the second year, and so on to 5 per cent in the fifth and final year. Proponents of site-value taxation recommend the transfer of the total property tax to the land (site), thus removing the disincentive to redevelopment and reducing land speculation; in practice this form of taxation has not worked well (for example, in western Canada).

The problems associated with blight are proliferating in modern cities because of the current pace of urbanization and the accelerated rates of social and economic change. The processes of economic and social change in pre-industrial societies were such that the periodic destruction and renewal of buildings could be accommodated in the gradual evolution of cities. The modern problem is simply that functional obsolescence is proceeding at a faster rate than physical deterioration; as a result functionally blighted areas are being created more quickly than their buildings can be economically renewed or modified for other uses. Moreover, in a period of rapid technological change vacant land in the urban fringe becomes even more attractive as the site for new structures.

The problems created by the out-migration of commerce, industry and high-income households to the suburbs have been compounded by the existence of divided political jurisdictions within metropolitan areas. The central city's share of metropolitan costs is directly proportional to the size of the suburban population but the tax bases of most central cities have been increasing at a rate which is inversely proportional to the growth of suburban municipalities. The heavier tax burden of the central city is also related to the large and growing incidence of tax-exempt property because of the downtown concentration of government offices, regional institutions, and various cultural and community facilities. In 1971, for example, 24 per cent of the City of Toronto's assessed property value was tax-exempt compared to the corresponding rates of between 9 and 16 per cent for the five boroughs which constituted the rest of Metro Toronto. In addition, and partly because of the zoning policies of suburban municipalities, the poor, the old, the unemployed and other disadvantaged people tend to cluster downtown, thus necessitating above-average expenditure on welfare, health, education, police protection and a variety of community services.

DOWNTOWN REDEVELOPMENT

There is a general tendency to equate progress with skyscrapers, and since 1960 the popularity of increasingly tall buildings has been the most universal characteristic of the redevelopment of Canadian city centres. In response to changes in their economic functions, down-towns are now frequently distinguished by large, impressive office towers, often set back from the street in landscaped plazas within multi-functional building complexes.

The new skyscrapers have had almost as many detractors as endorsers. The towers have been generally commended for the freshness of the open spaces created in cramped downtowns. (With the possible exception of Montreal, Canadian town centres have hitherto been largely devoid of public open areas.) The generous setbacks produce an almost park-like spaciousness where trees, foun-tains and an occasional vista offer a change from the walled canyons of the past. For tenants the tower provides commanding views and the convenience of a central elevator shaft. Critics of the contempor-ary skyscraper point mainly to the loss of the human scale, from a pedestrian's eye-view the towers are overscaled and appear like blank walls, while their landscaped grounds are often designed more to embellish the appearance of the building than to invite the passer-by. (The north-facing plaza of the Toronto-Dominion Centre in To-ronto, for instance, is little used and is a classic example of a lack of design consideration for pedestrians; in contrast the smaller south-facing plaza is much frequented.) Where before there were many pedestrian-directed activities along the sidewalk, the multi-func-tional complexes have re-grouped the horizontal arrangement of activities into a vertical system. The ground floor, which is set back from the sidewalk, is often a bare elevator lobby, whose empty spaciousness is designed primarily to cope with the rush-hour traffic; the offices are stacked vertically above the ground floor while most of the ancillary services such as banks, stores and restaurants, are removed to a subterranean level.

In contrast to the sterility of the new core's pedestrian environ-ment is the liveliness of the old downtown core. The new core is typically an office centre, and other uses, such as shops and restaur-ants, are merely ancillary activities which exist because they cater to the downtown work force. When the offices are closed in the evening, the new core is a dead area with few pedestrians. In contrast, the old core has a variety of activities which are not only interdependent but also independent; the bustle associated with its stores, banks and offices in the daytime gives way to the traffic generated by theatres, night clubs and restaurants in the evening. In the modern city there is a tendency towards increasing homogeneity in the areal segregation of functions, and the old core has often remained the only diversified district; in addition, the narrow streets, the continuity of store fronts, the variety of building types, and the low heights of buildings maintain the interest of the passer-by and contribute to the retention of the street's pedestrian character. It is doubtful whether the diversity of the old core, which to many people is the most attractive feature of the city centre, can be preserved by the unconstrained operation of the market. Downtowns are being systematically fragmented into special-purpose districts which are often too extensive or too widely separated for convenient pedestrian movement from one to another; typically the new multi-functional building complex is inward-looking and by catering to most daytime activities (offices, shops, restaurants) is capable of functioning as a self-contained community. It is only through public control that functional diversity can be maintained within the sub-districts of the city centre.

One of the more important planning objectives is to make the city centre attractive to pedestrians—workers, shoppers and tourists alike. More so than any other part of the city, downtown is the city's display window and it both reflects and creates the communal identity. Three objectives have been commonly pursued in designing a more attractive pedestrian environment: the provision of public open space, the creation of pedestrian precincts and walkways, and the preservation of historical buildings.

During the 1960s many Canadian cities initiated programs to renovate their historical areas which in almost every instance were located a short distance from the most active downtown core. In Victoria the attractive Bastion Square, located near the site of the first Hudson's Bay Company fort, between the downtown core and the Inner Harbour, emerged in 1965 from a cluster of nineteenth-century buildings which were formerly devoted to wholesaling and warehousing. The rehabilitation of the areas included the conversion of the buildings, which now house boutiques, professional offices and a maritime museum. Montreal's restoration program began officially in 1964 when a 100-acre area, corresponding approximately to the walled eighteenth century town, was designated as an historical precinct. The restoration of Quebec's Place Royale was begun in 1970 as part of a larger historical preservation program. In Vancouver the original 1870 townsite, now popularly known as Gastown, was designated an historical precinct in the late 1960s when it appeared that the area might undergo widespread redevelopment. In other cities, including Halifax and St. John's, the movement to preserve historical buildings is only in its formative stage. In Toronto, where the amount of downtown redevelopment has exceeded that of any other Canadian city, there is no official plan for the preservation of historical buildings. In every city the restoration of historical precincts has been recognized as important in promoting tourism while in the case of cities such as Victoria, Vancouver, Montreal, Quebec and Halifax there is the added attraction of re-emphasizing the waterfront, which first gave rise to the town but which was abandoned as a result of the construction of railway yards in the nineteenth century and of the dispersion of businesses in the modern automobile-oriented city.

A growing number of cities have tried to provide more comfort for pedestrians by removing conflicts with cars. One of the most frequently used methods involves the horizontal separation of foot and wheeled traffic by means of pedestrian precincts. In closing off a street from automobile traffic cities are in effect trying to create one large department store, thus duplicating the convenience of the suburban shopping centre. The downtown pedestrian mall was pioneered in Canada by Sparks Street, Ottawa; a typical commercial street in 1960, the mall has now emerged as a prestigious location for shops and offices, and a favourite place of relaxation for workers, shoppers and tourists. Calgary is the only other major Canadian city to convert one of its downtown streets (8th Street) into a pedestrian mall but many other cities have attempted experimental or temporary malls, including Toronto's annual mid-summer malls on Yonge Street and on Elizabeth Street in Chinatown. There is considerable potential for the creation of traffic-free zones in Canadian town centres; in dozens of European cities, especially in West Germany, the banning of cars from one or more downtown streets since the late 1960s has been proven to be both operationally feasible and commercially successful. Undoubtedly the creation of a pedestrian mall would generate problems for vehicular traffic but overall it would

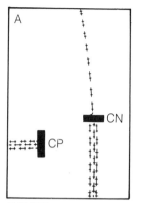 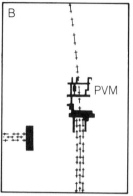 

FIGURE 9.7 Evolution of Montreal's underground pedestrian system. A: The two railway stations. B: The nucleus of the underground system, Place Ville Marie and Central Station, 1962. C: The opening of the subway system (1966) encouraged a significant extension of the system.

Source: ARCOP Associates, Halifax Waterfront Development Planning Study (1972), and the City of Montreal's Planning Department.

probably contribute to a more reasonable balance between vehicular and pedestrian accommodation in most Canadian town centres.

Although getting rid of cars is one way to create a more viable downtown core, many cities have been reluctant to turn traffic streets into pedestrian precincts and have instead promoted pedestrian comfort and convenience through the use of vertical separation. In Canada the subterranean walkway system was pioneered by Montreal's Place Ville Marie in 1962. Since its inception Montreal's underground pedestrian system has grown to almost two miles in length (Figure 9.7). The passages are mostly lined with shops and provide pleasant walks between the various activity zones to which they give access; in addition, the protected walkway is an inviting refuge from Montreal's severe winter. Toronto's underground system is in an earlier stage of development but is already the second most extensive in Canada. In cities such as Vancouver, where climatic conditions are not so harsh, an underground system is not considered appropriate. In this case the view of the mountains and the harbour is much more delightful than an escape from inclement weather; the city's concern for the comfort of pedestrians has instead been expressed in the campaign to encourage the use of outside

Courtesy City of Calgary Planning Department

*A pedestrian link in Calgary's "Plus-15" system.*

canopies by downtown merchants. Calgary is unique among Canadian cities (a more extensive system exists in Minneapolis) in adopting an elevated walkway system as a means of resolving pedestrian-automobile conflicts; its "Plus-15" system (i.e., 15 feet above street level) provides for free movement between buildings in weather-proof walkways. Since its inception in the late 1960s sufficient commitments have been made to assure reasonable prospects of success for this extensive and ambitious scheme.

The need for public open space in downtown areas is compelling in terms of both visual effect and physical relaxation. Because of the high value of downtown land the deficiency has in the past been difficult to remedy through public land acquisitions, but promising results have been achieved in many cities through the provision of open spaces in areas of private redevelopment. Most cities have bonus provisions (that is, additional floorspace allowances) in their zoning bylaws for the incorporation of public open space in any private redevelopment scheme; the reservation of open space is one reason why most cities favour the present trend towards large-scale projects. In the case of Calgary the adoption of the Plus-15 walkway system led logically to the encouragement of plazas at the 15-foot level rather than at ground level. One of the most practical proposals for remedying the deficiency of open space is a system of portable mini-parks; this involves the use of portable street furniture, plants in containers and modular paving systems. In most city centres there are many private properties which are kept vacant for varying periods of time while awaiting development; some of these can be used as interim parks if equipped with portable facilities. When the land is ready for development the park may be shifted to another vacant lot; in this way the park becomes more or less permanent although its location may change over time. In such cases the city normally leases the land for a nominal rent and assumes the responsibility for real property taxes. The system is not extensively used so far, but has been employed in both Toronto and Winnipeg (where it is known as port-a-park). In addition, there is considerable commercial-recreational potential in the use of alleys and lanes for shops, beer taverns, cafes and similar uses.

URBAN RENEWAL

The term urban renewal is generally restricted to programs in which the public sector is directly involved in the renewal of the urban environment. The need for government intervention in the redevelopment of some parts of the city centre may be justified mainly on the grounds that the presence of land use externalities disrupts the private development process. In an area of physically deteriorated buildings it would be unprofitable for an owner to upgrade his property unless all adjacent properties were also improved, and since there is no market mechanism for the coordination of private investment these districts often degenerate into slum areas where nearly all properties are similarly deteriorated. The interdependency of uses militates against a private sector solution to the problem, and necessitates the intervention of the government to coordinate the redevelopment process by eliminating the negative spillovers produced by the properties of non-cooperative owners. From a purely economic standpoint it is generally more profitable for an individual to maintain his property below rather than above the average standard for the neighbourhood.

Several other reasons for government intervention should be mentioned briefly. In order to encompass as much as possible of the spillover effects caused by the spatial proximity of urban uses, renewal schemes characteristically cover areas which are too large to be managed by private developers; alternatively, blight may be so widespread that private investors are discouraged by the inability of

Courtesy Information Services, Ontario Housing Corporation

*Regent Park, a high-density complex in Toronto.*

any one project to reverse the process of deterioration. Incompatible uses, such as a factory in a residential neighbourhood, may have to be removed by compulsory purchase through the use of the government's powers of eminent domain (the supreme power of the state over all property gives it the right of expropriation); similarly, land which is being held speculatively may have to be acquired by the public sector in order to facilitate the area-wide redevelopment process.

In Canada urban renewal may be said to have begun with the National Housing Act of 1944 which encouraged the redevelopment of old residential areas through the provision of grants for the acquisition and clearing of land suitable for low-cost housing, but the term was not used until it was incorporated into the 1954 National Housing Act. The first generation of urban renewal schemes ended in Canada in the late 1960s and it has since been extensively criticized (as has the United States' program) because of the widespread use made of bulldozer techniques. Regent Park North in Toronto was the first large-scale public housing scheme to be completed under the auspices of the 1944 Act; it was developed between 1948 and 1959 and includes 1,397 dwelling units on a six-block area (42.4 acres). Regent Park South, immediately adjacent to the earlier project, was built between 1957 and 1959, and contains 732 dwellings on a 26-acre site. Regent Park, north and south, contains about 9,000 people and has been widely condemned, along with similar large public housing projects, as a "ghetto of the poor." The social stigma attached to such large projects led to the withdrawal of public support in 1968 and their replacement by two programs: the acquisition of existing houses dispersed throughout the city for occupancy by low-income households, and the conservation-rehabilitation of deteriorated housing areas through neighbourhood-improvement and residential-rehabilitation programs.

There are essentially three ways of renewing an urban area: redevelopment, rehabilitation, and conservation. Redevelopment refers to the demolition, clearance and reconstruction of an entire area—the bulldozer approach. Rehabilitation involves the upgrading of existing property in order to meet prescribed standards. Conservation is the process of preventing the causes of blight and includes both the rehabilitation of properties and the redevelopment of small areas (spot clearance) in order to preserve the social structure of the neighbourhood while upgrading the quality of its physical facilities. The conservation-rehabilitation approach has replaced large-scale redevelopment in the federally supported program for improving deteriorated residential districts; residents are required to participate in the planning process (in both Canada and the United States) and funds are made available to help them do so effectively. Grants and loans are made available to landlords and homeowners for the repair and renovation of houses in the designated area, and money is also provided for upgrading neighbourhood services such as day-care centres and social and recreational facilities. The Canadian model for the conservation-rehabilitation of a deteriorating residential neighbourhood is Strathcona in Vancouver's east end; a less advanced but representative project is Toronto's Trefann Court.

Supporters of conservation-rehabilitation programs for downtown residential areas rightly emphasize that the principal fault of the large-scale redevelopment scheme lies in its bulldozer approach. The clearing of buildings and the subsequent reconstruction over a period of years puts an end to the original life of the neighbourhood; although all neighbourhoods undergo a continuous process of change it is usually impossible for them to accommodate rapid reconstruction while still retaining their individual identity. Conservation programs are adjusted to the human scale of change and do not cause severe disruption of family and neighbourhood associations; the direct participation of residents also assures that the necessary adjustments will be made at a pace which can be accommodated. Public participation in planning is generally most successful where preservation-improvement of the *status quo* is desired, in which case considerable benefits are derived from the involvement of residents in the rehabilitation of neighbourhoods.

Opponents of inner city residential rehabilitation generally emphasize two things: the disproportionate expenditure on the renovation of older housing, and the long-term disadvantages of preserving inner residential neighbourhoods for low-income groups. Although the rehabilitation of older housing is important it is frequently asserted that far more serious problems are engendered in the suburban fringe where in a growing city the bulk of residences must in any case be located. It is therefore contended that government programs should be directed towards solving the suburban housing problem, since the availability of a large supply of cheap suburban houses will accelerate the "filtering down" process (i.e., successive occupancies by households with increasingly limited incomes) and thus increase the quality of housing available to low-income households.

The more important criticism of inner city rehabilitation schemes is that the persistence of low-income housing in the city core may be unrealistic, since many of the jobs available to such households have already been transferred to the suburbs. Households locate in the low-rent inner city areas primarily because of the stock of inexpensive housing, and only incidentally because of proximity to employment centres. Historically, low-rent, high-density housing developed in close proximity to downtown work places because of the limited mobility of low-income households. The recent decentralization of industries to the suburbs has left the semi-skilled and unskilled residents of the city centre without easy access to the jobs which they can perform. These workers are less mobile (many have no car) than their suburban counterparts so that the effort required to reach a job in a distant and often unknown suburb is great. This "friction of distance" not only affects their economic ability to get to jobs but also interrupts the information flow about available jobs; many unskilled core residents depend on casual employment and information about such jobs is often relayed by word-of-mouth. As a result, in many metropolitan areas employment opportunities tend to occur farthest from those who need them most and often (particularly in the case of the ghetto residents of the United States) the blue-collar core resident travels further to work than the white-collar suburban worker. This tendency may be expected to increase in the future as more goods-moving activities move to the suburban fringe and service employment grows in the city centre. The foregoing criticisms may be somewhat exaggerated for two reasons: there are still many downtown service jobs which can be performed by unskilled workers and which may be expected to remain in a central location; and a number of downtown residents, including retired and unemployable people, are not members of the labour force (for instance, excluding the temporarily unemployed, this group made up 53 per cent of heads of households in Trefann Court, Toronto) and these groups benefit from a central location because of the convenient access on foot and by public transit to a wide variety of services.

Commercial redevelopment of city centres has been largely left to private enterprise but there are similar justifications for public sector involvement. Essentially, it is often necessary for government to coordinate private and public investment over an extensive area in order to control externalities and in so doing realize benefits that cannot be achieved by the operation of the private land market. One type of public involvement is the implementation of the "Norwich Plan" (named after the pioneering project in Norwich, England) which is a do-it-yourself face-lift or beautification scheme and which is often bolstered by the exhortations of organizations such as the Downtown Businessmen's Association. Victoria, Moose Jaw and Niagara Falls are among the Canadian cities which have successfully implemented beautification schemes. Without public cooperation private redevelopment may be impeded by a number of obstacles including: the difficulty of assembling the necessary land because of the small size of the landholdings; the obscurity of land titles; the possibility of holdouts (owners who demand payment well above the market price because of their awareness of the significance of the total project); and the possible failure to obtain public approval (after the land has been assembled) for rezoning, lane closings or whatever else is necessary for the development to proceed as planned. In practice, private developers may find it difficult to acquire all the land needed and usually the public sector is required to assist them with its power of eminent domain. In some Canadian provinces, municipalities may not acquire land except for public purposes and

Courtesy City of Hamilton. Department of Community Development

*Part of Hamilton's Lloyd D. Jackson Square — architect's model.*

may not, therefore, expropriate land on behalf of private individuals; even when such powers are available, municipalities may be reluctant for political reasons to support forced transfers of property between private owners.

Official, federally supported urban renewal schemes for commercial areas began and ended in the 1960s and there are few examples in Canadian cities. Hamilton's 43-acre Lloyd D. Jackson Square is one of the largest urban renewal projects in Canada, and is also typical of the conventional approach to the renewal of downtown commercial districts. At the time of its designation in 1965 the renewal area was on the declining edge of the central business district (the zone of discard) and included a blighted assortment of commercial, industrial and residential uses. The redevelopment program was of the bulldozer type and included the complete removal of existing buildings. The area was intended to function as a "civic centre" and a number of public buildings (including the Board of Education building, an auditorium, a convention centre, an art gallery, a library and the adjacent City Hall, completed in 1961) were located there in order to beautify the area and to act as catalysts for private development, which includes a 26-storey office tower, an enclosed shopping mall, two cinemas and underground parking facilities. Phase one was opened in 1972, and later phases, which are expected to be completed by 1978, will include a department store, a second office tower and apartment buildings.

In many Canadian city centres one of the most important factors encouraging redevelopment is the relocation of railway yards. A number of major cities, including Vancouver, Winnipeg, Quebec and Toronto, are at various stages in the relocation and redevelopment of downtown railway yards, while projects in Ottawa and, on a smaller scale, Saskatoon, are already completed. In Ottawa the railway relocation scheme was city-wide; 35 miles of railway track were removed and the railway station and freight terminal were relocated 2½ miles southeast of the city centre, with the result that a total of 251 acres of land were released for development. In the central area the old railway station was turned into a conference centre while the marshalling yards were redeveloped for a variety of uses, including the new National Defence Department headquarters. The former railway rights-of-way were mainly used for parkways (scenic drives) and the Queensway, a cross-town expressway which forms part of the Trans-Canada Highway. The Ottawa relocation program was made possible by federal funds (administered by the National Capital Commission) which had not been available to cities before the institution of a railway relocation program in 1973. In Saskatoon the relocation program was less ambitious and consisted of the removal of the downtown railway station and freight terminal; the railway station was relocated on the western edge of the city, the railway right-of-way was used for the construction of the Idylwyld freeway and the 26-acre downtown site was redeveloped for an auditorium and the Midtown Plaza, an enclosed shopping centre. Although in both Saskatoon and Ottawa relocation was proposed and financed by the public sector, the railway companies are often leading proponents of core area relocation (which requires the approval of the Canadian Transport Commission) in order to make way for redevelopment. A prime example is Toronto's 187-acre Metro Centre, a joint project of the two railway companies

Courtesy Midtown Plaza

*Saskatoon's Midtown Plaza—a city-centre redevelopment.*

(Canadian National and Canadian Pacific), and the largest railway relocation program in Canada.

The removal of railway service from the city core has both advantages and disadvantages. In its favour are transportation savings in time and money through the elimination of grade crossings and expensive overhead bridges. The redevelopment of the vacated land may also enhance both the aesthetic quality of the city centre (especially if cities are careful to exercise strict control) and the assessment rolls of the central city (for example, the property of the Canadian National Railway is tax-exempt, although grants-in-lieu of taxes are generally made). Arguments against railway relocation concentrate mainly on the removal of the downtown passenger station, which obviously eliminates the possibility of a convenient commuter train service as a means of easing peak-hour traffic congestion. In order to preserve downtown commuter service it is alternatively suggested that development take place above the railway tracks by the sale or lease of air rights as is the case in Montreal, Edmonton, Calgary and Vancouver. In Montreal commuter rail service is provided directly into Place Ville Marie (Central Station) while in Edmonton there are plans for the use of railway rights-of-way for the city's proposed rapid transit system.

TRANSPORTATION

Although transportation is of metropolitan-wide concern its worst consequences are concentrated in the city centre and it may appropriately be considered a central city problem. Although there is little concrete evidence, it is, for example, widely believed that the availability of rapid transit leads to the centralization of employment and indirectly to increased revenue for central cities; freeways, on the other hand, are generally cited as forces contributing to decentralization and downtown traffic congestion.

The transportation system is sometimes referred to as the "skeleton" of the city and land use as the "flesh." There is in fact such a close interrelationship between the two that neither can be understood or planned without reference to the other. Indeed, the land use structure of cities can be largely explained in terms of transportation technology (page 58). The pursuit of social and economic objectives in cities requires communication or interaction among individual units located within the urban area; the urban system may, therefore, be defined as a set of fixed activity nodes which are interconnected and supported by the flow of goods, people and information. The level of transportation-communications technology has a direct impact on the spatial structure of the urban functions. There are essentially two land use forces, operating in different directions, which give rise to the spatial segregation of urban activities: complementary or like uses benefit from proximity to each other and are drawn to the same location, while uses that have harmful effects on each other are located some distance apart. The degree to which uses become segregated as a result of these centripetal and centrifugal forces, is a function of communications technology — the less the cost of communication, the greater is the degree of spatial segregation by type of activity. Accordingly, the transportation system plays a vital role in accommodating and shaping the social and economic forces within cities.

Transportation systems must be publicly developed, and there has been a considerable amount of controversy over the suitability of

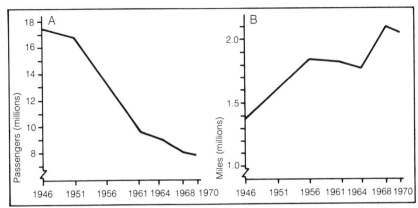

FIGURE 9.8    Changes in public transit use, Regina, 1946-1970. A: The annual number of passengers carried. B: The annual number of miles of route travelled.

*Source*: Planning Department, City of Regina.

various forms. Although the debate is frequently couched in terms of a choice between the car and public transit, a comprehensively planned system must strike some balance between private and public forms of transportation. A balanced transportation system implies that each mode of transportation does what it is best suited to, but in practice this means a trade-off between social and economic goals and between communal and individual benefits. The crux of the problem is that the automobile has a strong appeal to individuals but imposes social costs which cannot be recovered on a user-charge basis (therefore costs are borne by the community-at-large), while public transit is efficient from a community point of view but lacks market acceptance. In this respect transportation planning involves a trade-off between the self-interest of individuals and the general interest of the community; on the other hand, the achievement of social goals (e.g., clean air) frequently involves a loss of economic efficiency. Also important is the service which public transit provides for captive riders (those who do not own a car or who do not have a car available), many of whom are inner city residents.

Public and private transportation systems best fulfill different functions. Public transit is more capable of catering to high-density traffic corridors, while private transportation is more efficient in

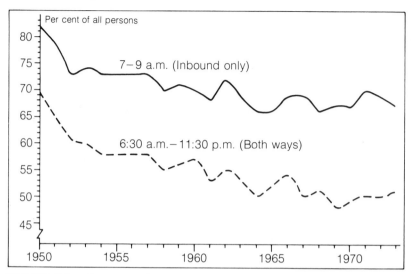

FIGURE 9.9    Persons using public transit as a percentage of all persons crossing the downtown traffic cordon, Toronto, 1950-1973.

*Source:* Toronto Transit Commission.

low-density traffic zones where journeys are dispersed in many directions. In large metropolitan centres rapid transit, including subways and commuter trains, is the most efficient means of coping with trips which are highly concentrated in space and in time; for example, peak-hour travel to frequent-destination zones such as the city centre. For widely dispersed destinations and for low-volume traffic some form of private transportation (car, bicycle or on foot) is generally more efficient and convenient. In practice, considerable care must be taken to maintain an optimal balance between private and public transportation, and this frequently means that a disproportionate effort must be made to increase the market acceptance of public transit through increased efficiency and convenience and lower operating costs. Figure 9.8 illustrates a common phenomenon in Canadian cities; rising public transit costs (as measured in miles travelled) are accompanied by decreasing numbers of passengers and therefore decreasing revenue. The decreasing proportion of people carried by public transit into downtown areas is a further cause for concern; this has been the case in Toronto despite the inauguration of a subway system in 1954 (Figure 9.9).

Public transit has suffered from its inability to meet its costs out of the fare box. It is almost impossible for public transit to amortize its capital costs out of passenger fares while maintaining a fare structure and level of service attractive enough to retain public acceptance. It has been argued that public transit should be provided as a free public service, although, in fact, it has been commonly observed that the demand for public transit is fairly unresponsive to price changes (there has, however, been very little experience with zero-priced situations). The failure of public transit to meet its costs arises partly because it is called upon to maintain service during off-peak, uneconomic hours and partly because it is prevented by traffic congestion from being efficient during the profitable rush hours.

The efficiency of public transit depends primarily on three things: the degree of interference from pedestrians and vehicles, the number of coaches that can be joined together (subway and commuter trains have the largest number of connected cars), and the density of population within the catchment area of the transit route. Within the urbanized area there are three types of transit, rated in terms of their carrying capacity. Buses operate with a maximum capacity of 3-6,000 persons per hour with speeds of less than 10 miles per hour, while subways have a capacity of 35-40,000 persons per hour and operate at speeds of over 20 miles per hour; a number of intermediate-capacity systems exist, including street-cars and elevated railways. A fourth type of public transit is the suburban commuter railway, which does not have a very high capacity (because of the low density of population within reasonable distances of its stations) but which serves a useful function because of the concentrated usage it receives during the rush hours. Commuter railways are rare in Canada; Ontario's GO (Government of Ontario) Transit, serving Toronto, is the most advanced experiment in Canada involving commuter rail service. In 1967 GO Transit began operating a 42-mile east-west commuter service between Pickering and Oakville; in 1970 the system was extended to Hamilton in the west and to Oshawa in the east by means of a feeder bus service. In 1974 GO Transit introduced a 30-mile rail service for the northwestern sector between Toronto and Georgetown. (In addition to its rail service GO Transit provides feeder buses from outlying communities to Toronto's suburban subway stations.)

One of the more difficult problems is the design of an intermediate-capacity transit system suitable for medium-sized cities, which are too large for a conventional bus system and yet too

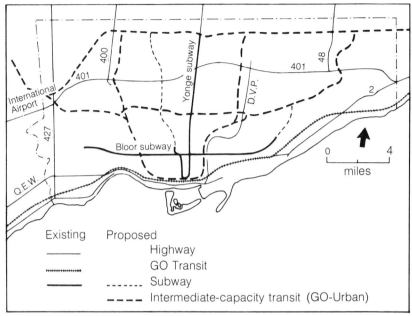

FIGURE 9.10 Proposed intermediate-capacity transit system, Metro Toronto (Municipality of Metropolitan Toronto).

*Source*: Government of Ontario.

small to support a high-capacity subway system; an intermediate-capacity system is also desirable in some suburban areas of large metropolitan centres where subway service may be uneconomical. The street-car, which is one of the cheapest intermediate carriers, was removed shortly after the Second World War from all Canadian cities with the exception of Toronto. One of the most imaginative plans for an intermediate-capacity system was proposed in 1972 by the Ontario government for Toronto, Ottawa and Hamilton. The elevated guide-rail system has a capacity of 10-20,000 persons per hour and uses automatic trains propelled by linear induction motors. The 56-mile network for metropolitan Toronto (Figure 9.10) will use rail and electric-transmission rights-of-way as well as median strips along major roads. The magnetic trains of the proposed system are, however, at an experimental stage of development.

A number of interim measures have recently been adopted in Canada for bridging the gap between a conventional bus system and

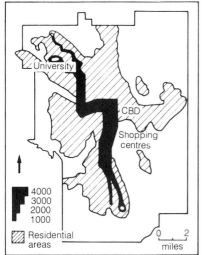 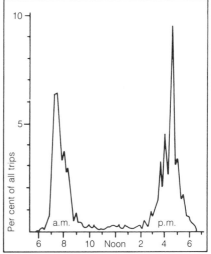

FIGURE 9.11. The Blue Arrow Bus Express System, Calgary. A: Daily passenger volumes. B: Trip frequency by time of day.

*Source*: Transportation Department, City of Calgary.

rapid transit facilities. Separate traffic lanes for buses were pioneered in Toronto in 1972; on major arterial routes the lane nearest the curb is reserved for buses during the rush hours, thus increasing their average speed and therefore their carrying capacity. A significant innovation is Calgary's Blue Arrow Bus Express System (BABES) which began operating in 1972. It operates along a proposed rapid transit alignment and, in contrast to a conventional bus system where passengers board and disembark along the entire route, it is specifically designed to provide a relatively direct service between the outer suburbs and the central business district. Its usage is accordingly highly specialized in terms of time, purpose and destination; in February 1973, for example, 81 per cent of all trips were made during the rush hours (7-9 a.m. and 4-6 p.m.), 80 per cent of all trips were to or from work, and 62 per cent of all trips terminated or originated in the CBD. In addition the Blue Arrow buses serve the University of Calgary and regional shopping centres (Figure 9.11). BABES does not yet operate on reserved lanes but various pre-emptions are under consideration, including a 5-second start on other traffic at some intersections and bus sensors which set up sequences of traffic lights.

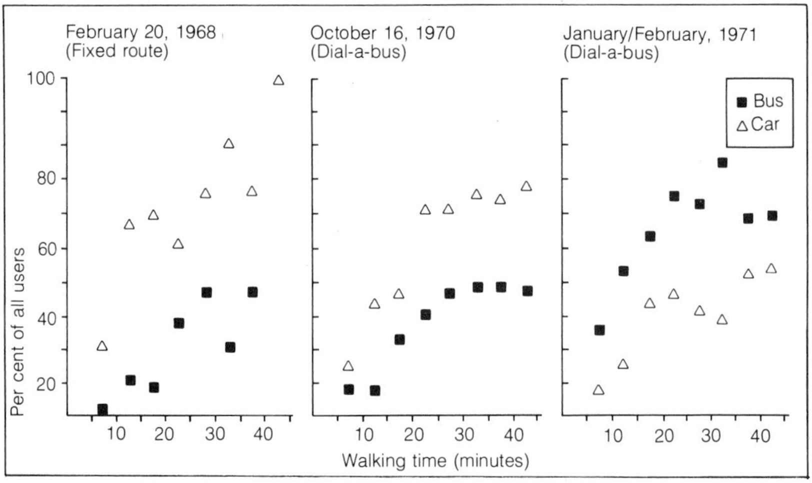

FIGURE 9.12  Access mode of GO train users in relation to walking time from the Bay Ridges station. (The percentages of people who walked are not shown.)

*Source:* Joint Technical Transportation Planning Committee, *A Proposed Dial-a-Bus Demonstration Project for Metropolitan Toronto* (Toronto, 1973).

In comparison with the private automobile public transportation suffers its greatest disadvantages in terms of convenience and flexibility. Public transit depends on some complementary means (car, bicycle or on foot) for assembling and distributing passengers to and from their ultimate destinations and origins while in theory the automobile provides door-to-door service. In high-density areas sufficient people may be within walking distance of transit stops to make the service both convenient and economical, but in the typical low-density suburb transit service is neither economical nor convenient for the majority of residents. The catchment area of a fixed bus route has been widely found to extend to a maximum of about 1,000 feet from transit stops. In order to attract a sufficient number of passengers transit service must be competitive with the private car in travel time and convenience as well as cost, and variable-route bus service may therefore be necessary in many low-density suburbs. Studies have repeatedly shown that the walking distance between the transit stop and the point of origin and/or destination is one of the most important factors influencing the decision of potential transit riders (i.e., excluding captive riders). In Calgary, for example, one of the principal aims of BABES was to replace as many automobile-based trips as possible, and in this the Blue Arrow buses were relatively successful since 24.5 per cent of users (February 1973) had in fact travelled by car prior to the introduction of this express service. Nevertheless, only 4 per cent of patrons had travelled by car to a boarding point—the remainder either walked (84 per cent) or transferred from feeder buses (12 per cent); these findings are typical of conventional bus systems.

A few Canadian cities have developed dial-a-bus services, which offer the door-to-door convenience of the private car as well as relatively low operating costs. Passengers arrange to be picked up at appointed times by means of a telephone call (or pre-book on a weekly basis), and are then ferried from their houses to one of a limited number of destinations, a transit stop, a railway station or perhaps a shopping centre. This system was pioneered successfully in Canada in Bay Ridges, twenty miles east of Toronto, where it was used as a feeder service for GO Transit. Bay Ridges is itself typical of modern low-density suburbs and over 90 per cent of its dwelling units are single-family houses arranged in a curvilinear street design; in other words both the low density and the street layout militated against a fixed-route solution to the transit demand. This service was introduced in July 1970 and its success may be gauged from the fact that 60 per cent of GO Transit passengers from Bay Ridges also made use of the dial-a-bus system compared to the corresponding proportion of 20 per cent for the former fixed-route feeder bus. Figure 9.12 indicates that within six months of the introduction of dial-a-bus service, the bus had replaced the car as the dominant mode of transport for GO Transit users who lived more than ten minutes walking distance from the station. Dial-a-bus services have also been successfully instituted in a number of other cities, including Regina (where it is known as Telebus), Stratford and Kingston. Another commonly used means of increasing the convenience of public transit for people who live beyond walking distance of transit stops is the provision of long-term parking facilities at suburban stations; these "park-and-ride" stations make it possible for the private car to be used for one part of the total trip.

The major perceived disadvantages of emphasizing private transportation are the excessive social and economic costs of freeways and

expressways. The social and environmental costs of urban expressways include air and noise pollution, the destruction of neighbourhoods, the demolition of houses, and, frequently, the loss of parkland because of the routing of expressways through river valleys. In
addition, the large land requirements contribute to construction
costs which often amount to $10-35 million per mile for a six-lane
freeway.

In the past, transportation systems were often designed solely in
engineering terms; physical capacity and technical efficiency were
the overriding concerns, and the primary goal was to move the
largest number of people in the shortest possible time. Insufficient
consideration was given to the transportation system's potential for
achieving social goals through its effect on the land use system. It
was not in fact until the late 1950s that the relationships between
transportation and land use were properly identified. The recognition of transportation as a function of land use (i.e., different types of
land use generate different types and amounts of traffic) led to the
development of more sophisticated transportation systems during
and after the late 1950s but it was not until another decade had
passed that transportation and land use planning were first coordinated in order to achieve specified community objectives. Evidence
of a lack of coordination between transportation and land use planning may be seen in a number of cities where urban freeways have
had to be expanded in response to land use changes in adjacent areas;
one of the classic examples in Canada is Toronto's Macdonald-
Cartier Freeway (Highway 401) which has undergone continuous
expansion since it was opened in 1956 as a four-lane freeway and
which now has up to twelve lanes in some sections.

Transportation planning, like all forms of urban planning, must
begin with community goal formulation and transportation engineers must therefore participate in the debate over the quality of
urban life and in the determination of the optimal trade-off between
economic efficiency and social welfare. Once the relationships between transportation and land use and the social, economic and
environmental impacts of alternative transportation systems are understood, the primary question becomes "what kind of a city does
the community want?" As is often the case with complex planning
issues, the transportation plan must strike an acceptable balance
among many goals, some of which may be incompatible; an em-

phasis on public transportation may, for example, reduce economic efficiency and personal convenience but increase social welfare.

One of the most serious transportation problems is the "peaking" of traffic in both space and time. Between 40 and 45 per cent of trips in most cities are made to and from work and these are mainly concentrated in only four hours of the day, the morning and after-noon rush hours; over 80 per cent of trips during the rush hours (7-9 a.m. and 4-6 p.m.) are generally to and from work. As the principal place of employment, the city centre bears the brunt of traffic congestion; according to the metropolitan Toronto transportation study, for example, 33 per cent of all trips made between 7:00 and 9:00 a.m. terminated in the central area (which generated only 5 per cent of the total number of metropolitan trips) and of these 90 per cent were journeys to work.

Two methods have frequently been used to ease traffic congestion during the rush hour: the staggering of work hours and the coordina-tion of traffic lights. Although the peaking problem is largely insolu-ble because of the social and economic advantages of a segregation of activities in both time and space, the capacity of the transportation system may be increased appreciably by an extension of the rush-hour period, even by half-an-hour. The savings in transportation as a result of the staggering of work-hours may, however, be accom-panied by a loss in economic efficiency. Since downtown uses are very interdependent, most firms benefit from common working hours in the expedition of their business dealings with each other, and any staggering of work hours would lead to some inefficiency; for example, a lawyer who begins work at 8:30 may on occasion have to wait until 9:30 when City Hall opens and his work day will thus be reduced from eight to seven hours. There are, however, some uses which form "economic complexes" and if their constituent firms have common working hours it may be possible to stagger these *vis-à-vis* other economic complexes; offices, for instance, may open one or two hours earlier than shopping-entertainment outlets. Major employers, such as government, also have a trigger effect on others and therefore have the principal responsibility in initiating a spread of working hours; in downtown Toronto, for example, the provin-cial government alone has about 10,000 employees. Toronto was one of the pioneers of computer-controlled traffic lights systems. For a comparatively small investment (compared to the outlay on roads

*Yonge Street at Eglinton, 1944.*

*Yonge Street at Eglinton, 1974.*

and subway construction) Toronto has substantially increased road capacity through the coordination of traffic signals at over 1,000 intersections.

A variety of other measures have been proposed or implemented to alleviate traffic congestion. Increasing residential densities throughout the city would have the effect of making public transit more efficient and of shortening the average length of trips. By dispersing work places, thus bringing home and work place closer, downtown congestion may be alleviated; the advantages of dispersing employment are questionable, since it inevitably reduces the savings which firms derive from locating in clusters. Specific measures applied to the downtown area may substantially increase its capacity: a ban on daytime loading; a one-way street system; strict regulation of street parking; and the discouragement of automobile-based trips. In Toronto's central business district (Dundas, University, Front and Jarvis streets) a parking-exemption policy has been in effect since 1959 and new buildings are not required to provide any parking space; this policy differs from that of all other parts of the city and is designed to encourage the use of public transit.

In large metropolitan centres where expensive subway construction is often necessary it is possible to reduce the cost of establishing such a system by taking advantage of the increased land values around subway stations. The dramatic effect of rapid transit on the value of neighbouring land is well illustrated by the commercial-apartment developments along Toronto's Yonge Street and Bloor Street subways. If the lands around the subway stations had been owned by the public sector their enhanced values would have offset most of the expenses incurred in subway construction. In Toronto part of the cost was recovered by the sale or lease of air rights over some subway stations but the amount earned was small compared to the total community-induced benefits. A program of land acquisition in the neighbourhood of subway stations (to be sold or leased to private developers) in conjunction with the strict control of land uses, would make subway construction cheaper and perhaps even profitable.

## Towards a National Urban Policy

Partly because municipalities are creatures of their provincial governments, urban policy in Canada has been concerned hitherto with the local rather than the national urban system. At the local level physical problems predominate; streets, buildings, sewers and other urban elements must be coordinated in order to promote efficiency, beauty, health and other social goals. At the national level, however, the inter-connectedness of the urban system may be more easily understood in economic terms, and problems at this level are frequently resolved by intercity discrimination in the allocation of resources. The problems of the two urban levels are obviously interdependent, and costs inevitably spill over from one to the other. Higher housing costs in Toronto (a local problem), which may result from rapid growth (a national problem), may be extended to the whole country in the form of higher prices for the city's goods and services. Theoretically, this should not occur in a competitive economy since producers should move to centres where production costs are lower; however, because of Canada's system of tariff protection, freight rate structures, scale economies and other locational advantages, the Quebec-Windsor corridor has a near-monopoly on certain high-order functions, including secondary manufacturing. It is possible that the unregulated growth of metropolitan centres within this area through the market allocation of resources may result in a less-than-optimal growth of national welfare by supporting a few selected centres at the expense of the rest of the country. The poverty of Maritime cities results, for example, from their slow growth; when a city grows too slowly it invariably experiences problems of unemployment, poverty and high dependency ratios (i.e., an above-average incidence of dependent or non-productive persons such as children and retired people) because of the selective out-migration of people and jobs, and this is likely to be intensified as the manufacturing area of central Canada is developed even further. In contrast, when a city grows too quickly congestion, rising land costs and other problems frequently follow; this may well be the prognosis for the cities of Ontario's Golden Horseshoe.

There is no national urban policy in Canada, although the first step was taken in 1971 when the Ministry of State for Urban Affairs was formed. Constitutionally, any agreement between the federal government and a municipality must be co-signed by the province concerned, and the consequent routing of federal urban affairs through each province has frustrated the development of a national urban policy. Traditionally, federal urban policy has been fragmented among a variety of special-purpose agencies, such as the Central Mortgage and Housing Corporation, and through the investment policies of various federal departments in particular cities. It was the recognition of this need for a coordinated approach to the resolution of urban problems which led to the creation of the Ministry of Urban Affairs. The constitutional limitations of the federal government are revealed in the circumspect wording of one of the Ministry's major mandates which was to "formulate and develop policies for implementation through measures within fields of federal jurisdiction in respect to the fostering of cooperative relationships in respect of urban affairs with the provinces and, through them, their municipalities."

Since the formation of the Ministry the federal government's urban policy has become both more selective and more multidimensional. The increased selectivity in the implementation of federal urban policy was indicated by the acquisition in 1972 of an 86-acre waterfront park in Toronto; there is no universal federal policy on the acquisition of urban parks and no single-purpose agency had been prepared to act alone. An example of the multidimensional approach was the designation of a 9,000-acre new town at Carlsbad Springs, Ottawa, in 1973; the federal government is to be involved with provincial and municipal governments not only as part-owner of the land but also in the detailed planning of the twenty-year development. In addition, a number of federal-provincial-municipal teams, known as tri-level action groups, have been formed at the instigation of the federal government in many large cities, including Montreal, Toronto, Vancouver, Winnipeg and Halifax. These groups are intended to ensure the close coordination of policies in key areas such as transportation and land assembly. The new approach may be contrasted with the traditional "universality" of federal urban policy. In 1964, for example, the federal government expanded its urban renewal program to include non-residential areas and agreed to pay 75 per cent of the cost of studies to identify areas in need of renewal. Until the cancellation of the program in 1968, the result was a spate of urban renewal studies in towns of almost every description, including a number in Saskatchewan with fewer than 1,000 people.

It remains doubtful whether a truly national urban policy will emerge, however, since this would require a level of intercity discrimination in the allocation of resources which might be both politically and constitutionally difficult to accomplish without accompanying changes in the institutional structure.

# Bibliography

## General

BERRY, B. J. L., and HORTON, F. E. *Geographic Perspectives on Urban Systems*. Englewood Cliffs, N.J.: Prentice-Hall, 1970.

CARTER, H. *The Study of Urban Geography*. London: Edward Arnold, 1972.

JACKSON, J. N. *The Canadian City: Space, Form, Quality*. Toronto: McGraw-Hill Ryerson, 1973.

JOHNSON, J. H. *Urban Geography: An Introductory Analysis*. Oxford: Pergamon Press, 1968.

LITHWICK, N. H., and PAQUET, G., eds. *Urban Studies: A Canadian Perspective*. Toronto: Methuen, 1968.

MURPHY, R. E. *The American City*. New York: McGraw-Hill, 1966.

SIMMONS, J. and R. *Urban Canada*. Toronto: Copp Clark, 1969.

THOMPSON, W. R. *A Preface to Urban Economics*. Baltimore: Johns Hopkins Press, 1965.

YEATES, M. H., and GARNER, B. J. *The North American City*. New York: Harper and Row, 1971.

## The External Urban System: National and Regional

### THE NATIONAL URBAN SYSTEM

BECKMAN, M. J. "City Hierarchies and the Distribution of City Size," *Economic Development and Cultural Change* 6 (1958): 243-48.

BERGSMAN, J., GREENSTON, P., and HEALY, R. "The Agglomeration Process in Urban Growth," *Urban Studies* 9 (1972): 263-88.

BERRY, B. J. L. "City Size Distributions and Economic Development," *Economic Development and Cultural Change* 9 (1961): 573-88.

——. "Cities as Systems within Systems of Cities," *Papers and Proceedings of the Regional Science Association* 13 (1964): 147-63.

——. "Relationships between Regional Economic Development and the Urban System: The Case of Chile," *Tijdschrift voor Economische en Sociale Geografie* 60 (1969): 283-307.

BORCHERT, J. R. "American Metropolitan Evolution," *Geographical Review* 57 (1967): 301-32.

DICKEN, P. "Some Aspects of the Decision Making Behavior of Business Organizations," *Economic Geography* 47 (1971): 426-37.

EVANS, A. W. "The Location of the Headquarters of Industrial Companies," *Urban Studies* 10 (1973): 387-95.

FRIEDMANN, J. *Urbanization, Planning and National Development.* Beverly Hills, Calif.: Sage Publications, 1973.

FRIEDMANN, J., and MILLER, J. "The Urban Field," *Journal of the American Institute of Planners* 31 (1965): 312-20.

GOODWIN, W. "The Management Centre in the United States," *Geographical Review* 55 (1965): 1-16.

GRAS, N. S. B. *Introduction to Economic History.* New York: Harper, 1922.

HARRIS, C. D. "The Market as a Factor in the Localization of Industry in the United States," *Annals of the Association of American Geographers* 44 (1954): 315-48.

JEFFERSON, M. "The Law of the Primate City," *Geographical Review* 29 (1939): 226-32.

KERR, D. "Metropolitan Dominance in Canada." In *Canada: A Geographical Interpretation*, edited by J. Warkentin. Toronto: Methuen, 1968.

LAMPARD, E. E. "The History of Cities in Economically Advanced Areas," *Economic Development and Cultural Change* 3 (1955): 81-136.

——. "The Evolving System of Cities in the United States: Urbanization and Economic Development." In *Issues in Urban Economics*, edited by H.S. Perloff and L. Wingo, JR. Baltimore: Johns Hopkins Press, 1968.

MAXWELL, J. W. "The Functional Structure of Canadian Cities," *Geographical Bulletin* 7 (1965): 79-104.

MEIER, R. L. *A Communications Theory of Urban Growth.* Cambridge, Mass.: M.I.T. Press, 1962.

PRED, A. *The Spatial Dynamics of U.S. Urban Industrial Growth, 1800-1914.* Cambridge, Mass.: M.I.T. Press, 1966.

RICHARDSON, H. W. "Theory of the Distribution of City Sizes: Review and Prospects," *Regional Studies* 7 (1973): 239-51.

TOWNROE, P. M. "Industrial Linkage, Agglomeration and External Economies," *Journal of the Town Planning Institute* 56 (1970): 18-20.

ULLMAN, E. "Regional Development and the Geography of Concentration," *Papers and Proceedings of the Regional Science Association* 4 (1958): 179-98.


THE REGIONAL URBAN SYSTEM

BERRY, B. J. L. "The Impact of Expanding Metropolitan Communities upon the Central Place Hierarchy," *Annals of the Association of American Geographers* 50 (1960): 112-16.

———. *Geography of Market Centres and Retail Distribution.* Englewood Cliffs, N.J.: Prentice-Hall, 1967.

BERRY, B. J. L., and PRED, A. *Central Place Studies: Bibliography and Review.* Philadelphia: Regional Science Association, 1964.

CHRISTALLER, W. *Central Places in Southern Germany.* Translated by C. W. Baskin. Englewood Cliffs, N.J.: Prentice-Hall, 1966.

HODGE, G. "The Prediction of Trade Center Viability in the Great Plains," *Papers and Proceedings of the Regional Science Association* 15 (1965): 87-115.

HUFF, D. L. "A Probability Analysis of Shopping Center Trading Areas," *Land Economics* 39 (1963): 81-90.

MARSHALL, J. U. *The Location of Service Towns: An Approach to the Analysis of Central Place Systems.* Toronto: University of Toronto Press, 1969.

Royal Commission on Agriculture and Rural Life. *Service Centres.* Report No. 12. Regina: Queen's Printer, 1957.

STABLER, J. C., and WILLIAMS, P. R. "The Changing Structure of the Central Place Hierarchy," *Land Economics* 49 (1973): 454-58.

ZIMMERMAN, C. C., and MONEO, G. W. *The Prairie Community System.* Ottawa: Agricultural Economic Research Council of Canada, 1971.

## Internal City Structure

### LAND USE THEORY

ALONSO, W. "A Theory of the Urban Land Market," *Papers and Proceedings of the Regional Science Association* 6 (1960): 149-57.

————. *Location and Land Use.* Cambridge, Mass.: Harvard University Press, 1964.

GOODALL, B. *The Economics of Urban Areas.* Oxford: Pergamon Press, 1972.

HAIG, R. M. "Towards an Understanding of the Metropolis," *Quarterly Journal of Economics* 40 (1926): 179-208.

HALL, P., ed. *Von Thünen's Isolated State.* Oxford: Pergamon Press, 1966.

HURD, R. M. *Principles of City Land Values.* New York: The Record and Guide, 1924.

RATCLIFF, R. U. *Urban Land Economics.* New York: McGraw-Hill, 1949.

WINGO, L. *Transportation and Urban Land.* Baltimore: Johns Hopkins Press, 1961.

### DESCRIPTIVE LAND USE MODELS

BERRY, B. J. L. "Internal Structure of the City," *Law and Contemporary Problems* 30 (1965): 111-19.

BURGESS, E. W. "The Growth of the City," *Proceedings of the American Sociological Society* 18 (1923): 85-89.

————. "The Growth of the City." In *The City*, edited by R. E. Park and E. W. Burgess. Chicago: University of Chicago Press, 1925.

HARRIS, C. D., and ULLMAN, E. L. "The Nature of Cities," *Annals of the American Academy of Political and Social Science* 242 (1945): 7-17.

HOYT, H. *The Structure and Growth of Residential Neighborhoods in American Cities.* Washington, D.C.: U.S. Government Printing Office, 1939.

————. "Recent Distortions of the Classical Models of Urban Structure," *Land Economics* 40 (1964): 199-212.

MURDIE, R. A. *Factorial Ecology of Metropolitan Toronto, 1951-1961.* Research Paper 116, Department of Geography. Chicago: University of Chicago Press, 1969.

————. "The Social Geography of the City: Theoretical and Empirical Background." In *Internal Structure of the City*, edited by

L. S. Bourne. New York: Oxford University Press, 1971.

NELSON, H. J. "The Form and Structure of Cities: Urban Growth Patterns," *Journal of Geography* 58 (1969): 198-207.

SIMMONS, J. W. "Descriptive Models of Urban Land Use," *Canadian Geographer* 9 (1965): 170-74.

## Urban Land Use Structure

### GENERAL

BLUMENFELD, H. "The Tidal Wave of Metropolitan Expansion," *Journal of the American Institute of Planners* 20 (1954): 3-14.

———. "The Urban Pattern," *Annals of the American Academy of Political and Social Science* 352 (1964): 74-83.

———.*The Modern Metropolis*. Cambridge, Mass.: M.I.T. Press, 1967.

BOAL, F. W. "Technology and Urban Form," *Journal of Geography* 57 (1968): 229-36.

BOURNE, L. S., ed. *Internal Structure of the City*. New York: Oxford University Press, 1971.

CHINITZ, B., ed. *City and Suburb: The Economics of Metropolitan Growth*. Englewood Cliffs, N.J.: Prentice-Hall, 1964.

DUE, J. F. *The Intercity Electric Railway Industry in Canada*. Toronto: University of Toronto Press, 1966.

HOOVER, E., and VERNON, R. *Anatomy of a Metropolis*. Cambridge, Mass.: Harvard University Press, 1959.

LOEWENSTEIN, L. K. "The Location of Urban Land Uses," *Land Economics* 39 (1963): 406-20.

MILLS, E. S. *Location of Employment in Urban Areas*. Baltimore: Johns Hopkins Press, 1970.

MOSES, L. N., and WILLIAMSON, H. F. "Location of Economic Activities in Cities," *American Economic Review* 57 (1967): 211-22.

NIEDERCORN, J. H., and HEARLE, E. F. R. "Recent Land Use Trends in Forty-eight Large American Cities," *Land Economics* 40 (1964): 105-10.

PUTNAM, R. G., TAYLOR, F. J., and KETTLE, P. G., eds. *A Geography of Urban Places*. Toronto: Methuen, 1970.

### MANUFACTURING

GOLDBERG, M. A. " Intrametropolitan Industrial Location: Some Empirical Findings," *Annals of Regional Science* 3 (1969): 167-78.

———. "An Economic Model of Intrametropolitan Industrial Location," *Journal of Regional Science* 10 (1970): 75-79.

KERR, D. P., and FIELD, N. C. *Geographical Aspects of Industrial Growth in the Metropolitan Toronto Region*. Toronto: Department of Treasury and Economics, Government of Ontario, 1968.

LEIGH, R. "Analysis of the Factors Affecting the Location of Industries Within Cities," *Canadian Geographer* 13 (1969): 28-33.

LEVER, W. F. "The Intra-Urban Movement of Manufacturing: A Markov Approach," *Transactions of the Institute of British Geographers* 56 (1972): 21-38.

LOGAN, M. I. "Locational Behavior of Manufacturing Firms in Urban Areas," *Annals of the Association of American Geographers* 56 (1966): 451-66.

PRED, A. R. "The Intrametropolitan Location of American Manufacturing," *Annals of the Association of American Geographers* 54 (1964): 165-80.

STEED, G. P. F. "Intrametropolitan Manufacturing: Spatial Distribution and Locational Dynamics in Greater Vancouver," *Canadian Geographer* 17 (1973): 235-58.

RESIDENTIAL

BERRY, B. J. L., SIMMONS, J. W., and TENNANT, R. J. "Urban Population Densities: Structure and Change," *Geographical Review* 53 (1963): 389-405.

BOURNE, L. S. "Market Location and Site Selection in Apartment Construction," *Canadian Geographer* 12 (1968): 211-26.

BOURNE, L. S., and BERRIDGE, J. D. "Apartment Location and Developer Behaviour: A Reappraisal," *Canadian Geographer* 17 (1973): 403-11.

DAVIES, W. K. D., and BARROW, G. T. "A Comparative Factorial Ecology of Three Canadian Prairie Cities," *Canadian Geographer* 17 (1973): 327-53.

JOHNSTON, R. J. *Urban Residential Patterns*. London: Bell, 1971.

KAIN, J. F. "The Journey to Work as a Determinant of Residential Location," *Papers and Proceedings of the Regional Science Association* 9 (1962): 137-60.

MUTH, R. F. "The Spatial Structure of the Housing Market," *Papers and Proceedings of the Regional Science Association* 7 (1961): 207-20.

———. *Cities and Housing: The Spatial Pattern of Urban Residential*

*Land Use*. Chicago: University of Chicago Press, 1969.

NADER, G. A. "Some Aspects of the Recent Growth and Distribution of Apartments in the Prairie Metropolitan Areas," *Canadian Geographer* 15 (1971): 307-17.

ROSSI, P. *Why Families Move*. New York: The Free Press, 1955.

SIMMONS, J. W. "Changing Residence in the City: A Review of Intra-Urban Mobility," *Geographical Review* 58 (1968): 622-51.

STEGMAN, M. A. "Accessibility Models and Residential Location," *Journal of the American Institute of Planners* 35 (1969): 22-29.

TIMMS, D. W. G. *The Urban Mosaic: Towards a Theory of Residential Segregation*. Cambridge: The University Press, 1971.

WEBBER, M. M. "The Urban Place and the Nonplace Urban Realm." In *Explorations into Urban Structure*, edited by M. M. Webber. Philadelphia: University of Pennsylvania Press, 1964.

WOLFORTH, J. R. *Residential Location and the Place of Work*. Vancouver: Tantalus Research Ltd., 1965.

COMMERCIAL

ARMSTRONG, R. B. *The Office Industry: Patterns of Growth and Location*. A Report of the Regional Plan Association. Cambridge, Mass.: M.I.T. Press, 1972.

BERRY, B. J. L. *Commercial Structure and Commercial Blight*. Research Paper 85, Department of Geography. Chicago: University of Chicago Press, 1963.

BOAL, F. W., and JOHNSON, D. B. "The Functions of Retail and Service Establishments on Commercial Ribbons," *Canadian Geographer* 9 (1965): 154-69.

CAROL, H. "The Hierarchy of Central Functions Within the City," *Annals of the Association of American Geographers* 50 (1960): 419-38.

COWAN, P. *The Office: A Facet of Urban Growth*. London: Heinemann, 1969.

GODDARD, J. B. "Office Communications and Office Location: A Review of Current Research," *Regional Studies* 5 (1971): 263-80.

MCKEEVER, J. R. *Shopping Centres: Principles and Policies*. Washington, D.C.: Urban Land Institute, 1958.

VANCE, J. E., JR. "Emerging Patterns of Commercial Structure in American Cities." In *Proceedings of the I.G.U. Symposium in Urban Geography*, edited by K. Norborg. Lund, Sweden: Gleerup, 1962.

## The City Centre

BOURNE, L. S. "Comments on the Transitional Zone Concept," *Professional Geographer* 20 (1968): 313-16.

BOWDEN, M. "Downtown Through Time: Delimitation, Expansion and Internal Growth," *Economic Geography* 47 (1971): 121-35.

DAVIES, D. H. "The Hard Core of Cape Town's Central Business District," *Economic Geography* 34 (1960): 53-69.

_____. *Land Use in Central Cape Town: A Study in Urban Geography.* Cape Town: Longmans, 1965.

GODDARD, J. B. *Office Linkages: A Study of Communications and Spatial Patterns in Central London.* Oxford: Pergamon Press, 1973.

GOTTMAN, J. "Why the Skyscraper?" *Geographical Review* 56 (1966): 190-212.

HORWOOD, E. M., and BOYCE, R. R. *Studies of the Central Business District and Urban Freeway Development.* Seattle: University of Washington Press, 1959.

MURPHY, R. E. *The Central Business District.* Chicago: Aldine-Atherton, 1972.

MURPHY, R. E., and EPSTEIN, B. J. "Internal Structure of the CBD," *Economic Geography* 31 (1955): 21-46.

MURPHY, R. E., and VANCE, J. E., JR. "Delimiting the CBD," *Economic Geography* 30 (1954): 189-222.

_____. "A Comparative Study of Nine Central Business Districts," *Economic Geography* 30 (1954): 301-36.

PRESTON, R. E. "The Zone in Transition: A Study of Urban Land Use Patterns," *Economic Geography* 42 (1966): 236-59.

PRESTON, R. E., and GRIFFIN, D. W. "A Restatement of the Transitional Zone Concept," *Annals of the Association of American Geographers* 56 (1966): 339-50.

RANNELLS, J. *The Core of the City.* New York: Columbia University Press, 1956.

VERNON, R. *The Changing Economic Function of the Central City.* New York: Committee for Economic Development, 1959.

## Selected Aspects of Canadian Development to 1867

ALBION, R. G. *Forests and Sea Power: The Timber Problem of the Royal Navy, 1652-1862.* Cambridge, Mass.: Harvard University Press, 1926.

CURRIE, A. W. *Canadian Economic Development*. Toronto: Thomas Nelson, 1963.

EASTERBROOK, W. T., and AITKEN, H. G. J. *Canadian Economic History*. Toronto: Macmillan, 1963.

EASTERBROOK, W. T., and WATKINS, M. H., eds. *Approaches to Canadian Economic History*. Toronto: McClelland and Stewart, 1967.

GLAZEBROOK, G. P. DE T. *A History of Transportation in Canada*. 2 vols. Toronto: McClelland and Stewart, 1964.

INNIS, H. A. *The Fur Trade in Canada: An Introduction to Canadian Economic History*. Toronto: University of Toronto Press, 1956.

KERR, D. G. G., ed. *A Historical Atlas of Canada*. Toronto: Thomas Nelson, 1960.

LOWER, A. R. M. "The Trade in Square Timber." In *Approaches to Canadian Economic History*, edited by W. T. Easterbrook and M. H. Watkins. Toronto: McClelland and Stewart, 1967.

MACMILLAN, D.S., ed. *Canadian Business History: Selected Studies, 1497-1971*. Toronto: McClelland and Stewart, 1972.

## Canadian Urban Development

BEAULIEU, A., and MORLEY, W. F. E. *La Province de Québec*. Canadian Local Histories to 1950: A Bibliography, vol. 2. Toronto: University of Toronto Press, 1971.

BOUCHETTE, F. *The British Dominions*. London, 1831.

————. *A Topographical Dictionary of the Province of Lower Canada*. London, 1832.

BOURNE, L.S., and MACKINNON, R.D., eds. *Urban Systems Development in Central Canada*. Toronto: University of Toronto Press, 1972.

CARELESS, J. M. S. "Frontierism, Metropolitanism and Canadian History," *Canadian Historical Review* 35 (1954): 1-21.

————. "Aspects of Metropolitanism in Atlantic Canada." In *Regionalism in the Canadian Community, 1867-1967*, edited by M. Wade. Toronto: University of Toronto Press, 1969.

CHAMBERS, E. J., and BERTRAM, G. W. "Urbanization and Manufacturing in Central Canada, 1870-1890." In *Papers on Regional Statistical Studies*, edited by S. Ostry and T. K. Rymes. Toronto: University of Toronto Press, 1966.

CLARK, A. H. *Three Centuries and the Island: A Historical Geography of Settlement and Agriculture in Prince Edward Island, Canada*. Toronto: University of Toronto Press, 1959.

————. *Acadia: The Geography of Early Nova Scotia to 1760.* Madison: University of Wisconsin Press, 1968.

————. "Acadian Heritage in Maritime 'New France'," *Geographical Magazine* 45 (1972): 219-27.

CRAIG, G. M. *Upper Canada: The Formative Years, 1784-1841.* Toronto: McClelland and Stewart, 1963.

CREIGHTON, D. *The Empire of the St. Lawrence.* Toronto: Macmillan, 1956.

GENTILCORE, R. L. "Ontario Emerges from the Trees," *Geographical Magazine* 45 (1973): 383-91.

GILMOUR, J. M. *Spatial Evolution of Manufacturing: Southern Ontario, 1851-1891.* Toronto: University of Toronto Press, 1972.

HARRIS, R. C., and WARKENTIN, J. *Canada Before Confederation: A Study in Historical Geography.* New York: Oxford University Press, 1974.

HOWELL-JONES, G. I. "A Century of Settlement Change: A Study of the Evolution of Settlement Patterns in the Lower Mainland of British Columbia." Unpublished M.A. thesis, University of British Columbia, 1966.

HUGO-BRUNT, M. "Two Worlds Meet: A Survey of Newfoundland Settlement." Part 1: "The Great Fishery and Early Settlement," *Plan Canada*, vol. 5, no. 1 (1964): 22-36; Part 2: "Development in the 19th and 20th Centuries," *Plan Canada*, vol. 5, no. 2 (1964): 59-83.

KERR, D. "Metropolitan Dominance in Canada." In *Canada: A Geographical Interpretation*, edited by J. Warkentin. Toronto: Methuen, 1968.

LESSARD, M. "Bibliographie des villes du Québec," *Recherches Sociographiques* 9 (1968): 143-209.

LESSARD, M., and MONTMINY, J. *L'urbanisation de la société canadienne-française.* Quebec: Laval University Press, 1967.

MACNUTT, W. S. *New Brunswick: A History, 1784-1867.* Toronto: Macmillan, 1963.

————. *The Atlantic Provinces: The Emergence of Colonial Society, 1712-1857.* Toronto: McClelland and Stewart, 1965.

MASTERS, D. C. "Toronto vs. Montreal: The Struggle for Financial Hegemony, 1860-1875," *Canadian Historical Review* 22 (1941): 133-46.

MORLEY, W. F. E. *The Atlantic Provinces.* Canadian Local Histories to 1950: A Bibliography, vol. 1. Toronto: University of Toronto Press, 1967.

_____. *Ontario*. Canadian Local Histories to 1950: A Bibliography, vol. 3. Toronto: University of Toronto Press, 1969.

ORMSBY, M. A. *British Columbia: A History*. Toronto: Macmillan, 1958.

OSLER, C. F. "The Process of Urbanization in Canada, 1600-1961." Unpublished M.A. thesis, Simon Fraser University, 1968.

PARKER, W. H. "The Towns of Lower Canada in the 1830s." In *Urbanization and Its Problems*, edited by R. P. Beckinsale and J. M. Houston. Oxford: Pergamon Press, 1968.

PEEL, B. *A Bibliography of the Prairie Provinces to 1953*. Toronto: University of Toronto Press, 1956.

PROWSE, D. W. *The History of Newfoundland*. London: Macmillan, 1895.

RAWLYK, G. A., ed. *Historical Essays on the Atlantic Provinces*. Toronto: McClelland and Stewart, 1967.

SPELT, J. *Urban Development in South-Central Ontario*. Toronto: McClelland and Stewart, 1972.

STELTER, G. A. *Canadian Urban History: A Selected Bibliography*. Sudbury: Laurentian University Press, 1972.

STONE, L. O. *Urban Development in Canada*. Ottawa: Queen's Printer, 1967.

URQUHART, M. C., and BUCKLEY, K. A. H., eds. *Historical Statistics of Canada*. Toronto: Macmillan, 1965.

WAKSTEIN, A. M., ed. *The Urbanization of America: An Historical Anthology*. New York: Houghton Mifflin, 1970.

## *Urban Planning, Municipal Finance & Metropolitan Government*

### URBAN PLANNING

BABCOCK, R. F. *The Zoning Game*. Madison: University of Wisconsin Press, 1966.

Bureau of Municipal Research. "Neighbourhood Participation in Local Government: A Study of the City of Toronto," *Civic Affairs*, January 1970.

CHAPIN, F. S., JR. *Urban Land Use Planning*. Urbana: University of Illinois Press, 1965.

CLAWSON, M., ed. *Modernizing Urban Land Use Policy*. Baltimore: Johns Hopkins Press, 1973.

CLAWSON, M., and HALL, P. *Land Planning and Urban Growth: An Anglo-American Comparison*. Baltimore: Johns Hopkins Press, 1973.

DENNIS, N. *Public Participation and Planners' Blight*. London: Faber and Faber, 1972.

FALUDI, A. *Planning Theory*. Oxford: Pergamon Press, 1973.

FRIEDEN, B. J., and MORRIS, R., eds. *Urban Planning and Social Policy*. New York: Basic Books, 1968.

GALLION, A. B., and EISNER, S. *The Urban Pattern*. Princeton, N.J.: Van Nostrand, 1963.

GERTLER, L. O., ed. *Planning the Canadian Environment*. Montreal: Harvest House, 1968.

GOODMAN, W. I., and FREUND, E. C., eds. *Principles and Practice of Urban Planning*. Washington, D.C.: International City Managers Association, 1968.

HUGO-BRUNT, M. *The History of City Planning: A Survey*. Montreal: Harvest House, 1972.

JOYCE, J. G., and HOSSÉ, H. A. *Civic Parties in Canada*. Ottawa: Canadian Federation of Mayors and Municipalities, 1970.

KAPLAN, H. *The Regional City*. Toronto: Canadian Broadcasting Corporation, 1965.

MASSON, J. K., and ANDERSON, J. D., eds. *Emerging Party Politics in Urban Canada*. Toronto: McClelland and Stewart, 1972.

MILNER, J. B. "Town and Regional Planning in Transition," *Canadian Public Administration* 3 (1960): 59-75.

————. *Community Planning: A Casebook on Law and Administration*. Toronto: University of Toronto Press, 1963.

RICHARDSON, N. H. "Participatory Democracy and Planning: The Canadian Experience," *Journal of the Town Planning Institute* 56 (1970): 52-55.

Royal Architectural Institute of Canada. *Reflections on Zoning*. Report of the Zoning Study Committee. Ottawa: The Institute, 1964.

SENIOR, D. *The Regional City: An Anglo-American Discussion of Metropolitan Planning*. London: Longmans, 1966.

SEWELL, J. *Up Against City Hall*. Toronto: James Lewis and Samuel, 1972.

MUNICIPAL FINANCE

Advisory Commission on Intergovernmental Relations. *State-Local Taxation and Industrial Location*. Washington, D.C.: The Commission, 1967.

BEACH, D. "Industry: A Childless Ratepayer," *Canadian Tax Journal* 12 (1965): 431-36.

BEEMAN, W. J. *The Property Tax and the Spatial Pattern of Growth Within Urban Areas.* Washington, D.C.: Government Printing Office, 1969.

Cities of Alberta and the Alberta Urban Municipalities Association. *Urban Crisis: Alberta Municipal Finance Study.* Edmonton, 1968.

FINNIS, F. H. "Slums and Property Taxation," *Canadian Tax Journal* 16 (1968): 154-58.

GOFFMAN, I. J. *The Burden of Canadian Taxation.* Toronto: Canadian Tax Foundation, 1962.

HARDY, E. "Municipal Finance in Canada," *Canadian Banker*, vol. 73, no. 2 (1966): 53-66.

MARTIN, J. "Real Property Taxation: Stirrings of Reform," *Canadian Tax Journal* 20 (1972): 437-52.

Ministry of Treasury, Economics, and Intergovernmental Affairs. *Analysis of Income and Property Taxes in Guelph.* Ontario Tax Paper No. 7. Toronto: Government of Ontario, 1972.

NETZER, D. *Economics of the Property Tax.* Washington, D.C.: The Brookings Institution, 1966.

————. *Impact of the Property Tax: Effect on Housing, Urban Land Use and Local Government Finance.* Washington, D.C.: Government Printing Office, 1968.

Ontario Committee on Taxation (Smith Committee). *Report.* Toronto: Queen's Printer, 1967.

PECHMAN, J. *Fiscal Federalism for the 1970's.* Washington, D.C.: The Brookings Institution, 1971.

PICKARD, J. P. *Taxation and Land Use in Metropolitan and Urban America.* Washington, D.C.: Urban Land Institute, 1966.

PLUNKETT, T. J. *The Financial Structure and the Decision-making Process of Canadian Municipal Government.* Ottawa: Central Mortgage and Housing Corporation, 1972.

QUINDRY, K. E., and COOK, B. D. "Humanization of the Property Tax for Low-income Households," *National Tax Journal* 22 (1969): 357-67.

RAWSON, M. *Property Taxation and Urban Development: Effects of the Property Tax on City Growth and Change.* Washington, D.C.: Urban Land Institute, 1961.

ROSTVOLD, G. N. "Property Tax Payments in Relation to Household Income: A Case Study of Los Angeles County," *National Tax Journal* 15 (1962): 197-99.

SILVER, S. "Feasibility of a Municipal Income Tax in Canada," *Canadian Tax Journal* 16 (1968): 398-406.

SLATER, D. W. "Urban Growth and Municipal Finance," *Canadian Banker*, vol. 70, no. 2 (1963): 5-17.

METROPOLITAN GOVERNMENT

Bureau of Municipal Research. "The 101 Governments of Metro Toronto," *Civic Affairs*, October 1968.

BURNS, R. M. "Intergovernmental Relations in Canada," *Public Administration Review* 33 (1973): 14-22.

COOK, G. C. A., and FELDMAN, L. D. "Approaches to Local Government Reform in Canada: The Case of Winnipeg," *Canadian Tax Journal* 19 (1971): 216-25.

FELDMAN, L. D., and GOLDRICK, M. D., eds. *Politics and Government of Urban Canada*. Toronto: Methuen, 1972.

KAPLAN, H. *Urban Political Systems: A Functional Analysis of Metro Toronto*. New York: Columbia University Press, 1967.

MILES, S. R., ed. *Metropolitan Problems: International Perspectives*. Toronto: Methuen, 1970.

Ontario Royal Commission on Metropolitan Toronto (Commissioner H.C. Goldenberg). *Report*. Toronto: Queen's Printer, 1965.

PLUNKETT, T. J. *Urban Canada and Its Government*. Toronto: Macmillan, 1968.

_____. "Structural Reform of Local Government in Canada," *Public Administration Review* 33 (1973): 40-50.

REDCLIFFE-MAUD, LORD. *Royal Commission on Local Government in England*. 3 vols. London: H.M.S.O., 1969.

ROBSON, W. A. "Metropolitan Government: Problems and Solutions," *Canadian Public Administration* 9 (1966): 45-54.

ROBSON, W. A., and REGAN, D. E. *Great Cities of the World: Their Government, Politics and Planning*. 2 vols. London: Allen and Unwin, 1972.

ROSE, A. *Governing Metropolitan Toronto: A Social and Political Analysis, 1953-1971*. Berkeley: University of California Press, 1972.

ROWAT, D. C. "Planning and Metropolitan Government," *Canadian Public Administration* 1 (1958): 43-47.

_____. *The Canadian Municipal System: Essays in the Improvement of Local Government*. Toronto: McClelland and Stewart, 1969.

SMALLWOOD, F. *Metro Toronto: A Decade Later*. Toronto: Bureau of Municipal Research, 1963.

TENNANT, P., and ZIRNHELT, D. "Metropolitan Government in Vancouver: The Strategy of Gentle Imposition," *Canadian Public Administration* 16 (1973): 124-38.

WOOD, R. C. *1400 Governments: The Political Economy of the New York Metropolitan Region.* Cambridge, Mass.: Harvard University Press, 1961.

## Urban Problems and Public Policy

GENERAL

ANDREWS, R. B. *Urban Land Economics and Public Policy.* New York: Free Press, 1971.

BANZ, G. *Elements of Urban Form.* New York: McGraw-Hill, 1970.

BOLLENS, J. C., and SCHMANDT, H. J. *The Metropolis: Its People, Politics and Economic Life.* New York: Harper and Row, 1970.

CRECINE, J. P., ed. *Financing the Metropolis: Public Policy in Urban Economics.* Beverly Hills, Calif.: Sage Publications, 1970.

JACOBS, J. *The Death and Life of Great American Cities.* New York: Random House, 1961.

KRUEGER, R. R., and BRYFOGLE, R. C., eds. *Urban Problems: A Canadian Reader.* Toronto: Holt, Rinehart and Winston, 1971.

LITHWICK, N. H. *Urban Canada: Problems and Prospects.* Ottawa: Central Mortgage and Housing Corporation, 1970.

MAYER, A. *The Urgent Future.* New York: McGraw-Hill, 1967.

NETZER, D. *Economics and Urban Problems.* New York: Basic Books, 1970.

PERLOFF, H. S., and WINGO, L., eds. *Issues in Urban Economics.* Baltimore: Johns Hopkins Press, 1968.

RICHARDSON, B. *The Future of Canadian Cities.* Toronto: New Press, 1972.

RICHARDSON, H. W. *Urban Economics.* Harmondsworth, Middlesex: Penguin, 1971.

VERNON, R. *The Myth and Reality of Our Urban Problems.* Cambridge, Mass.: Harvard University Press, 1966.

URBAN FRINGE

BRYANT, G. W. R. "Land Speculation: Its Effects and Control," *Plan Canada*, vol. 5, no. 3 (1965): 109-21.

Bureau of Municipal Research. "The Toronto Region's Privately Developed New Communities," *Civic Affairs*, no. 2 (1972).

———. "Land Banking: Investment in the Future," *Civic Affairs*, no. 1 (1973).

CARVER, H. *Cities in the Suburbs*. Toronto: University of Toronto Press, 1962.

Central Office of Information. *The New Towns of Britain*. London: H.M.S.O., 1972.

CLAWSON, M. "Urban Sprawl and Speculation in Suburban Land," *Land Economics* 38 (1962): 99-111.

———. *Suburban Land Conversion in the United States: An Economic and Governmental Process*. Baltimore: Johns Hopkins Press, 1971.

CRERAR, A. D. "The Loss of Farmland in the Growth of the Metropolitan Regions of Canada." In *Resources for Tomorrow*. Supplementary volume. Ottawa: Department of Northern Affairs and National Resources, 1962.

EVANS, H. *New Towns: The British Experience*. London: Charles Knight, 1972.

GOLANY, G. *New Towns Planning and Development: A World-wide Bibliography*. Research Monograph No. 20. Washington, D.C.: Urban Land Institute, 1973.

GOTTMANN, J., and HARPER, R. A., eds. *Metropolis on the Move: Geographers Look at Urban Sprawl*. New York: Wiley, 1967.

HALL, P., *et al*. *Urban and Metropolitan Growth Processes or Megalopolis Denied*. The Containment of Urban England, vol. 1. London: Allen and Unwin, 1973.

HARVEY, R. O., and CLARK, W. A. V. "The Nature and Economics of Urban Sprawl," *Land Economics* 41 (1965): 1-9.

HIND-SMITH, J. "The Impact of Urban Growth on Agricultural Land: A Pilot Study." In *Resources for Tomorrow*. Ottawa: Department of Northern Affairs and National Resources, 1962.

HOWARD, E. *Garden Cities of Tomorrow*. Edited by F. J. Osborn with an introductory essay by Lewis Mumford. London: Faber and Faber, 1965.

JACOBS, P. "The Urban Fringe: Resolving Its Problems, Developing Its Potentials," *Habitat* 15 (1972): 30-35.

KRUEGER, R. R. "The Rural-Urban Fringe Taxation Problem: A Case Study of Louth Township," *Land Economics* 33 (1957): 264-69.

————. "The Disappearing Niagara Fruit Belt," *Canadian Geographical Journal* 58 (1959): 102-13.

KURTZ, R. A., and EICHER, J. B. "Fringe and Suburb: A Confusion of Concepts," *Social Forces* 37 (1958): 32-37.

LANGLOIS, C. "Speculation and Sprawl," *Canadian Geographer*, vol. 5, no. 3 (1961): 1-11.

MERLIN, P. *New Towns: Regional Planning and Development.* Translated by M. Sparks. London: Methuen, 1971.

Montreal. *Urbanization: A Study of Urban Expansion in the Montreal Region.* Technical Bulletin No. 5. Montreal: City of Montreal, 1969.

OSBORN, F. J., and WHITTICK, A. *The New Towns: The Answer to Megalopolis.* London: Leonard Hill, 1969.

PEARSON, N. *What Price Suburbia.* New Westminster, B.C.: Lower Mainland Regional Planning Board, 1967.

PRYOR, R. J. "Defining the Rural-Urban Fringe." In *Internal Structure of the City*, edited by L. S. Bourne. New York: Oxford University Press, 1971.

RANICH, M. T. "Land Value Changes in an Area Undergoing Urbanization," *Land Economics* 46 (1970): 32-40.

RODWIN, L. *The British New Towns Policy: Problems and Implications.* Cambridge, Mass.: Harvard University Press, 1956.

SCHAFFER, F. *The New Town Story.* London: Paladin, 1972.

SCHMID, A. A. "Suburban Land Appreciation and Public Policy," *Journal of the American Institute of Planners* 36 (1970): 38-43.

SINCLAIR, R. "Von Thünen and Urban Sprawl," *Annals of the Association of American Geographers* 57 (1967): 72-87.

STEIN, C. *Toward New Towns for America.* Liverpool: University of Liverpool Press, 1951.

THOMAS, D. *London's Green Belt.* London: Faber and Faber, 1970.

THOMAS, R. *London's New Towns.* London: Political and Economic Planning, 1969.

United Nations. *Planning of Metropolitan Areas and New Towns.* New York: United Nations, 1967.

WEHRWEIN, G. S. "The Rural-Urban Fringe," *Economic Geography* 18 (1942): 217-28.

WISSINK, G. A. *American Cities in Perspective: With Special Reference to the Development of Their Fringe Areas.* Assen: Royal Van Gorcum, 1962.

CENTRAL CITY

AGAPOS, A. M., and DUNLAP, P. R. "Elimination of Urban Blight Through Inverse Proportional Ad Valorem Property Taxation," *American Journal of Economics and Sociology* 32 (1973): 143-52.

ANDREWS, R. B., ed. *Urban Land Use Policy: The Central City*. New York: Free Press, 1972.

BERRY, D. S., *et al. The Technology of Urban Transportation*. Evanston, Ill.: Northwestern University Press, 1963.

BOURNE, L. S. *Private Redevelopment of the Central City*. Research Paper 112, Department of Geography. Chicago: University of Chicago Press, 1967.

HALLIDAY, J., ed. *City Centre Redevelopment*. London: Charles Knight, 1973.

LEA, N. D., and Associates. *Urban Transportation Developments in Eleven Canadian Metropolitan Areas*. Ottawa: Canadian Good Roads Association, 1966.

LOWDEN, J. "A Case Study of Community Rehabilitation: The Strathcona Rehabilitation Project," *Plan Canada* 13 (1973): 136-40.

MEYER, J. R., KAIN, J. F., and WOHL, M. *The Urban Transportation Problem*. Cambridge, Mass.: Harvard University Press, 1965.

MOSES, L. N., and WILLIAMSON, H. F. "Value of Time, Choice of Mode, and the Subsidy Issue in Urban Transportation," *Journal of Political Economy* 71 (1963): 247-64.

NEEDLEMAN, L. "The Comparative Economics of Improvement and New Building," *Urban Studies* 6 (1969): 196-209.

OWEN, W. *The Metropolitan Transportation Problem*. Washington, D.C.: The Brookings Institution, 1966.

VANCE, J. E., JR. "Focus on Downtown." In *Internal Structure of the City*, edited by L. S. Bourne. New York: Oxford University Press, 1971.

WILSON, J. Q., ed. *Urban Renewal: The Record and the Controversy*. Cambridge, Mass.: M.I.T. Press, 1966.

# Index